HANCOCK AT GETTYSBURG...*and beyond*

A. M. Gambone

**First Edition
Butternut and Blue
1997**

Copyright 1997 by A. M. Gambone

No part of this book may be reproduced
in any form or by any means without the
written consent of the publisher

ISBN 0-935523-59-6

Printed in the United States of America
on acid-free paper.

Published in 1997
as the eighteenth volume of
the *Army of the Potomac Series*

by

**Butternut and Blue
3411 Northwind Road
Baltimore, MD 21234
410-256-9220**

Cover Artwork: *Cemetery Hill*, courtesy of Don Troiani, Southbury, CT.

DEDICATION

TO THE MEMORY OF MY SISTERS, ANN & GLADYS, AND MY BROTHER FRANK.

OTHER BOOKS BY A. M. GAMBONE:

• *Major-General John F. Hartranft, Citizen Soldier and Pennsylvania Statesman.*

• *"...if tomorrow night finds me dead," The Life of General Samuel K. Zook.*

THOUGHTS ON GENERAL HANCOCK

"If you will sit down and write the best thing that can be put in language about General Hancock as an officer and a gentleman, I will sign it without hesitation."

General William Tecumseh Sherman, USA.

* * * * * * * * * * * * * * * * * * *

"But the men who stood with him on the summit of the hill that day, and who cheered him in triumph as he rode along their lines, scarcely mourn his loss today more sincerely than do those whom he opposed. A mighty man has fallen...."

Charleston News and Courier

Contents

PAGE

List of Photographs and Drawings i

List of Maps iv

Preface v

Acknowledgments xxi

Abbreviations and Definitions xxiv

CHAPTER ONE
    A Changing Order *and tense moments* 1

CHAPTER TWO
    "Terminological Inexactitude" 21

CHAPTER THREE
    "I'd Be God Damned..." 76

CHAPTER FOUR
    "Tell General Hancock" 112

CHAPTER FIVE
    "I may never see you again" 165

CHAPTER SIX
    "The citizens of Louisiana...cherish the memory" 188

CONTENTS

PAGE

Appendix — A: Thanks of Congress 224

Appendix — B: General Order No. 40 225

Endnotes 227

Bibliography 286

Index 303

LIST OF PHOTOGRAPHS AND DRAWINGS

PAGE

Major-General Winfield Scott Hancock .... *frontispiece*
Almira Hancock ix
Ada Hancock x
Hancock and Son Russell xi
Hancock between Generals Hunt and Couch xii
Major-General Winfield Scott Hancock 10
Major-General Joseph Hooker 11
Major-General Darius N. Couch 12
Major-General George Gordon Meade 29
Major-General Winfield Scott Hancock 30
Major-General John F. Reynolds 31
Major-General Oliver Otis Howard 32
Major-General Henry W. Slocum 33
Major-General Abner Doubleday 34
Brigadier-General John Buford 35
The Gateway on Cemetery Hill 36
Brigadier-General Charles H. Morgan 37
Brigadier-General William G. Mitchell 38
Hancock's Marginal Notes In the *Journal of Military Service Institution* 51
Hancock's Marginal Notes In the *Journal of Military Service Institution* 52
Major-General Daniel E. Sickles 80
Brigadier-General Samuel K. Zook 86
Lieutenant-Colonel Henry C. Merwin 89
Colonel Eliakim E. Sherrill 93
Brigadier-General William Barksdale 94
Brigadier-General Winfield Scott Hancock 96
Monument to the First Minnesota on Cemetery Ridge at Gettysburg 99
Major-General Samuel S. Carroll 103
The Leister House 108
Major-General Winfield Scott Hancock 125

List of Photographs and Drawings

PAGE

Brigadier-General Henry J. Hunt 126
General Hunt in the painting *Battle of Gettysburg* 127
    by Paul Philippoteaux
Painting: *Battle of Gettysburg—Pickett's Charge* 149
    by Peter F. Rothermel
General Hancock in the painting *Battle of Gettysburg* 150
    by Paul Philippoteaux
Hancock shortly after he was wounded 151
Hancock being removed from the field 151
Monument marking spot of Hancock's wounding 152
Brevet Major-General Alexander S. Webb 153
Surgeon, Major Alexander N. Dougherty 154
Henry H. Bingham 155
Major-General George E. Pickett 156
Brigadier-General Lewis A. Armistead 157
Monument marking where Armistead fell 158
Photograph thought to be John Hancock 159
Nail comparison 160
An 1859 McClellan saddle pommel 161
X-ray of an 1859 McClellan saddle pommel 162
Major-General Winfield Scott Hancock 171
Bullet trajectory 172
Hancock's wound 173
The bullet that hit Hancock 174
Home of Hancock's parents 175
Dr. Louis W. Read 176
Hancock in Norristown 177
Modern site of the home of Hancock's parents 178
Hancock in civilian clothes 185
Harper's engraving of a defeated Hancock 186
A corpulent General Hancock 190
Major-General Winfield Scott Hancock 191
Hancock and family on Governor's Island 192
Hancock's residence on Governor's Island 192
Hancock at the head of Grant's funeral 193
Hancock at Gettysburg 194

PREFACE

This volume developed as a result of a late night telephone conversation with my publisher, Jim McLean, of Butternut and Blue. During that discussion, Jim asked me to consider a monograph on the activities of Major-General Winfield Scott Hancock at Gettysburg, a battle the general always felt should have destroyed Lee's army.[1] Jim indicated that based upon his extensive readings, there still remains a substantial want of detail related to Hancock's contributions at Gettysburg plus a need for a better understanding of the controversies in which he became embroiled. With some early research on my part, it became clear that much data are indeed still lacking regarding Hancock's activities, disputes and even his wounding during that great ordeal. In addition, and beyond, there also unfolded an uncanny lack of particulars related to his final infirmity, death and funeral. Therefore, the attempt to fill those conjugated voids serves as the primary objective of this work. But, let the reader be warned that Gettysburg controversies are virtually endless on both sides, and reading this composition is similar to embarking on the study of Philosophy 101. To the unsuspecting student, that topic might be eagerly anticipated as the long-sought answer for life's many complex questions. In reality, the astute pupil soon realizes that the introduction to philosophy raises far more questions than providing answers. In part, and unfortunately, because of the nature of this subject matter, so it is with this book. Because the entire battle is such a massive human epic, the reader will soon appreciate that the name Gettysburg is synonymous with the terms controversy and confusion.

It might be helpful to further caution the reader that it is impossible to complete such a volume without some repetition of earlier efforts. Unfortunately, to place key people, issues and events in their proper perspective, it is absolutely necessary to have some reiteration. However, to avoid a significant repetitive commentary, I have adopted a posture that assumes the reader to have at least a primary knowledge of the Gettysburg battle and some of its major personalities. That license permits me to dwell on original or obscure data more rapidly. Also, while I have made a concerted effort to introduce as much unpublished or little-known material as possible, wherever that was not practical, I have attempted to utilize a fresh view upon well-documented data.

Preface.

It is also important to understand that this work is not driven by a desire for revision-based history. Instead, it is an honest attempt to establish facts that frequently clash with commonly held myths. Such an attempt is a major problem with much Civil War literature and the results of such efforts are not always easy to accept, and frequently more difficult to accomplish. Too, in terms of precautionary statements, the author readily acknowledges that he is not a battlefield expert and those details herein are primarily meant to fix the time and positions for General Hancock and his related happenings. This volume is not another treatise about the military technicalities of the conflict, because the battle of Gettysburg has already received far better attention, in that regard, than this author might ever offer. Rather, this effort is devoted to a better understanding of some of the key personalities at Gettysburg, and mainly General Hancock, in an attempt to understand how and why their actions, or lack of, created lasting disputes. For those with a thirst for a broader or more technical view of the fight, the author encourages them to pursue the many excellent volumes and profiles listed in the bibliography.

This book strives to lift off the pages the one-dimensional, parochial view that biographies frequently tend to produce of people. Since this battle is a vast human tapestry, if we remove that human factor, we are left with absolutely nothing. Consequently, today, we are forced to make some intelligent value judgments in an attempt to determine who was right, wrong, good or bad in this monumental event. And while no one can be all right or all wrong at all times, there are obviously those who were more right or wrong in their battle decisions and actions than their peers. It falls to the serious history student to make the resulting analytical distinctions. To purposely avoid such trials and difficulties can only be described as historical prostitution.

If these pages are read carefully, most will properly conclude that General Winfield Scott Hancock was a very human, successful, and effective field commander. This simple definition demands that we also appreciate that he had very strong emotions and convictions which were coupled with a large ego and confidence factor which are absolutely necessary for such achievements. Hancock possessed the clear, decisive vision necessary for a good field commandant. He definitely understood that to fight battles successfully, a general must be perfectly willing to sacrifice life and limb from his most precious command though that fact does not render *carte blache* for the incompetent. It is folly to believe that any field general can attain military greatness and not win battles; and battles-won means *killing* the enemy. Today, such bluntness may not be appealing nor politically correct, but this grisly candor is absolutely basic for any good soldier. Hancock was such a soldier, which led one comrade

Preface.

and neighbor to state: "...he was emphatically a fighter."[2] However, he was human!

Interestingly, Hancock was born of English, Scots and Welsh ancestry and sprang from a passive Quaker religious background on Valentine's Day, February 14, 1824.[3] Unlike Lupercus, for whom his birthday was named, he was raised in the budding metropolis of Norristown, Pennsylvania, along with his twin brother, Hilary. Later, both boys were joined by another brother, John, who served as an assistant adjutant in Winfield's renowned II Corps at Gettysburg. These were the only children of Benjamin Franklin Hancock and Elizabeth Hoxworth Hancock. Continuing a family tradition of bestowing illustrious names, infant Winfield was titled for the hero of the War of 1812, General Winfield Scott. The senior Hancock admired that Virginia-born commander and even briefly served his country during that war with England. While allegedly demonstrating a proclivity for the military as a lad, Hancock's lawyer-deacon-father reluctantly accepted a rather serendipitous appointment to West Point for his son.

When his 16-year-old scion took leave of home, the elder Hancock sent him off with a copy of the United States Constitution and Sir William Blackstone's *Commentaries*, "a systematic, clear, and elegant description of the state of English law...[which] In England and America...became the basis of university legal education."[4] Benjamin Hancock charged his offspring to read each piece at least once a year, which was probably done with some regularity, if not precisely as ordered.

Young Winfield entered the Academy on July 1, 1840 and during his four years there, he came to know some future key war participants who were destined to serve on both sides of the Mason-Dixon line: Simon Bolivar Buckner, Don Carlos Buell, Abner Doubleday, Richard B. Garnett, John Gibbon, Ulysses S. Grant, A. P. Hill, George B. McClellan, Lafayette McLaws, John Pope, Kirby Smith, Earl Van Dorn and others. Graduating July 1, 1844, Hancock ranked 18 in a class of 25 and had managed to gather an impressive 307 demerits during his tenure.[5]

Like many other ante-bellum professional officers, Hancock saw duty in the War with Mexico, the third Seminole War in Florida and then off to Fort Leavenworth, in Kansas. But, just like all of his contemporaries, nothing in his military education or limited combat experience prepared him for the size and complexities of the unprecedented commands that erupted during the Great Rebellion. Because the Civil War was on the threshold of the old clumsy Napoleonic style of fighting, versus the modern engineering tactics it fostered, only those officers and men capable of making and executing such a critical transition rose rapidly, owing to their extraordinary results with developing modern warfare. Hancock proved to be so adaptable and became such a soldier and field executive.

In 1850, Hancock married beautiful Almira Russell of St. Louis, an accomplished organist, composer and socialite, who was devoted to her husband and followed him and his career wherever he was assigned.[6] While little is known about Almira, according to one newspaper report, when a youthful Hancock stopped in St. Louis on his way to the West, he was smitten by the beautiful young lady he noticed on the porch of a large home. Hancock made it his business to ride past each morning and one day he saw the pretty woman and her father drive off in a carriage. He followed them to the home of a friend and brazenly entered and requested his friend to introduce him. Apparently, his bizarre antics won him the favor of Mr. Russell, who invited the young officer to call upon his daughter at their home. It didn't take long before Winfield and Almira were engaged and married.[7] Immediately following her death in 1893, Hamilton Fish, the noted New York politician who was very close to the Hancocks, described Almira as "so bright, so gay, so full of sunshine..."[8]

The Hancock nuclear family grew to include two children, a son Russell, and a daughter Ada. During the two years prior to the war, the Hancocks were stationed in California where they furthered their warm relationship with fellow officers, including Lewis Armistead and Dick Garnett. Both of those men later sided with the South and attained the rank of brigadier in the Confederate Army. Hancock's relationship with Armistead in particular has been highly glamorized and, at times, even fantasized beyond practical bounds. There are no known written records, from either individual, that offer testimony to such a romanticized relationship as is currently held. Yet, their purported, melodramatic, deep bond does reflect the horror of brother-against-brother inherent with any civil war.[9] Nonetheless, there is little doubt that the three men, like so many others, shared some form of camaraderie. Unfortunately, they were forced to set their warmth aside for the higher interest of duty, which poignantly forced them to confront each other on the bitter, bloody battlefield at Gettysburg on July 3, 1863.

As the war progressed, so did Hancock's military talents, which furthered his own understanding and transition of war technology earlier noted. This was evident when he eagerly purchased a dozen Gatling guns for his noted II Corps, a new tool frowned upon by most Civil War general officers. Even earlier, as a young captain in California, Hancock showed his tolerance for change when he became the army's first officer, under Secretary of War Jeffer-

Mrs. Almira Hancock

Preface.

Miss Ada Hancock

The only daughter of the Hancocks, Ada died on March 28, 1875 at the age of eighteen. She is buried in the tomb with the general. (Circa 1874)

Hancock and His Son Russell

A young Lieutenant Hancock and his son Russell. (Circa 1852)

Hancock Between Generals Hunt and Couch

Brigadier-General Winfield Scott Hancock seated between General Henry Hunt on the left and General Darius N. Couch on the right. This photograph was taken in November 1862 at Warrenton, Virginia.

Preface. xiii

son Davis, to test the suitability of camels in the American desert.[10] He welcomed challenging technology and traditions even if they were not always popular and successful.

Aesthetically, Hancock was every inch the professional soldier while inculcated by his father with high ideals of national pride and everlasting Union. After the Civil War broke out in the spring of 1861, he returned to the East in September and Major-General George B. McClellan recommended him for an appointment to brigadier and promptly gave him command of the Third Brigade, VI Corps, in the division belonging to William "Baldy" Smith. That promotion also meant that the obscure, 37-year-old quartermaster officer made an instant leap from captain to brigadier-general, which could not sit well with everyone.[11]

Nonetheless, at the battle of Williamsburg, in the spring of 1862, during McClellan's now famous Peninsular Campaign, Hancock first demonstrated his suitability for high field command. Holding his line against a strong Confederate attack led by Brigadier-General Jubal A. Early, he ordered a swift and costly bayonet countercharge which caused his attackers to retire and count their 600 casualties.[12] In the process, one of his junior officers, Second Lieutenant George A. Custer, captured the first Confederate flag of the war for the Union. That evening, as General McClellan sent a message to his wife, Mary Ellen, he gave the new brigadier a life-long sobriquet when he wired, "Hancock was superb today."[13] In September of 1862, at the battle of Antietam, Hancock succeeded the mortally wounded Major-General Israel B. Richardson and took command of the First Division of the II Corps. That ascension also won him promotion to the rank of major-general of volunteers. In December of 1862 and again in May of 1863, he repeatedly distinguished himself during the sanguinary battles of Fredericksburg and Chancellorsville while serving directly under the quiet but capable Major-General Darius N. Couch, commander of the II Corps. By that time, Hancock's military character had matured and he had become well known for his intrepid personal traits and idiosyncrasies. One of his aides, Colonel George Shallenberger, clearly recalled that whenever Hancock prepared for "a forward movement everything was made doubly sure... [and] woe be to the man who shirked or in any sense failed to meet and perform his duty." He demanded total commitment to performance and insisted that his officers understand that "in your department there is no such word as *can't*."[14]

Following the Union debacle at Chancellorsville, General Couch resigned his post rather than serve any further under Major-General Joseph Hooker, whom he deemed incompetent. Because of that vacancy, on June 9, 1863, Hancock was appointed commander of the distinguished II Corps, which

Preface.

he would lead into battle at Gettysburg. There, his confident leadership won him the admiration of the Union, and belatedly, the coveted Thanks of Congress*, which was awarded to only 15 Union Army officers during the entire war. Regrettably, Hancock was never to know independent command and, while Gettysburg was destined to mean laurels for him, it also became a platform of controversy and lasting debate.

As a native of Norristown, I was pleased with Jim McLean's request, since I consider writing about Hancock a distinct honor. Initially, I thought that because of his high rank and visibility, voluminous personal records on the general would be readily available to facilitate such a project. Not true! As with many participants in that war, new, meaningful Hancock data, and personal letters in particular, are difficult, if not impossible to locate. This makes it all the harder to fully crystallize his personality which was highly volatile, complex but coupled with an extremely quick mental capacity. It is safe to understand that he did not win military fame because he was timorous on or off the battlefield. Instead, he was dynamic, forceful, resolute, bold, crude, obstinate, harsh, and sometimes too quick in his judgments, but always dedicated to victory. He was a demanding disciplinarian and, at times, perhaps too particular in this area. The fact is, most everyone who won well-earned fame during that or any other war shared most of these traits. Effective soldiers are not cut from the same cloth as the idyllic mother. They are a holy, or different, breed and the greater their professional talent, the more unacceptable they might be to society during their most productive moments. Real soldiering is bloody work and Hancock understood that perfectly! One of his peers wrote: "...his eye was warm and genial, but in the hour of battle [they] became intensely cold...[his] nervous, [his] moral, and [his] mental systems were all harmoniously stimulated, and that he was, therefore, at his very best on the field of battle."[15] Still, in spite of such soldierly attributes, his parental influence and passive heritage were not totally lost upon his mature life. Instead, he respected and followed the writings of an ancient scribe who patiently counseled a time for everything:

> A time to kill, and a time to heal;
> a time to tear down, and a time to build.
> A time to love, and a time to hate;
> a time of war, and a time of peace.[16]

---

* *See Appendix — A.*

Preface. xv

Since Hancock was very human, he could be mercurial, and while he was very sensitive, he definitely placed limits on his patience. Accordingly, he could display a very quick temper, but while he held few grudges, they were not a total void in his life. While many glowing and exaggerated stories about him grew out of his services, many can be discounted and considered 19th century creations. However, one factual aspect that was always a constant was his love of discipline. He also had a passionate disdain "for either laggards or cowards in his service."[17] During and after the war, he steadfastly tried to avoid fighting any kind of battles or disputes in the newspapers, which became very common, apparently because he felt it unprofessional if not immature. Nonetheless, whenever he was forced into such a public platform, his posture was direct, consistent and curt.

Despite efforts by some who might claim otherwise, he naturally made his share of mistakes but generally acknowledged them. On balance, his tally of military errors was far less than his successes. Throughout his entire military career, his very presence commanded attention and respect, leading one of his staff members, Captain Henry H. Bingham, to comment: "One felt safe when near him."[18] Major-General George Gordon Meade also added his praise when he noted: "No commanding General ever had a better Lieutenant than Hancock, he was always faithful and reliable."[19]

As a dedicated American, Hancock was totally committed to his youthful nation and flag, traits that unfortunately have been strongly diluted in present times. At Gettysburg, his military zenith, some of his decisions are understandably contested while others are predictably deemed to be farsighted. For example, his assuming command from Major-General Oliver Otis Howard, as ordered, on the first day has precipitated a lasting controversy. On the second day, he essentially sacrificed the already emaciated 1st Minnesota Regiment to gain precious minutes by staving off disaster from some of Lee's approaching forces.[20] On the third day, during the great Confederate cannonade, he ordered return fire from Union batteries that were just ordered to cease fire to conserve long-range ammunition. That command instantly became controversial and won him the lasting enmity of Brigadier-General Henry J. Hunt, whose very title, Chief of Artillery, and scope of authority, is still subject to debate. Hunt charged that Hancock had overstepped his bounds and that he alone had command of the Reserve Artillery, including that which was serving on the II Corps commander's line. That entire episode led to another acrimonious dispute which saw both men to their respective graves.

As is so often the case with distinguished individuals, Hancock-related fact and fantasy began to meld together, making precise delineation difficult if not impossible. A good example of such exaggeration is attributed to President Lincoln, who, when supposedly told that the II Corps would be employed in mortal combat, said to a group of White House visitors: "I am afraid Hancock is going to be killed to-day."[21] Unfortunately, there appears to be no basis for such a claim, though Hancock obviously had a warm relationship with the Lincolns as witnessed by a note sent him by Mrs. Lincoln. The general was to call at the White House but the President decided that a rest was necessary so he made arrangements for him and Mary to attend Grover's Theatre. Not wishing to miss his visit, Mary immediately sent off a note to General Hancock, asking him to "stop in Box No. 2–& see us–which will please the President very much."[22] Another indication of Hancock's friendly association with the President is the following comment made by Mr. Lincoln:

> Some of the older generals have said to me that he [Hancock] is rash, and I have said to them that I have watched General Hancock's conduct very carefully, and I have found that when he goes into action he achieves his purpose and comes out with a smaller list of casualties than any of them. If his life and strength be spared I believe that General Hancock is destined to be one of the most distinguished men of the age.[23]

Physically, Hancock has been described in a variety of discordant accounts, but we can be certain that during the war, he stood about six feet one or two inches tall with broad, square shoulders, standing erect with a barrel chest and "a great large forehead and most commanding [soldierly] presence."[24] His hair was fair, fine and straight, usually hanging just over his ears and parted on the right. He had deep blue penetrating eyes with fleshy pockets on their underside, which emphasized their glare when ignited. His cheeks were clean-shaven, though he wore a mustache which met the beard of his chin. Just below his lower lip, he had a distinctive tongue of hair, which provided character to his face. When desired, he could employ a deep booming voice that dictated unquestioned authority to his field commands. If historians will allow for a character parallel, then we can view Hancock as closer to a swaggering, earthy John Wayne as opposed to a punctilious *Lone Ranger*. One of his close friends fondly wrote: "The dignity of command sat perfectly upon him, for the simplicity and sincerity of his nature robbed it of arrogance and gave it a grace that was all his own."[25] Another aide noted that in battle, "It was his habit to re-

Preface. xvii

main mounted at all times...encouraging all to stand fast & give no ground."[26] Obviously, war was his stage!

His personality was pleasant, his mind quick and insightful. He was something of an artist, amateur scientist, botanist and he even wrote some verse.[27] He had a striking but calming physical bearing; he was handsome with a good sense of humor, though frequently and excessively profane in his language. At least one cleric, Father William Corby of the Irish Brigade, noted that while Hancock was "addicted" to profanity, he still "showed a respect for religion in respecting its ministers."[28] But not everyone was as tolerant of such a character flaw as Father Corby. In 1862, the Chaplain for the 145th Pennsylvania, Reverend J. H. W. Stuckenberg, wrote, but did not send, a plea to Hancock to stop his free use of oaths before the troops. Stuckenberg wanted to remind his brigadier-general: "...you were uttering the most horrid oaths in the presence of our regiment yesterday morning...some looked upon their worthy and so much honored General as giving them a license for their profanity, whilst others were in danger of learning profanity from your lips...what can my feeble labors accomplish, when in conflict with [your] example of so high authority."[29] Is it possible that Reverend Stuckenberg had second thoughts about provoking his volatile commander's unbridled wrath?

Despite his love and frequent use of profanity, Hancock was still sensitive and a soldier's soldier. Once, he had a guard detail from the 148th Pennsylvania Infantry around his headquarters and one of their members complained bitterly to him that the bread rations for that particular day were paltry indeed. That incident led to a brief discussion and Hancock asked the man:

> "Do you get half enough?"
> "Yes," replied the soldier.
> "Then," said Hancock, "damned poor soldier that can't steal the other half."

The next morning, when the general's waiter went to call him for breakfast, men from the 148th stole into his tent and cleaned the table of its contents. A few days later, Hancock called on the colonel of the regiment and told him what a fine command he had. Hancock went on to say: "...if [I] could get them within a mile of Richmond they would steal the city."[30]

In another incident, Private David H. Young of Company D, also with the 148th Pennsylvania, had been wounded at Chancellorsville and was recuperating in a military hospital. Young reported that General Hancock was a frequent visitor to the hospital and he had been passed over while Hancock had stopped at the bed of every other soldier to speak with them. Somewhat distressed by what appeared to be a snub, Young insisted to a nearby orderly: "Please tell General Hancock that he spoke to every soldier in the ward except me, and be sure to tell him that I consider myself as good a man as he is." The "orderly" said he would immediately pass Young's comments along to the general. But, the soldier's lament was overheard by a nearby nurse who berated the private for his boldness in addressing the general and the "orderly" in such a manner. Nonetheless, within a half hour, Hancock reappeared with the "orderly," who introduced the general to Private Young. Hancock warmly took the hand of the wounded soldier, which reassured Young he had intended no insult. Then, probably with a broad smile, Hancock introduced the private to the "orderly," who was really Brigadier-General John Gibbon.[31]

Fastidious about his person and dress, Hancock often confounded his comrades by always wearing freshly starched white shirts into battle. According to Colonel J. William Hofmann of the 56th Pennsylvania, Hancock's apparently endless supply of starched shirts were the result of his English valet, "Mr. Shaw," who reportedly spent much of his time over the scrubbing board.[32] Like his father, the general was a life-long Democrat, which was considered undesirable by some in the Union's Republican administration. He was born into the Baptist Church, became a Mason, and belonged to the Norristown Royal Arch Chapter #190 and Charity Lodge Chapter #190. Still, his final Episcopal religious ceremony belied his 25 years as a Masonic Brother.[33]

Hancock's life did not end with the close of the war. Indeed, he was destined for many demanding assignments, including that of military governor of Texas and Louisiana during the Reconstruction era. In that post, he issued his famous General Order No. 40,* which restored civil law and won him the lasting respect and admiration of the Southern people, which continues to this very day.[34] For that brief, but enlightened service as a benevolent military dictator, one newspaper wrote: "No man ever won more completely the confidence of a community, and no man could possibly carry with him, in fuller degree, the blessings and good wishes of a grateful people."[35] More than a decade after he left that position, General Hancock was in New Orleans when that City and the State honored him with Concurrent Resolutions and invited him to address the Senate and House of the State of Louisiana.[36]

---

* *See Appendix — B.*

Preface.

After the war, the relationship between Hancock and General Ulysses S. Grant became estranged, mainly because of Grant's opposition to General Order No. 40. But, before that sad breakdown, in 1864, Grant had proposed a restructuring of the eastern armies. He suggested to President Lincoln that Hancock should take command of the Army of the Potomac.[37] In his memoirs too, Grant was perhaps overly gracious when he noted: "Hancock stands the most conspicuous figure of all the general officers who did not exercise a separate command...his name was never mentioned as having committed in battle a blunder for which he was responsible."[38]

In the postwar period, Hancock served on the Ordnance Board in Washington and strongly recommended that the Federal Government adopt a standardized .45 caliber rifle.[39] He spent time on the plains fighting Indians, and his last assignment sent him to Governor's Island in New York City Harbor for 14 years. There, he commanded the Division of the Atlantic where he actively promoted the growth of the National Guard, was the first National Commander of MOLLUS, and served as president of the Military Service Institution and the Mexican War Fraternity Aztec Club of 1847. Like General Ambrose E. Burnside before him, he also served as president of the financially troubled National Rifle Association during the year 1881–1882.[40] Politically, Hancock was always considered a conservative and a man of his own mind. In 1880, he was the Democratic candidate for President of the United States but lost to James A. Garfield by a scant 7,023 popular votes and 59 electoral votes. His running mate was William H. English of Indiana, and some attributed their loss to "dirty politics" in New York City.[41] During his acceptance speech, Hancock coined the phrase, "A public office is a trust," which later became the battle cry for the successful bid of President Grover Cleveland.[42]

Despite his loss, during the campaign period, Hancock touched the hearts and minds of many Americans in the South and proved to be very popular with both blacks and whites. One newspaper noted: "In Montgomery County [Alabama], where the colored vote is larger than the white, the Democratic editor is a colored man, and the colored Hancock club had over six hundred members. In Richmond, Va., the colored Hancock club numbers over five hundred members...Winchester has a colored Hancock club with nearly as large a membership..."[43]

While dubious political ethics in the North may have played a part in his brief civic career, his personal integrity was not lost upon the thinking people of the nation. President Cleveland's Secretary of State, Thomas F. Bayard, likened Hancock to the first President when he said: "...[Hancock] like Washington, never forgot he was a citizen."[44]

Preface.

After fighting the many battles of bullets, ballots, shot and shell, Winfield Scott Hancock died on February 9, 1886 of an apparent, protracted case of diabetes. After brief ceremonies in New York City, his remains were transported back to his home turf in Norristown. There, on February 13th, one day before his 62nd birthday, he was laid to rest in a tomb he personally had constructed of local stone in Montgomery Cemetery.[45] In it already lay his beautiful daughter Ada, who preceded her father in death by nine years when she was only eighteen. In fact, just 14 months prior to his own death, Hancock had also lost his son Russell, who died at age 32 and was buried at Bellefontaine Cemetery in St. Louis, at the request of his mother.

When the train carrying the general's body arrived in Norristown, it was met by a group of local and national dignitaries for the final obsequies. Without the benefit of any religious ceremony at his vault, a simple spray of flowers from his beloved but distraught, absent wife Almira stood as her personal perfumed sentinel. The heavy, cold, damp winter air was suddenly broken by the four salvos issued from thirteen minute guns which were the command signal for the bugler's strain of taps. When the last note ended, the gate to the vault was closed and General Hancock became another member of the annals of history.[46]

A. M. Gambone
Myrtle Beach, South Carolina
November 10, 1996

ACKNOWLEDGMENTS

I would like to take this opportunity to thank the following individuals and institutions for their assistance with this effort. First, my publisher, Jim McLean, for the entire concept of this work; Ms. Bea Savage of Gettysburg for her extensive research assistance and enthusiasm for this project; Mr. D. Scott Hartwig and Cindy Stouffer of the Gettysburg National Military Park [GNMP] for their direction and assistance with research and Mr. Hartwig's critical review; the National Archives and the Library of Congress for their records and photographs; the Infantry School Library at Fort Benning Georgia. Researcher Mr. Sam Flocca of Salado, Texas, and a particular debt of gratitude to the entire staff at the Public Library of Woodbury, Connecticut. Every author should be so blessed with such a cooperative, productive library staff. The Kent Library in Suffield, Connecticut; the Pequot Library Association of Southport, Connecticut; Yale University in New Haven, Connecticut, plus Messrs. Steve Wright and Blake Magner of the Civil War Library and Museum in Philadelphia, along with archivist Steve Zerbe, for all their research and photographic assistance; author Michael Cavanaugh for his constructive guidance. The entire staff of the Historical Society of Montgomery County at Norristown [HSMC], for their files on the general and, in particular, Mr. Edward T. Addison, Jr., President, Dr. Joseph Riemer and Mrs. Judith Meier, for their constant assistance; the warm consideration from Dr. Richard J. Sommers, Louise Arnold-Friend and the photographic department of the United States Army Military History Institute [USAMHI] at Carlisle Barracks for their nearly endless files, volumes, newspapers and photographs, along with the Pennsylvania Historical and Museum Commission, the Pennsylvania State Archives and the State Museum of Pennsylvania. Mr. Brian C. Pohanka for generously sharing his Hancock photographs and files from his personal collection; Mr. George R. Stammerjohan, State Historian for California; Irish Brigade author, Kevin E. O'Brien of Scottsdale, Arizona, for sharing Hancock data from his manuscript; Mr. D. Scott Hartzell of Downingtown, Pennsylvania, for sharing his original Hancock letters; Mr. and Mrs. Ronald Shireman for their research efforts; Mr. William Barrante, for all of his editing assistance; Mr. Michael Phipps, historian, author and Gettysburg battlefield guide for his important

Acknowledgments

manuscripts; Mr. Timothy Buchanan, Chairman of the Pennsylvania Historical and Museum Commission, for the use of his personal photograph collection; Civil War artist, Don Troiani for his research data and permission to use his painting, *Cemetery Hill*, that graces the dust jacket. Mr. Paul Korzynski of New Hartford, Connecticut, a re-enactor and member of the First Company, Governor's Horse Guard; Mr. Hank Kluin at F. Burgess & Co., from Red Bank, New Jersey and Nick Nichols, a saddle expert, from Virginia, for their invaluable assistance with the research on the McClellan saddles and their fabrication. Dr. Harry W. Pfanz for his critical and important review of some early drafts; Mr. Albert Henry Wunsch, III and son of Englewood Cliffs, New Jersey, for the use of their letters; Mr. Timothy Smith, Gettysburg battlefield guide and author, for his research assistance and critical reviews; Mr. Charles Euston, owner of the Woodbury Blacksmith & Forge Company, for his education on the art of making nails and Mrs. Maria Allen for the kind use of her photographs.

The Hartford Public Library; The New Haven Free Public Library; Ms. Judith A. Sibley, Assistant Archivist at the United States Military Academy; The Mortensen Library of the University of Hartford; Ms.Candace Barth of the Silas Bronson Library in Waterbury, Connecticut, who rendered much help; Ms. Susan Ravdin of Bowdoin College for the O. O. Howard papers. To Mr. William M. McCain, for his research assistance in the Norristown area; Mr. Paul Koons and his daughter Karin Jones, who head up the Hancock Restoration Committee of the HSMC, for their many records and photographs. The Pennsylvania State Archives; Mr. Richard Seltzer, President of the Hancock Fire Company in Norristown; The Joyner Library of East Carolina University at Greenville, North Carolina; The Hamilton College Library at Clinton, New York; the Clement C. Maxwell Library of Bridgewater State College, Bridgewater, Massachusetts; the Bridgeport Public Library, Bridgeport, Connecticut; The Williams College Library at Williamstown, Massachusetts; The Carnegie Library of Pittsburgh; photographer and HSMC member, Joseph F. Morsello; my good friend Mr. Andy DeCusati of Gettysburg, for his research assistance and photographs; and the 27th Connecticut Volunteers, A Uniformed Historical Society. Mr. Wayne Motts, historian, Gettysburg battlefield guide and Lewis Armistead biographer, for his research efforts and manuscript reviews; The Adams County Historical Society at Gettysburg [ACHS], for their cooperation with photographs from the William H. Tipton Collection plus their volumes and newspaper collection; the Western Reserve Historical Society in Cleveland, Ohio; and Mr. Robert George of Prospect, Connecticut, for all of his photographic assistance; and Ms. Carol Resch of Bellefontaine Cemetery in St. Lou-

Acknowledgments

is. The medical team that afforded me so much help, Dr. Dean Mesologites; Mr. and Mrs. Tom and Jane Brown, Ms. Jonna Racela and Maryellen Woolley for her anatomical drawings; The American Civil Liberties Union Library in New York City; Ms. Marsha Rader for sharing her Hancock records and photographs; Ms. Karen Giustino and Maureen D. Hynes for their research at the New York City Public Library; Hancock interpretive re-enactor and Valley Forge Supervisory Park Ranger, Mr. Bruce Stocking; the National Rifle Association; the Library of Congress; Mr. and Mrs. Anthony J. Saraceni for their demanding work on the maps along with Matt and Heather Philbin for the use of their Hancock records.

Since this volume deals primarily with personalities related to the battle, the author has been most fortunate to have had the opportunity to discuss those many facets with a number of knowledgeable individuals. For those invaluable discussions, I would like to acknowledge the verbal contributions of D. Scott Hartwig, Dr. Richard Sommers, Wayne Motts, Timothy Smith, David A. Keough, Bruce Stocking and Karlton Smith. As always, I am especially grateful for the time, assistance and enormous patience that my wife Nancy affords me and my work. I alone assume full responsibility for any errors or omissions herein, and to anyone that I might have failed to notice, please accept my sincere apology.

Abbreviations and Definitions

ACHS.......... Adams County [Pennsylvania] Historical Society.

CWLM........ Civil War Library and Museum at Philadelphia, Pennsylvania.

CWRT......... Civil War Round Table.

GNMP......... Gettysburg National Military Park.

H. R .... House of Representatives.

HSMC......... Historical Society of Montgomery County at Norristown, Pennsylvania.

Joint Committee Report: This is the investigating Committee on the Conduct of the War which was established in December, 1861. According to *Civil War Dictionary*, they were empowered to investigate contracts, expenditures and military affairs. The Committee investigated all of the commanders of the Army of the Potomac and published their findings in *Reports of the Joint Committee on the Conduct of the War*.

MOLLUS.... Military Order of the Loyal Legion of the United States.

Abbreviations and Definitions

O. R. ....*War of the Rebellion, Official Records of the Union and Confederate Armies.*

S.H.S.P. ...... *Southern Historical Society Papers.*

USAMHI..... United States Army Military History Institute at Carlisle, Pennsylvania.

WSH............Winfield Scott Hancock

CHAPTER ONE

A Changing Order *and tense moments*

The bloody battle of Chancellorsville that had taken place during the first four days of May was now over, and the result was a masterful success for Confederate General Robert E. Lee and his storied Army of Northern Virginia. Along with that victory, the moderating 1863 spring weather began to dry and firm the Virginia roads, which naturally bolstered the spirits of the Southern army and its leaders. Eager to provide some relief to the war-torn Virginia countryside, and perhaps with a hope to facilitate Confederate recognition from England and France, Lee decided upon a bold second invasion of Northern soil. Candidly, all of the possible reasons for Lee's decision to move north are the subject of debate that will not soon end. These arguments are of no great concern today because Lee's decision was made and the reasons, in a sense, really do not matter. Once the Confederate invasion was officially sanctioned by Richmond, a battle such as the one fought at Gettysburg was preordained and nothing, save an impossible reversal of Lee's plans, could have prevented it. On June 3, with his plan winning an authoritative nod, Lee ordered his 75,000-man Army of Northern Virginia, with more than 280 cannon, to begin its march northward, away from the Fredericksburg and Chancellorsville areas. The very next day, portions of the 85,000-man Union Army of the Potomac, under Major-General Joseph Hooker, began to move in the shadow of its mortal enemy with over 350 cannon in its ranks. All of that stirring was to begin a march in excess of 200 miles for both armies and the crack Union II Corps as well.[1]

At that time, within the Federal Army, many of the ranking officers stood in chorus with their disdain for the colorful but defeated Union commander, "Fighting" Joe Hooker. An 1837 graduate of West Point, Hooker was regarded as a flamboyant, boastful individual given over to wine, women and song. Nonetheless, he impressed President Abraham Lincoln, and following the Union defeat at Fredericksburg in December of 1862, he was appointed to the high command though many considered him rather hedonistic. With his appointment, Lincoln emphatically warned Hooker against rashness. Despite his Chancellorsville failure, however, Hooker's strategy in the thickly wooded Virginia wilderness must be viewed as most creative and could well have been Lee's Waterloo if the Federal commander had not lost his nerve. But, such are the fickled fortunes of war and history which never celebrate a good strategy poorly executed.

One of the principal Union field officers upset with General Hooker was his long-time consort, Major-General Darius Nash Couch, commander of the II Corps.[2] A native of New York State and 1846 West Point graduate, Couch had developed an enviable military reputation owing to his intrepid though deceptively quiet nature. He suffered miserably from a long-standing bout of dysentery which he contracted during the Mexican War, and his resulting less-than-robust health gave him chronic problems. Unfortunately for the 41-year-old officer, medical science then could only commit him, and many others like him, to a life of related ongoing sufferings.

Shortly after the battle of Chancellorsville, General Couch took leave and went to Washington ostensibly to tend to his recurring malady. During his stay of approximately three weeks, Couch had at least two meetings with President Lincoln, the second occurring on May 22. During those meetings, Couch never attempted to hide his professional disdain for Hooker and he boldly, if callously, told the President that he thought Hooker incompetent. While it was uncharacteristic for Lincoln to defend himself during those kinds of trying moments, it is easy to appreciate that such stinging candor carried some measure of personal discomfort for the President, especially since Hooker had been his personal choice. Couch undoubtedly recognized that executive discomfort and later observed that his directness appeared to make the President "despondent." Nonetheless, Couch maintained that his blunt posture was necessary for the good of the army and the nation. After listening carefully to General Couch's condemning but honest words, Lincoln undoubtedly surprised the normally placid officer when he asked, "what about you?," meaning Couch as Hooker's replacement. Initially flattered, Couch knew that his impaired physical vigor could not accommodate such a demanding position and he definitely wanted no part of all the Washington political interference inherent with such an appointment. Consequently, he gracefully declined.

Couch suggested to the President that Major-General George Gordon Meade, of Philadelphia, commander of the V Corps, would make an excellent choice for the position. Then, perhaps to underline his own confidence in the recommendation, Couch told Lincoln that while Meade was his junior, he would be only too pleased to serve under him without regard to his own seniority.[3] When that meeting concluded, Couch left the President and would not see

A Changing Order *and tense moments.*

him again until November of that year when Lincoln delivered his famous Gettysburg address and the general was invited to sit on the platform. The President obviously thought well of Couch's suggestion because shortly after that meeting, Lincoln was overheard to say, "I tell you I think a great deal of that fine fellow Meade."[4]

Meanwhile, portions of the Union Army were still on the banks of the Rappahannock River near Fredericksburg, Virginia, and 39-year-old Major-General Winfield Scott Hancock commanded the First Division of Couch's II Corps. Hancock too was disgruntled over the Chancellorsville disaster, which he felt "should have been a brilliant [Union] victory." Hancock had just written to his wife Almira, whom he affectionately called Allie, and told her that "I do not know what will be the next turn of the wheel of Fortune, or what Providence has in store for this unhappy army. I have the blues ever since I returned from the campaign." Then, anticipating Almira's fears about his being appointed to the post of high command, Hancock wrote: "I have been approached again in connection with the command of the Army of the Potomac. Give yourself no uneasiness—under no conditions would I accept the command. I do not belong to that class of generals whom the Republicans care to bolster up. I should be sacrificed."[5] Actually, if Hancock was considered at all, he had little to fear since he was too junior an officer and, as he alluded to Almira, as a Democrat, he was affiliated with the wrong political party. But his concerns about any new commander grew as rumors of others he thought incompetent were mentioned as potential successors to the hapless Hooker. So, like many other soldiers, he was forced to simply wait until Washington made a decision.

Hooker too was certainly feeling the sting from all the vicious public and negative military reaction to his loss at Chancellorsville, despite Washington's official position of restraint. Perhaps as a public facade, President Lincoln and General-in-Chief Henry W. Halleck arrived at nearby Falmouth, Virginia, on May 7, to bolster the army's morale and they were soon participating in a grand review. But such visits did little for the unforgiving Northern public, who did not generally fathom the capricious fortunes of war. So, in typical American fashion, they created a new vilifying cocktail, "Hooker's Retreat." Newspapers in the North became polarized about the vanquished Union commander and, initially, even Horace Greeley's *Tribune* made attempts to support him though in the end, Greeley had to agree that Hooker's defeat and retreat were a shameful shock. In Washington, the *Daily Morning Chronicle* maintained full and unswerving support while the *National Intelligencer* saw Hooker as totally inept.[6]

Even though Hooker and Hancock were good friends, Hancock's dismay over Hooker's poor performance continued to simmer within him and he wrote Allie that the army commander had failed to utilize two of his vital corps at Chancellorsville, in spite of repeated suggestions to do so. He continued: "He would not do it. Now the blame is to be put on [General John] Sedgwick for not joining us; as if it were possible to do so with one corps, when we had six corps, and this force was considered strong enough to attempt to unite with Sedgwick, without risk to the command."[7] But all that backward speculating was nothing more than an emotional vent. The only real source of solution was, at that moment, quietly watching the proud but shaken ranks of his blue-coated army pass in review.

During their Falmouth visit, Lincoln and Halleck eventually invited General Meade to join them for lunch, which the President utilized as a platform to familiarize himself with the potential new army commander. Meade reported that during their extended luncheon, the three men discussed "all sorts of things" and that "he [Meade] did not blame any one" for the Chancellorsville debacle.[8] Meade's low profile and prudent attitude were undoubtedly a welcome respite for the President, who probably had already decided upon Meade but continued to wait to be fully comfortable with his decision.

Meanwhile, an irritated General Couch had hoped his earlier meetings with the President would precipitate a quick change in the top command for the Army of the Potomac. When those wishes appeared to be stalled in political red tape, in an unusually impatient move, Couch asked to be relieved and Washington promptly accommodated him. As a dubious reward for his faithful service, Couch was placed in charge of the newly created Department of the Susquehanna, which had been formed to defend Harrisburg in the event of Rebel invasion.[9] Later, Francis Walker recorded: "It is a matter of regret that General Couch did not, for a little while longer, possess his soul in patience. A few weeks more would have seen the army commanded by an officer in whom he had the utmost confidence..."[10]

On the day Couch resigned, May 22, Hancock was appointed, with equal dispatch, to assume command of the II Corps and its 13,000 men. Indicative of Washington's endless bureaucracy at the time, it took until June 25 before the terse official notification of Hancock's appointment was sent to General Hooker: "The President has assigned General Hancock to the command of the Second Corps."[11]

Hancock's promotion resulted in the subsequent appointment of Brigadier-General John C. Caldwell, a former schoolteacher from Lowell, Vermont, to command his First Division. As so often happens in the military, Caldwell's

A Changing Order *and tense moments.* 5

appointment also suffered no want of speculative comments, and one young lieutenant in General Samuel K. Zook's 57th New York wrote home and told his sister: "Upon Hancock assuming command of the Corps after Chancellorsville, the Division devolved up [*sic*] Caldwell, in which capacity he has been ever since. He is quite a favorite among the boys (so good natured) but there is nothing very brilliant [*sic*] about him." [Emphasis in original][12]

Over the next month, details on Hancock are few though we can safely assume he made every effort to understand his new command and to be understood. During the time span between June 21 through the 25th, the II Corps and Hancock remained in the Thoroughfare Gap area where little happened in the way of serious fighting.[13] Hancock informed headquarters that he was in "a strong position," and while there was some Confederate cavalry in the locale, he confidently reported that "you need have no fears of this position."[14] June 22nd might be considered as significant because that day reportedly saw the first death of an American involved in what was to become the infamous battle of Gettysburg. According to Dr. William D. Hall, a physician with the 1st New York Cavalry:

> At the little village of Greencastle Penn, and on June 22nd, 1863—was killed the first man who was fated to fall on Penn soil—Corpl Wm. H. Rihl of Co. C 1 NY Lincoln Cav'y. Capt Boyd had left Chambersburg with his Co. C 1 NY S Cav'y with intention of finding Lee's advance. We ran upon a squadron of [Brigadier-General A. G.] Jenkins Cav'y 5 miles out from Chambersburg—charged them and drove them into Jenkins command at Greencastle—We were met by a terrific fire and Corpl Rihl fell dead—the first man killed on Penn's soil during the war. His remains were buried by the Confederates by the side of the road were [*sic*] he fell and two days afterwards the citizens of Greencastle buried him in one of the burial lots in the village...A lad of about 19 years...[15] [Emphases in original]

Before the end of July 3rd, a mere 11 days away, there would be approximately 53,000 more casualties which would mark the bloodiest conflict ever fought on the North American continent. But, the 22nd also saw a growing Rebel frenzy in the North which dictated some new and drastic measures for some. In compliance with the edict of the Mayor of Harrisburg, all the saloons in the capital city were forced to close.[16]

During the 23rd, Hancock encountered some frustrations with Major-General Julius Stahel, a Hungarian-born soldier whom General Hooker had assigned to General Couch to command the cavalry for the Department of the Susquehanna. Hancock had requested from Stahel between 200–300 cavalrymen to assist in keeping the roads open and free of Rebels. Instead of troopers, his request only received the following response. "I regret not being able to accommodate you."[17] An angry Hancock then turned to headquarters but that did not improve his fortunes. Understandably upset, later that evening, he sent the following to General William H. French:

> General:
>
> Notwithstanding my application to General Stahel for cavalry, 200 or 300, he declined leaving any. I have made application to headquarters of the army for cavalry, but the reply I received was such as to deter me from asking again. I will use all the cavalry I have to scour the roads, keeping none in reserve.
>
> The men captured this afternoon were taken to Hay Market [sic]. They have all been recaptured. They were pumped dry.
>
> There is nothing new.
>
> Winf'd S. Hancock[18]

On the morning of the 25th, General Hooker ordered Hancock and his new corps to march to Edwards's Ferry via Sudley Springs and onto Gum Springs.[19] In doing so, the II Corps blocked the forward movement of Major-General "JEB" Stuart's famed Confederate cavalry at Haymarket. Stuart judiciously pulled his ranks off the roadway to a safe distance but proceeded to annoy the Yankees with his artillery, which resulted in three Federal casualties before they were finally driven off.[20] While this event did not evolve into a major conflict, Hancock sent word to General Hooker that "The enemy with... 6,000 men, with one battery of artillery...have driven in my cavalry, but nothing further as yet." As a result, this time Hancock was soon reinforced

A Changing Order *and tense moments.* 7

with a brigade of Union cavalry and Stuart soon prudently retired to an even safer distance.[21]

Hancock's ranks next entered Centreville, which was garrisoned by the brigade belonging to Brigadier-General Alexander Hays, another Pennsylvanian and West Point classmate of General Hancock. Apparently, some of the II Corps men were less than sterling soldiers, which caused General Hays to boldly order Hancock, his superior, to move his ranks away. Hancock listened carefully, then prudently agreed with his subordinate-friend as he moved his troops. Hays later said that he had ordered his own command to shoot any members of the II Corps who might create any further havoc. As it turned out, it would only be a matter of mere hours before General Hays and his command were absorbed into the ranks of the II Corps as Hancock's Third Division.[22]

Also during the 25th, Brigadier-General Alexander S. Webb came into the midst of the II Corps camp seeking General Hancock as he wished an assignment that would assure him of some battlefield exposure. It happened that at the same time, General Gibbon, commander of Hancock's Second Division, had just placed Brigadier-General Joshua T. [Paddy] Owen, who commanded the "Philadelphia" or Second Brigade, under arrest for unidentified causes. When Webb finally located General Hancock, the two men spoke briefly and, according to Major Francis Walker, Hancock placed Webb in Owen's stead, "because he [Hancock] knew the man."[23] Little did anyone realize that in less than ten days, General Webb, a former math teacher, would be at the focal point of the great Confederate assault.

On the evening of the 26th, Hancock and his command crossed the Potomac at Edwards's Ferry, which was very close to the 1861 Union disaster known as Ball's Bluff. The weather had been miserable all day and heavy rains plagued those weary II Corps soldiers who had been marching for 18 hours. Just as soon as they crossed the river, they "lay down to sleep, the men badly used up, many of them missing." Remaining in that area until 3:00 on the afternoon of the 27th, they were then ordered to start their march anew.[24] From Edwards's Ferry, Hancock wired General Hooker, who was still in command, and informed him that General Sedgwick and part of his command had arrived in that area and they too were crossing the river.[25]

At 3:00 a.m. on June 28, General Meade was asleep in his tent at Frederick City, Maryland, when he was suddenly aroused by a courier from Washington. While Meade never tells us why, his first fleeting thought was that Hooker was having him arrested or relieved and he was astonished to learn that his caller was Colonel James A. Hardie from the War Office in Washington. Hardie lit a candle and perhaps heightened Meade's anxiety when he told him that he had come "to give him trouble." Of course, that "trouble" was exactly what some Union generals did not want to hear about themselves. President Lincoln was finally appointing the dour Pennsylvanian commander of the Army of the Potomac and relieving General Hooker.[26]

In fairness to General Hooker, his removal was brought about in part by his own offer to resign when Halleck supposedly refused his request to allow him to absorb command of the troops at Harpers Ferry. Commensurate with his lack-luster personality, "Old Brains," as Halleck was derisively known, sent a telegram to a subordinate of General Hooker, advising him: "Pay no attention to General Hooker's orders." Yet, following the coming battle at Gettysburg, the changeable Federal Government would bestow upon the derided Hooker the coveted Thanks of Congress.[27] In spite of all his disenchantment with the Washington intrigue, it must have been a very bitter experience for "Fighting Joe" when Hardie, along with General Meade, showed up at his tent unannounced. Hooker did not need any special preamble to know the purpose of the Washington visitor and to his credit, he bowed out with much grace.[28] His final ignominious chapter on being relieved from command followed shortly when General Halleck had Hooker arrested for visiting Washington without leave.[29]

Almost one year after he was assigned to his new command, General Meade offered the following about his predecessor and his own general strategic ignorance:

> When I assumed command of the army [sic] of the Potomac, on the morning of the 28th of June, it was most around Frederick, Maryland; some portions of it, I think, were at that time at Middletown; one or two corps were the other side of a range of mountains between Frederick and Middletown. I had no information concerning the enemy beyond that fact that a large force under General Lee, estimated at about 110,000 men, had passed through Hagerstown, and had marched up the Cumberland Valley; and through information derived from the public journals I had reason to believe that one corps of the rebel [sic] army, under General Ewell, was occupying York and Carlisle, and threatening the Susquehanna at Harrisburg and Columbia.

A Changing Order *and tense moments.*

My predecessor, General Hooker, left the camp in a very few hours after I relieved him. I received from him no intimation of any plan, or any views that he may have had up to that moment. And I am not aware that he had any, but was waiting for the exigencies of the occasion to govern him, just as I had to be subsequently.[30]

While Meade would not have to wait long for governing exigencies, his appointment was generally welcomed by the officers and troops of the Union army. General Alexander S. Webb was one of those delighted and he wrote to his father, "Rely on Meade. He is the man we have been looking for. The best we have discovered." [Emphasis in original][31]

During the day of the 28th, portions of Hancock's II Corps began to filter into the area of Frederick City, having completed a Hooker-initiated march from Sugar Loaf Mountain, in pursuit of Lee's northward move. Hancock's hometown friend, General Zook, was part of that spearhead which entered the area with his Third Brigade of Caldwell's First Division. Soon after Zook had established a camp for his ranks, an unidentified soldier approached Zook's picket line with all the proper signs, claiming that he had "important news for General Hancock."[32] That important news was confirmation that General Lee was already in the Pennsylvania town of Chambersburg. While that information was disturbing, it was not too surprising since Hancock had been plotting Lee's forward movement with his daily reports to General Hooker. Perhaps it was after obtaining that news about General Lee's position when General Hancock was confronted with a new dilemma. A Confederate spy had been caught with a complete account of the Union troops. The man was quickly tried, confessed and was found guilty. Someone suggested that the spy should be sent to Washington so the authorities there could deal with him. Hancock immediately disagreed and said "No! If you send him to Washington they will promote him." The man was soon suspended from a tree.[33]

Actually, by the time Hancock received the confirmation about Rebel locations, Lee had been in Chambersburg for about four days and one of his lieutenants, Major-General Jubal A. Early, had already made his headquarters further north in York. Meanwhile, in response to all of that Rebel movement, General Meade had notified Washington that he intended to move his army "as promptly as possible on the main line from Frederick to Harrisburg..."[34] Meade was already mentally prepared for battle though it was anything but clear where or when it might occur.

Major-General Winfield Scott Hancock

A Changing Order *and tense moments*. 11

Courtesy: Massachusetts Commandery MOLLUS and the USAMHI.

Major-General Joseph Hooker

Major-General Darius N. Couch

A Changing Order *and tense moments.* 13

Sometime during the evening of the 28th, both Hancock and General Gibbon went to see General Meade to offer their congratulations on his appointment. While Meade was pleased to see both men, he appeared to be "very anxious" and he even chided Gibbon about speaking of him as the new army commander. After their visit with Meade, Hancock and Gibbon then called on the deposed General Hooker, whom Gibbon understandably described as not "in a good humor at all."[35]

General Gibbon was a close associate of Hancock and he was destined to play a large part in activities at Gettysburg. The two men shared a great mutual confidence and trust. Unfortunately, in 1864, even that warm relationship was to erode over Hancock's charge that Gibbon failed to properly execute one of his commands near Petersburg. Born in Philadelphia and raised in Charlotte, North Carolina, Gibbon was graduated from West Point in 1847 and when he became of age, he changed his family name from *Gibbons* to *Gibbon* for reasons known only to him. Perhaps because he was raised in the South, he had a tendency to be quiet about his home and some thought him moody and morose. But, overall, there is little question about Gibbon's fighting qualities and after the war he was sent to the west. There, following the 1876 disaster at Little Big Horn, John Gibbon led the troops that rescued the survivors and buried the mutilated dead belonging to Custer's command.[36]

Perhaps about the same time that Hancock and Gibbon were visiting with General Meade, back in Chambersburg, General Lee was reluctantly speaking with Henry Thomas Harrison, a scout employed by General Longstreet to gather intelligence. Since Lee had little confidence in the credibility of such men, he was extremely reluctant to make any critical decisions based upon Harrison's information. Finally though, Lee became convinced that Harrison's data, telling that General Meade now led the Army of the Potomac which was rapidly closing upon his own forces, had to be heeded.[37] Despite his reluctance, the Rebel commander fatefully ordered his far-flung corps to converge on the tiny village of Cashtown, or near the slightly larger village of Gettysburg.[38]

While still enroute to Frederick, Father Corby recorded an incident about General Hancock, which warrants attention. When the II Corps entered Maryland, Hancock issued a very stern warning to his ranks that they were not to molest or destroy any private property in a loyal State. While riding through his camp one evening, the general spotted several soldiers chasing a sheep, which infuriated him to think that his orders were being violated. According to the cleric, when Hancock caught up to the men, the sheep was no where to be seen and he roared with a string of oaths, "Blank, blank, you blank, blank, scoundrels!" Hancock continued and increased his cursing when suddenly, the sheep reappeared but quickly ran off. Immediately, Hancock's entire attitude inexplicably changed and he suddenly began to speak in more civil tones: "I take it all back. I am glad you have not transgressed my orders." So quick a change certainly perplexed his soldiers but Father Corby, who had become a witness, noted: "Gen. Hancock was a...polished gentleman and had a keen sense of propriety. Addicted merely through force of habit to the use of profane language, when excited, he would invariably stop short when he discovered the presence of a clergyman."[39]

On the 29th, Hancock was ordered to begin a march to Frizzelburg at 4:00 a.m., but an errant headquarters clerk failed to deliver the order, causing a three-hour delay.[40] Predictably, that delay angered the intolerant Hancock and he later reported to General Meade: "The man in question has already been brought to punishment. I took every precaution...I shall try to make up the most of it by short cuts and rapid marching."[41] Despite the late start, as promised, Hancock drove his men relentlessly through the heat, at least 32 miles and until 10:00 that evening, when they finally made camp at Uniontown, about two miles short of their original objective. Today, it is difficult to fully appreciate the physical demands of such a forced march, including the enormous effort to keep an eight-mile-long wagon train moving with all of the troops.[42] But, Hancock's ranks accomplished much though they grumbled and complained as loud as any in either army. For example, the men of General Zook's brigade cried that Hancock "would not stop until he got to Harrisburg...[and] a thousand men in the Second Corps were physically disabled for weeks thereafter."[43] Typical infantry bitching!

Upon his arrival in Uniontown, Lieutenant Josiah Favill of Zook's 57th New York noted: "Uniontown is a pretty secluded village, patriotic, but paralyzed just now by the nearness of the rebel [sic] army."[44] Hancock also soon learned that JEB Stuart was again nearby in Westminster with a considerable force and a number of field guns.[45] Stuart had arrived in the area late that afternoon with 125 wagons and brushed away some stubborn resistance from two determined companies of Delaware cavalry, who counted 67 casualties for their defiance. As Stuart started receiving local reports, he probably realized that he was smack in the middle of the marching Federal army, so on the 30th he moved toward Hanover, only to encounter Judson Kilpatrick's Union cavalry.[46] While Stuart never posed a serious problem to Hancock on the 29th, the Union undoubtedly lost a golden opportunity to destroy the flower of the Confederate cavalry. When Hancock learned of Stuart's position, he immediately notified headquarters, which did nothing. That inaction was probably caused by the Union cavalry commander, Major-General Alfred Pleasonton,

A Changing Order *and tense moments.* 15

who told General Meade that Hancock must be mistaken because his forces were already in control of the area.[47] Consequently, Stuart remained unmolested and the confusion of Gettysburg was already beginning to crystallize.

During the night of the 29th, Meade finally found time to write his wife Margaret, and told her of the bizarre experience surrounding his appointment. While Margaret had presumably read about her husband's promotion in the Philadelphia newspapers, Meade informed her: "I was aroused from my sleep by an officer from Washington entering my tent, and after waking me up, saying he came to give me trouble...then handed me a communication to read; which I found was an order relieving Hooker from command and assigning me to it." Then expressing the fear of all who thought they might be so appointed, Meade added, "you know how reluctant we both have been to see me placed in this position...I had nothing to do but accept and exert my utmost abilities to command success."[48] But while Meade expressed his personal trepidations, many within the ranks were thrilled about Hooker's removal, if not Meade's appointment. One II Corps officer confided to his diary:

> This evening we hear Hooker has been relieved of the command, and that General Meade from the Fifth corps [*sic*] is appointed in his place. There is not an officer in the army, I think, who does not rejoice at the news. We saw enough of Hooker at Chancellorsville to assure us he was not capable of commanding an army like this.[49]

Gilbert Frederick, a sergeant in the 57th New York, perceptively noted: "It was a dangerous thing to change commanders on the eve of a battle, but the authorities in Washington seemed unwilling to trust General Hooker with the enemy so near the capitol."[50] Whatever the feelings or problems related to his appointment, one of Meade's first official acts was to elevate three young cavalrymen from the rank of captain to brigadier-general. Those troopers were George A. Custer, 23, Elon John Farnsworth, 26, and Wesley Merritt, 29. That trio of fortunate, young officers was destined to become known as the "boy generals." As might be expected, not everyone delighted in those elevations, including Brigadier-General John Buford, commander of the First Cavalry Division.[51]

Despite command changes and dubious promotions, the Union army continued northward and those demanding marches took a great toll on the Yankee soldiers who wore those oppressively hot, heavy, woolen uniforms. However, there were some occasional benefits inherent with those marches and uniforms. One member of the 1st Minnesota noted in his diary entry of June 30 that as he and his comrades marched through Maryland, they found it to be "top shelf." Many of the local residents gave those Yankees a kind reception and the boys certainly appreciated flirting with the "nice girls in particular." The diarist also wrote: "Gen. Hancock issues an order [and] compliments us for our 'vigorous exertions' in marching 'full thirty miles' yesterday, and saying that such a march was 'required by the Maj. Gen. commanding, on account of urgent necessity.'"[52]

Also on the 30th, General Couch, in his new position, was receiving reports on how General Early demanded of the small town of York $100,000 cash, 150 barrels of flour, 40,000 pounds of beef plus 50 bags of coffee and assorted other staples. While Early was to receive most of the demanded supplies, the small town could only offer him $28,600 in cash.[53]

Because of all the growing tension, that day also saw the Union President bombarded by recommendations he could have done without. No matter the critical nature of the national crisis at that moment, sponsoring men still attempted to put forward their favorites. Examples:

Philadelphia, June 30, 1863.
His Excellency Abraham Lincoln
President of the United States:

In my judgment, it is essential that McClellan be placed in charge of the forces in Pennsylvania not now attached to the Army of the Potomac. I speak as a friend.

J. Edgar Thomson[54]

A Changing Order *and tense moments.*

Philadelphia, June 30, 1863.

His Excellency Abraham Lincoln
President of the United States:

...Unless we are in some way rescued from the hopelessness now prevailing, we shall have practically an inefficient conscription, and be powerless to help either ourselves or the National Government. After free consultation with trusted friends of the Administration, I hesitate not to urge that McClellan be called here. He can render us and you the best service, and in the present crisis no other consideration should prevail...

A. K. McClure[55]

New York, June 30, 1863

His Excellency Abraham Lincoln
President of the United States:

Our citizens generally have great confidence in the military capacity of General Franklin, and think he can render good service at the North. He is willing to serve wherever he can be useful. Will you not detain him for duty here?

Waldo Hutchins
Prosper M. Wetmore
Jos. Wadsworth[56]

Meanwhile, Early's very presence in York further fueled the Union newspapers, which were already bursting with excitable reports. From all over the northeast came warnings of a Rebel invasion, imploring the populace to dire preparations and sacrifices. Matters had reached a fever pitch in the Northeast as the pages of the local gazettes were frantically emblazoned:[57]

Philadelphia: One more appeal is made to you in the name of duty, and manhood...Close your manufactures, workshops and stores, before the stern necessity for common safety makes it obligatory...Let no one refuse to arm who will not be able to justify himself before man and God...

Philadelphia: The Corn Exchange raised five companies this morning...The merchants have resolved to raise a million of dollars. All the stores are to be closed, and the men employed in them forwarded for the defence [sic] of the city and the State. The men who leave their employment are to be paid their usual salaries during their absence.

Honesdale, PA.: A large meeting is assembled here to-night to raise militia companies. The Delaware and Hudson Canal Company gives five thousand dollars towards the movement in this county.

Harrisburg: Great anxiety is felt for the safety of the Pennsylvania railroad. The enemy's movements show that they are endeavoring to reach thirty or forty miles west of the place.

Trenton: Gov. [Joel] Parker forthwith took measures to call out the militia of New Jersey...Troops are arriving here, hourly, and will proceed at once to Pennsylvania.[58]

Norristown, PA.: Hancock's home was not to be left out in the cold and they too responded to the call. On the 28th, that budding metropolis noted that "The manufacturers have determined to close their works until the rebels are driven from the State, and have raised $10,000 to pay the wages of all who volunteer during their absence. Five hundred men will leave for Harrisburg in the morning."[59]

In concert with all of this concern, General Meade issued a circular to all of his senior officers that stated in part:

A Changing Order *and tense moments.*

The commanding general has received information that the enemy are advancing, probably in strong force, on Gettysburg. It is the intention to hold this army pretty nearly in the position it now occupies until the plans of the enemy shall have been more fully developed.[60]

The Yankee nation was electrified and the news of impending battle, wherever it might occur, overshadowed everything else. On June 30th, General Meade, certain that battle was imminent, issued another statement to his officers:

>Headquarters Army of the Potomac
>June 30, 1863
>
>The commanding general requests that previous to the engagement soon expected with the enemy, corps and all other commanding officers address their troops, explaining to them briefly the immense issues involved in this struggle. The enemy are on our soil. The whole country now looks anxiously to this army to deliver it from the presence of the foe. Our failure to do so will leave us no such welcome as the swelling of millions of hearts with pride and joy at our success would give to every soldier of this army. Homes, firesides, and domestic altars are involved. The army has fought well heretofore; it is believed that it will fight more desperately and bravely than ever if it is addressed in fitting terms.
>
>Corps and other commanders are authorized to order the instant death of any soldier who fails in his duty at this hour.
>
>By command of Major-General Meade:
>
>S. Williams
>*Assistant Adjutant General*[61]

Hancock too issued an appeal to his own new command, which made perfectly clear his expectations when he concluded: "To the patriotic and brave

I have said enough. Upon those who desert their post in the hour of trial let instant death be inflicted by their comrades."[62]

The public attention, especially in the Northeast, was overwhelmingly preoccupied with the Rebel invasion. On the same day that General Meade issued his circular to his officers, another sad event was also taking place. Fifty-seven-year-old Rear Admiral Andrew Hull Foote, the intrepid Yankee sailor who became affectionately known as the "Gunboat Commodore," had been quietly laid to his rest in New Haven, Connecticut.[63] Even so solemn a final tribute to the hero of Forts Henry and Donelson could not momentarily divert the Yankee attention from the hysteria caused by the impending Rebel conflict.

CHAPTER TWO

July 1, 1863
"Terminological inexactitude."
—Winston Churchill

After resting at Uniontown, Maryland, the entire last day of June, Hancock and his II Corps were ordered to march the short seven miles to Federal headquarters in Taneytown on July first. They arrived there about 11:00 a.m., probably under an overcast sky with a moderate temperature of about 74 degrees.[1] Obviously intrigued by the old town, Hancock told Major St. Clair Mulholland, commander of the 116th Pennsylvania and a future regimental chronicler, a brief tale about his grandfather, who was an officer in George Washington's Continental army. Apparently, Hancock's ancestor had been sent to Taneytown to collect Revolutionary War prisoners that had been captured from British General John Burgoyne's ranks, and ordered to deliver them to the American commander at Valley Forge.[2] Unfortunately, nothing further is known about the matter, though we can safely assume that Hancock's interest in Taneytown sprang from a family tradition which he must have heard many times over.

Once settled, Hancock promptly reported to General Meade, who was already beginning to receive preliminary reports from the field at Gettysburg, a battle site not yet formally selected and just developing. During an intense but cordial meeting, Meade informed his II Corps commander that based upon the local maps and topography, he felt it best to engage Lee at Pipe Creek, just south of Taneytown. Meade detailed his thoughts and later, Hancock left us the following comments:

> While I was there General Meade told me all his plans. He said he had made up his mind to fight a battle on what was known as Pipe creek; that he had not seen the ground but judging from the map it presented more favorable features than any other position that he could see; that he had sent his

engineers there to examine the position and note all its strong features, and that he was preparing an order for that movement.³

Shortly after Meade completed his review, disturbing word arrived from Major-General John F. Reynolds that matters at Gettysburg were already getting very hot and the enemy was attacking in force.⁴ It was about 11:30 a.m.

Until his meeting with the new army commander, Hancock had been completely unaware that matters in Gettysburg had become pretty challenging ever since 7:30 that morning. According to tradition, at that moment, Lieutenant Marcellus Jones, of the 8th Illinois Cavalry, fired the opening shot of the fight. That report also became the signal to Hancock's good friend, Brigadier-General John Buford, that the Confederate division belonging to Major-General Henry Heth was advancing up the Chambersburg Pike.⁵ The historic, confusing and controversial battle of Gettysburg was irreversibly under way!

Anxious about having only a thin line of cavalry to defend against the pressing mass of Rebel infantry he knew were soon to arrive, General Buford sent an aide to locate the approaching General Reynolds and rush him to the front. Reynolds had been placed in charge of the army's left wing, which included the I, III and XI Corps plus a cavalry division under Buford's command.⁶ Just about two miles south of the village, Reynolds was found personally leading the I Corps to Buford's aid. When Reynolds learned about the unfolding battle, he directed his ranks to move quickly as he personally hurried forward to meet with his cavalry commander. When he entered the village, Reynolds stopped briefly at the home of Mr. George to seek directions. Taking only a few moments there, he was off shortly but destined to return soon.⁷

According to Buford's aide, Lieutenant Aaron B. Jerome, Reynolds found the 37-year-old Buford in the cupola of the Lutheran Seminary, west of town. After some quick pleasantries, the two officers promptly made their way onto the field, making decisions for deployment of the I Corps the moment it should arrive. In the process, it didn't take Reynolds long to make an accurate evaluation of developing conditions. Turning to an aide, Captain Stephen M. Weld, he instructed him to ride back to General Meade and inform him that "the enemy are advancing in strong force, and that I fear they will get to the heights beyond the town before I can." To emphasize the urgency, Reynolds told the aide: "Don't spare your horse—never mind if you kill him."⁸ It was

Weld who made that 11:30 report to General Meade as the army commander finished his morning meeting with Hancock.

The I Corps finally arrived upon the field about 10:30 that morning, and on both sides of the Chambersburg Pike, fighting became intense and, in some areas, developed into a hand-to-hand struggle. On the field only about 20 minutes, Reynolds was moving a blue column from the Iron Brigade's 2nd Wisconsin into the Herbst Woods, near the top of Eastern McPherson's Ridge, hollering: "Forward into line at the double quick!" That blue line was momentarily stunned by a Rebel volley but Reynolds again urged the black-hatted soldiers: "Forward! For God's sake forward and drive those fellows out of those woods." In an instant he was killed by a bullet to his head and in all probability, he was dead before he hit the ground.[9] According to his orderly, Charles H. Veil, "I have seen many men killed in action, but never saw a ball do its work so <u>instantly</u> as did the ball which struck General Reynolds..." [Emphasis in original] The dead I Corps commander was less than 90 days away from his 43rd birthday. Taking charge of his commander's remains, Veil again stopped briefly at the home of Mr. George before proceeding to Taneytown.[10] With Reynolds down, Captain John P. Corson, of the 1st Maine Cavalry, found Major-General Abner Doubleday, commander of the Third Division, and informed him he was now in command of the field.[11]

Back in Taneytown, after Weld related Reynolds's message to Meade, its impact was immediately appreciated by the army commander and he exclaimed, "Good God! if the enemy gets Gettysburg, we are lost."[12] Shortly after, Meade received another report from General Buford which had been sent at 10:10 that morning, informing him: "I am positive that the whole of A. P. Hill's force is advancing."[13] Serious pressure was then mounting on Meade.

About the same time that the I Corps entered the field, Major-General Oliver Otis Howard, commander of the XI Corps, was also coming into the area with his escort, in advance of his ranks. General Reynolds had ordered Howard and the XI to Gettysburg earlier that morning and by eight o'clock, the one-armed commander was leading his men up the Emmitsburg Road from the town with the same name. Unaware that Reynolds was down and anxious to locate him, Howard was led to a building at the intersection of Baltimore and Middle Streets, by an 18-year-old Gettysburg native, Daniel A. Skelley.[14] That location was known locally as Fahnestock's Observatory, and once on the balcony of that building, Howard had an excellent vista of the entire unfolding conflict. Within moments of his arrival, Howard looked down and saw Major William Riddle, Reynolds's aide-de-camp, who told him that Reynolds had been wounded. Riddle quickly departed and soon found that his commander had in fact been killed and he went off to report matters to General Meade. Minutes later, another aide appeared before Howard, telling him: "General Reynolds is dead, and you are the senior officer on the field." Howard, who then superseded General Doubleday, made his way to Cemetery Hill, near the large brick gateway to the Evergreen Cemetery where he would establish his headquarters.[15] From that position, he would also have a commanding view of the entire field at that time. According to General Howard, the time was approximately 11:30 a.m. General Meade was soon to learn about the death of General Reynolds.

In Taneytown, when Meade finished with Hancock, the latter returned to his own tent and was probably not too surprised to learn of the rapidly developing Gettysburg events. While Meade was still digesting the earlier Reynolds and Buford messages, Major Riddle arrived with the sad news that Reynolds had been killed. That revelation shocked Meade.[16] Perhaps it caused him to reflect for a moment on his very own morning message to Reynolds: "The Commanding General cannot decide whether it is his best policy to move to attack until he learns something more definite of the point at which the enemy is concentrating. This he hopes to do during the day."[17] As it turned out, unfolding events at Gettysburg, far beyond Meade's or anyone else's control, actually determined the best policy.

It was the mournful report of Reynolds's death, plus Meade's belief that he needed a better informed commander to take control of the challenging events at Gettysburg, that decided his next actions. With his chief-of-staff, Major-General Dan Butterfield, in tow, Meade made his way to Hancock's headquarters and undoubtedly surprised his II Corps commander when he ordered him to immediately move to Gettysburg and *assume command* of the field.[18] Hancock recorded that Meade sent him "because he [Meade] had [just] explained his views to me, and had not explained them to the others; that I knew his plans and ideas, and could better accord with him in my operations than anybody else."[19] Not surprisingly, from an army always crawling with rumor, claims that Meade had selected Hancock because he had little confidence in Howard, who was technically next in line to succeed General Reynolds, developed very rapidly. While Meade leaves us an incomplete commentary on the matter of his selection, all of the precise reasons for his selection of Hancock will probably never be known, though he clearly expressed his admiration for the Norristown general long before that particular moment.[20] By the same token, Meade had not stated any known prior reservations about Howard though General Doubleday was definitely not a favorite of his. Meade always thought the reputed founder of baseball "slow and pedantic" and held him in great disdain.[21]

Naturally, there must have been at least some brief discussion among the generals when Hancock realized that Meade's order to *assume command* carried a military impropriety. Since such a directive would place him in a position of authority over a senior officer, he mentioned it to Meade, who was not moved to change.[22] Instead, the army commander also instructed Hancock to turn command of the II Corps to his Second Division commander, Brigadier-General John Gibbon, who was junior to Brigadier-General John C. Caldwell of the First Division. None of that trampled protocol seemed to bother Meade because he had recently received Washington's authority to handle army assignments as he saw fit, license absolutely denied to General Hooker.[23] During the coming battle, General Meade would make several unconventional staff decisions, including his failure to fully utilize his second most senior and competent general officer, Major-General John Sedgwick.[24] Obviously, the Federal commander acted to meet all the crises at hand without precise concern for seniority or protocol because, when he was appointed, Meade was instructed: "You are authorized to remove from command and to send from your army, any officer or other person you may deem proper, and to appoint to command as you may deem expedient."[25] While Meade was to exercise this license, the most important questions at that moment were, should he finalize preparations for battle near Pipe Creek, or, did matters at Gettysburg now dictate otherwise? He was not a man to be obsessed with picayune feelings while a potentially great battle was unfolding and minute-by-minute increasing in ferocity. As a result of the pressing question of where to prepare for battle, at 1:10 p.m., Meade ordered Hancock to proceed to Gettysburg and "*assume command* of the corps there assembled, viz., the Eleventh, First and Third [commanded by Major-General Daniel E. Sickles], at Emmitsburg...in consequence of the death of Major-General Reynolds." [Emphasis added] General Meade also instructed Hancock to "make an examination of the ground in the neighborhood of Gettysburg, and report to me...the facilities and advantages or disadvantages of that ground for receiving battle."[26] A copy of Meade's order was sent to General Howard and Meade soon issued a second order at 1:15 p.m., instructing Hancock and now, Gibbon: "Hold your column ready to move."[27] In Hancock's own words, his interpretation of Meade's directive was: "If the ground was suitable, and circumstances made it wise, I was directed to establish the line of battle at Gettysburg."

Whatever else may be written about Hancock's posture on this touchy matter of *assuming command*, he did not shirk the responsibility or the potential of hurt feelings. He made his position perfectly clear when he stated: "Of course it was not a very agreeable office for me to fill to go and take command of my seniors. However, I did not feel much embarrassment about it, because I was an older soldier than either [Howard or Sickles] of them."[28]

Shortly after that second impromptu meeting concluded, Hancock was on the road north accompanied by his chief-of-staff, Lieutenant-Colonel Charles H. Morgan, Major William G. Mitchell, a few personal aides and a small group from the Signal Corps under Captain James S. Hall, 53rd Pennsylvania.[29] By 1:30 that afternoon, General Gibbon had the long blue line of the II Corps begin its hot, dusty, 13-mile march toward Gettysburg as well. That advancement toward the battlefield was testy for all the men that humid, sultry afternoon. Driven by nervous officers and the natural anxiety of impending combat, one II Corps soldier wrote:

> The march...of July 1 was exceedingly nagging, as it was made in quick time. The distant booming of cannon soon increased the heart beat. The heavy Enfield rifle, accouterments, knapsacks, haversacks and canteen were no longer burdensome. Tired limbs, blistered feet and sore muscles no longer absorbed our thoughts or drew upon the will power; the whole man was changed as by magic; quickened and apparently refreshed to a degree not explainable, and hardly to be appreciated by those who have never experienced the wondrous power of a battle already begun, and toward which one is rapidly marching.[30]

Hancock departed Taneytown in an ambulance so he could study the existing period maps of the area and read the recently issued orders from General Meade. No doubt that ride was bumpy, hot, slow and trying on his nerves, which made him anxious to take to his own sorrel. But, he persevered and a few miles outside of Gettysburg, his party encountered the ambulance bearing the body of a slain soldier. Not realizing the wagon's precise contents, Hancock asked the attendant whose remains were in the blanket. The sole officer-guard replied, "General Reynolds, sir."[31] That melancholy meeting had an immediate dulling effect on everyone's spirits, since the death of Reynolds seemed to underscore their own mortality. Perhaps it was at that moment when Hancock sent Major Mitchell ahead to locate and inform General Howard of his

"Terminological inexactitude."

impending arrival. Once located, Mitchell remained with Howard until his commander arrived.

Shortly after passing Reynolds's remains, Hancock's party mounted and soon began to encounter a road-clog of XI Corps wagons and pack animals, which were creating confusion. The first of his many commands to restore organization was to promptly order those wagons to the rear so that arriving troops and supply trains could pass with greater ease.

By mid-afternoon, mounting Confederate pressure was being applied to the Yankee lines. Concerned about what he perceived as a total lack of leadership on the field, and unaware of Hancock's impending arrival, at 3:20 p.m. the Kentucky-born General Buford penned a quick note to Major-General Alfred Pleasonton: "At the present moment the battle is raging on the road to Cashtown...General Reynolds was killed early this morning. In my opinion, there seems to be no directing person." Then, plaintively he added, "P.S.—We need help now."[32] Later, Howard was to respond to Buford's message: "I do not wonder that he was full of apprehension and he judged me when our troops were giving way...I believe the dispositions are what the emergency called for..."[33] Hancock was later informed that Buford supposedly sent another written or verbal dispatch [the source could not recall which] to General Meade, urgently requesting: "For God's sake send up Hancock, everything is going at odds and we need a controlling spirit."[34] However, this author finds no record of such a message.

The timing of Hancock's arrival on the field at Gettysburg is not precise. While it would be helpful to have such detail, the lack of same does not alter his actions and accomplishments once he did arrive. Nonetheless, in both his battlefield report and testimony before the Joint Committee, Hancock indicates his arrival as 3:00–3:30 p.m. while General Howard noted the time as 4:30. Judging from a variety of sources, it appears likely that his arrival occurred between 4:00 and 4:30 p.m.[35] Once on the field, his discriminating eye was obvious to many on both sides. One Confederate officer noted: "With the perception of a great general he [Hancock] saw the strength of the position [Cemetery Hill], seized upon it, reformed broken corps and reported to his chief that he had a favorable position." Unable to resist the temptation though, this Rebel eyewitness went on to boldly speculate: "Had Stonewall Jackson been alive and in [Lieutenant-General Richard S.] Ewell's stead, as he would have been, Hancock would not have been able to rally on Cemetery Hill."[36] While the impact of Jackson's absence might be forever debated, one unchallenged point is that when Hancock came upon the field, he was very impressive.

From Lieutenant Francis Wiggin, of the 16th Maine: "When the shattered forces of the First Corps reached the [Cemetery Hill] Ridge, one of the first things we saw, was the magnificent form of General Hancock...He was surrounded by his staff...busy issuing orders...He had quickly grasped the situation and had gotten matters so well in hand that the Confederates would certainly have met a very warm reception..."[37] Another Maine man, Captain Greenlief T. Stevens of the 5th Maine Battery, noted that as he and his battery approached the cemetery gate, General Hancock called out for their commanding officer. Stevens immediately presented himself to the general, who charged the captain to "take your battery on to that [Culp's] hill and stop the enemy from coming up that ravine." The captain naturally asked, "By whose order?" Perhaps with one of his broad smiles came the reply, "General Hancock's."[38] Stevens moved promptly!

The most eloquent appraisal of Hancock's arrival was offered by President Lincoln's personal secretaries, John Nicolay and John Hay. In their monumental ten-volume work on Lincoln, the two men noted:

> His presence immediately exerted a remarkable calming and encouraging effect. All accounts agree as to the extraordinary influence wielded by Hancock upon the battlefield, an influence not wholly attributable to prestige or to great intellectual power. The vague phrase "personal magnetism" is the one most frequently chosen by observers to express it. He was then in the flower of his youth, a man of singularly handsome presence, tall and stalwart, with the eye and profile of an eagle, a strong voice, and a manner expressive throughout of soldierly resolution and ardor. His arrival alone, at that critical moment, was like the reenforcement of an army corps.[39]

While everyone will never totally agree on the profile of any individual, the reader can be confident that most Hancock observers, friend and foe alike, all tend to gravitate toward the same adjectives to describe him. Still, while Hancock's arrival may have inspired, it also signaled the cause of controversy and since the first day of the battle, rumor, fiction, bias and personal pride have all been joined together to give rise to the Gettysburg debate known as:

"Terminological inexactitude."

Major-General George Gordon Meade

Major-General Winfield Scott Hancock

Major-General John Fulton Reynolds

Major-General Oliver Otis Howard

"Terminological inexactitude."

Major-General Henry Warner Slocum

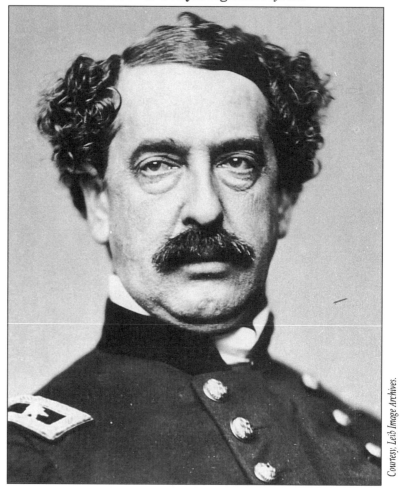
Major-General Abner Doubleday

Brigadier-General John Buford

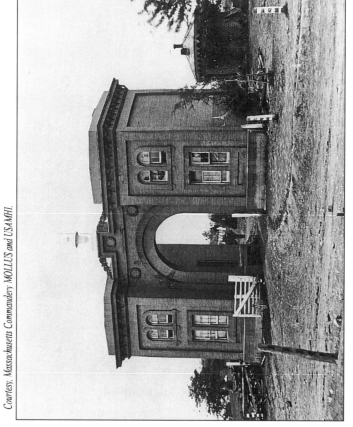

Courtesy, Massachusetts Commandery MOLLUS and USAMHI.

The Cemetery Gate

Brigadier-General Charles H. Morgan

During the battle of Gettysburg, Morgan was a senior aide on General Hancock's staff.

Brevet Brigadier-General William G. Mitchell

During the battle of Gettysburg, a younger Major Mitchell was an aide to General Hancock.

"Terminological inexactitude."

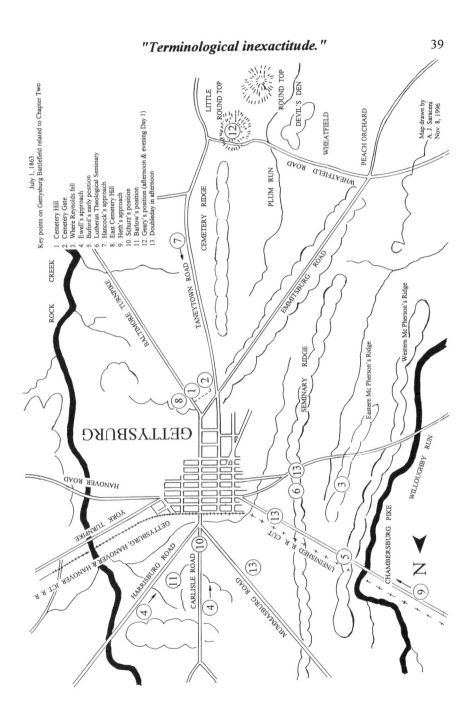

July 1, 1863
Key points on Gettysburg Battlefield related to Chapter Two

1. Cemetery Hill
2. Cemetery Gate
3. Where Reynolds fell
4. Ewell's approach
5. Buford's early position
6. Lutheran Theological Seminary
7. Hancock's approach
8. East Cemetery Hill
9. Heth's approach
10. Schurz's position
11. Barlow's position
12. Geary's position (afternoon & evening Day 1)
13. Doubleday in afternoon

Map drawn by
A. J. Saraceni
Nov. 8, 1996

Hancock at Gettysburg...*and beyond.*

THE HANCOCK–HOWARD CONTROVERSY.

General O. O. Howard was a native of Leeds, Maine. He graduated from Bowdoin College in 1850 and then promptly entered West Point, graduating fourth in his class of 1854. He was an openly devout Christian, which won him the army sobriquet of "Old Prayer Book Howard." Even President Lincoln warmly referred to him as the "Christian general."[40] At First Bull Run, Howard led a brigade which, like so many others that day, was routed, but soon after, he received a brigadier's star. On the second day of Fair Oaks, he was severely wounded which led to the amputation of his right arm. After he returned to the field at Antietam, in September, 1862, he assumed command of the Second Division of Major-General Edwin V. Sumner's II Corps when Major-General John Sedgwick was wounded and taken from that field. In November of 1862, he was promoted to major-general and commanded the Second Division, II Corps at Fredericksburg. Afterward, he was in charge of the entire II Corps for only 11 days. He then succeeded the popular but mediocre, German-born Major-General Franz Sigel in command of the XI Corps just before the fateful battle of Chancellorsville. There, on May 2, 1863, Stonewall Jackson sent his II Corps smashing into the unprotected right flank of the Yankee XI Corps, sending Howard's heavily populated German ranks fleeing in total pandemonium. After that disastrous battle, Lincoln considerately defended Howard from his numerous detractors who sought to have him removed. In a very paternal manner, the 16th American President told them: "Give him time, and he will bring things straight."[41] By the time the battle of Gettysburg was concluded, Howard had somehow won Lincoln's trust and the President even utilized him as something of a mediator when the President wished to express his disappointment with General Meade.[42]

After Gettysburg, Howard went to the west under General William T. Sherman and led the northern column on the latter's famous March to the Sea, where his performance appears not to have improved greatly. For at least one Federal soldier who fought at the Howard-directed battle of Pickett's Mill, Howard simply proved himself to be totally inept.[43] He remained in the army after the war and became a commissioner for the Freedman's Bureau, which was rampant with corruption though no scandal ever touched Howard. He founded a Congregational Church in Washington, D.C., and was very instrumental in the creation of Howard University, serving as its president between the years 1869–1874. In 1872, President Ulysses S. Grant appointed him a peace commissioner to the Apache Indians under Cochise, and he later led expeditions

"Terminological inexactitude."

against the Nez Percé, Bannocks and Paiute Indians. In 1880, he served as the superintendent of West Point and his final assignment was commander of the Division of the East, which he held until his retirement in 1894. In 1893, he was awarded the Medal of Honor for his heroic action at Fair Oaks. During his life he would write no less than seven books plus numerous newspaper and magazine articles.[44] Consequently, whatever human and military failings Howard may have had, he was an individual of some very impressive energies and accomplishments.

When Howard took command of the field at Gettysburg, he passed charge of his XI Corps to German-born Major-General Carl Schurz, his Third Division commander. In turn, the Prussian-born Brigadier-General Alexander Schimmelfennig, a former German revolutionary, took command of Schurz's division. At that time, the Union infantry line was bent in an arc from the Hagerstown Pike on the left, and Howard extended it all the way around to the Heidlersburg Road [another name for the Harrisburg Road] on the right. The far left of that line was held by General Doubleday and his I Corps, which was having a difficult time with the Confederate divisions belonging to Major-Generals Henry Heth and Robert E. Rodes.

Between the hours of noon and two o'clock that afternoon, an uncanny lull settled over the battlefield. But, at 1:00 p.m., General Schurz brought Howard confirmation of General Buford's earlier report that Confederate Lieutenant-General Richard S. Ewell was advancing southward from York with his entire II Corps.[45] This meant that soon, the Federal line would be forced to defend itself against the seasoned divisions of Major-General Robert E. Rodes, Major-General Jubal A. Early and Major-General Edward Johnson, known affectionately as "Old Allegheny." With that pressing news, Howard sent urgent messages to General Sickles at Emmitsburg and Major-General Henry W. Slocum at Two Taverns to bring up their ranks as quickly as possible.[46] He then ordered General Schurz to "push forward [with] a thick line of skirmishers, to seize the point...as a relief and support of the First Division." In response, Schurz ordered "General Schimmelfennig...to advance briskly through the town, and to deploy on the right of the First Corps in two lines." Shortly afterward, Schurz also ordered Brigadier-General Francis C. Barlow and his First Division, XI Corps, to take up a position "on the right of the Third Division," while the Second Brigade was to be held to the rear of the First.[47] With those movements under way, General Howard set off to closely evaluate General Doubleday's line, finding him about a quarter of a mile beyond the seminary.[48]

About 2 o'clock a new Confederate assault began in earnest, pushing the Federal lines off McPherson's Ridge and back onto Seminary Ridge. There was heavy fighting between the two lines of Blue and Gray with the Confederates continually gaining the upper hand. About 3:30 p.m., General Early had personally arrived in the area and he ordered Brigadier-General John Brown Gordon's brigade to attack the right flank of General Schurz's First Division.[49] No matter that he had pressed his men over 14 grueling miles to get to Gettysburg, Gordon wasted no time as he sent his 1,200 Johnnies successfully reeling into Schurz's lines. Gordon's thundering assault was a veritable Confederate military elixir and it rekindled the enthusiasm for at least portions of Brigadier-General George Doles's Brigade which had just been repulsed by the Yankees. General Schurz noted that "Suddenly the enemy opened upon the First Division from two batteries...It was now clear that the two small divisions under my command, numbering hardly over 6,000 effective men...had a whole corps of rebel [sic] army to contend with."[50] According to Professor Edwin B. Coddington, "...Gordon's attack indeed appeared to be a signal for all Confederate forces to close in on Federal positions stretching from the Fairfield to the Heidlersburg Road."[51] Gordon's attacking ranks began to buckle Schurz's line, who was soon forced to acknowledge that it was time for, "A movement to the rear..." Matters were no better for General Doubleday's far left, which was being hit hard by Heth's and Major-General William Dorsey Pender's divisions. According to one report, "about 4 p.m. Heth attacked Doubleday's center, and that Ewell pressed with three of Rhodes' [sic] brigades between Schurz and Doubleday and that Early, coming down from the northeast, struck Barlow's right flank..."[52] When Ewell's forces were placed into line, the Confederates had a numerical superiority of nearly two-to-one[53] over their Yankee foe and Doubleday noted: "It was evident Lee's whole army was approaching us..."[54] That "movement to the rear" or "retrograde" became somewhat confused as the I and XI Corps began to push into the village for whatever protection they might find. It is obvious that once into the town, discipline within some Union ranks broke down quickly. According to one eyewitness, "There the troops of the eleventh corps [sic] appeared in full retreat, and long lines of Confederates...were sweeping forward in pursuit...It was a close race which could reach Gettysburg first, ourselves, or the rebel [sic] troops..."[55] In a letter home to his mother, General Barlow told her: "We ought to have held the place easily, for I had my entire force at the very point where the attack was made— But the enemies skirmishers had hardly attacked us before my men began to run— No fight at all was made...During this time the whole of our line had been driven back, both the Ist Corps and the 11th..."[56]

"Terminological inexactitude."   43

As Hancock was approaching the area near Cemetery Hill on the Taneytown Road, he encountered portions of those retreating Federal troops, some of whom were forming near that roadway. But any sense of formation could not have been too great since one eyewitness description noted: "the road was literally full of men...going to the rear." After offering hard resistance to the Confederates for nearly five hours, at 4:10 p.m., Howard ordered the "First and Eleventh Corps to fall back gradually, disputing every inch of ground..." Actually, his order had already been anticipated and was being executed as Doubleday noted: "The enemy...advanced in large numbers...[and] It became necessary to retreat."[57] The specifics of that Union retreat turning into a general rout is another heated controversy connected with the battle of Gettysburg. Whatever the debated details of that moment, there is ample evidence that at least portions of those Yankee lines retired in good order, returning fire as they made a deliberate retrograde. Another eyewitness recorded what is probably a very accurate profile: "...there was no organization as far as I could see. Neither was there any great hurry."[58] Still, during those very moments, at least some portions of the I and XI Corps were running through the streets of Gettysburg with a variety of Rebel regiments in hot pursuit. It is easy to imagine the intense confusion.

Hancock and his staff moved among those scattered I Corps ranks huddled along Taneytown Road as they assisted the efforts to reorganize a defensive line along one of the stone walls near the roadbed.[59] Despite any pandemonium, Hancock saw that for the moment the worst of the Rebel attack was over and an effective line of resistance had to be quickly established to prevent another successful Rebel assault.[60] With that in mind, he moved forward and found Howard on Cemetery Hill, which Howard had already selected as a focal point. The foresight of his selection was later noted by a subordinate who correctly stated: "Howard selected the position on Cemetery Hill as a rallying point, and the next two days of fighting showed the wisdom of this selection."[61]

With all of the confusion and pockets of fighting still in progress, Hancock quickly saw that some of the best resistance on the entire field was being offered by Buford's sorely tried cavalry. Even in his battlefield report, Hancock noted: "The cavalry of General Buford was occupying a firm position on the plain to the left of Gettysburg, covering the rear of the retreating corps."[62] Almost immediately upon his arrival, Hancock began to exercise his authority. On his way to meet General Howard on Cemetery Hill, on the northwest portion of that prominence, he encountered the Second Brigade of Brigadier-General Adolph W. A. F. von Steinwehr's Second Division, which was then being led by Colonel Orland Smith, who recorded the following:

> [Hancock] immediately rode along my lines and complimented the men and the dispositions. He saw Captain Madeira and inquired who commanded that brigade. On being told, he desired to see me. I was called and introduced. "Said He: My corps is on the way but will not be here in time. This position should be held at all hazards. Now Colonel, can you hold it?" Said I, "I think I can." "Will you hold it?" "I will." And we did.[63]

According to Hancock, when he did arrive on Cemetery Hill, he found that Howard had attempted "...to stop and form some of his [own] troops there—what troops he had formed there I do not know. I understood afterwards, and accepted it as the fact, that he had formed one Division there prior to this time."[64] This then was the state of matters when Hancock rode up to General Howard, and sets the backdrop for the dispute. The heart of this controversy is generally thought to be General Howard's reluctance, if not complete refusal, to yield command to General Hancock when he arrived on the field. Despite this commonly held view, like the Roman god Janus, the controversy actually has two distinct faces or questions. First, did General Howard refuse or impede the transfer of command to General Hancock? Second, what was Howard attempting to accomplish with his numerous, written justifications about his Cemetery Hill meeting with Hancock.

Segment One

The most widely accepted version of an onerous meeting between Hancock and Howard is based upon the dubious report of Captain Eminel P. Halstead, Assistant Adjutant General of General Doubleday's staff, who wrote:

> ...I [Halstead] returned to where General Howard sat, just as General Hancock approached at a swinging gallop. When near General Howard, who was then alone, he saluted, and with great animation, as if there was no time for ceremony,

"Terminological inexactitude."

said General Meade had sent him forward to take command of the three corps. General Howard replied that he was the senior. General Hancock said: "I am aware of that, General, but I have written orders in my pocket from General Meade, which I will show you if you wish to see them." General Howard said: "No, I do not doubt your word, General Hancock, *but you can give no orders here while I am here.*" Hancock replied: "Very well, General Howard, I will second any order that you have to give, but General Meade has also directed me to select a field on which to fight this battle in rear of Pipe Creek." Then casting one glance from Culp's Hill to Round Top, he continued: "But I think this the strongest position by nature upon which to fight a battle that I ever saw, and if it meets with your approbation I will select this as the battlefield." General Howard responded: "I think it a very strong position!" "Very well, sir, I select this as the battlefield."[65] [Emphasis added]

    The reader should appreciate that it would have been perfectly normal for General Howard, or any senior officer, to have had some reluctance about yielding command to a junior officer. When viewed in that light, Halstead's comments offer little evidence that any meaningful controversy occurred between Hancock and Howard regarding the passing of authority except for the reputed comment about Hancock's not being permitted to issue any orders. Further, the scenario that Halstead offers regarding Hancock's willingness to "second" any of Howard's orders, paints a pandering posture for the II Corps commander, which sounds too foreign to his personality. It is also at odds with Hancock's earlier statement about his not feeling embarrassed about assuming command. Let the reader beware!

    While the author is certainly no apologist for Howard, the greater source of fermentation here is definitely not rooted in Captain Halstead's report [no matter any inaccuracies], but rather, the puzzling embellishments and efforts of General Doubleday. After Halstead reported back to his commander, Doubleday, for precise reasons known only to him, eagerly promoted and later chronicled that Halstead clearly *overheard* Howard's blatant refusal to acknowledge Hancock's authority to command, and the controversy was born.[66] In his official report, Doubleday also notes that shortly after Hancock arrived on the field, and after he announced himself to Howard, there was at least one attempt by Howard to countermand a Hancock order.[67] This author finds no such data.

Despite Halstead's claim that he was the sole witness, there is another reported first-hand version of that Hancock-Howard meeting that warrants some consideration because it is probably a little closer to the truth than Doubleday's version of Halstead's comments. It was reported by Captain J. O. Kerby of the Signal Corps, who was then attached to the Headquarters of the Cavalry Corps and also claimed to have been a witness. Unfortunately, his reasons for being on Cemetery Hill at that time are not known.

According to Kerby, when Hancock found Howard, the XI Corps commander was "biting his finger nails, evidently...much rattled..." [This is something that Halstead does not report.] Hancock hollered: "Howard, let's get them behind that stone fence, they can never get us out of that."[68] According to Hancock, General Howard had made earlier attempts "to reform some of the Eleventh corps as they passed over Cemetery Hill...[but] it had not been very successful."[69] Kerby continues that when Hancock spoke to Howard, he "said something in a low voice...which I *took* to be an acquiescence with Hancock's suggestion." [Emphasis added] The two commanders were soon joined by General Doubleday, whom Hancock ordered to place his men behind the nearby stone fence as well. Captain Kerby was involved with those placements and reportedly was close enough to Hancock and Howard, who were in the midst of "animated conversation." Kerby reported that he heard Howard answer to something said by Hancock:

> *"Hancock, you cannot command here to-day."*[70] [Emphasis in original]

Despite Halstead's and Kerby's versions, the author is convinced that the central issue here is not Howard's supposed refusal to relinquish his command, but instead an earlier message *reportedly* sent by Howard to Meade stating: "...the First Corps has fled without fighting." That alleged message understandably infuriated General Doubleday, who lamented that it "created the greatest feeling against the [I] corps, who were loudly cursed for their supposed lack of spirit and patriotism."[71] Apparently, as a result of that disparaging comment, Doubleday sought some form of retribution for what he considered an intemperate remark by Howard, though, again, there is not the slightest evidence that Howard ever sent such a message. What did reach Meade was a later comment sent by General Hancock, who informed the army commander that *Howard had told him* that the I Corps had given way. For that comment, Doubleday never showed Hancock any of the disdain that he afforded Howard.

In terms of exposure for the various versions of the Hancock–Howard meeting, Doubleday's promoted story would understandably receive more attention owing to his rank and relative fame over Captain Kerby. It must be understood that the day of the first proved to be an embarrassment for Doubleday too, which was later evident in his lament: "He [General Meade] never asked me a single question in relation to the operations of that day."[72] For a man who had held actual command of the entire field, even for a short while, some attempt to save face is all too familiar, if not understandable.

Despite any distortion from Doubleday, it would be unfair to create a totally innocent profile for General Howard's contribution to the controversy. Candidly, he was still smarting from his great discomfiture about Chancellorsville when his XI Corps was soundly routed by Stonewall Jackson's surprise attack. That sad event undoubtedly led him to search for an opportunity for redemption and, now, the potential to retrieve his standing was being removed by Hancock's unanticipated appointment. That certainly could not sit well, especially since he thought he was doing his very best to hold the Union position that afternoon.

This entire dispute cannot be fully appreciated without some understanding of General Doubleday's evaluation of General Howard's Chancellorsville performance. In that regard, Doubleday was blunt and severe with his evaluation in his 1881 volume, *Chancellorsville and Gettysburg*. Therein, his assaults upon Howard were painful though not exactly inaccurate. He takes Howard to task for being surprised by Stonewall Jackson and lays the blame directly at his feet since Howard failed to post pickets, even *after* he had been warned of a possible attack. Doubleday quotes a writer from *Harper's*: "The rout of Howard's corps was possible only from the grossest neglect of all military precaution." Yet, despite his harsh criticism, Doubleday also objectively and fairly notes: "Howard exerted himself bravely then, and did all he could to rally the fugitives..." In the end, however, Doubleday accurately sums up General Howard's Chancellorsville performance by quoting a French military writer: "It is permissible for an officer to be defeated; but never to be surprised."[73] How many historians have echoed those feelings over the past 135 years?

Irrespective of Doubleday's opinion, Howard remains the most confusing part of this entire controversy. He was bright, well-educated, devout, and a dedicated [if not the most exacting] soldier. But his performance in the East was not always impressive. When Bruce Catton wrote of Sherman's ability to develop fighting men, he noted that Howard "never showed a sign of anything but diligent mediocrity but that when he was transferred west...he presently became an army commander."[74] Even this modestly flattering evaluation appears to be in question. For example, Captain F. C. Winkler, who served in General Schurz's division, positively wrote that Howard checked into every department and was most polite and even said thank you to his orderlies. However, three days later, Winkler noted that "very little confidence is felt in General Howard." When Howard was placed in command of the IV Corps, near Atlanta, Winkler again noted: "The news was received with profound regret."[75] Howard simply appears to have possessed an inordinate amount of talent for alienating the soldiers. A member of the 71st Pennsylvania angrily noted: "His [Howard's] incompetency at Gettysburg was but a repetition of his conduct at Chancellorsville."[76]

From a more modern evaluation, Albert Castel, who authored *Decision In the West*, felt that while Howard was intelligent and brave, he was favored by Grant and Sherman because of his dedication and not because of his precise military talent. In fact, Castel states: "Howard should consider himself lucky to hold any command at all, much less that of a corps. Not only had he allowed his troops to be surprised at Chancellorsville; his performances at Gettysburg and Chattanooga had at best been mediocre. He is a poor tactician, unenterprising, and so ostentatiously pious that the troops call him Old Prayer Book."[77]

Perhaps the most perplexing aspect of General Howard was his selected proclivity toward distorting, or avoiding, the truth. For an openly religious man, he clearly demonstrated that trait at Chancellorsville when he claimed he had not received an important precautionary message from General Hooker. Later, Howard's claim was challenged by General Schurz, his Third Division commander, who confirmed the receipt of that warning and that he personally delivered it to General Howard. At Gettysburg, Howard again made a similar claim and declared that he did not receive a copy of Meade's 1:10 p.m. message appointing Hancock to command. Regrettably, this Gettysburg cry smacks of *déjà vu*.[78]

In his volume *Chancellorsville and Gettysburg*, Doubleday offered his most popular version of the Hancock–Howard Cemetery Hill meeting which is, according to that author, a repeat of Halstead's earlier report. Let the reader be aware that Doubleday significantly modified some of Halstead's comments and, fortunately, his book was printed while Hancock was still alive. When he read that work, the former II Corps commander made some important, critical

"Terminological inexactitude."

marginal notes which clearly demonstrate why some historians are uncomfortable with Doubleday's credibility since some of his points are commonly contested and others are in blatant error. Despite those failings, however, it would be imprudent to deem his work as completely useless as some detractors cry. Nonetheless, in 1911, Hancock's marginal notes on Doubleday's book were discovered and published in the ***Journal of Military Service Institution***. The following extracts are direct quotes written by Doubleday with Hancock's marginal responses. They offer us some clear insight into one portion of this controversy. [See photos on pages 51 and 52.]

Doubleday: "...General Meade superseded Howard by sending his junior officer, General Hancock, to assume command of the field and rally the First Corps—who needed no rallying, as they were all fighting in line of battle. He also ordered General John Newton of the Sixth Corps to take command of the First Corps."[79]

Hancock: "I had no such orders! had not heard of such conditions of officers."

Doubleday: "Owing to the *false dispatch* Howard had sent early in the day, Meade was under the impression that the First Corps had fled without fighting, and Hancock had orders to rally them."

Hancock: "NO!"[80]

Doubleday: "Howard *refused* to submit to Hancock's assumption of authority, and *quite a scene occurred.** He [Howard] said, 'Why, Hancock, you cannot give any orders here! I am in command, and I rank you!'† Hancock replied that he was sent by order of General Meade, but *Howard said he should refuse to acknowledge his authority*.‡ Hancock then said he would go back to headquarters and report, but Howard asked him to remain and help him organize the troops. Hancock then rode over to me, perhaps a little doubtful whether I would join Howard in not recognizing his right to command."

Hancock: "This is all wrong, General Howard made no objections whatever—no scene occurred!"[81] [All emphasis added]

---

* Note that Captain Halstead did not include any statement about a "scene" in his report.

† Note the difference between Halstead's and Doubleday's comments here.

‡ Howard, never made this statement! [See photo on p. 52.]

Certainly, these marginal Hancock notes will lead any serious observer to question Doubleday's details and motives. While Hancock's notes definitely cast aspersions upon Doubleday, another Gettysburg veteran left a fanciful account that would have further angered General Doubleday. Second Lieutenant Sidney G. Cooke of the 147th New York, part of Doubleday's own command, noted that during their retreat "Hancock was there to meet the crisis... Every man knew how hopeless resistance would be, but Hancock sat his horse, superb and calm as on review; imperturbable, self-reliant, as if the fate of the battle and of the nation were not his to decide. It almost led us to doubt whether there had been cause for a retreat at all."[82]

Since the objective of this chapter is the Hancock–Howard controversy, we must conclude that both Doubleday and Howard had personal reasons, real or imagined, to fuel their mutually antagonistic rhetoric. This was amplified when we note that both men leave several articles each about those critical Hancock–Howard moments on Cemetery Hill, though none are exactly identical in detail. In general, Doubleday's writings tend to disparage Howard while Howard's articles are written as face-saving vehicles against Hancock's assuming command. After castigating Howard, Doubleday would have us believe that he promptly embraced Hancock's authority when facts appear to indicate otherwise. One example is an incident related by an aide to General Hancock.

Upon his arrival on Cemetery Hill, Hancock promptly began to increase the defense of the entire area. He ordered his aide, Lieutenant-Colonel Morgan, to take a brigade from the I Corps and occupy Culp's Hill. Morgan immediately went over to General Doubleday and informed him of Hancock's wishes. Doubleday bristled at the order and was described as showing "beaten demeanor...protested that his men were worn out, cut up, [and] had no ammunition..." As it happened, Hancock was within hearing distance and rode over and unceremoniously told Doubleday: "General...I want you to understand that I am in command here, send every man you have." With that encouragement, Brigadier-General James S. Wadsworth was ordered to place his entire First Division into position.[83] This move receives Howard's confirmation when he wrote: "After General Hancock left me on the highest point of the ground, he went directly to Doubleday...What he said to him I do not know but in a few moments I saw that Wadsworth's Division...was detached and led off to the right..."[84] In Hancock's opinion, the movement of Wadsworth's ranks, plus the batteries sent with him, became the real deterrent for General Ewell's later, fateful decision not to "carry the hill."[85]

Doubleday's credibility was also sarcastically challenged by yet another of his subordinates after the general noted: "I waited until the artillery had

"Terminological inexactitude." 51

> Hancock, to assume command of the field and
> Corps—who needed no rallying, as they were i
> line of battle. He also ordered General John
> Sixth Corps to take command of the First Cor[
> The head of the Eleventh Corps reached (
> 12.45 P.M., and the rear at 1.45 P.M. Schir
> division led the way, followed by that of Barl
> were directed to prolong the line of the Firs
> right along Seminary Ridge. The remaining
> of Steinwehr, with the reserve artillery under M
> were ordered to occupy Cemetery Hill, in rear (
> as a reserve to the entire line. Before this dis
> be carried out, however, Buford rode up to n
> formation that his scouts reported the advar
> corps from Heidlersburg directly on my right
> a staff officer to communicate this intelligen
> Howard, with a message that I would endeav
> ground against A. P. Hill's corps if he could
> the Eleventh Corps, keep Ewell from attack
> He accordingly directed the Eleventh Corps to
> to meet Ewell. As it did so, Devins's caval
> back and took up a position to the right and r
> just south of the railroad bridge.
> The concentration of Rodes's and Early's
> one from Carlisle and the other from York—t(
> great exactness; both arriving in sight of Get
> same time. The other division, that of Jol
> longer route from Carlisle by way of Greenw
> the trains, and did not reach the battle-field
> Anderson's division of Hill's corps was also ba
> in the mountains on the Chambersburg road.

Photo Credit, Steve Zerbe.

**Hancock's Marginal Notes Published In
the *Journal of Military Service Institution***

This is a photograph taken from the 1911 edition of the *Journal* which shows General Hancock's disagreement with General Doubleday's comments made in *Chancellorsville and Gettysburg*. Hancock's note here states: "I had no such orders! had not heard of such conditions of officers."

Hancock at Gettysburg...*and beyond.*

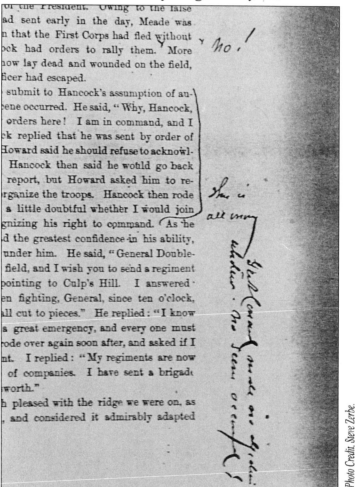

**Hancock's Marginal Notes Published In
the *Journal of Military Service Institution***

In this marginal note, General Hancock states: "No! This is all wrong. General Howard made no objection whatever—no scene occurred!"

"Terminological inexactitude." 53

gone [retreated] and then rode back to the town with my staff. As we passed through the streets, pale and frightened women came out and offered us coffee and food, and implored us not to abandon them."[86] To this claim, Captain R. K. Beecham, a member of the First Brigade, First Division of the I Corps, mused:

> It would be interesting to one old veteran to know when the retreat began as heretofore spoken of, or where General Doubleday "waited until the artillery had gone." We of the Black Hat [Iron] Brigade did not wait a second after taking in at a glance the full peril of our situation, but dashed down the Chambersburg Pike. While we were running our very best... the artillery...passed us...but we saw nothing of General Doubleday and his staff...
>
> Of course it stirs the heart of an old veteran to have his General speak in words of commendation of himself and comrades; nevertheless, we must conclude that a number of us left Seminary Ridge some time after our General, for when we arrived in the city, there were no "pale and frightened women on the street," with coffee and cookies for us.[87]

Still, Doubleday remained consistent about his support of Hancock's assigned authority on July first. Almost 30 years after the battle, he publicly declared:

> Toward the end of the contest Hancock rode up and told me he had been sent to *assume command* of the field. He was our good genius, for he at once brought order out of confusion and made such admirable dispositions that he secured the ridge and held it. As he was junior in rank to General Howard, he had no right, technically speaking, to supersede the latter. Meade had assigned him to that duty, it is true, but under the law only the President himself could place a junior general over a senior. Howard did not recognize him as a superior...[88] [Emphasis added]

These considerations aside, Hancock clearly recorded some of his immediate impressions of matters on Cemetery Hill when he noted: "I presume there may have been 1,000 to 1,200 at most, organized troops of that corps [XI], in position on the hill. Buford's cavalry, in a solid formation, was showing a firm front in the plain just below (in line of battalion in mass, it is my recollection) Cemetery Hill, to the left of the Taneytown Road."[89]

As Hancock sat there mounted near the gate, the blue ranks continued to stream back into the village and onto Cemetery Hill. Another member of the decimated Iron Brigade, Sergeant Jerome A. Watrous, was now approaching the hill in an ammunition wagon and, upon seeing Generals Hancock and Howard, he naturally moved toward the commanders and as he approached, he saluted. Surprised by the sight of the wagon, Hancock exclaimed, "Great God, what have you got here? What have you got a wagon here for? You haven't been out into the action?" Watrous replied: "Yes sir, just came back with the rear guard." Holding his breath, Hancock queried: "...did you lose all your ammunition?" Proudly, the sergeant replied: "No sir; distributed nearly all of it." Hancock then asked: "Lose any of your wagons?" Watrous responded: "Well, I got back with some of them." By this time, Hancock was incredulous about Watrous's success and sympathetically told him: "You did well, Sergeant. Just move your wagons down there and report to me in half an hour." Watrous moved away as ordered and later recalled: "It makes it rather personal, but that is one of the things that a non-commissioned, or a commissioned officer would never forget when we take into account the character of the man that Hancock was."[90]

Meanwhile, the issue of Ewell's lack of pursuit against Cemetery Hill is yet another Gettysburg controversy which certainly touches upon Hancock and deserves some brief attention here. In 1878, Hancock addressed a letter to Fitzhugh Lee wherein he stated that "...in my opinion, if the Confederates had continued the pursuit of General Howard on the afternoon of the 1st July at Gettysburg, they would have driven him over and beyond Cemetery Hill." Hancock's quote here has been used by some in an attempt to prove that if Ewell had made his attack, he would have been successful. But, immediately following the above statement, Hancock adds: "After I had arrived upon the field, *assumed the command*, and made my dispositions for defending that point (say 4 P.M.), I do not think the Confederate force then present could have carried it." In this evaluation, Hancock also has the agreement from Colonel John B. Bachelder, the noted Gettysburg historian.[91] [Emphasis added]

In 1877, a lengthy Gettysburg article by former Lieutenant-General James Longstreet appeared in the Philadelphia *Weekly Times*. While this piece caused a hailstorm of Southern criticism because Longstreet was critical of Lee's performance, he also addresses the Ewell issue as well: "If General Ewell had engaged the army in his front at that time (say 4 o'clock) he would have prevented their massing their whole army in my front..." Longstreet continues his belief that even as late as 5 o'clock that afternoon, Ewell still could have succeeded in pushing the Federals out of their position.[92] Lee's "old war horse" receives some support from General Gordon, who quoted General Hancock in his *Reminiscences of the Civil War*: "The rear of our troops were hurrying through the town, pursued by the Confederates. There had been an attempt to reform some of the Eleventh Corps as they passed over Cemetery Hill, but it had not been very successful." Then, with a lamenting sigh, Gordon concluded: *"And yet I was halted,"* from storming the hill.[93] One Confederate who definitely disagrees with both Longstreet and Gordon is artillerist, Colonel E. P. Alexander. In his *Personal Recollections* Alexander notes: "This delay [Ewell's] has been sometimes criticized. I think *any* attack we could have made that afternoon would have failed."[94] Assuming a time factor of 4 o'clock or beyond, this author agrees. [All emphases added]

More important, when we study Hancock's comments closely, we find that he was referring to a potential Confederate success *before* his arrival, not *afterward*. This delineation is not meant so much as a personal laud for Hancock but rather praise for his effective placement of the troops. The question of Ewell's unwillingness to attack Cemetery Hill has been addressed numerous times and virtually any desired decision can be orchestrated or constructed. Yet, when viewed without emotion there is general agreement between North and South that somewhere about 4:00 to 5:00 o'clock that afternoon, any such attempt would have been futile. This author believes that the Gettysburg time pieces are far too erratic for anyone to pontificate with absolute certainty in regard to the final timing of Ewell's decision. Bear in mind that Ewell's prior performance speaks to a bold and decisive brand of leadership which is too frequently ignored when defining his actions at Gettysburg. For those who believe that his personality changed dramatically after he lost his leg, his work in the Valley and at Brandy Station has been deemed as brilliant. Too, he was widely known for his intrepid posture and "it was said that to him war meant fighting and fighting meant killing." All of that hardly speaks to an impaired warrior.[95] Ewell gets some support from General Doubleday, who noted in a letter to a friend, "Hancock's dispositions...were calculated to impress the enemy with the idea that we had been reinforced. This prevented them from attacking us. They thought we had a long line."[96]

All the reasons for his lack of attack are not yet fully understood and certainly the time-related considerations are far too conflicting to prove Ewell remiss. While Ewell prudently refused to permit General Gordon to pose a solitary attack with his weary brigade, Gordon relates that he would have joined forces with Major-General Edward Johnson's division, which was nearing the village. In all fairness to Ewell, Bachelder puts the time of Johnson's arrival at 6 o'clock and after Johnson's division completed a "fatiguing" 25-mile march.[97] Such a forced march would have left the fighting quality of Johnson's ranks in serious question and by the time of Johnson's arrival, Cemetery Hill was well fortified. Ewell tends to confirm this when he noted: "The enemy had fallen back to a commanding position known as Cemetery Hill...[which] was not assailable from the town...Before Johnson got up, the enemy was reported moving to outflank our extreme left..."[98] Again, in support of Ewell, General Doubleday noted: "The dispositions made by Hancock were calculated to deceive the enemy and make them think that we had been largely reinforced..."[99] All of this speaks directly to the wise strategy of Hancock's decisions on Cemetery Hill. One last intriguing, and little publicized, comment from General Ewell made to General Meade after the war about the entire matter: "Gen. Lee [directed] him to assume the defensive and not to advance."[100]

Returning to Hancock's dispositions, when he was coming into town he saw from the Taneytown Road, the two hills, the Round Tops, to his left could be easily reached with a pistol. It was clear that they were extremely vital but highly vulnerable and he promptly ordered Brigadier-General John W. Geary to take his Second Division of the XII Corps down to the protection of the Round Tops. Hancock himself stated: "I came up on the Taneytown road only an hour before or so before Geary appeared...I sent Geary there immediately, as a precaution, to prevent our left from being turned..."[101] According to one report, the commander told Geary: "That knoll is a commanding position, and we must take possession of it, and then a line of battle can be formed here and a battle fought. If we fail to fight here we will be compelled to fall back about seven miles. In the absence of Slocum I order you to place your troops on that knoll."[102] Geary moved accordingly and that was the emergence of the famous "fish hook" configuration which was so vital to the Union success. But, Hancock's advent upon the hill did not evoke some miraculous-like immediate return to order. Throughout the rallying process on and around Cemetery Hill, some confusion continued, which led one eyewitness to record that the Yankees were "a most unmilitary crowd that Hancock and Howard met and rallied on Cemetery Hill. Organization had temporarily melted away."[103]

"Terminological inexactitude."

To bring order to chaos was the greatest challenge that confronted General Hancock.

Not long after his arrival, Hancock and Howard were joined by Major-General Gouverneur K. Warren, Chief Engineer for the Army of the Potomac and Meade's unofficial "Acting Chief of Staff."[104] General Buford was also there and he watched as Hancock barked commands directing the placement of various troops. When he wrote his report, Buford stated that after he had arrived on Cemetery Hill, "...General Hancock arrived, and in a few moments he made superb disposition to resist any attack that might be made."[105] Once Hancock established a defensive line on and around Cemetery Hill and Little Round Top, the battle site of Gettysburg had been irrevocably established. When order began to be restored, Warren and Hancock jointly reviewed the general vicinity, and Warren later testified before the Joint Committee that Hancock's presence "did a great deal toward restoring order." He further stated: "I went over the ground with General Hancock, and we came to the conclusion...it would be the best place for the army to fight on if the army was attacked."[106] It seems highly unlikely that the insightful Warren would make such an evaluation and decision with an officer who was *not* in command.

But, some pandemonium continued and portions of the XI Corps were having difficulties pulling back. To the northeast of Cemetery Hill, Brigadier-General Francis Barlow, commander of the First Division, had been severely wounded and erroneously left for dead on the field. His command fell to Brigadier-General Adelbert Ames, who reported that the "whole division was falling back with little or no regularity..."[107]

About 5:00 p.m., Captain Edward N. Whittier of the 5th Maine Battery, which was also known as "Leppien's old battery," made his way out of Gettysburg and up to Cemetery Hill. There he found Hancock surrounded by a group of officers handing out orders. In want of direction for his own battery, Whittier rode up and when Hancock saw him, he saluted and asked him what he needed. Whittier replied that he and his six 12-pounders had just come out of the village and he wanted to know where they were needed most. Hancock turned quickly and, pointing to the northwest slope of Culp's Hill, he said, "Do you see that hill, young man? Put your battery there and stay there." Before taking his leave, Whittier could not help but notice Hancock's "clean and white...collar...and...wristbands..." Once into position, Whittier's guns could sweep Benner's Hill, the Rock Creek Valley and be within easy canister range of East Cemetery Hill.[108] Whittier's battery was joined by another from General Howard's command and they both proceeded to open a galling fire which gave the Rebels further cause for canceling any further thoughts about an advance.

About the same time, General Carl Schurz came upon Cemetery Hill. He and Hancock took a moment to sit upon one of the several stone fences on the hilltop. Schurz candidly admitted that all the Confederate infantry and artillery activities that they could see made him nervous. He also reports: "It was soothing to my pride, but by no means reassuring to our situation, when General Hancock admitted that he felt nervous too."[109]

Hancock then received word that Slocum and his XII Corps were just south of Gettysburg and he sent Lieutenant-Colonel Morgan to ride over and view their position. On the way, Morgan met General Slocum, who told him that as he approached the village, he encountered "an enormous number of stragglers, principally from the 11th Corps." Despite that depressing news, Morgan told the general that Hancock was waiting and prepared to turn total command over to him. At first, Slocum felt that was not a good idea since Hancock undoubtedly knew more about the conditions of the terrain and troops. But, when Morgan told him that his assumption of command was Meade's desire, the future New York Congressman promptly agreed.[110]

Finally, the unchecked flow of men heading back toward the safety of the Baltimore Pike was controlled and regiments and brigades began a meaningful process of reforming. Creating a solid defense line brought a greater sense of order and confidence to the Union soldiers, and between 5:30 and 6:00 p.m., Hancock turned the field command over to General Slocum. Slocum would again "receive command" from General Howard, who submitted same around 7:00 p.m. To that double reception, Professor Coddington noted: "Slocum, a graduate of West Point though a lawyer by profession, had demonstrated the spirit that wins cases at the bar, not battles."[111] In fairness to General Slocum, what else could he have done but accept command from both Hancock and Howard? General Slocum was not the problem.

SEGMENT TWO

In terms of General Howard's position about matters on July first, that becomes a bit more complex. Basically, Howard steadfastly and correctly refused to acknowledge anything even close to a "scene" between him and Hancock as Doubleday reports. Between the years after the battle and his death, Howard repeatedly wrote that instead of an argument or refusal to turn over command, he and Hancock, in a most unmilitary manner, strangely "shared" in the command. Candidly, Howard's problem is simply that he could not admit that Hancock *was in command*. We have already seen how he refused to acknowledge the warning at Chancellorsville. Howard also claimed, and Gen-

"Terminological inexactitude." 59

eral Slocum vehemently denied, that on the first, when he summoned Slocum to the field, the XII Corps commander was either slow or refused to advance in a timely manner.[112] Clearly, there were times when General Howard had difficulty with the truth.

But, Hancock and Howard do agree on the issue of "no scene." In fact, in his Gettysburg report, Hancock candidly noted that after he arrived in Gettysburg, he "received material assistance from Major-General Howard..."[113] Still, Hancock maintained his position about authority and when he testified before the Joint Committee on the Conduct of the War, he informed them: "I told General Howard I had orders to take command in the front. I did not show him the orders, because he did not demand it. *He acquiesced*." [Emphasis added] One other point here deserves brief attention. Over the years there has been debate over who selected Cemetery Hill as a defensive Union position. For this author, there appears to be no valid argument on this matter since General Howard had already established his headquarters there and that's where General Hancock found him. Howard selected Cemetery Hill as a rallying position and to debate the matter further is pointless.

But, starting with his battlefield report, Howard embarked upon a baffling life-long denial of Hancock's bestowed authority. While the author feels that we will never know all the details that drove Howard accordingly, a large factor must have been his attempt to avoid another grave embarrassment like Chancellorsville. Apparently, and simply, he could not bring himself to acknowledge that his superiors might not hold him in adequate esteem to handle the complex and critical issues rapidly developing at Gettysburg. If nothing else, though, Howard remained consistent in his professed belief that Hancock was not sent to assume command, nor did he ever assume full command.

Howard had his supporters too and, recently, Dr. John A. Carpenter, who authored a Howard biography, ***Sword and Olive Brach***, defended the XI Corps commander. In his work, Dr. Carpenter states that when Hancock arrived on the field, "The two generals worked together harmoniously..."[114] This author believes that Dr. Carpenter's phrase here is very misleading. While there may have been some mutual cooperation, the reader must not accept Dr. Carpenter's statement to mean a shared authority or an ambiguous leadership role on the part of Hancock. That was absolutely not the case!

Another source of support for Howard was Colonel Charles S. Wainwright, commander of the Artillery Brigade for the I Corps, First Division. Wainwright kept a military diary and noted that after the first day, "I have since heard it said that General Hancock claims to have been in command at this time. I neither saw nor heard anything of him, and the troops certainly were posted as General Howard told me he meant to put them." It is interesting that Wainwright should make this comment when two pages before, in his diary, he noted: "While I was with General Doubleday, one of Howard's German aides rode up, and told him that General Hancock, who succeeded Reynolds in command of the two corps, wished that Cemetery Hill should be held at all hazards." Also, while Wainwright makes no mention of Hancock in his Gettysburg battlefield report, the editor of his diary, Professor Allan Nevins, viewed Hancock in a much more authoritative and productive light. In fact, Professor Nevins comments: "Fortunately for the Union cause, General Winfield S. Hancock arrived at this critical moment, not with his Second Corps, but alone, with full power to *assume command* until Meade came. He soon restored order, and oversaw the placing of the Union forces..."[115] [Emphasis added] Whatever his sources of support, in his battlefield report Howard specifically stated that Hancock came to him about 4:30 p.m. and

> ...said General Meade had sent him on hearing the state of affairs: that he had given him instructions while under the impression that he was my senior. We agreed at once that that was no time for talking, and that General Hancock should further arrange the troops, and place the batteries upon the left of the Baltimore pike, while I should take the right of the same.[116]

That's not nearly the way Hancock viewed matters because in his battlefield report, he clearly states: "At 3 p.m., I arrived at Gettysburg and *assumed command*."[117] [Emphasis added] In addition, it should be noted that General Meade never acknowledges that he wrongly believed that Hancock was Howard's superior as General Howard indicates. Too, in response to General Howard's claim that the two shared the command, Hancock emphatically stated: "The only pretext for his statement of such an understanding is, that as I was about riding away to the left I understood him to indicate to me that he would prefer the right, where his troops were then posted, for his own position, and he said that he would be found there personally; *but there was no division of command between General Howard and myself.*"[118] Further, while Hancock might have attempted a diplomatic approach with Howard, it would have been entirely out of his character for him not to execute Meade's clear directive,

"Terminological inexactitude."

"*assume command*." [Emphases added] On another plane, it is interesting to ponder General Meade's deafening silence on the position of either officer.

It is also curious to note that one of General Hancock's antagonists, General Henry Hunt, actually supported Hancock's position of the first. In his profile for Century Company, General Hunt wrote the following:

> As they [members of the XI Corps] reached the [Cemetery] hill they were received by General Hancock, who arrived just as they were coming up from the town, under orders from General Meade to *assume command*. His person was well known; his presence inspired confidence, and it implied also the near approach of his army-corps. He ordered Wadsworth at once to Culp's Hill to secure that important position, and aided by Howard, by Warren who had also just arrived from headquarters, and by others, a strong line, well flanked, was soon formed.[119] [Emphasis added]

More than a decade after the war, and after years of relative silence on the entire Gettysburg issue, General Howard again brought the entire Cemetery Hill meeting to the surface in an article published in the *Atlantic Monthly* entitled "Campaign and Battle of Gettysburg." Even before Hancock had a chance to read Howard's comments, he felt certain that the former XI Corps commander was probably attempting to again justify his posture of July first and he wrote to General Hooker:

> Shortly, I expect to read Howards Statement, [*sic*] and will notice it so far as I may think necessary to correct untruthful assertions or to resist exaggerated claims where they may conflict with the honors properly belonging to me or to the troops I commanded. From the stir made by this publication there must be something in it which I should read.[120]

In that *Atlantic Monthly* article, Howard states: "General Hancock greeted me in his usual frank and cordial manner, and used these words: 'General Meade has sent me to *represent* him on the field.'" To this use of the word "represent," and a whole new implication of his assignment, Hancock vehemently replied: "I assert positively that I never implied in any conversation with General Howard that when I arrived at Gettysburg on that occasion I was to *represent* Meade as Butterfield, the chief of staff would have done, on the field of battle." Howard lamely continues that "It did not strike me that Hancock...was doing more than directing matters as a temporary chief of staff for Meade." But, after he acknowledges receiving Meade's order [at 7:00 p.m.] placing Hancock in command, he states: "I was of course deeply mortified, and immediately sought General Hancock and appealed to his magnanimity to represent to General Meade how I had performed my duty on that day..."[121] Howard also states, in substance, that Hancock told Vice President Hannibal Hamlin, of Maine: "The country will never know how much it owes to your Maine general, Howard."[122] [All emphasis added]

    Howard then continues and presents a weak justification for General Meade, claiming that it was Major-General Dan Butterfield who suggested that Hancock go forward and take command. "Meade assented, and Butterfield then drew the order accordingly..." Howard then concluded in a sophomoric manner: "From these statements it is now easy to understand General Meade's attitude toward me."[123] [Author's note: If Howard honestly believed this statement, it is tantamount to an acknowledgment of Hancock's authority over him.] This Butterfield scenario hardly fits Meade, who really wanted General Warren as his chief of staff and actually removed Butterfield on July 5th. Allowing Butterfield to make such an important decision does not appear likely, especially when we consider that the two men already had a strained relationship.[124]

    In addition to all of this, Meade issued several other orders confirming Hancock's appointment. For example, at 4:45 p.m. he wired General Sickles: "General Hancock has been ordered up to *assume command* of the three corps—First, Eleventh, and the Third." Then, at 6:00 p.m., with ample time to collect his thoughts, if necessary, Meade informed General Halleck that *he* had appointed Hancock to *assume command.*[125] [All emphasis added]

    Still, General Howard proceeds in his narrative that when General Meade arrived on the battlefield "The first words he [Meade] said to me were in substance that 'he was very sorry to have seemed to cast any discredit upon me; he had no blame to affix.'"[126] Meade leaves no record of such a statement but, if one was made, it is important to remember that by the time of his arrival at Gettysburg, Meade had already read Howard's plaintive message about his being mortified with Hancock's appointment. It is entirely possible, indeed natural and probable, that Meade might have said something to assuage Howard's bruised feelings.[127] Note that Meade does not offer Howard any succor

"Terminological inexactitude."

about altering his earlier appointment of Hancock though he also fails to support Hancock's appointment with his usual authority.

After having read Howard's *Atlantic Monthly* article, and probably with his blood pressure building, Hancock fired off another letter to General Hooker wherein he stated:

> I made my official report of the Battle [sic] when the facts were fresh in my mind, was examined by the committee on the Conduct of the war [sic] soon afterwards, and since have avoided any publication concerning the subject. It may be that Gen. Howards [sic] statement may force me to depart from that reticence. Gen. Howard made an official report and I believe was examined by the committee on the conduct of the war [sic] but he does not seemed satisfied although a dozen years have passed. What has caused General H. to appear in print at this time I do not know. I was prepared to leave the history of the Battle [sic] with the Historians [sic] of the future....[128]

Howard's *Atlantic Monthly* piece finally caused Hancock to decide on a rare but vigorous public response, published in the December, 1876 edition of *The Galaxy*, entitled "Gettysburg Reply to General Howard." Hancock first cites Meade's 1:10 and 1:15 p.m. orders and telegrams, directing him to *assume command*, as his basic authority. Then he strikes out at Howard's comment regarding his *representing* General Meade: "But to be more explicit: I assert positively that I never implied in any conversation with General Howard that...I 'was to *represent* Meade...'" [All emphasis added] Hancock then offers his comrade the benefit of doubt regarding Howard's statement that he did not receive Meade's order appointing Hancock until 7:00 p.m. But, Hancock also properly points out: "...it [the 7:00 message] was not the first...opportunity to see that order, because...I offered to show him the original...he said he did not desire to see it..." In terms of Howard's statement regarding Hancock's alleged comment to Vice President Hamlin, the former II Corps commander stated: "...I am well satisfied that if the gentleman [Hamlin] informed General Howard that I made the [those] remarks concerning him...he either misunderstood my meaning, and applied what I said of the Maine *men* to General Howard personally..."[129] [Emphasis in original]

Hancock at Gettysburg...*and beyond.*

Then, in a July 23, 1876 letter to General Hooker, Hancock again addresses Howard's comments about Hamlin and stated: "...I never made use of language to Vice President Hamlin or to any one else—conveying the idea set forth. I never had such views as to the importance of Gen. Howard's services at Gettysburg as to make it possible that [I] could have made use of such an expression."[130] Hancock also properly points out that if, as Howard claimed, he received Meade's formal order appointing Hancock at 7:00 p.m., then the XI Corps commander was in no position to transfer any command to General Slocum since it rightly belonged to General Hancock and not him. Ever mindful of military propriety, as he had been when Meade appointed him, Hancock reminds the reader of critical military protocol that Howard "knew I was exercising authority which no staff officer would *dare* to personally exercise under any circumstances."[131] Clearly, Hancock knew that for any subordinate officer to take it upon himself to *assume command* over superiors, without official authority, it would be a suicidal act. Hancock's comments in *The Galaxy* and those written to General Hooker are the last known record of any rebuttal he offered Howard, or anyone else, regarding the controversy. [All emphases added]

But, that was not the case with General Howard, and in 1888 he wrote, but did not send, a letter replying to an article that had appeared in the July 2nd issue of *The New York Times*, which rehashed the old controversy of a "scene" on Cemetery Hill. Howard's position had not changed much though it was probably the closest he ever came to acknowledging Hancock's authority. He thought of responding:

> General Hancock did come to me...on Cemetery Hill...while skirmishing was yet going on. He and I did have an interview near the Cemetery gate but *no* controversy whatever. [Emphasis added]
>
> ...he was sent by General Meade...So that with this understanding, though I was his senior, I should have most cheerfully conformed to any instructions that he gave me, but he gave me no instructions whatever...
>
> We arranged together in an instant that he should take one side of the Baltimore Pike and I the other, for rushing the troops into position.[132]

Then, the 58-year-old Howard aptly noted: "It has been frequently sought by people who have brighter imaginations than memories to represent a quarrel between me and General Hancock on the field at Gettysburg. Such a quarrel never existed."[133] This statement is certainly correct; but, again, Howard simply could not bring himself to acknowledge that Hancock *was* in command. He might have exercised some of his own philosophical advice.

Fifteen years later, in 1903, Howard again reiterated his same basic position when he addressed the graduating class of Syracuse University. Of those critical Gettysburg moments, he told those young students: "Just at this juncture General Hancock without his men joined me near Baltimore Pike. The bullets were flying and I replied to Hancock's message from Meade, 'There is no time to talk. Hancock, you take the left side of the road and I will take the right and put in these troops.' Without a further word Hancock rallied the troops to the left of the pike and led them into place."[134] This reference to a "message from Meade," is the second closest moment Howard ever came to acknowledging an order from the commander appointing Hancock to take command of the field. Upon reflection, if he knew Hancock had a message [order] from General Meade and he refused to review same, that might be understood as insubordination.

In 1907, a 77-year-old Howard published his two-volume autobiography and again he addresses his meeting with Hancock on Cemetery Hill:

> ...between 4 and 5 P.M., General Hancock joined me near the Baltimore Pike; he said that General Meade had sent him to *represent* him on the field. I answered...'All right, Hancock, you take the left of the Baltimore pike and I will take the right, and we will put these troops in line.' After a few friendly words between us, Hancock did as I suggested.[135] [Emphasis added]

Here again, note the word *represent* which is not part of Hancock's related vocabulary but one that Howard adopted from General Meade. The reader should also take careful note of Howard's modest but important variants within his multiple representations of the first of July.

Returning to matters on July 1, 1863, at 5:00 that afternoon, Howard sent a message to General Meade providing the army commander with an encapsulation of his activities that day. He ends that note with the revealing statement that "General Hancock arrived at 4 p.m., *and communicated his instructions.* I am still holding on at this time. Slocum is near but will not come to assume command."[136] Since Hancock's instructions were to *assume command*, Howard's statement here only raises more questions about his sense of propriety about the entire matter. Perhaps Janus was simply peeking through the clouds! [Emphasis added]

It might be helpful to crystallize a few key points here before proceeding. First, there can be no doubt that General Hancock was sent forward to *assume command* and that is precisely what he did, to the great dismay of General Howard. Second, there is every indication that Howard turned over his command to Hancock without any real hesitation, though it is understandable that he was personally upset by the selection of a junior officer. Nonetheless, Howard was a professional officer and followed orders. Third, there is also no doubt that the entire issue of a Hancock–Howard "controversy" over the change of command on Cemetery Hill is the result of General Doubleday's dubious objectives. Unfortunately, Doubleday's seeds are exacerbated by Howard's inability to be truthful about Hancock's appointment to command.

But, we also have the nagging questions regarding those reports supposedly heard and definitely reported by Halstead and Kerby, that Hancock could not command while Howard was on the field. It appears logical that whatever Halstead and Kerby may have heard, it was incomplete. The two officers tell similar, though not exact, versions and with so much noise and excitement on Cemetery Hill at the time, variants are to be expected. Candidly, that the two men related essentially the same comments about Hancock's inability to issue orders while Howard was on duty cannot, at this time, be fully explained. However, it is doubtful that either commander, Hancock or Howard, would shout at each other regarding such sensitive issues and that would further restrict Halstead's and Kerby's hearing. This author believes that both of their comments are highly suspect and Doubleday himself offers some insight into the possible linguistic elasticity when he later addressed Kerby. Doubleday also indicated the possibility of other witnesses being present on Cemetery Hill:

> You appear to have been the only witness to the scene who was not either a staff officer of Howard's or Hancock's, and you have, no doubt, told a straight story. You know, staff officers *will lie* for their chiefs.[137] [Emphasis added]

"Terminological inexactitude."

Perhaps the last troubling issue is why Howard carried his denial so far and for so long. Without question, he must have been mentally comfortable with his synthetic posture, though it was counter to his professed religious fervor. Yet, religiosity is no assurance of veracity, so Howard's reasons appear to have been buried with him. Nonetheless, the only practical answer appears to lie in his wish to avoid another embarrassing repeat of the Chancellorsville fiasco.

Another curious aspect of the entire controversy is the relatively warm, occasional correspondence between the key participants during the balance of the war and thereafter. Perhaps this is simply indicative of nineteenth century manners and a good example would be Hancock's letter to General Howard, dated March 14, 1864. In it, Hancock is responding to a recent letter from Howard regarding the possibility that he might have authored an article in the Philadelphia *Evening Bulletin*. Note the cordial nature of Hancock's unflattering response:

> ...I have not written anything for the press concerning the battle of Gettysburg, nor am I responsible for anything that has been written...I have my views concerning the battle of Gettysburg, but I have not yet put them in print, nor shall I do so, so far as I know now. I have seen many things in print which I consider unjust, but I do not think it wise to reply to them...I have always done justice to your gallantry on the field of battle, on every occasion when it was proper for a friend to do so.[138]

Returning to July 1, 1863, another important consideration evolves in the latter portion of the day through a sequence of related messages. At 5:25 that afternoon, with the fighting beginning to end, Hancock sent a report via his aide, Captain I. B. Parker, to General Meade:

> When I arrived here an hour since, I found that our troops had given up the front of Gettysburg and the town. We have now taken up a position in the cemetery, which cannot well be taken; it is a position, however. easily turned. Slocum is now coming on the ground, and is taking position on the

right, which will protect the right. But we have as yet no troops on the left, the Third Corps not having yet reported; but I suppose that it is marching up. If so, his [Sickles] flank march will in a degree protect our left flank. In the meantime Gibbon had better march on so as to take position on our right or left, to our rear, as may be necessary, in some commanding position. Gen. G.[ibbon] will see this despatch. The battle is quiet now. I think we will be all right until night. I think we can retire; if not, *we can fight here, as the ground appears not unfavorable with good troops.* I will communicate in a few moments with General Slocum, and transfer the command to him. *Howard says that Doubleday's command gave way.** General Warren is here. [All emphasis added]
    Your obedient servant,
        WINFIELD S. HANCOCK
        Maj. Gen'l., Com'dg. Corps.[139]

In response to this message, General Meade later stated: "...[it] caused me at once to determine to fight a battle at that point..."[140] Despite all the demands and concerns confronting him that day, at 6:00 p.m., General Meade sent an aide to Frederick to wire a descriptive message to General Halleck in Washington. In part, that telegram stated: "The First and Eleventh Corps have been engaged all day in front of Gettysburg. The Twelfth, Third and Fifth have been moving up...General Reynolds was killed this morning...I immediately sent up General Hancock to *assume command*."[141] [Emphasis added]

At about the same time, Meade sent another message to both Hancock and Doubleday, which would soon precipitate even more ire from General Howard owing to its obvious omission:

    HEADQUARTERS ARMY OF THE POTOMAC
        July 1, 1863 — 6 p.m.
Major-Generals Hancock and Doubleday:
    If General Slocum is on the field, and I hope he is, of course he takes command. Say to him I thought it prudent to

---

* This or some variant is undoubtedly the key statement to the Doubleday-Howard strain at Gettysburg.

"Terminological inexactitude."

leave a division of the Third Corps at Emmitsburg, to hold in check any force attempting to come through there. It can be ordered up to-night, if necessary. Sedgwick is moving up here, and will be pushed forward in the night if required. It seems to me we have so concentrated that a battle at Gettysburg is now forced on us, and that, if we get up all our people, and attack with our whole force to-morrow, we ought to defeat the force the enemy has.

Very respectfully, &c.,
GEO. G. MEADE
Major-General Commanding[142]

Shortly after 7:00 that evening, Howard sent a telegram to Meade, which tends to reveal a lot about his mind-set. It is, perhaps, the central reason why General Meade began to use the phrase that Hancock was sent to *represent* him. Because of its importance, the following is Howard's entire message:

HEADQUARTERS ELEVENTH CORPS
July 1, 1863

General: General Hancock's order, in writing, to *assume command* reached here at 7. At that time, General Slocum being present, having just arrived at this point, I turned over the command to him. This evening I have read an order stating that if General Slocum was present he would assume command. I believe I have handled these two corps to-day from a little past 11 until 4, when General H. assisted me in carrying out orders which I had already issued, as well as any of your corps commanders could have done. Had we received re-enforcements a little sooner, the first position assumed by General Reynolds, and held by General Doubleday till my corps came up, might have been maintained; but the position was not a good one, because both flanks were exposed. and a heavy force approaching from the northern roads rendered it untenable, being already turned, so that I was forced to retire the command to the position now occupied, which I regard as a very strong one.

> *The above has mortified me and will disgrace me. Please inform me frankly if you disapprove of my conduct today, that I may know what to do.*
> I am, general, very respectfully, your obedient servant,
> O. O. Howard
> Major-General, Commanding.
> Major-General Meade,
> Commanding Army of the Potomac[143] [Emphasis added]

Hancock categorically denied Howard's comment regarding his assistance: "Now, I had no such understanding with General Howard, and I did not so assist him in carrying out orders which he had already issued." To Howard's comment about turning over command to General Slocum, Hancock properly noted: "...if he pretended to transfer the command to General Slocum at 7 p.m., when, he says, 'General Hancock's order to assume command' reached him in writing, he was doing that which he had no authority to do."[144]

Howard's cry of mortification to General Meade apparently touched a soft spot in the normally irascible commander. Regrettably, Meade again leaves us no record of his response but there is the strong possibility that once he read Howard's comment's about being disgraced, Meade uncharacteristically altered his earlier decisiveness about Hancock's orders to *assume command*. This change in posture began with Meade's own battlefield report wherein he stated: "About the time of this withdrawal, Major-General Hancock arrived, whom I dispatched to *represent* me on the field..."[145] This is not what his original orders stated! When he testified before the Joint Committee on March 4, 1864, General Meade again does not specifically state that he sent Hancock forward to *assume command*. Instead, he states that "I directed Major General Hancock...to proceed without delay to the scene of the contest; and, having in view this preliminary order which I had issued to him, as well as to the other corps commanders..."[146] That "preliminary order" instructed Hancock to *assume command* but for whatever reasons, Meade failed to articulate that important fact for the Committee. [All emphasis added]

It certainly appears that General Howard liked the word "represent" because it became a part of his own lexicon. The change in Meade's language definitely clouds the issues because the two directives, *assume command* and *represent* have two different implications, which certainly troubled Hancock as well. Assuming command has a certain finality about it while representing an individual is certainly not as authoritative. Still, Hancock never changed his

"Terminological inexactitude."

position nor did he change the selection of the key words. But General Meade's adoption of the word *represent* clearly granted General Howard great linguistic and mental license, even if innocently.

Whatever the style of argument regarding Meade's decision and language, General Doubleday offers an excellent observation on the army commander's flexible attitude. Writing to a friend in 1874, Doubleday noted that while testifying before the Joint Committee, Meade stressed "the absolute necessity of recognizing an officer's rank in the army as the very cement of all discipline and organization. He obtained his object on that occasion but I have never forgotten the urgency of his appeal or the way in which he changed his views when he had the power to change the rank of other officers."[147] Obviously, Doubleday was referring to Meade's directive appointing Hancock to *assume command* over Howard and General John Newton, a subordinate, to replace himself.

About 7:00 p.m., Major Mitchell, Hancock's aide, arrived in Taneytown to report to the army commander. Mitchell told Meade how the troops at Gettysburg had been positioned and that Hancock "would hold the position until night." By doing so, Hancock wanted to afford his commander the courtesy of ample time for maneuvering in the event he desired a change. In response, Meade apparently told Mitchell, "I will send up the troops."[148]

By this time, the entire northeast portion of the United States was gripped by mortal fear and confusion, believing that threatening Rebels were lurking under every rug. A Reading, Pennsylvania, newspaper was calling for farmers to drop their plows and take up arms in defense of their state. Martial law had been declared in Baltimore and the populace was informed: "To save the country is paramount to all other considerations." In Albany, Governor Horatio Seymour ordered that 30 regiments be immediately raised and trained. In Columbus, Ohio, Governor David Todd warned that he had information which told of a scheduled Rebel invasion within the month, while Kentucky braced for an anticipated crush of 15,000 butternut-clad soldiers. Oddly enough, the city of Harrisburg was then breathing a relative sigh of relief as it reported that "There is no excitement in the city."[149] At 10:30 that evening, believing the Federal army already in peril, members of the Philadelphia Union League implored Secretary of War Edwin Stanton: "...we do urge upon you to call instantly upon the Governors of all States east of us to send whatever soldiers are at the moment available."[150]

About 6:00 p.m., in line with General Meade's orders, Hancock passed command of the field to his senior, General Slocum, and he soon caught sight of the lead elements of the III Corps approaching Gettysburg. No doubt, that body of troops gave him even greater confidence. He remained on the field for a little while, but feeling certain that the Union line was now secure, Hancock headed back to Taneytown to report to his commander. The time was approximately 8:00 p.m. when he left Gettysburg and just about three miles south of the village, he encountered his own corps and ordered General Gibbon to halt their march for the night and act as a rear guard.[151]

Before leaving his II Corps, Hancock had some discussion with Gibbon and some of the other commanders who were all eager for any information about the battlefield. In the process, Colonel Samuel S. Carroll, First Brigade, Third Division, asked Hancock if the Union position was a good one. Hancock responded: "If Lee does not attack before all our forces are up, we can hold the position I have selected against the whole Confederacy."[152] After some further but brief discussions, he continued his difficult ride of 13 miles and when he arrived in Taneytown, about 9:00 p.m., he found Meade in the midst of preparing to leave the area. Reportedly somewhat preoccupied by his search for a pair of misplaced spectacles, Meade listened to Hancock's report of the day's activities and told him that he had already ordered up the balance of the troops to Gettysburg. Meade planned to leave Taneytown as soon as their discussion was complete. It was about 10:00 p.m.[153]

When he finished reporting to Meade, Hancock realized that he was exhausted from the physically demanding day. He had risen before dawn, ridden the seven miles to Taneytown, then another thirteen miles to Gettysburg, where he encountered the grinding demands of battle, and then returned the thirteen miles to Taneytown. As a result, he understandably felt the need to settle himself down to get at least a couple of hours of sleep. But, his sleep was short and perhaps, before falling off into quiet slumber, he may have shuddered with the realization that if the Confederates had pressed their pursuit earlier that afternoon, they would have driven the Yankees "over and beyond Cemetery Hill."[154] While precise details of any other activities during those few resting hours are unknown, an aide indicates that Hancock left Taneytown for Gettysburg about 1:00–2:00 a.m., on the second. That same aide also tells us that the hard pace and riding of that first day killed nearly "every horse belonging to the General or his staff..."[155]

Meanwhile, back on Cemetery Hill, General Howard had earlier sent an aide to the gatehouse to request dinner for himself and some of his fellow commanders. Mr. Peter Thorn, the gatekeeper, was in the Union army, but not at Gettysburg, and his wife agreed to Howard's request. After baking bread all day long for the Yankees, Mrs. Thorn gladly cooked the special dinner "but they did not come until midnight and with General Howard was Generals

Slocum and Sickles." Apparently, Mrs. Thorn's meal proved to be memorable for on December 12, 1902, Howard sent her a letter stating: "General Sickles and I still remain to remember the only meal we had after early sunrise during that ever-memorable first day of July over forty-one years ago."[156] When the meal and discussion were concluded, Generals Howard and Slocum agreed that no more could be accomplished, and they laid themselves upon the floor where they "slept side by side."[157] July 1 and all of its confusion had finally drawn to an end, though the endless debates were just beginning to bud. Perhaps the only comprehensive statement that explains the Union fate that day was expressed by an unidentified aide to General Slocum, who said: "On the first day we were pounded into a splendid position."[158]

Meade had not yet come upon the field and while there is another dispute over exactly what time he did arrive, it appears to have been between midnight and 1:00 a.m. of the second.[159] Whatever the precise time, upon his arrival, the commander was quickly joined by Generals Slocum, Howard, Sickles, Warren, Hunt and other officers and staff members. After a brief tour through the public cemetery, Meade turned to Howard and asked: "Well Howard, what do you think; is this the place to fight the battle?" Howard was quick to respond, "I think the position a good one, General Meade." According to Howard, General Sickles then added his thoughts and told Meade: "It is a good place, General, to fight from." No doubt, with a matter-of-fact tone, the commander responded: "I am glad to hear you say so, for I have already ordered the other corps to concentrate here and it is too late to change." Shortly thereafter, Meade made an inspection of the entire area and appears to have captured little or no sleep that night.[160] Despite current popular belief, Hancock was not present.

As is so common with many historical events, there can be many conflicting aspects to specific points, and the selection of Gettysburg as a battlefield and the hero thereof is no exception. Almost immediately after the battle, numerous claims were made that challenge the tradition that Hancock made the battlefield selection. One report claimed that General Adolph von Steinwehr, commander of the Second Division of the XI Corps, made the fateful decision to hold Cemetery Hill. Supposedly, Steinwehr said to General Howard, "General, we must hold this position under all circumstances. This will be the key to the whole battle."[161]

Another view was offered by a veteran of the 2nd New Hampshire in a letter dated March 5, 1886. Therein, the soldier noted that "[General] Daniel E. Sickles...he was the savior of that battle if anyone was[,] not Gen. Hancock, as they wish us to believe at this late day after the old ones are all dead. They make the next generation believe Hancock was the Hero [sic] but we don't take any stock now, not but Hancock was a good General, but I believe in giving credit where credit is due."[162]

Whatever the source of the many claims, the evidence clearly demonstrates that the unexpected clash between the troops of Generals Buford and Heth really made the selection of the battlefield. Once that occurred, both armies were simply forced to fight, reinforce and prepare for further engagement. There can be no doubt that General Howard was intent on fortifying Cemetery Hill, which was completed by General Hancock. Hancock certainly did not act alone and he never made such a claim, In fact, according to one recent and practical evaluation, "...Hancock, Slocum, and Meade all endorsed Howard's tactical strategic view of the battle and his choice of ground...[and] no one can gainsay his [Howard's] pivotal contribution to the three-day struggle."[163] As for the credit of selecting the battlefield, we must recognize that such speculation is futile and the reality is that fate and fate alone dictated the bloody field of Gettysburg. In terms of battlefield heroes, this author has counted at least 150,000.

When the first finally came to an end, many of both sides on that field were upset, discouraged, angered or jubilant about the day's events. One of those perturbed soldiers was none other than General Robert E. Lee, who expressed his views about General Ewell's decision not to attack Cemetery Hill:

> General Ewell was therefore instructed to carry the [Cemetery] hill...if he found it practicable but to avoid a general engagement until the arrival of the other divisions of the army...He decided to await Johnson['s] division, which...did not reach Gettysburg until a late hour. In the meantime the enemy occupied the point [and]...Under these circumstances it was decided not to attack until the arrival of Longstreet...
>
> It had not been intended to deliver a general battle so far from our base unless attacked, but coming unexpectedly upon the whole Federal army, to withdraw through the mountains with our extensive trains would have been difficult and dangerous...A battle therefore had become, in a measure unavoidable....[164]

"Terminological inexactitude."

The news media were, as always, eager to offer concluding positions following monumental events such as the battle of Gettysburg. Frequently, in their haste to be first, they make significant errors. The year 1863 was no exception but at least one newspaper writer came close to the truth as the morning of the second began to emerge: "The news of his [Reynolds's] death, and the defeat of the first day reached us in Philadelphia...adding to the popular gloom, and aggravated by ten thousand rumors the intelligence of the Confederate victory."[165]

For General Hancock, his precautionary statement of 1876 still rings true with all its attending complexities: "The historian of the future who essays to tell the tale of Gettysburg undertakes an onerous task, a high responsibility, a sacred trust."[166] As for the entire Hancock–Howard controversy, Hancock also left us a clear message about his thoughts on General Howard's performance that first day of July. While students and scholars may disagree with his actions and evaluations, they cannot argue about the clarity of his forceful opinion: "...I have always considered that Gen. Howard claimed too much for his services at Gettysburg and has received greater honor for the same than he is legitimately entitled to...."[167]

"Knowledge, as has been shown, consists in the perception of the agreement or disagreement of ideas".
John Locke.

CHAPTER THREE

July 2, 1863
"I'd be God Damned..."

The second day at Gettysburg was much different than the first for General Hancock because it did not focus upon a particular individual, event or controversy. Instead, it demanded all of the mental agility the II Corps commander could muster, as his important interactions encompassed a variety of individuals and demanding crises. While much of that day proved to be very uneventful, once matters began to unfold, the fast pace of battlefield events simply swept Hancock into a veritable vortex over those critical hours. If ever there was a moment in his military life that proved him suitable for independent command, July 2, 1863 was certainly that test of fire.

By dawn on the second, General Meade had established his headquarters in the small, white, wooden Leister home, located immediately east of Cemetery Ridge. No doubt, the new army commander had many concerns of potential threats that morning, including his initial fear that Lee might move upon the Yankee left. Such a move was exactly what General Longstreet had urged upon his commander, Robert E. Lee, which some now consider "sound military sense."[1] Meanwhile, Hancock left Taneytown "sometime after daylight [and] I again reported to Genl. Meade at Gettysburg."[2] In his battlefield report, Hancock mentions that the march of his II Corps was continued at daylight and he rejoined them even before they arrived at Gettysburg. General Gibbon later recalled that the II Corps arrived on the field at "6 o'clock" that morning, while Lieutenant Frank Haskell noted that the II Corps was awake at three and in the early morning mist, the "men looked like giants..."[3] All indications are that the II Corps came onto the field between 6:00–6:30 a.m., which receives further confirmation from General Hunt.[4] When the II Corps did arrive, Hancock reported they were faced to the north owing to General Meade's altered belief that Lee might now attack his right. But, "shortly afterwards we marched over to the position [Cemetery Ridge] which we held during the subsequent battle."[5] Hancock recalled: "The troops were soon placed in position, the right resting near the Emmitsburg road, to the west of Cemetery Hill, connecting there on

"I'd be God Damned..."

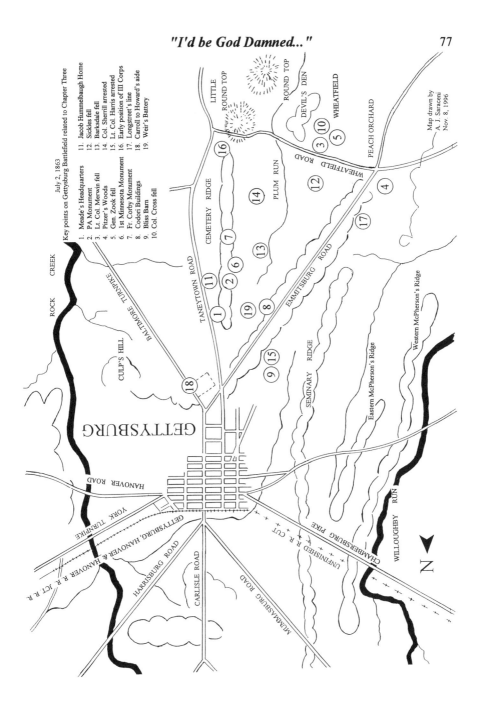

the right with the Eleventh Corps and on the left with the Third Corps..."[6] This means that when all three of those corps were in position, the Union line extended from the Emmitsburg Road, just south of town, down to the Round Tops, a distance of approximately two miles. Again, according to Haskell, just before 8 o'clock that morning, the II Corps was completely in position with its skirmishers posted as well.[7]

When the placement of his ranks was complete, Hancock's Third Division, under Brigadier-General Alexander Hays, was on the far right, near the angle of the stone wall and Ziegler's Grove. Next, General Gibbon's Second Division took the center near the copse of trees, and Brigadier-General John C. Caldwell's First Division took the far left. To support his infantry, Hancock placed his artillery batteries as follows, from his right to left: Lieutenant George A. Woodruff's Battery I, 1st U.S., at Ziegler's Grove; Captain William A. Arnold's Battery A, 1st Rhode Island directly east of General Meade's headquarters; Lieutenant T. Fred Brown's Battery B, 1st Rhode Island just north of Hancock's open-air headquarters; and Captain James McKay Rorty's Battery B, 1st New York about 100 yards south of Brown's battery. All of those II Corps batteries were west of the Taneytown Road and under the overall direction of Captain John G. Hazard.[8] Hancock recorded that the morning of the second "remained comparatively quiet...except the enemy attacked Genl. Slocum..."[9]

According to General Meade, his initial plan for the second was to hurl his V, VI and XII Corps against Lee's left. That contemplative attack was to commence the moment the fast marching VI Corps arrived on the field. But, like so many things during any battle, Meade's plan had to be scrapped when General Slocum sent word that "the character of the ground in [his] front was unfavorable to making an attack." Consequently, Meade was forced to look for an alternate strategy.[10]

About 8:00 a.m., Meade took time to hold a brief meeting with the Virginia-born Major-General John Newton, commander of the Third Division, VI Corps. The army commander obviously considered that 40-year-old engineering officer as very dependable, if not spectacular, and felt he was far better qualified to lead the I Corps than Doubleday. When Newton reminded his commander that Doubleday outranked him, Meade again dismissed that notion and simply invoked his new license from Washington. General Meade insisted that Newton take command of the I Corps despite any chagrin on Doubleday's part.[11] Such appointments, no matter how prudent, have fueled controversy throughout the years. We must be mindful that the battle participants did not necessarily share the same high or low opinions of their comrades that we might hold today. They did not have our advantage of critical hindsight.

"I'd be God Damned..."

When General Sickles had arrived on the first, he brought with him Major-General David B. Birney and his First and Second Brigades of the First Division. Those ranks spent the night in the low area immediately north of Little Round Top, and they were joined that morning by Colonel P. Regis de Trobriand's Third Brigade and the balance of the III Corps. General Birney was to play a conspicuous part in the events impacting on the III Corps that day. He was a citizen-soldier, born in Huntsville, Alabama, though raised in Cincinnati, Ohio. Well-educated at Andover, Birney later passed the bar in Upper Saginaw, Michigan. His father, James G. Birney, had been a slaveholder, but before moving to Cincinnati, he freed his chattels and became a champion for emancipation. In 1840 and 1844, the senior Birney was the Presidential candidate for the Anti-Slavery Liberty party. General Birney had succeeded General Philip Kearny to command of the First Division when that one-armed officer was killed at Chantilly. That also made Birney second-in-command to General Sickles, and some of his peers felt that he was too interested in promoting his own interest. Regrettably, Birney developed malarial fever in the fall of 1864 and was sent home to Philadelphia, where he died at age 39.[12]

Soon after his meeting with Newton, the Union commander sent his son and aide, Captain George Meade, to see General Sickles with instructions to position his III Corps to the left of Hancock's line. The youthful Meade reported that he personally delivered his father's message and General Sickles informed him that his ranks were presently coming into the area and they "would be in position shortly."[13] About 11 o'clock that morning, Sickles rode over to speak with General Meade because he felt that his assigned ground was "unfit for infantry, [and] impractical for artillery." But Meade, perhaps preoccupied, only repeated his earlier directive and ordered that the III Corps remain as assigned. In response, Sickles strongly expressed his concerns with the poor topography of his position. Since Meade could not personally get away to view the area, Sickles requested permission to move his ranks on his own judgment. To that, Meade replied in vague terms: "Certainly, within the limits of the general instructions I have given you." But, as a measure of his concern for Sickles's adherence to his orders, and in response to the New York general's laments, the army commander sent General Henry Hunt back to view the position of Sickles's batteries.[14]

As the two generals rode back to the III Corps position, Sickles detailed to Hunt how he felt certain that an attack was imminent on his left and that his current location did not offer him a good defensive position. Hunt could plainly see Sickles's concern but remained cautious. While he felt the assigned position was indeed too low and strewn with boulders, Hunt also felt

Major-General Daniel E. Sickles

"I'd be God Damned..."

it improper to condone a forward move of approximately 1,200 yards as Sickles proposed. It was abundantly clear to Hunt that such an independent move would expose the left of the II Corps and leave both III Corps flanks highly vulnerable. In the end, Hunt would not approve any move, but told Sickles that he would urge Meade to take a personal look at his problem, and then he returned to the Leister House. Before leaving, however, Hunt suggested that Sickles might send some troops forward to reconnoiter Pitzer's Woods in his front, which appeared to be harboring some Rebel infantry. Shortly thereafter, Sickles sent one regiment of Colonel Hiram Berdan's green-suited sharpshooters, plus the 3rd Maine, to investigate. Indeed, those Yankees found stiff resistance from the ranks of Brigadier-General Cadmus M. Wilcox's Brigade of A. P. Hill's III Corps. When General Meade failed to show, General Sickles became impatient with what he considered Meade's lack of concern. About 2 o'clock, he took it upon himself to begin a fateful, unauthorized forward movement of his ranks to take advantage of the high ground at the Peach Orchard.[15]

July 2 would prove to be a very nervous, testy day for General Hancock and one where he demonstrated an inordinate sense of irritation and an especially low tolerance for incompetence. While he was always demanding on a battlefield, this day appears to have been exceptional in that regard. No doubt, it was the many intense demands and critical pressures that kept him on edge, causing him to be more short-tempered with some of his subordinates. A good example:

Around 10 o'clock that morning, about half of the 1st Delaware was under heavy Confederate fire, making it difficult for them to hold onto the Bliss Barn. According to Lieutenant L. Brady of that regiment, his boys had temporarily lost sight of their commander, Lieutenant-Colonel Edward P. Harris, whom they curiously found inside the relative safety of that structure. When Brady informed Harris of the struggle he was having with the Rebels, the colonel sheepishly made a superficial evaluation and decided to personally "lead" a portion of the regiment that was in little or no danger. That left Brady and the balance of the regiment to fend for themselves as best they could, which was not easy. Lieutenant Brady and his small command were again sharply engaged by the enemy, and, this time, the Rebels killed at least two of his fellow officers while several others were captured. Meanwhile, Harris was making his way, unmolested, into a nearby apple orchard when his craven movement caught the angered eye of General Hancock, who immediately rode over and confronted him. Just then, a beleaguered Brady appeared on the scene. He saw an enraged Hancock standing erect in his stirrups, cursing Harris for his poor example. In a final explosion, Hancock "ordered [Harris] under arrest for cowardice in the face of the enemy."[16] "...woe be to the man who shirked or in any other sense failed to meet and perform his duty." The balance of that morning and early afternoon proved to be rather quiet for the II Corps commander. During that time, he undoubtedly prepared his line for battle, conferred with peers and subordinates, and simply waited for events to develop.

About 2 o'clock, the forward ranks of Major-General John Sedgwick's 18,000-man VI Corps began to enter upon the field. "Uncle John," as General Sedgwick was affectionately known, had driven his men 37 miles from Manchester, Maryland, over the last 17 hours because he told General Meade on the first: "I will be at Gettysburg with my corps at 4:00 tomorrow afternoon." As usual, Sedgwick did not fail his commander even though many of his men suffered from their liberal consumption of rye whiskey they found in Manchester.[17] As evening approached, the bulk of "Uncle John's" exhausted troops arrived on the battlefield. Once present, they were ushered to the front in order to bolster the ranks of the II, III, and V Corps troops who were already locked in deadly combat.[18]

Just before 4:00 p.m., General Hancock returned to his line on Cemetery Ridge after attending a meeting of corps commanders with General Meade at the Leister home. He was met by General Gibbon, who began to provide him with an update on matters.[19] As the two commanders spoke, their attention was suddenly diverted by a host of activity on their left. That bustle was the unauthorized forward movement of Humphreys's division of Sickles's III Corps. The two general officers were simply astonished. Neither commander could fathom that move since General Sickles had never bothered to notify them of his plans.[20] As the two watched, "Hancock was resting on one knee, leaning upon his sword; he smiled and remarked: Wait a moment, you will soon see them tumbling back."[21] Later, Hancock recalled that "...the object of Genl. Sickles moving to the front I could not conceive."[22] Lieutenant William P. Wolson, a member of General Caldwell's staff, confirmed Hancock's impression when he wrote that the general commented that while the movement was beautiful, the III Corps would not be in their new position long. To that, the Philadelphia-born Gibbon commented that while Sickles's lines were well-formed, "...it is not war." Then, Gibbon compared the pageantry of Sickles's move to the "Charge of the Light Brigade" at Balaklava.[23] Noticing that on Humphreys's left there rested a body of woods, Gibbon turned to Hancock and almost aimlessly asked: "Do you suppose the enemy has anything in that woods?" According to General Gibbon, the time was 4 o'clock.[24] Another eyewitness, Lieutenant Frank A. Haskell, noted that the impressive move of the III Corps was "magnificent." But, he also commented:

Gnl. [sic] Sickles supposed he was doing for the best; but he was neither born nor bred a soldier. But one can scarcely tell what may have been the motives of such a man,—a politician, and some other things, exclusive of the Barton Key affair,*—a man after show, and notoriety, and newspaper fame, and the adulation of the mob! O, there is a grave responsibility on those in whose hands are the lives of ten thousand men; and on those who put stars upon men's shoulders, too! Bah! I kindle when I see some things that I have—it developed the battle;—the results of the move to the Corps itself we shall see. O, if this Corps had kept its strong position upon the crest...[25]

General Sickles had also ordered General Birney forward with the reassuring, but empty, promise that both the II and V Corps had offered one division each to stand ready to support him in the event of any problems. As a result Birney placed Brigadier-General J. H. Hobart Ward's Second Brigade on his left, almost touching Little Round Top, while de Trobriand's Third Brigade took the center in the Wheatfield. Brigadier-General Charles K. Graham's First Brigade was placed on the far right, extending to the Emmitsburg Road.[26] When they were in their final positions, Birney's entire First Division formed a crescent facing south and west. Sickles's forward move exposed both of his III Corps flanks plus the left flank of Hancock's II Corps. Unwittingly, the flamboyant New York commander created a ripe opportunity for the Confederate attack soon to be delivered by General Longstreet's I Corps.[27] The entire move was to prove costly to the III Corps and at least 40% of its ranks that were present and fully equipped were destined to wind up on the casualty list that afternoon.[28]

While that move was still under way, and shortly after 4:00 p.m., an angered General Meade rode over to the position of the Union III Corps and spoke directly with General Sickles. An aide to General Sickles recorded the following details:

General Sickles saluted with a polite observation. General

---

* In 1859, Sickles shot and killed Barton Key, son of Francis Scott Key, for having a love affair with his beautiful wife, Teresa.

Meade said: "General Sickles, I am afraid you are too far out." General Sickles responded: "I will withdraw if you wish, sir." General Meade replied: "I think it is too late. The enemy will not allow you. If you need more artillery call on the reserve artillery."[29]

Hancock later testified that while he certainly expected a fight to begin somewhere along the Union line that day, he simply could not comprehend the move being made by General Sickles. What did become clear was that a fight was now imminent in his front, which he felt would be "disadvantageous to us." Certainly, the resulting casualties that day proved him right, and soon Longstreet's assaulting lines engulfed "everybody along the line."[30] At those very moments, another eyewitness on the field remarked that while the III Corps was moving, all was quiet. Then, suddenly, someone yelled, "There!" and pointed "to where a puff of smoke is seen rising against the dark green of the woods. Another and another cloud is seen until the whole face of the forest is enveloped and the dreaded sound of artillery comes loud and quick..."[31] Longstreet had ordered his attack to begin.

The aide to General Sickles goes on to relate that one of those Confederate cannon shells fell nearby and "frightened the charger of General Meade..." As it happened, that specific horse was not Meade's faithful "Old Baldy," but a mount that belonged to his cavalry commander, General Alfred Pleasonton. When the shell exploded, the horse simply let off for parts unknown, and the aide later commented of the beast, "let him run, and run he would, and run he did."[32]

While those events were unfolding, matters were also heating up on the crest of Little Round Top, which was destined to plunge some of those participants into the forefront of history. In particular, Colonel Joshua Chamberlain and his 20th Maine Regiment were to win the praise of General Hancock and many others. More than 20 years after the battle, Hancock wrote General Walker that "the enemy did attempt to turn our position on the 2nd, and would have done so, but for the final, decisive action in which Chamberlain was the left." But while his praise was high for the Maine boys, Hancock also demonstrated a typical sense of balance when he mentioned that the actions [North and South] on Little Round Top "showed a devotion to duty, and a quality of independence of character on the part of the subordinate, detached commanders of both armies, which merits the highest praise."[33]

"I'd be God Damned..." 85

About 5:00 p.m., an aide from General Meade's staff rode up and instructed Hancock, who was still not yet engaged, to send a division to assist Major-General George Sykes and his V Corps. Sykes had succeeded Meade to command of the V Corps when Meade was promoted, and he was now located on Hancock's far left around Devil's Den. Sykes, who was a professional soldier, has perhaps been unfairly viewed, owing to his West Point sobriquet, "Tardy George." He too was tainted by another obscure Gettysburg controversy on July 3rd when his corps reportedly failed to follow up on the Union victory.[34] Debates aside, Sykes's troops played a key roll in the defense of the Union left that day.

In response to Meade's order, Hancock quickly turned and said to General Caldwell, "...get your division ready."[35] After the war, Hancock recalled, "I imagine that the reason it [Caldwell's division] was ordered to report to General Sykes was that after General Sickles advanced, General Sykes was ordered to hold Round Top, and probably his own troops had not gotten up."[36] Promptly, most of Caldwell's First Division were on the move. Included in Caldwell's marching line was Colonel Patrick Kelly's Irish Brigade, consisting of the 28th Massachusetts, 63rd, 69th and 88th New York and the 116th Pennsylvania. Many of those boys happened to be Roman Catholic. As their blue line began to pass just south of the modern Pennsylvania Monument site, Father William Corby mounted a large rock and momentarily halted their ranks. In a paternal manner, the future two-time president of Notre Dame University urged those men to express a "heartfelt sorrow for the sins by which we have ungratefully offended the Divine Author..." When he finished his brief entreaty, Father Corby raised his right hand and, using the universal Latin language of the church, he granted the men a general absolution.[37] Despite the building, crushing noise and anxiety caused by Longstreet's thunderous attack, Kelly's men savored those precious moments to reflect on their probable, impending meeting with their God. As Corby faced that small sea of pensive faces, he could see that General Hancock was in the rear, mounted, and waiting out of respect. Corby later commented that "Hancock removed his hat, and, as far as compatible with the situation, bowed in reverential devotion."[38] Rather romantically, Colonel St. Clair Mulholland, who would win the Medal of Honor for his heroics at Chancellorsville, noted: "Nearby stood, Hancock, surrounded by a brilliant array of officers, who had gathered to witness this very unusual occurrence, and while there was profound silence in the ranks of the Second Corps, yet over to the left...where [Stephen H.] Weed, [Strong] Vincent and [Charles E.] Hazlett were dying, the roar of the battle rose..."[39] With those brief devotions complete, Caldwell's line continued its move, believing it was

Brigadier-General Samuel K. Zook

Mortally wounded in the Wheatfield on July 2, 1863.

"I'd be God Damned..." 87

headed directly toward Devil's Den. Actually, owing to the smoke and confusion on the field, Caldwell had inadvertently moved into the Trostle Woods.[40]

Shortly before Father Corby's absolution, Colonel Edward E. Cross, commanding Hancock's First Brigade, First Division, had just given some of his personal affects to Dr. William Child and bid him a terse good-bye. Cross then prophetically added: "It will be an awful day. Take care of yourself, I must go into the fight, but I fear I shall be killed. Good-by!"[41] This was at least the second time within the past several days that Cross had such morose feelings. On the march to Gettysburg, he told an aide, Lieutenant Charles A. Hale, "I wish you to attend to my books and papers...After the campaign is over, get it at once, dry the content, if damp, and then turn it over to my brother Richard." As he was preparing his brigade to move, General Hancock rode up with his staff and addressed Cross, who was standing at his horse. "Colonel Cross, this day will bring you a star." Perhaps fully attuned to his earlier intuitions, and with a black kerchief instead of his usual red identifying cloth tied to his forehead, Cross laconically replied: "No, General, this is may last battle."[42]

Just after Father Corby's absolution, Hancock's hometown friend, Brigadier-General Samuel K. Zook, commander of the Third Brigade, First Division, with whom he had developed legendary cursing matches, was being implored by Major Henry E. Tremain of General Sickles's staff. Tremain begged Zook to pull out of Caldwell's line and move to the aid of the pummeled III Corps in the Wheatfield. Earlier that morning Zook had been asked by one of his soldiers to hold his money during the coming battle because he had a foreboding of death. After agreeing to accommodate the request, the new brigadier thought better and told the soldier he had better find someone else because he too felt that he would be killed that day.[43] For Zook, also, that premonition of death was not new. Nonetheless, after some quick discussion and thought, Zook consented to Tremain's pleas and, fatefully, pulled his brigade out of line and ultimately headed for a spot known as Stony Hill in the Wheatfield. Within the hour, both Cross and Zook would both be mortally wounded. Cross died around midnight, while Zook died during the late afternoon of the third.[44] Unfortunately, battlefield demands do not allow for the mourning of such heroes during the heat of conflict. Meanwhile, the full force of Longstreet's attack, led by Major-General John Bell Hood, was now under way. Lieutenant Haskell left the following record:

> The fire all along our crest is terrific, and it is a wonder how anything human could have stood before it, and yet the mad-

ness of the enemy drove them on, clear up to the muzzle of the guns,—clear up to the lines of our Infantry,—but the lines stood right in their places.[45]

The total impact of General Sickles's move has long been debated and shows no signs of abating soon. The entire event is yet another Gettysburg controversy that has polarized participants, students and buffs. For example, while General Warren was busy with his own challenges that afternoon, he nonetheless was fully aware of Sickles's inexplicable decision. After the battle, when he was testifying before the Joint Committee, Warren was asked if he thought Sickles was an officer who could "bring his corps into a fight well?" Thinking carefully, Warren offered this balanced, if not political, reply:

> I do not think that General Sickles would be a good man to fight an independent battle, which a corps commander would often have to do. I do not think General Sickles is as good a soldier as the others, but he did the best he could...When you come down to the details of a battle, General Sickles has not had the same experience which others have had. The knowledge of those details do not make a soldier, but he should be possessed of them as much as he is of his own language.[46]

Unfortunately, the era, politics and dictates of the American Civil War period had a tendency to promote and utilize too much incompetence on both sides of the conflict. That failing is probably a testimony to the youthful state of the nation, its traditions and military machinery.

About 5 o'clock, the thinned ranks of the 27th Connecticut, led by Lieutenant-Colonel Henry C. Merwin, were preparing to enter the fray in the Wheatfield. That Connecticut regiment had fought under Hancock at Fredericksburg, where the general successfully charged them not to bring any shame upon their state. Now, after less than nine months of active service, their ranks that day could not count more than a mere 75 intrepid men. Not allowing their paltry numbers to deter them, in they went and, by dark, their numbers dwindled by another 11 men, including their commander, Colonel Merwin, who was killed in the charge.[47]

In a return to Fredericksburg for a moment, that battle and the days

Lieutenant-Colonel Henry C. Merwin

This commander of the 27th Connecticut was killed in the Wheatfield on July 2, 1863.

before and after also served as an added, important record of Hancock's personality. Included in his ranks of the First Division were the stalwart men of the noted Irish Brigade and one member left a particularly revealing testimony to the martinet general:

> ...General Hancock was fiery and excitable, iron-willed and, in many instances, harsh and tyrannical to the volunteer troops under his command. He expected that they...should already have attained that perfection in military discipline and drill which only regular troops...reach. ...I cannot hide the fact that General Hancock reached the highest degree of perfection in cursing at his volunteer troops.[48]

Continuing with this personality insight a bit further, on November 22, 1862, Hancock was inspecting the 116th Pennsylvania when Private William McCarter witnessed the following incident involving a comrade known only as "Richmond Dick." Unfortunately, that sad soldier's dress and countenance were described as "no way reasonably clean," which did not please his division commander.

> Next came my own [inspection]...Company "C." Oh, no! Stop, watch the fiery eye of Hancock as it catches the first sight of something down the line, stowed away among the men of Company "D." It was no less a personage than "Richmond Dick." Nearer and nearer the dreaded inspector got to him. Now Dick was reached. He presented a dirty musket to the chief, who took hold of it, looked at it suspiciously, then stared at its owner, scanning him for a moment from head to foot...Half a minute later, the clear, loud voice of the general, was heard, "What in the devil are you doing here?"
>
> Then the weapon was dashed to the ground. The dirty, slovenly soldier was seized by the coat collar and dragged out of the line by the powerful arm of Hancock. The scene caused a tittering of laughter by all the troops there. The offender now received one of the general's not to be forgotten tongue-

"I'd be God Damned..."

thrashings, never lacking in profanity. Dick was then sent spinning towards his quarters by a kick on the posterior from the toe of one of the general's heavy-soled army boots...next morning, he [Dick] could not be found anywhere within the Union lines...[49]

"...woe be to the man who shirked or in any sense failed to meet and perform his duty."

According to General Birney, around 6:00 p.m., as the fury in the Wheatfield continued, General Sickles was over by his headquarters, the Trostle home, taking every opportunity to encourage his embattled troops. Sickles had just returned to that area and had just finished speaking with Generals Birney and Humphreys, when a cannon ball ripped into his right leg, all but severing the limb except for a few pieces of remaining flesh.[50] Completely disabled by the dreadful wound, Sickles told his aide, Major Tremain, to turn command over to General Birney and he was carried off the field on a stretcher, puffing away on a cigar. When Meade heard of Sickles's wounding and his subsequent appointment of Birney to succeed him, he thought differently. Instead, Meade promptly appointed Hancock to assume command of the III Corps. Twenty-five years later, General Sickles still confidently reflected on his unauthorized move at Gettysburg and was quoted as saying: "I would do tomorrow under the conditions and circumstances that then existed exactly what I did on July 2, '63." For his "extraordinary" performance on the field that day, General Dan Sickles was awarded the Medal of Honor.[51] So much for politics!

"All are not soldiers that go to war."[52]

Hancock was not pleased with Meade's decision to give him that new assignment. After the battle, the general commented: "I never really exercised any command over any part of the 3d Corps in action, save the fragments of Genl Humphreys command." Because of his new appointment, Hancock dutifully turned the II Corps back to General Gibbon.[53] According to Gibbon, Hancock was "...uttering some expressions of discontent at being compelled at such a time to give up command of one corps in a sound condition to take command of another which...had gone to pieces."[54]

Returning to the issues on Cemetery Ridge, somewhere around 7:00 p.m., south of Ziegler's Grove, General Hancock was personally leading his Third Brigade, Third Division, under Colonel George L. Willard, to assist General Birney's crumbling ranks.[55] Birney himself told Hancock that "his troops had all been driven to the rear, and had left the position to which I [Hancock] was moving." Hancock further recalled that Birney then went to the rear in an attempt to collect his broken command, which had sustained over 2,000 casualties that afternoon. Despondent over his heavy losses and the poor condition of his command, later that evening a broken Birney was overheard to say, "I wish I were already dead."[56]

About the same time, Hancock could also see that General Humphreys's Second Division was being forced back, though according to that commander, his troops were "slowly firing as [they] retired." It was perfectly clear to Hancock that at that time, most of the III Corps was "all gone as a [fighting] force, for that occasion." Despite that critical analysis, he thought that General Humphreys's command was handling itself as well as might be expected and he ordered Humphreys to place his men in the position vacated earlier by General Caldwell's First Division.[57] Then, he directed Willard's brigade to fill the void to Humphreys's left, where General Birney had withdrawn.

Just then, another crisis was developing in Hancock's front, as the brigade belonging to General Wilcox was headed for Humphreys's center, while Brigadier-General William Barksdale's Brigade was headed for Willard's flank. Hancock obviously felt comfortable about Humphreys's ability to handle himself, and he chose to stay near Willard's ranks. As Willard's men began their move to meet Barksdale, the Confederates were attempting to break his right and also threatened to turn his entire flank. Hancock was watching this and he spurred his horse to the rear of Willard's line to find reinforcements. There he found Colonel Clinton D. MacDougall and his 111th New York, whom Willard had placed in reserve; Hancock ordered MacDougall forward!

Meanwhile, the left of Willard's line was hotly engaged, and a Rebel shell took away a part of the brigadier's face, killing him instantly. Colonel Eliakim Sherrill, a former U.S. Congressman, took his place.[58] Concurrently, MacDougall had arrived into his position on the right and drove the Confederates back, "almost into the mouth of their own batteries..." But, his efforts were costly, and of 390 men MacDougall led into that fray, 180 were either killed or wounded within 20 minutes.[59]

During the heavy exchange of fire between Willard's and Barksdale's ranks, the 41-year-old Confederate general was mortally wounded. Earlier, the proud Barksdale had broken through the Yankee line and had been an import-

Colonel Eliakim E. Sherrill

Brigadier-General William Barksdale, CSA

ant factor in the Confederate gain of the Peach Orchard that afternoon. The indomitable politician then hurled his ranks against Willard's forces. Perched upon his white horse, he presented a target that simply begged for attention. Among the several Federal regiments which claimed to have brought Barksdale down were the men of the 11th New Jersey, Company H. Those Yankees allegedly fired a volley and five balls soon knocked Barksdale from his saddle, tearing into his left breast and breaking his left leg. The Southern political-general was given attention by Surgeon Alfred Thornley Hamilton of the 148th Pennsylvania, who described Barksdale as possessing a firm mental makeup with "quick perception and ability to succeed..."[60] According to some traditional accounts, Barksdale's last audible words were: "I am killed. Tell my wife and children I died fighting at my post."[61] Actually, his time had not come just yet and his last words were not to be quite so poetic.

William Barksdale was another of the many interesting people that comprise the complex tapestry of the American Civil War. He was born in Rutherford County, Tennessee, and studied law as a young man. Always an ardent pro-slavery man, Barksdale entered the Mexican War as an enlisted man and attained the rank of captain. But politics was the dominant factor in his life and he served in the U.S. Congress between 1853–1861, representing the state of Mississippi. Some claim that when his colleague, Preston Brooks of South Carolina, caned the abolitionist senator from Massachusetts, Charles Sumner, on the Senate floor, Barksdale prevented bystanders from rendering any assistance to the pompous Sumner. With the outbreak of civil war, Barksdale first served as quartermaster-general of his state's army and then led the 13th Mississippi. He quickly earned a reputation as an intrepid, competent regimental commander, which was furthered at the battle of Malvern Hill. There, General Lee took particular notice of him and he was promoted to brigadier in August, 1862 and assigned a brigade. Throughout most of the major eastern battles, including Antietam, Fredericksburg and Chancellorsville, Barksdale led his proud Mississippians. General Lee thought enough of him to remark that he displayed "the highest qualities of the soldier."[62]

Immediately following that successful Union repulse of Barksdale's Brigade, Sherrill stopped to reform his lines in the Plum Run Valley. Then, for reasons known only to him, Sherrill inexplicably decided to take his command back to their original position near the Bryan House, up near Ziegler's Grove. According to Lieutenant-Colonel James M. Bull, of the 126th New York, Sherrill was simply carrying out the designs of the dead Willard.[63] But, as Sherrill began his march, General Hancock watched in disbelief, feeling certain that he was going to hold the defended position instead. Urging his horse for-

Brigadier-General Winfield Scott Hancock

This is a photograph by Mathew Brady. (Circa 1862)

"I'd be God Damned..."

ward to the head of the moving column, Hancock encountered Sherrill. There, in a fit of rage, and no doubt amidst a shower of ripe expletives, Hancock had Sherrill placed under arrest. In his stead, the general appointed Colonel MacDougall to take command. The next day, however, Hancock restored Sherrill at the behest of General Alexander Hays and Colonel MacDougall.[64]

With that crisis now under control, Hancock rode a little further north, between the Wheatfield Road and the copse of trees. There he could see a continuing dilemma on his front, and he immediately sent to Generals Gibbon and Hays for reinforcements. At the same time, portions of Birney's III Corps were making a run for the rear. In concert with other officers, Hancock attempted in vain to organize those dispirited Yankees, but close on the heels of the retreating Federals were the 1,600 men belonging to General Wilcox's Brigade. Close to the II Corps commander was his aide, Captain W. D. W. Miller, and it didn't take long before the approaching Confederates were sending their lead in the general's direction. Two of those balls found their mark in Miller. After sending his aide to the rear for medical attention, Hancock began to search desperately for a temporary means to stall the approaching enemy.

With his adrenaline now flowing and anxiety growing, all Hancock could see were 262 men of the 1st Minnesota, the only regiment from that state with the Army of the Potomac.[65] While he was not certain, Hancock assumed that they had been sent to him by General Gibbon, and he cried out, "My God! Are these all the men we have here?" Then, turning to the first available officer, Colonel William Colvill, Jr., Hancock asked, "What regiment is this?" Colvill immediately replied, "First Minnesota," part of General Gibbon's First Brigade.[66] Losing not a second more, Hancock pointed toward the approaching Rebel banners and said to Colvill, "Colonel, Do you see those colors?" "Yes, sir," Colvill replied. "Well, capture them." Immediately, Colvill saluted Hancock and was off as ordered.[67]

None of those Minnesota men required any written script to know that Hancock's order meant certain death or maiming for most if not all of them. Colonel Colvill ran to the front of his line and hollered, "Forward, double-quick..." With their bayonets fixed, the 100-yard-wide line of blue began yelling as they rushed down the incline into a veritable wall of Confederate lead. Within moments, Colvill went down with a wound to his leg. He was soon followed by Lieutenant-Colonel Charles Adams, who was brought down by six Rebel balls. But the conviction of those determined Minnesota boys simply stunned the attacking Confederates, who were soon halted in their pursuit. In five minutes, the successful Yankee attack was over and Hancock gained his precious time.[68]

But the field was now strewn with the bodies of those Midwestern boys, and one survivor recorded: "What Hancock had given us to do was done thoroughly. The regiment had stopped the enemy...But at what sacrifice!...Of the two hundred and sixty-two men who made the charge, two hundred and fifteen lay upon the field...forty seven were still in line, and not a man was missing."[69] For their bloody valor, the Minnesota boys took some comfort in the knowledge that they had helped to save the ridge and had certainly earned a hard-won, enviable reputation and, reportedly, some of the colors belonging to Wilcox's Brigade.[70] According to Hancock, that Rebel offensive was the "furtherest advanced point at which any of the enemy appeared on the second day."[71] However, it appears that CSA Brigadier-General Ambrose R. Wright's Brigade might really hold that distinction. Nonetheless, Hancock's selection of the 1st Minnesota provides the stage for another of the many battle ironies. On June 28, while marching to Gettysburg, Hancock's aide, Colonel Morgan, had Colonel Colvill arrested because some of his men balked at the crossing of a stream. Colvill was not released from that sentence until the 1st Minnesota arrived on the field on the morning of July 2nd.[72]

Whatever the strange details attached to that heroic defense, according to one postwar account, Hancock told the Senator from Minnesota, Morton Wilkinson: "I had no alternative but to order that regiment in. Troops had been ordered up and were coming on the run, but I saw that in some way five minutes must be gained or we were lost. It was fortunate that I found so grand a body of men as the First Minnesota. I knew they must lose heavily, and it caused me pain to give the order for them to advance, but I would have done it if I had known every man would be killed. It was a sacrifice that must be made. No soldiers, on any field, in this or any other country, ever displayed grander heroism."[73] When he addressed a reunion of the 1st Minnesota after the war, Hancock told those members: "...you accomplished results which will make the name 1st. Minn. immortal, if valor and devotion to a cause continue to be prized by your countrymen."[74] Despite those warm words, few living Americans know or appreciate the heroics of those brave men.

They come like sacrifices in their trim,
And to the fire-eyed maid of smoky war
All hot and bleeding we will offer them.
Shakespeare[75]

Monument to the First Minnesota on Cemetery Ridge at Gettysburg

It was in this area where their heroic attack was made.

With the charge of the 1st Minnesota coming to an end, Hancock now faced a new problem. Shortly after he ordered Colvill to attack, he moved northward along the line and was astonished to find that one of his batteries, which he had personally placed, was now abandoned. Battery C, 5th U.S. Artillery, under Lieutenant Gulian V. Weir, was now deserted along with the assigned protective infantry, and the Rebels were intending to help themselves.[76] With enemy shells falling in the area, Hancock realized that matters were again dire. Looking around once more, Hancock saw Brigadier-General George J. Stannard's Third Brigade, Third Division, I Corps headed his way by orders of General Doubleday. Hancock quickly spoke with Colonel Francis V. Randall of the 13th Vermont and explained his newest dilemma. He asked that Vermont colonel if he thought he could retrieve those vital field pieces. Because the Rebels were so close, Hancock certainly appreciated the hazard involved in such a request and undoubtedly that made him reluctant to order another costly attack similar to the one made by the 1st Minnesota. But Randall made matters easy when he accepted the challenge, and five of his companies were soon rushed forward. In a matter of minutes those Green Mountain boys saved the guns and took some Confederate prisoners as a bonus.[77] Throughout that entire episode, Hancock remained on the field to watch and was himself observed by those attacking Southerners.[78]

Despite his pleasure with Randall's success, Hancock was furious about the abandonment of those guns and he had every intention of addressing the matter with General Hunt. Unfortunately, matters on the third day put a temporary hold on that issue.[79] However, the final chapter of the incident was closed 23 years later when a repentant and despondent Weir put a bullet through his heart.[80]

Conditions on the field had now become horrific and macabre. But oddly enough, even during such trying times, some humans have a way of employing their humor. For example, in the midst of all that fighting and carnage, one unidentified Rebel soldier yelled out: "Have we got all creation to whip?" Not to be surpassed by his foe, an equally unidentified Yankee soldier replied: "Attention Universe! Nations into line! By Kingdoms! Right Wheel!"[81] Even if such reports are not completely accurate, they do reflect the vent of mental frustrations of the common soldier.

Hancock next ordered up the 19th Maine from Gibbon's Second Division. He wanted them posted along Cemetery Ridge, in front of Meade's headquarters. As Colonel Francis E. Heath was moving those Maine men accordingly, a battery that Hancock had ordered forward was also in motion and the two units became entangled. Heath prudently ordered his men back to allow the battery to pass. Hancock had watched the meshing of those two bodies and became highly irritated and "gave way to a curious outbreak of temper." Furious at the confusion, Hancock rode up to the battery and "in a good deal of passion," told the battery officer: "...if I commanded this regt. I'd be God Damned if I would not charge bayonets on you—"[82] Unfortunately, Colonel Heath does not leave us any further details, and we can only assume it was an uncomfortable moment for everyone involved.

Hancock next moved to fill the void that was left when Sickles's III Corps had vacated earlier in the day. He sent back to General Meade for new units to anchor themselves to the left of his II Corps. His request was soon answered when portions of the Second Brigade, First Division, XII Corps, under Brigadier-General Henry H. Lockwood, showed up and secured the area. Shortly thereafter, Hancock again encountered General Humphreys and ordered him to place his two brigades to the left of the II Corps, which Humphreys quickly did. Joined by some of Hancock's troops and artillery, any pursuing Rebels were driven from that part of the field.[83]

Late in the day, Hancock received erroneous word that General Humphreys had been killed. Hancock had also gotten some preliminary reports and even General Sykes curiously told him that his old division, the First, had performed poorly in their attempt to assist his battered V Corps. Hancock became very upset to think that his old command, now led by General Caldwell, would not stand such a test. However, he soon learned that the fatal report on Humphreys was incorrect and that Caldwell's ranks had indeed performed most admirably.[84] In fact, they fought so well that as he was being improperly briefed, Colonel Cross and General Zook both lay mortally wounded. Soon after, Hancock ordered Caldwell's battered ranks back to their original position, where they "lay on our arms until the morning of the 3d."[85]

As the heated fighting across the Union left and center began to recede, General Ewell began a concerted effort to break the Union lines on Culp's Hill and Cemetery Hill. Ewell had ordered General Edward Johnson's division to take some of the works that Slocum's men vacated when they went to help restore order on the Union left. In addition, General Early sent two of his brigades, belonging to Brigadier-General Harry T. Hays and Colonel Isaac E. Avery, against Howard's ranks on East Cemetery Hill. As Early's lines moved up the slope, they overpowered the Yankees and captured some of their field guns, and continued their way to the crest. Again, Howard's ranks had come to the precipice of defeat and embarrassment.[86]

All of that heavy Rebel firing along Howard's line convinced Hancock that the Union right was seriously threatened. While Howard had not requested any help as yet, Hancock, who was standing next to General Gibbon, felt the danger too real and, without requesting permission from General Meade, he turned to Gibbon and said: "We ought to send some help over there. Send a brigade, send Carroll!"[87] With that, Gibbon promptly directed Colonel Samuel S. Carroll and his First Brigade, Third Division, also known as the Gibraltar Brigade, to move. This newest challenge for Hancock was caused mainly by the reluctance of Brigadier-General Adelbert Ames's Second Brigade, First Division, XI Corps, to move forward. That unit had just been repulsed by the Confederate assault and were very reluctant to reenter the fight.[88] According to Captain James F. Huntington, commander of the Third Volunteer Brigade, Reserve Artillery, when Carroll reached Cemetery Hill in the growing darkness, he asked Huntington where the enemy was and immediately moved forward and saved Batteries F and G belonging to Captain R. Bruce Ricketts.[89] Carroll wasted no time and when he and his ranks fell upon the Confederates, their ranks broke and ran "pell mell" down the east slope of Cemetery Hill.[90] In his own words, Carroll noted, "We found the enemy up to and some of them in among the front guns of the batteries on the road...it being perfectly dark...I had to find the enemy's line entirely by their fire...by changing the front of the Seventh West Virginia, they were soon driven from there."[91] According to a grateful Ricketts:

> At about 8 p.m. a heavy column of the enemy charged on my battery, and succeeded in capturing and spiking my left piece. The cannoneers fought them hand to hand with handspikes, rammers, and pistols, and succeeded in checking them for a moment, when a part of the Second Army Corps charged in and drove them back. During the charge I expended every round of canister in the battery, and then fired case shot without the fuses. The enemy suffered severely.[92]

Long after the battle, Carroll wrote to Hancock: "Had Howard's lines not been reinforced as they were it is quite certain that he would have lost cemetery hill [sic], and the army [sic] of the Potomac its position for the enemy was in Howard's batteries, and Slocum's line had been penetrated..."[93] Certainly, while Carroll's charge is far less known, it was equal to the superb timing of those led by Colonels Vincent and Chamberlain on Little Round Top. Carroll pushed back the initially jubilant Rebels and thwarted the designs of

Brevet Major-General Samuel Sprigg Carroll

reinforcements, who were already on their way to lend support. Immediately after his success, Colonel Carroll sent an aide to find Howard to request that he assign troops to meet up with both of his flanks. Unable to locate Howard, the aide instead found General Ames, who enjoyed an enviable reputation but instructed Carroll to stay put, "as he could not rely on his [own] troops..." That sad response only infuriated Carroll, who in turn told Ames, "damn a man who had no confidence in his troops..."[94] When the fighting was all over, about 10:20 p.m., General Howard insisted that Carroll and his ranks remain in their position for the rest of that night. As it turned out, Howard pleaded that Carroll's brigade stay in that same position throughout the third as well, and while they saw little or no action that day and their absence from the II Corps line highly irritated Hancock and Carroll both.[95] Sometime during the night of the second, Ames's ranks finally anchored themselves to Carroll's right and left.[96]

For Carroll's quick and decisive action, which undoubtedly saved Cemetery Hill that evening, Generals Hancock and Gibbon, always remained high in their praise for that commander's bravery and accomplishments. Long after the war, while Hancock was on Governor's Island, he sent a retired Major-General Carroll a copy of his *Official Reports*, which made proud mention of Carroll's name. On the frontispiece, the former corps commander warmly inscribed the slim volume:

"To: Maj Genl. S. S. Carroll with kind regards, W. S. Hancock."[97]

Unfortunately, Howard treated Carroll's success with an indifferent attitude, and in his battlefield report, he simply stated that Carroll "went into position just in time to check the enemy's advance." Such a bland statement for Carroll's important results also irritated General Gibbon. In February, 1864, Gibbon wrote to Carroll: "It has come to my attention that you have failed to receive from Maj. Gen. Howard the official acknowledgment to which you and your Brigade are entitled...the reports which reached me at the time and afterwards of your timely arrival at and prompt recovery of a critical point...preventing the enemy from obtaining a foothold on...Cemetery Hill." After Gibbon's letter was published, Howard wrote Carroll and acknowledged his valuable service on July 2nd.[98] However, it must be noted that General Howard did write Carroll a warm letter of thanks shortly after the battle.[99] It is highly likely that General Gibbon was never aware of that note. Nonetheless, even to this day, the important contribution of Colonel Carroll and his brigade are still not fully appreciated, though one cannoneer on the hill that evening left us this

"I'd be God Damned..."

comment: "I never saw Carroll's Brigade in battle except for 20 minutes that moment on Sundown of July 2, 1863...The way they walked into that wreck and set things straight was something that one who saw it can never forget."[100] The entire matter is another testimony to Hancock's executive field abilities.

When the day's fighting finally came to an end, General Hancock noted that "although the enemy had actually gotten in our line at more than one place, yet when night came we had managed to repulse them, and had driven them back, so that we held exactly the same position we had started out with, which was the direct line from Cemetery Hill to Round Top." However, he also sadly noted that the Federals did not hold any of that advanced ground west of Cemetery Hill despite the desperate and costly fighting that occurred that day.[101]

As the welcomed protection of darkness fell over the field, the grisly task of gathering the wounded began for both sides. One eyewitness recorded the following:

> Then was heard the rumbling of wagon wheels behind, and soon hundreds of ambulances were drawn up in rear of the lines, and with them came surgeons, hospital stewards, and stretcher-bearers without number. With their lighted lanterns they passed to the front and scattered over the valley, seeking out the wounded, and everywhere finding a full harvest. From the other side came the Confederate surgeons and their assistants, who scattering likewise over the hither fields, soon filled the mile-square space between the two armies with wandering jets of light...These wandering lights were seen all through the night, and when morning came the work of relief was still unfinished.[102]

But the common dictates of the battlefield never stop for such noble efforts, and by 11:00 that evening, Meade's corps commanders were all assembled in the small wooden Leister House for a council of war. Present for that session were Generals Birney, Gibbon, Hancock, Howard, Newton, Pleasonton, Sedgwick, Slocum, Sykes, Warren and Brigadier-General Alpheus S. Williams, also of the XII Corps.[103] Catching a glimpse of Hancock, Lieutenant Frank Haskell gave us the following description:

106   **Hancock at Gettysburg...***and beyond.*

Hancock is the tallest, and most shapely, and in many respects is the best looking officer of them all. His hair is very light brown, straight and moist, and always looks, well,—his beard is of the same color, of which he wears the moustache and a tuft upon the chin; complexion ruddy, features neither large nor small, but well cut, with full jaw and chin, compressed mouth, straight nose, full deep blue eyes, and a very mobile, emotional countenance. He always dresses remarkably well, and his manner is dignified, gentlemanly and commanding. I think if he were in citizens clothes, and should give commands in the army to those who did not know him, he would be likely to be obeyed at once, and without any question as to his right to command.[104]

As the men gathered into that small, sparsely furnished eastern room, it didn't take long before the air became thick with the cigar smoke. General Gibbon described the room as being "not more than ten or twelve feet square, with a bed in one corner, a small table on one side, and a chair or two."[105] Some sat while others walked, and at least two made themselves comfortable upon the only bed in the house. General Warren, "suffering from a wound in the neck...lay down in a corner of the room and went sound asleep..."[106] Warren's sleep was so deep that when he later testified before the Joint Committee on the Conduct of the War, he told them that he did not remember anything "like a definite council of war...a part of that evening I was asleep, being very tired..."[107]

Details on Meade's council are not very plentiful, and those that do exist must be viewed on a holistic basis and not interpreted on a word-for-word evaluation. General Gibbon reported that the meeting opened with a rather casual discussion, and each commander reviewed the status of his troops. In 1891, General Slocum recalled: "I remember each corps commander was first asked as to his losses during the day and the number of fighting men he could put into battle the next morning. These questions answered, then came the commanding general's all-important query: What shall be the order of the day for to-morrow?'" General Newton surprised some by his statement that "this was no place to fight a battle..."[108] General Slocum went on to draw a parallel between the battles of Waterloo and Gettysburg, and during the discussion General Meade was frequently interrupted with reports from various parts of

"*I'd be God Damned...*" 107

the field.[109] Finally, Meade posed three critical questions, which his chief of staff, General Dan Butterfield, had developed and recorded:

1. Under existing circumstances, is it advisable for this army to remain in its present position, or to retire to another nearer its base of supplies?
2. It being determined to remain in present position, shall the army attack or wait the attack of the enemy?
3. If we wait attack, how long?[110]

According to papers found in Meade's files after his death, the following responses were made to each corresponding question:

Gibbon: 1. Correct the position of the army, but would not retreat.
          2. In no condition to attack, in his opinion.
          3. Until he moves; until enemy moves.
Williams: 1. Stay.
          2. Wait attack.
          3. One Day.
Birney, same as General Williams.
Sykes, same as General Williams.
Newton: 1. Correct position of army, but would not retreat.
          2. By all means not attack.
          3. If we wait, it will give them a chance to cut our line.
Howard: 1. Remain.
          2. Wait attack until 4 p.m. tomorrow.
          3. If don't attack, attack them.
Hancock: 1. Rectify position without moving so as to give up field.
          2. Not attack unless our communications are cut.
          3. Can't wait long, can't be idle.
Sedgwick: 1. Remain, and wait attack at least one day.
Slocum: Stay and fight it out.[111]

After two hours of deliberation and discussion, the generals were clear in their decision to stay and wait for the enemy's certain attack, though Newton and Gibbon felt that some changes to the Union position might be needed. However, neither one gave the slightest hint of retreat, and General Meade noted that Hancock was "Puzzled about [the] practicability of retiring" and felt certain that the army could not remain static for long. Meade concluded the

108   **Hancock at Gettysburg**...*and beyond.*

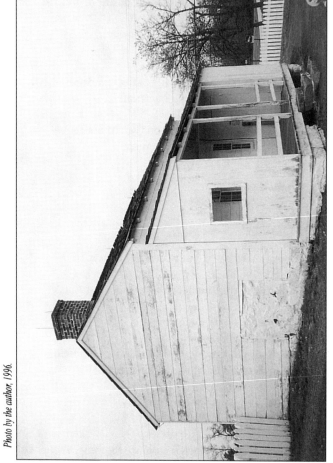

Photo by the author, 1996.

The Leister House at Gettysburg

This was General Meade's headquarters where he held his council of war on the night of July 2, 1863.

"I'd be God Damned..."

session with the statement: "Such then is the decision."[112] Before the generals left the Lesiter House, two important things happened. First, General Gibbon overheard Generals Meade and Birney in a tense discussion where Meade curtly snapped: "Gen. Hancock is your superior and I claim the right to issue the order." Gibbon noted that he thought Meade's angry tone resulted because General Birney was displeased that Hancock, and not he, was assigned command of the III Corps.[113] Second, Gibbon and Meade exchanged a few thoughts which were prompted by the junior officer's expression of gratitude at having been invited to the meeting. Meade told the 36-year-old Gibbon that "I wanted you here" and then perceptively added: "If Lee attacks to-morrow, it will be in your front." When Gibbon asked him why he thought so, Meade replied: "Because he has made attacks on both our flanks and failed, and if he concludes to try it again it will be on our center."[114] However, Meade's conviction here was to waiver somewhat over the next twelve hours.

When General Meade finished with Gibbon, perhaps he privately reflected on the many aspects of the day, but he most certainly reflected upon the unauthorized move by General Sickles. Five years after the war, Meade still burned with disdain for his former III Corps commander who continued the justification for his move in the newspapers and journals. When Meade responded to one newspaper article on the matter, he succinctly concluded his retort with the following:

> Sickles's movement practically destroyed his own corps, the 3d, caused a loss of 50 per cent in the 5th Corps, and very heavily damaged the 2d Corps, as I said before, producing 66 per cent of the loss of the whole battle, and with what result—driving us back to the position he was ordered to hold originally...If this is an advantage—to be so crippled in battle without attaining an object—I must confess I cannot see it.[115]

About midnight, with the long, exhausting day now over, Hancock, like everyone else on that field, was simply physically and mentally drained. Again, aching for at least a little rest, he climbed into an ambulance that was parked just south of the Leister House. There, he found Generals Gibbon and Newton already inside. He probably grunted a few words and promptly went off to sleep.[116] But sleep was not foremost on the minds of everyone that evening, and one member of the 126th New York left his recollections as he went onto the field that night:

> Nothing could be more dismal and appalling than searching over a battle-field in a dark night for a friend or comrade. To turn up one dead cold face after another to the glimmering light of a lantern, and see it marred with wounds and disfigured with blood and soil, the features, perhaps, convulsed by the death-agony, the eyes vacant and staring,—surely that friendship must be, indeed, stronger than death which would prompt to such an office, yet it was often undertaken, and even by women! Dismal, too, the sight of the dark battleground, with lanterns twinkling here and there, "like the wisp on the morass!"[117]

While the main field of Gettysburg had become relatively quiet with the welcome mist of slumber, inside the numerous makeshift hospitals, the ghoulish labor of the surgeons continued unabated. Just outside the white clapboard home of Jacob Hummelbaugh, near the Taneytown Road, lay the mortally wounded General Barksdale. Inside, Union surgeons were busy plying their sanguinary talents and sometime during that murky night of the second, or early morning of the third, the adjutant of the 148th Pennsylvania, J. W. Muffly, recorded his own gruesome testimony to that day's brutal fight:

> ...as I approached the little house— now the field hospital— I stepped upon something that felt so peculiar that I stopped and picked it up. It proved to be an arm. Happening to look at the west window I saw an outline of a pyramid of some sort, which on examination I found was a pile of hands, arms, feet and legs which the surgeons had thrown out in their work and which now reached the window sill. In front of the house lay General Barksdale...his breast torn and one leg shattered...begging for water, which a drummer boy was giving him with a spoon, and cursing the Yankees, it was a most pathetic scene...[118]

───────────── ♦ ─────────────

"I'd be God Damned..."

"Ye say, a good cause will hallow even war?
I say unto you; a good war halloweth every cause."
F. W. Nietzsche, 1885.

CHAPTER FOUR

July 3, 1863
"Tell General Hancock..."

The early morning sky of the third saw a complete covering of billowing stratocumulus clouds that proved to be the precursor of heavy thunder showers much later that day. By 7:00 a.m., the temperature was already a bearable 73 degrees, and while a gentle breeze made an attempt to fan the field, the air was already becoming thick with humidity.[1] The clouds would soon pass and, for the better part of the daylight hours, the sun would appear to focus its heat solely upon the small village of Gettysburg.

Hancock was awake well before dawn, having spent the short night between the ambulance and the small porch of the Leister House. When he did arise, he freshened himself and prepared for what some thought might be a relatively quiet day after two days of hard battle. In his own words, Hancock explained that his line on Cemetery Ridge "consisted of the 1st, 2d, and 3d corps, of which I had the general command. I commanded that whole front."[2] In terms of personal matters, the general recalled that he wore a stiff black felt hat [not a slouch hat] with general officer's cord, and a coat that he described as "undress." He also noted that "I was in the habit of wearing my coat only buttoned in the upper front, opened towards the waist," without a sash. He wore his sword belt under his coat and he carried only a light rapier.[3]

Despite the many demands inherent with his extended command, at some point that morning, Hancock found time to send Almira, who was visiting her parents in Saint Louis, a brief telegram informing her, "I am all right, so far." According to Mrs. Hancock, her husband frequently telegrammed her from the field with similar messages while battles raged.[4] Apparently, his brief battlefield missives assuaged Almira's anxieties.

The first major military focus that morning was to the northeast of Hancock's line on Culp's Hill where General Slocum's artillery began firing upon the Confederate forces of General Ewell's II Corps, around 4:30 a.m.[5] That heated contest lasted until nearly 11:00 a.m. when the Rebels were finally forced back across Rock Creek. Then, a relative lull fell over the field.

"Tell General Hancock..."

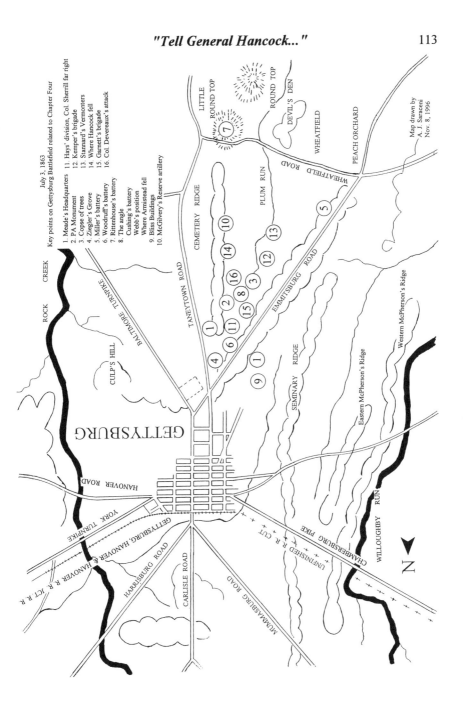

But, well before the conclusion of that Culp's Hill fight, and about 8:00 that morning, Hancock rode along the line of his II Corps ordering his men to fortify their positions. Following behind the general, several supply wagons passed along and men threw out shovels, picks, axes and other tools to facilitate that grunt work. By 11:00 a.m., the boys of the 148th Pennsylvania, reported that: "We had built a six-foot breastwork a few feet high and well lined..."[6]

On the other side of the field, if matters appeared quiet, they were not exactly dormant. West of the Emmitsburg Road, 28-year-old, Georgia-born Colonel E. Porter Alexander had been up since 3:00 that morning placing his artillery into position which would soon pound the Union center. Alexander recalled that while he was directing that work, he found himself amused that the Yankees actually watched him station his pieces without any attempt to dissuade him.[7] The total number of those Confederate cannon would eventually swell to about 172 and they were represented by a patchwork of Napoleons, 12-pound howitzers, Parrots and even two Whitworths. Like so many other particulars at Gettysburg, Alexander had been improperly instructed that his focal point was a copse of trees on Cemetery Ridge, which was, he was told, the local cemetery.[8] Little did anyone realize how famous that clump of trees was destined to become.

Sometime later that morning, Hancock rode over to speak with Colonel John Rutter Brooke, who was now leading the newly created Fourth Brigade of his First Division. During their conversation, Brooke mentioned to Hancock the heroics of the remaining small band of the proud 27th Connecticut. Brooke reported that those New England boys had lost their colonel in the Wheatfield the day before and emphasized that he felt they were worthy of some special praise. Hancock agreed and he addressed the regiment of only 64 surviving soldiers: "Stand well to your duty now, and in a few days you will carry with you to your homes all the honors of this, the greatest battle ever fought on this Continent."[9] Perhaps a sense of pride engulfed those depleted ranks of Nutmeggers and Hancock's prediction was soon realized by all of them and many more.

Even though a quiet day was contemplated, just before noon, Hancock continued his usual high vigilance and went forward to inspect and encourage another group of his men on the front line of Cemetery Ridge. There, he came upon the men belonging to a raw, unidentified regiment. When Hancock approached their line, those enthusiastic novices began to cheer him repeatedly and cried out eagerly to be led against the enemy. Knowing their innocence, the general warmly challenged them, instead, to simply hold their position in the event of an enemy attack. With that charge, several of those uninitiated soldiers naively called to him: "General we'll never leave this ground until you order us away." Adjusting himself in the saddle and displaying a broad grin at that comment, Hancock replied: "That's right my men, that's right, your line is entirely safe now, for I'll *never* order you away." Some nearby II Corps veterans watched that entire event with amused interest and noticed that when the meaning of the general's facetious retort really became clear, the smiles worn by those untested soldiers were soon replaced with troubled contemplation.[10]

At about the same time, 63 cannon belonging to General A. P. Hill's III Corps opened fire upon the northern end of Hancock's line. The Rebel objective was to halt the attacks of the 14th Connecticut that had just captured the Bliss house and barn, which had become a haven for Confederate snipers. Brigadier-General Alexander Hays of Hancock's Third Division had sent two earlier attacks against those buildings and he now ordered them cleared, which resulted in the capture of a band of Rebel prisoners. Hancock had been keeping his eye on those activities and after Hays's second advance, he sent his aide, Captain Henry H. Bingham, of the 140th Pennsylvania, to instruct Hays to burn the buildings and return to his line on Cemetery Ridge. Since the buildings were not strategically critical, neither Meade nor Hancock wished them to become the cause of a general engagement. When Bingham informed Hays of Hancock's order, Hays pleaded for permission to continue his attacks and asked: "Major, please return to General Hancock and say to him that that old barn is my 'Reb' trap. I have caught more than one hundred & fifty in it this morning and if he will only allow me to withdraw my line so that they will come into it again and then let me take one more dash at it – I will willingly burn it as he directs."[11] [Emphasis in original] But, Hancock's orders prevailed. Hays, who would be killed at the Wilderness in less than one year, then ordered the complete destruction of the barn and house, which was carried out by the 14th Connecticut, under the command of Major Theodore G. Ellis. After those Yankees fired the buildings, they found it impossible to resist the temptation of "requisitioning" a few prized chickens to take back to their lines, which had been thinned by 160 comrades, compliments of those Confederate sharpshooters.[12] When the 14th finished their candescent work, a second and rather beguiling sense of quiet and calm fell over the entire field.

Taking advantage of that respite, Hancock accepted the welcomed invitation of General John Gibbon, who decided to host a luncheon in the rear of his line. Among others who would eagerly accept Gibbon's thoughtful offer were Generals Meade, John Newton, who now headed the I Corps, and Alfred Pleasonton of the cavalry, plus a number of their aides. Since Gibbon was unable to offer his guests a cherry wood table and crystal goblets, the general officers gladly accepted a couple of crude wooden stools and a table hurriedly fashioned from a mess-chest. For the repast, they joyfully feasted on boiled potatoes, bread, and an enormous pan of stewed chicken, which was described as "large and in good running order." [Emphasis in original] Following that "elegant" battlefield meal, the generals sat, smoked and debated where Lee might attack next. Throughout the entire occasion, Hancock's aide, Captain Bingham, slept soundly on the nearby ground oblivious to the feast, talk and imminent events. Years later, the then unsuspecting Bingham would win the Medal of Honor for his distinguished gallantry at the battle of the Wilderness.[13] But, for now, he was completely engulfed in a delightful phantasmagoric state.

During those relaxed moments, General Meade expressed some understandable uncertainty since he felt Lee might again attack his left while he also worried that a frontal assault might be possible. Perhaps he simply wished to consider all the possibilities for any Rebel attack, though Meade was now confident that any assault, no matter where, would occur much later in the day. Meade also told Hancock that if his center happened to be the focal point of an attack, he would order the V and VI Corps to fall upon the Rebel flanks.[14] Throughout that entire morning, Hancock felt equally certain that any Confederate thrust would definitely be made against his front, the center of the Union line.[15] But, since no one was able to divine any of Lee's definitive thoughts or movements, Hancock turned to more mundane matters. He momentarily left the clustered officers and again went forward. This time he ordered the relief of Colonel Wheelock G. Veazey and his 16th Vermont, which had been on picket duty in front of Cemetery Ridge. After that, he rode a little further south where he again encountered the men of the 148th Pennsylvania, and one of those men recorded the following: "About this time General Hancock rode along our line encouraging the men and informed us that the enemy was going to make a charge on our line and that he wanted every soldier to stand at his post."[16] When he finished with those Vermont and Pennsylvania boys, Hancock started back toward the group of generals who had now gathered near Meade's Headquarters at the Leister House. On the way, he began dictating a memo to Lieutenant-Colonel Charles H. Morgan about the distribution of fresh beef.[17]

At that moment, 1:00 p.m. according to Colonel E. P. Alexander, across the field toward the Emmitsburg Road and north of the Peach Orchard, Colonel J. B. Walton of the Washington Artillery was responding to General Longstreet's command, "Let the batteries open."[18] By prior arrangement, Walton ordered his two signal guns from Captain Merritt B. Miller's battery, located in the Peach Orchard, to open fire. Almost instantly, the first gun, under

Sergeant W. T. Hardie, boldly announced the warning, "Be on your Guard," as its shell reportedly went smashing into a Union caisson. A defective friction primer caused a slight delay in the second scheduled report. Nonetheless, that next shot was soon fired by the gun belonging to Sergeant P. O. Fazende, and with it the heavy, quiet air was shattered by the screaming shells from a long line of thundering Confederate cannon. As the noise from the shrieking missiles rose to a crescendo, Colonel Alexander would soon note that "The enemy replied rather slowly at first, though soon with increasing rapidity."[19]

Hancock's instinctive reaction was to complete his fragmentary beef memo but those Southern shells began arriving with such increased frequency that the resulting bloody confusion made that impossible. Instead, it appears that he dismounted and began to give out orders. While in that process, the wagon, which moments earlier had held the welcomed luncheon food, was suddenly pulled away when the attached horses broke and "ran wildly about," killing the driver.[20] Hancock sent an aide to ask General Gibbon, who was now standing in front of the copse of trees, what his assessment of the cannonade might be. Gibbon sent his compliments to Hancock and told him that he felt it was either the prelude to a retreat or the beginning of an assault. Gibbon added that whichever was the case, he felt that his line was properly prepared to meet any demands.[21] But, the surprise of the barrage caused some pandemonium on the Union field, and of that moment, Colonel Francis A. Walker, historian for the II Corps, noted:

> The air shrieked with flying shot, the bursting shells sent their deadly fragments down in showers upon the rocky ridge and over the plain behind; the earth was thrown up in clouds of dust as the monstrous missiles buried themselves in the ground, or glanced from the surface to take a new and, perchance, more fatal flight...All that is hideous in war seemed to have gathered itself together...upon Cemetery Ridge.[22]

Similarly, a Confederate officer recorded that he had never heard or seen anything even close to the horror of that cannonade. He philosophically, but pragmatically, wrote: "Some of the enthusiasts back in the Commissary Department may speak of it as grand and sublime, but unless grandeur and sublimity consist in whatever is terrible and horrible, it was wanting in both these qualities."[23]

All of that horrendous artillery noise rudely interrupted Captain Bingham's nap. Upon awakening, however, he promptly appreciated the reason for all the excitement. Quickly borrowing a horse, Bingham immediately set out to find Hancock for instructions and when he got up to the Battery I belonging to Lieutenant George A. Woodruff, at Ziegler's Grove, he was struck in the head by a spent minie ball. Fortunately, while the ball probably created quite a headache, it was not a serious wound and after a surgeon quickly dressed it with "cuttings of sticking plaster," Bingham was back on the field in search of his commander.[24]

Meanwhile, when Hancock went to remount his favorite sorrel, which he had ridden all that morning, he found that his normally steady animal had become unmanageable because of the deafening cannonade. He immediately turned to his Commissary of Musters, Captain Edward P. Brownson, and said: "You can afford to have a horse of this kind, Captain, on such an occasion as this, but I can not." Brownson naturally gave up his mount for that of Hancock, who later described that borrowed animal as a "very tall light bay, with a white stripe on its face or nostril."[25]

Hancock first rode toward the far right, north of his line, along with Major Mitchell plus Captains Isaac Parker and Brownson. Also included in that party was Private James Wells, of the 6th New York Cavalry, who carried the corps banner and was later described, by the general, as a "short stout Irishman."[26] The air had become laden with humidity, and the oppressive nature of the 87-degree heat was only put off by the intense, fearful chorus of concussions and thick sulfurous smoke. Having reached the end of his line at Ziegler's Grove, Hancock turned southward, dispatching staff members off to various points until it was just he and Wells riding down the line in a slow and deliberate manner. Typical Hancock, this was his moment and he clearly took advantage of the dire circumstances to inspire his men by speaking calm, steady, reassuring words of encouragement to many as he passed, his ever present brilliant, white starched shirt peeking out of his sleeves and bursting forth from his open coat. To many of those terrified men, his mere presence had a paternal calming effect as they watched him slowly evolve from the acrid billows of gray battlefield smoke. If possible, he made the treacherous moment electrifying and one that many, of all ranks, would never forget for the rest of their lives. General Abner Doubleday, for example, was one who was still enthralled by those stirring moments even after Hancock's death:

"Tell General Hancock..."

I can almost fancy I can see Hancock again as he rode past the front of his command, just previous to the assault, followed by a single orderly, displaying his corps flag, while the missiles from a hundred pieces of artillery tore up the ground around him.[27]

Captain Bingham was another who became caught up in that moment and later recalled:

It was a gallant deed of heroic valor, such as a knight of olden time might have performed & withal not a reckless exposure of life without object, for the noble presence and calm demeanor of the commander as he passed through his line during that fiery crisis, encouraging his men set an example before them which an hour later cropped out and served their stout hearts to win the greatest & bloodiest battle ever fought on American soil.[28]

Future President Rutherford B. Hayes, who was not at Gettysburg, but drew from eyewitness accounts, added his pen to the praise of Hancock during those dramatic moments:

During the tremendous artillery fire which swept our line on the third day, just previous to the charge, knowing well that some desperate movement of the enemy was to follow the heavy firing, Hancock rode along his line, through the furious storm of shot and shell, his daring heroism and splendid presence giving the men new courage....[29]

The entire episode, no matter the source, had a distinct Shakespearean aura about it:

"The pride, pomp and circumstance of glorious war."[30]

As he and Wells rode southward, Hancock was reportedly approached by a brigadier-general, "an old [unidentified] neighbor," who pleaded with him that "the corps commander ought not to risk his life that way." Realizing it was far more important for his men to *see* their leader, Hancock *allegedly* replied with his classic statement, "There are times when a corps commander's life does not count."[31] Hancock wasted no time and promptly continued down the line to his extreme left and came upon some of the officers of Caldwell's division, including Colonel John Rutter Brooke and Major Octavius Bull, both of the 53rd Pennsylvania. There, he spent some time and spoke with his men when he sheepishly realized that he had been rather intolerant of some during recent days. Just before departing, he apologetically told those officers: "Before leaving you I wish to say I speak harshly sometimes. If I have at any time ever said anything to offend or hurt the feelings of any one of you I wish now to offer an apology." Just prior to leaving, he also told General Caldwell, "If the enemy's attack strikes further to your right, I want you to attack on their flanks..."[32]

During the opening moments of the Confederate barrage, General Hunt had been viewing the position of the Union guns from the vantage point offered by the crest of Little Round Top. He was with Battery D, Fifth U.S. Artillery and Lieutenant Benjamin F. Rittenhouse, who had succeeded Lieutenant Charles E. Hazlett, who was killed on the second. Looking out over the field, Hunt saw that "All their [Rebel] batteries were soon covered with smoke, through which the flashes were incessant, whilst the air seemed filled with shells, whose sharp explosions, with the hurtling of their fragments, formed a running accompaniment to the deep roar of the guns."[33] He soon made his way down the hill and to the artillery park located at the rear area of Cemetery Ridge, to instruct his Reserve Artillery to be prepared to move up on a moment's notice. Then, he moved directly to the front line to assume personal command of the Reserve Artillery. Moments later, the Union guns began a deliberate reply to the Rebel fire as if "making target practice out of it."[34] Hunt had judiciously instructed those guns to begin firing about fifteen minutes after the Rebel bombardment began, to conserve ammunition and to allow for a better understanding of their objective. With the two sides now blaring at each other with more than 250 big guns, the noise was reportedly heard as far away as 150 miles. For the better part of two hours, the incredible cannonade bellowed, rumbled, screeched, maimed, killed and thundered along normally quiet, rolling, gentle hills and rich Pennsylvania farmland.

Beyond its deadly potential, however, it was the queer, unexpected trance-like cadence of the cannonade that sent some Yankee soldiers into a peculiar state of *dolce far niente* and even slumber. From one eyewitness: "The men lay close to the earth and sought every inch of shelter their light works afforded, while the shell burst over their heads, tore through their ranks and filled the air with that awful rushing sound which causes the firmest hearts to quail as in the very presence of Death."[35] Incredibly, some Yankees found it difficult to resist the hypnotic rhythm of the artillery duel and were lulled to sleep, in spite of the horrendous noise.[36] Indeed, Confederate General Longstreet appears to have succumbed to the trance since he admits to "resting" during the heated exchange and was actually seen sleeping.[37] Colonel Veazey observed that among his men "...I think a majority, fell asleep, and it was with the greatest effort that I could keep awake myself..."[38]

About one hour after the barrage began, Hunt began to worry sorely about his dwindling long-range ammunition supply and went in search of General Meade to discuss the matter. Unable to find the Union commander, who actually shared his concern, Hunt took it upon himself to order the Federal guns to cease firing to conserve those important shells. It was now perfectly obvious that the Rebel barrage was nothing more than a softening prelude to an infantry attack and Hunt wanted adequate firepower to meet that occasion, whenever it might occur. In response to the Union slackening, the Confederate fire also began to relax since they became convinced that the Federal guns were being destroyed.[39]

Unaware of Meade's concern and subsequent order to Hunt to reduce fire and conserve ammunition, Hancock became very angry and concerned about the costly negative impact the quitting of the Union guns would have upon the morale of his men.[40] There can be little doubt that his anger was also fueled by the thought that any subordinate would dare alter his orders on his line. Consequently, he sent an aide to instruct the silent artillery to reopen their fire. The most quiet segment of the Union artillery line belonged to Lieutenant-Colonel Freeman McGilvery and his First Volunteer Brigade of Artillery Reserve. When Hancock's aide instructed McGilvery to reopen his guns, the colonel simply ignored the messenger. Enraged by such impudence, Hancock personally rode to that line and while articulating some of his finest expletives, he demanded that McGilvery reopen his guns. But, McGilvery steadfastly refused and Hancock even threatened him and his men with force.[41] Still, the corps commander had little success and McGilvery later noted: "I was not under Gen. Hancock's orders, and I could not see why the Second Corps could not stand the fire as well as the other corps..." But, the batteries to the north, belonging to Captain John J. Hazard, did reopen because, Hunt later wrote, Hazard's command "was under Gen. Hancock's [direct] orders." Hunt later claimed that Hazard's compliance impaired his plan for "an artillery crossfire that would have stopped it [the advancing infantry attack] before it reached our lines..."[42] A recent Hunt biographer noted that "Hancock's order [to reopen the fire] ensured that Hunt would be unable to subject the rebel infantry to the sort of cross fire that might well have crippled their [Confederate] assault beyond repair *before* their attack was fairly under way."[43] [Emphasis added]

It is all of these technical artillery and authority issues that give rise to yet another ongoing Gettysburg dispute known as:

THE HANCOCK–HUNT CONTROVERSY.

The total scope of details surrounding this debate will probably never be known. Nonetheless, if we are to understand the conflict at all, we must first define its margins, and the key issue is definitely one of authority. Not surprisingly, while this point is central to the issue, there are other related problems that will become more evident as the controversy unfolds. It is important to understand that General Hancock had full authority over his line that day and even General Hunt granted as much. At least, Hunt did so once when he noted: "General Hancock's claim that he commanded all the troops of every description posted on his part of Cemetery Ridge is perfectly valid. It cannot be disputed, and I never questioned it; but all commands must be exercised subject to the established principles for the government of armies."[44]

Unfortunately, Hunt's statement here is not part of a trail of personal consistency and that failing only clouds the entire debate. Over the years and decades following Gettysburg, Hunt frequently challenged Hancock's authority and argued that he, and not Hancock, had command over the Reserve Artillery on the II Corps line that day. In one of his many written articles, Hunt states: "Major General Hancock's repeated assertions that I did not command the Reserve Artillery at Gettysburg, are made with usual audacity and in the face of official evidence to the contrary..."[45] In light of this chameleon-type posture, the entire ordeal becomes more confusing and perhaps a matter of who was "more" right, Hancock or Hunt? In fairness, we should consider both points though the reader must understand that space limitations dictate only a synopsis.

We must first acknowledge the timeless argument of one school of thought versus another, i.e., there are always two sides to every story. Then, we must be cognizant about passing time and its potential changes to recollection of details from eyewitnesses about events of years past versus their writings of a much later day. Coupled with these factors, there is the strong influence of personal pride and ego which can and does affect and prejudice just about any memory bank. Still, despite all of these concerns, we are anything but poverty-stricken on this debate owing to the substantial amount of correspondence, reports and voluminous writings of General Hunt and his supporters. Hunt literally "spilled" gallons of ink justifying his position to his dying day. Conversely, Hancock attempted to remain aloof of the debate, letting his successful performance of July 3, 1863 speak for itself, though he certainly had his own school of supporters. Whatever the source of particular thought or writings, both sides offered strong and sometimes convincing arguments to bolster their own positions. In the final analysis, like any debate, it is impossible for both sides to be equally right and it should be noted that General Hunt did not only have problems with General Hancock and, because of his antagonistic proclivities, he should be viewed in a holistic manner.

This entire controversy is focused upon two of the Union's most capable officers and it must be understood that both men had high opinions of their talents, plus equal tempers and temperaments that allowed for little flexibility. Perhaps it is those very difficult traits that made both officers excel in their respective efforts. Yet, Hancock *was* the commanding officer of the "Left Center" that fateful day and if the results justify the means, there is very little to argue about. But, such a simplistic, definitive posture would offer no real appreciation for Hunt's contribution and no sensitive evaluation of his viewpoint. Therefore, a closer scrutiny is necessary and some background on Hunt will be helpful.

General Henry J. Hunt was a native of Detroit, Michigan, a professional soldier and a descendant of a long line of conservative military men. Like himself, his forebearers were all known as "Old Army."[46] He entered West Point at age 16 and was graduated in 1839, 19th out of a class of 31. His entire military career was associated with the artillery, where he developed a most distinguished reputation beginning with the Mexican War, where he was wounded. He assisted in revising the light artillery tactics that were utilized during the entire Civil War. With rumor of war, Hunt prepared the defense and preparations for destruction of Harper's Ferry, if required. After the Union rout at Bull Run, Hunt's artillery command played an important part in deterring any real attempt at Confederate pursuit. At Malvern Hill, he directed the fire of at least 100 field pieces which reeked absolute havoc upon the Confederates and, at Antietam, he "served with distinction." At Fredericksburg, Hunt commanded the 147 Union guns that pummeled the town and he sent forward the boats that made the initial landing on the far side of the Rappahannock. During the battle of Gettysburg, he was 44 years old and undoubtedly, and correctly, felt that he was at the pinnacle of his career. On the second day, he placed about 72 guns along Wheatfield Road, which was most instrumental in securing the Peach Orchard. On the third, he was key in the death and destruction delivered by the Union artillery upon the lines of Pickett's Charge. After the war, Hunt remained in the army and commanded the Frontier District from Fort Smith, Arkansas. He also disarmed and disbanded the Irish revolutionaries known as the Fenians, who were active along the Canadian border. In 1880, he was assigned to command the Department of the South and in 1883, he retired from the military. Moving to Washington, D.C., Hunt accepted the position of governor of the Soldier's Home, which he held until his death on February 11, 1889.[47] Consequently, no reasonable evaluation of General Hunt can fail to realize his important talents and contributions.

Unfortunately, for all of General Hunt's background, education, talent and technical ability, he can only be viewed as a *prima donna*. If he didn't get his way he would threaten to take his proverbial "bat and ball and go home." In one of his letters regarding Gettysburg, Hunt alludes that he had become disenchanted with the army and that he was considering resigning. Later, in that same note, he does some reversing, but note his associated dictates: "It is now probable I shall remain long with the Army in my present position. There will probably and possibly be some trouble between Gen M.[eade] and myself. I have asked to be relieved from his Staff and will insist upon it unless he *meets my views* as to my department and if he does meet them, it will bring him to War with many of his Generals."[48] [Emphasis added] This is typical Henry J. Hunt personality.

When Hunt went searching for General Meade to discuss his ammunition concerns, he first encountered General Howard, who agreed with his assessment to stop the firing.[49] Shortly thereafter, he also encountered Hancock's aide, Captain Bingham, who had been sent by General Meade to order Hunt to "observe great care with their ammunition."[50] Later, Hunt also discovered that Meade's Chief Engineer, General Warren, also felt it was propitious to cease the artillery fire to conserve ammunition. After the battle, Hunt wrote about all of these details and individuals and further emphasized that Meade sent his concerns via one of Hancock's own staff officers and that Meade's direct contact with him was proof that he *was* in overall charge of the Reserve Artillery and not Hancock.[51] Hunt does concede, however, that the artillery permanently assigned to the II Corps, and, in particular, the brigade belonging to Captain Hazard, did indeed report directly to Hancock and not him.

For clarification, Captain Hazard commanded the II Corps artillery

Major-General Winfield Scott Hancock

Brigadier-General Henry J. Hunt

"*Tell General Hancock...*" 127

Courtesy, Albert H. Wunsch, III and Son Collection.

General Hunt on Cemetery Hill, July 3, 1863

General Henry J. Hunt, far left, on Cemetery Ridge during the Confederate attack on July 3, 1863. Taken from the painting, *Battle of Gettysburg*, by Paul Philippoteaux.

brigade which consisted of 28 guns and five batteries as follows:

>1st New York Light, Battery B,
>   Captain James McKay Rorty*
>1st Rhode Island Light, Battery A,
>   Captain William A. Arnold
>1st Rhode Island Light, Battery B,
>   Lieutenant T. Fred Brown
>1st United States, Battery I,
>   Lieutenant George A. Woodruff*
>4th United States, Battery A,
>   Lieutenant Alonzo H. Cushing*

In his battlefield report, Hazard confirms that his command did consume "all their [long-range] ammunition, excepting canister..."[52]

Before proceeding, the reader should be aware that the seeds for Hunt's acrimony, and certainly a strong contributor to the command confusion, began during the Chancellorsville campaign, under Major-General Joseph Hooker. That commander effectively demoted Hunt from a line to a staff position and in his own subsequent report, the snubbed artillerist insubordinately noted that:

> The command of the artillery, which I held under Generals McClellan and Burnside, and exercised at battles of Antietam and Fredericksburg, was withdrawn from me when you assumed command of the army, and my duties, made purely administrative, circumstances very unfavorable to their efficient performance...I doubt if the history of modern armies can exhibit a parallel instance of such palpable crippling of a great arm of the service in the very presence of a powerful enemy... It is not, therefore, to be wondered at that confusion and mismanagement ensued...[53]

---

* Killed or mortally wounded on July 3, 1863.

Obviously, Hooker's move with Hunt, for whatever his reasons, caused a lasting enmity between the two. In addition to Hunt's problems with Hooker, after the battle of Chancellorsville, Hancock had been rather critical in his perception of poor performance from the Hunt-led Reserve Artillery at Antietam and Chancellorsville. Understandably, those unflattering comments would not serve to endear Hancock to Hunt either. But, demonstrating a distinct pattern, immediately following the battle of Gettysburg, Hunt also found himself censured by General Meade for his impudence.[54] Consequently, while the issue of precise authority between the II Corps commander and General Hunt is key to this Gettysburg debate, an equally large factor is Hunt's unremitting pride, impudence and obstinate personality.

On the particular point of authority over the artillery, it is perfectly clear that even after Chancellorsville, Hooker *never* restored Hunt to his full prior command of that arm, though Hunt made assumptions otherwise. An example of those dangerous assumptions are obvious when after a meeting on May 5, 1863, General Hooker ordered Hunt to "post enough guns to clear a lane of withdrawal..." Hunt took that as perfect evidence of his being restored to his former authority. But, even a recent Hunt biographer can only guardedly state, of that order: "This latest *directive* seemed to *indicate* clearly that Hunt had been restored to full authority..." There was no such precise order of restoration from Hooker, and in the end, Hunt himself agreed that he was not *definitely* reinstated to his prior position. Further, there is no record that General Meade, after assuming command, ever restored or appointed Hunt to his full former position. Again, Hunt's recent biographer states that after Meade asked him to "inspect the lines...It *seemed* to *indicate* that Meade *intended* to reinstate him to full authority." When Meade later requested Hunt to fill a gap in General Henry Slocum's line, the same biographer further extrapolates that request to mean: "There was no doubt now: Meade *had* restored him to full power." This, despite the fact that Meade did **not** restore Hunt and shortly after the battle of Gettysburg, Hunt became so disenchanted with Meade that he threatened to resign on July 26.[55] All of Hunt's assumptions about his scope of authority can be disastrous in the military, then and now. It is obvious that his presuppositions are a key factor in his difficulties with his superiors and peers. [All emphases are added.]

Again, existing records do not show that General Meade ever made any official recognition or restoration for Hunt during the battle of Gettysburg. Indeed, in a letter to General Webb, Hunt confides: "Now, I was by no means a favorite with Meade; he rarely consulted me as a Chief of Artillery is consulted...He did not take me into his confidence."⁵⁶ By the same token, it is also true that Meade never made any announcements of a reduced posture for Hunt. The facts are simply that General Hunt was demoted at Chancellorsville and was *never* officially fully restored to prior power by either Hooker or Meade until *after* the battle of Gettysburg. While General Meade might have been too new to command to attend to such a detail, we today cannot summarily assume what he had in mind.⁵⁷ Last, relative to the entire argument of General Hunt's authority, let the reader be mindful that he was a brigadier-general while Hancock was a major-general. To the civilian community, this detail may have little impact but, to the military mindset, this becomes vitally important despite General Hunt's claim to the contrary.⁵⁸

From their respective writings, Hunt clearly felt that he and his Reserve Artillery were solely responsible to General Meade, while Hancock logically felt that his authority encompassed anyone or any unit posted along his line, including any Reserve Artillery. Despite his earlier noted agreement regarding Hancock's line authority, Hunt also steadfastly maintained that:

> The assumption by General Hancock that artillery engineer troops assigned to army-corps and divisions are made by the new regulations independent commands under officers of their own arm, in any different sense from that in which this has always been the case is entirely gratuitous. Under certain circumstances they must be more under the control of their special chiefs, than of other commanders, and in some cases, as in sieges, and the attack and defence [*sic*] of entrenched lines, often are and must be under the exclusive control of those chiefs.⁵⁹ [Emphasis in original]

Hunt then adds to his lengthy epistle the following regulations which he felt further supported his position and gave him potential command of *all* artillery:

> The duties of the chief of artillery of the army, are both administrative and executive. He is responsible for the condition of all the artillery; wherever serving, respecting which he will keep the commanding general fully informed.

"Tell General Hancock..."

<u>Through him</u>, the commanding general of the army will take the proper steps to insure the efficiency of the artillery for movement and action, <u>and its proper employment on the field of battle</u>.

<u>All artillery</u>, not attached to other troops will be <u>commanded by the Chief of Artillery</u> xxx <u>In battle</u> he will under the instruction of the Major General Commanding distribute and place in position the Reserve Artillery and when so directed <u>select positions for the batteries attached to troops</u> conveying to the commander of the troops the directions of the Commanding General.[60] [All emphases in original]

From Hunt's perspective, all of this clearly gave him full command of all the Reserve Artillery, no matter where they might be placed or to which commander they may be temporarily assigned. However, he conveniently avoids the lack of his specific appointment and authority by Generals Hooker and Meade. Nonetheless, during the battle of Gettysburg, the Reserve Artillery consisted of one regular and four volunteer brigades. Of particular interest for this consideration will be the First Volunteer Brigade led by Lieutenant-Colonel Freeman McGilvery, who commanded the following:

- Massachusetts Light, 5th Battery,
    Captain Charles A. Phillips.
- Massachusetts Light, 9th Battery,
    Captain John Bigelow.
- New York Light, 15th Battery,
    Captain Patrick Hart.
- Pennsylvania Light, Batteries C and F,
    Captain James Thompson.[61]

McGilvery's command boasted 33 guns and on the third, his line was to the left of the II Corps, running north–south. Once the Confederate guns opened, it was soon clear to every experienced Union field officer that Lee planned a "not uncommon ruse," a heavy barrage followed by an infantry attack. Later, Hunt recalled his precise instructions to his battery commanders as he:

...warned them against being led into a hasty [artillery] reply...They were specially instructed to withhold their fire at least for 10 or 15 minutes after the enemy opened...They were further directed to fire deliberately and slowly, as at target practice...that we might have at least half our ammunition on hand to meet the assault which would follow....[62]

Irrespective of the Hancock–Hunt debate, the Union artillery response on July 3rd delivered devastating results upon the Rebel lines and Hancock was always high in his praise for their work.[63] Federal artillery and its ammunition had long been recognized as vastly superior to its Confederate counterpart and the terrific exchange that day only proved the issue beyond any doubt. Colonel Joseph C. Mayo of the 3rd Virginia recorded that soon after the two opening Confederate shots, the Yankees replied and "Nearly every minute the cry of mortal agony was heard above the roar and rumble of the guns...Over us, in front of us, behind us, in our midst and through our ranks, poured solid shot and bursting shell dealing out death on every hand..."[64] This does not mean to imply that the Confederate fire rendered no valuable service, because one Union report shows that while many of their bombs fell behind the Yankee line, "The shells swoop down among the Battery horses...their vitals and blood smear the ground. And these shot and shells have no respect for men either. We see the poor fellows...with the mangled stump of an arm or leg, dripping their life blood away, or with a cheek torn open, or a shoulder smashed."[65]

As all of that hell-fire was occurring, Hunt recalled that the concerns of General Meade and him were heightened when they learned that General Hancock had failed to bring up about one-half of his artillery trains, which potentially held critical reserve ammunition. They soon discovered that General Sickles had also committed the same error. Despite the possible gravity of those missing wagons, those two failings set a perfect sophomoric stage for Hunt, who took great pride in surprising General Meade by his ability to divine such a possibility. Obviously delighted with himself, Hunt announced that he had made provisions to cover such an eventuality by secretly creating a special ammunition train to carry an extra 20 rounds for "every cannon in the army..."[66] Despite that good news, Meade and Hunt both fretted that those absent wagons contained important reserve ammunition which might soon be required. Fortunately, in fairness to both of those corps commanders, the lack of their wagons does not appear to have created any significant problems for the Union that day.

"Tell General Hancock..."

When those noisy Union batteries began to respond to Hunt's cease fire order, Hancock instinctively moved to learn the reasons why! He was concerned that as long as the Confederates continued their bombardment, his infantry would be demoralized without their own guns firing in response, a complaint that some Hunt-led artillery officers later dismissed as very common. Such disparity of thought might dictate that only actual experience on such a battle line can properly determine which school of thought was correct.

Some of those affected by Hunt's order were Battery B of the 4th United States Artillery, commanded by Captain James Stewart. Stewart and his guns were located on the highest portion of Cemetery Ridge and were ordered silent by an aide from Hunt's staff.[67] Another Yankee officer, Colonel Edwin E. Bryant of the 3rd Wisconsin, recorded that in his opinion, General Hunt had wisely ordered the silencing of his guns, which he felt duped the Confederates into believing that they were in fact destroying the Federal artillery. Bryant then wrote that Hunt certainly knew that an infantry attack would follow and he sent "word along our line to withhold our reply."[68] Another, later, source of support for General Hunt came from Colonel Charles S. Wainwright, commander of the I Corps, Artillery Brigade. In his diary, Wainwright noted that "...Hancock I think, nearly ruined himself by insisting that the batteries along his line keep up a heavy fire, after he, Hunt, had ordered them to cease. The consequence was they expended all their ammunition, and had none when the tug came."[69] Wainwright's comment here is essentially correct as it relates to II Corps long-range ordnance.

As the Union guns began to fall silent, Colonel E. P. Alexander later recalled that "there was a decided falling off in the enemy's fire, and as I watched I saw other guns limbered up and withdrawn. We frequently withdrew from fighting Federal guns in order to save our ammunition for their infantry. The enemy had never heretofore practised [*sic*] such economy."[70] While Alexander was pondering that newfound Federal frugality, Hancock angrily approached some of the various battery commanders in an effort to get them to resume their fire. When he spoke directly to Lieutenant-Colonel McGilvery, Hancock was told that Hunt had ordered the guns to cease fire and conserve ammunition. That statement only served to fuel Hancock's anger and he even threatened to use force if necessary to have those guns open fire.[71] McGilvery and several other pro-Hunt participants left their recollections of their encounter, real or contrived, with the fuming Norristown general:

CAPTAIN PATRICK HART, Commander, 15th New York Light Battery:

Hart proved to be eternally vicious about Hancock and even 14 years after the battle, he referred to the general as a "traitor" and one capable of "treachery." In one of his many acrimonious letters to General Hunt, Hart wrote his past commander that he [Hunt] had saved the second day of Gettysburg when General Sickles "lost" it and again on the third when "a greater traitor in Hancock" also threatened to destroy the Union army. Hart went on to state that on the third, when Hancock approached him to reopen fire, "he did not use threats but his language was profane and Blasphemous such as a drunken Ruffian would use..." Then, coiled for the *ad hominem*, Hart lashed out: "let us look back to 1864 and can we see one battle in which Hancock took a part in that was not a defeat—let us look at Deep Bottom, Reims [*sic*] Station and the Weldon Rail Road, and do we find anything else but confusion and defeat under his command...?" Poised with a modicum of bravado that was commensurate with plenty of safe distance, Hart proudly proclaimed to Hunt: "*I am the Captain who refused to fire when General Hancock ordered me to do so.*"[72] [Emphases added]

CAPTAIN JOHN BIGELOW, Commander, 9th Massachusetts Battery:

For the most part, Bigelow left an account that essentially recapitulates some of the difficulties Colonel McGilvery reportedly had with Hancock. He recounted that McGilvery "told me that during the cannonade by the enemy Gen'l Hancock came riding up to him in hot haste and wished him to reply to the enemy with his batteries, giving the old excuse that it was necessary in order to keep his men steady." McGilvery refused to obey the II Corps Commander though "[Captain John G.] Hazard, however, did not withhold his fire." Bigelow concludes that "McGilvery always stoutly maintained that had Gen'l Hancock not interfered, and had Hazard reserved his fire as you instructed, the enemy could not have got a handful of men through the crossfire, which Hazard and he would have poured over the open field in front of the Second Corps."[73]

CAPTAIN CHARLES A. PHILLIPS, Commander, 5th Massachusetts Battery:

Phillips's report lacks the venomous attitude inherent with most other commanders under Lieutenant-Colonel McGilvery and General Hunt. In his report, Phillips stated that "About 1 o'clock the enemy opened a heavy fire from a long line of batteries, which was kept up for an hour, but beyond the noise which was made no great harm was done. Having received orders from General Hunt and from you [McGilvery] not to reply to their batteries, I remained silent for the first half hour, when General Hancock ordered us to open. We then opened fire on the enemy's batteries, but in the thick smoke probably did very little damage."[74]

LIEUTENANT-COLONEL FREEMAN MCGILVERY, Commander, First Volunteer Brigade, Reserve Artillery:

Unfortunately, McGilvery, who was a professional sailor and described as an "old sea dog from Maine," died in 1864 of an overdose of chloroform which was being administered while undergoing surgery to remove his left forefinger.[75] Consequently, he did not participate in the extended, bitter postwar letter campaign. However, in his Gettysburg report, McGilvery arrogantly noted that "About one-half hour after the commencement, some general commanding [Hancock] the infantry line ordered three of the batteries to return the fire. After the discharge of a few rounds, I ordered the fire to cease..."[76]

According to some reports, when Hancock demanded that McGilvery reopen his guns, that Maine officer allegedly looked him square in the eye and brazenly told him to "go to hell."[77] Let the reader be aware that this author sorely doubts that Hancock would have sustained such insubordination either personally or professionally.

What can be concluded from all of this hyperbole? That is not an easy question to answer and arguments will undoubtedly continue, *ad infinitum*. But, it is proper to first acknowledge that perhaps never before in the Civil War had the Union artillery been used so effectively as it was at Gettysburg. Not even the big Confederate muzzles at Fredericksburg were as deadly as the ultimate horseshoe arrangement of Union guns that caught the unsuspecting Confederates on the third and simply belched wholesale agony and death into their ranks.[78] It must also be acknowledged that General Hunt made a very valid point in his desire to husband long-range ammunition in anticipation of the Rebel infantry attack. Further, Hunt's claim that had such economy been executed, fewer Confederate troops would have come close to the wall, resulting in reduced Union casualties, is also very logical and valid. General Hancock clearly understood, appreciated and acknowledged these points.[79] But Hancock steadfastly maintained that the sound of those Union guns was critically important for the morale and confidence of his infantry.

The ultimate problem is not mechanics because General Hunt's major difficulty was definitely not his combat theory, technical competence or his stated concerns and intent. Rather, it was simply a matter of his style and personality. Upon close consideration, it is something of a wonder that Hunt was not court-martialed, or worse, for insubordination. For a man with the capacity to "get mad at his own brother," as Hancock was known, General Hunt was indeed a fortunate insubordinate officer not to have felt the full fury of Hancock's unbridled wrath.[80] His actions on the third, which were contrary to Hancock's, all demonstrate a decided lack of cooperation and respect for the wishes and orders of the commanding officer on that portion of the field. Further, Hunt's writings reveal an unauthorized, insubordinate attempt to act as an independent artillery commander, a license to which he was definitely not entitled. Too, let us be mindful that Hancock's expanded scope of authority at Gettysburg made him the most important commander in the entire Army of the Potomac except for General Meade. Prudently, this is not the individual you want to challenge!

General Hunt simply assumed too much about his scope of responsibility, though in all fairness, he makes a similar complaint about General Hancock as it relates to the Reserve Artillery.[81] It is plain that Hunt's field of authority was at best undefined and certainly not on a par with any corps commander, let alone a corps commander who was, in effect, in charge of almost one-half the entire Union army. Ever since he had been demoted by General Hooker, Hunt's official position was, unfortunately, vague and therefore precarious and he did little to help matters. While General Hunt was a very capable, technical line officer, with diplomatic matters of interfacing with superiors, he permitted his own obstinance to interfere with the execution of military protocol and prudence. Regrettably, Hunt's handling of matters with Generals Hooker, Hancock and even Meade clearly show he did not posses the demanding politico inherent with military life and its high command. If he was technically correct on July 3, 1863, and there appears to be little doubt of that, he was absolutely wrong in his style of execution. In the military, as well as the high corporate world, failings of that nature can be as deadly as any bullet or cannonball.

Of added interest to this entire debate is the view held by Colonel E. P. Alexander, the Confederate artillery chief. In his personal recollections written after the war, Alexander made two key observations related to this debate. First, in terms of who should have ultimate authority of the line, Alexander states: "I think a corps commander should be supreme in his corps, & the army chief must submit, or get the commander in chief to interpose & overrule the corps commander." Second, he then offers his thoughts on the business of Hunt's shutting down the Union guns: "I rather think too that I concur with Gen. Hancock's idea that the Federal policy at Gettysburg should have been to keep their batteries firing at least as long as ours were."[82]

The total result of Hancock's attempt to have all the Reserve Artillery reopen fire is not clearly known though it was obviously far from complete. Dependable data are scarce and battlefield reports from participants tend to avoid the use of any inflammatory accusations. It is the letters and testimonies after the battle that provide the best detail, though they too can be very self-serving and misleading. A good example of those difficulties is all the vitriolic statements made by Captain Hart. In the final analysis, his letters, in particular, suffer from his gross macho imagination since Hancock usually sent subordinates to the lines to deliver his orders, thereby precluding his direct contact with every battery officer. But even if he were directly approached by the general, it is fair to believe that Captain Hart only found safety in time and distance as it relates to the bravado he heaped upon Hancock, who had absolutely no tolerance for his type of arrogance.[83]

When the great cannonade ended, it was quickly destined to become a part of the American Civil War lexicon. For those killed or wounded in the duel, its horror could never be diminished in the slightest. However, on the grand scale of results-oriented military history, one Union participant wryly noted:

> The artillery duel of the third day is chiefly remarkable as the only really great exhibition of strength of that arm of the service made by the army of Northern Virginia. On no other field during the entire war did Gen. Lee develop a force over 100 guns in line, or maintain a grand cannonade for more than one hour. As a demonstration, or rather a spectacle, it was superb, but as a military operation it was not effective...[84]

Around 3:00 p.m. the guns of both sides fell silent and as the blue-gray smoke began to rise from the concave field, the sounds from the clanking and creaking of Rebel batteries moving toward the rear could be plainly heard. On Cemetery Ridge, Hancock and his line waited nervously for the infantry advance that was certain to follow. They were not disappointed! About 3:10 p.m., the Yankees were provided with a delightful visual banquet of pageantry which probably had not been seen since the Napoleonic Wars. From behind the line of trees nearly a mile away, about 12,000 Confederates stepped out in parade fashion and made a wonderful, awe-inspiring spectacle. With flags and banners flying, bands playing, "Pickett's Charge" was about to commence. One Rebel soldier noted:

> Now we hear the murmur and jingle of a large corps in motion. Colonels on horseback ride slowly over the brow of the ridge; followed by a glittering forest of bright bayonets... The rustle of thousands of feet amid the stubble stirs a cloud of dust...The flags flutter and snap—the sunlight flashes from the officers swords...and thus in perfect order, this gallant array of gallant men marches straight down in the valley of Death![85]

According to the II Corps historian, Francis Walker, Hancock rode along the line and when he saw that line of Confederate troops, he smiled and

"Tell General Hancock..."

told his staff: "Gentlemen, that is meant for us."[86]

As the nearly mile-wide line of butternut-clad soldiers began to move forward, in the Confederate right rear, Brigadier-General Lewis A. Armistead led his brigade. Watching from the low stone wall on the Union side, someone in the ranks of General Gibbon's Second Division was heard to cry out, "Here they come! Here they Come! Here comes the infantry!"[87] Later, the II Corps commander recalled:

> It looked, at first, as if they were going to attack the center of my line, but after a little they inclined somewhat to the left, as if their object was to march through my command and seize Cemetery Hill, which, no doubt, *was* their intention. They attacked with wonderful spirit; nothing could have been more spirited. The shock of the attack fell upon the 2d and 3d Divisions of the 2d Corps, assisted by a small Brigade of Vermont troops, together with the artillery of our line; these were the troops that really met the assault. No doubt there were other troops that fired a little; but these were the troops that really withstood the shock of the assault and repulsed it. The attack of the enemy was met by about six Brigades of our troops, and was finally repulsed after a terrific contest at very close quarters, in which our troops took about thirty or forty colors, and some four or five thousand prisoners, with great loss to the enemy in killed and wounded. The repulse was a most signal one, and decided the battle.[87] [Emphasis in original]

As the approaching Rebels closed in upon the wall, Hancock, with only his flag bearer, was in the vicinity of the interface between the I and II Corps. Specifically, he was near the Third Brigade, Third Division of the I Corps, belonging to Brigadier-General George J. Stannard. While in the rear of those Vermont boys, Hancock met up with Stannard and directed him to send troops to enfilade the right flank of Brigadier-General James L. Kemper's advancing Confederate brigade, as soon as it came upon the Yankee line. Stannard would respond by sending forth his 13th and 16th Vermont Regiments, led by Colonels Francis V. Randall and Wheelock G. Veazey respectively. Both of those units were nine-months volunteers who had never before seen battle.[89] Upon Stannard's command, those two Green Mountain regiments, assisted by Colonel William T. Nichols and his 14th Vermont, would move rapidly to meet the oncoming Rebel line.

During those same moments, Kemper's forward line was already taking a withering frontal fire from the remnants of Brigadier-General William Harrow's brigade. It was during those fearful seconds when General Kemper was severely wounded and shot from his horse.[90] Meanwhile, a little to the north, General Garnett was leading his 1,427 men directly toward the angle of the low stone wall. As he encouraged his lines forward, they were greeted by an implacable wall of blue wool and gray steel. One eyewitness noted that the Union men steadfastly stood as they "shouted and killed—hatless, coatless, drowned in sweat, black with powder, red with blood, stifling in the horrid heat, parched with smoke and blind with dust, with fiendish yells and strange oaths they blindly plied the work of slaughter."[91]

Almost simultaneously, Hancock had just ridden back to Meade's headquarters and, finding it vacated, he moved toward the front. As he approached the line, he could see that the determined Rebels were going to attempt a crossing of the stone wall. Spurring his horse forward, Hancock came upon a body of men and he impatiently ordered them: "Forward, men! Forward! Now is your chance!"[92] He then met Colonel Arthur F. Devereaux of the 19th Massachusetts, who later recalled that he could hear the rush of Hancock's horse, and as the general came up, Devereaux cried: "See, their colors; they have broken through. Let me get in there." Hancock, clearly aware of the threat, fired back, "get in godamned quick." In response, Devereaux, in concert with the 42nd New York Tammany Regiment, "went in on the run," probably filling a void created by the hasty withdrawal of the 71st Pennsylvania.[93] With that momentary crisis under control, Hancock headed back toward Stannard's line when General Gibbon was brought down, reportedly by a sharpshooter's bullet which penetrated his left shoulder.[94]

At the same time, Brigadier-General Alexander S. Webb, located in the immediate area and north of the copse of trees, was leading parts of his Second [Philadelphia] Brigade, which included the 69th, 71st, 72nd and Companies A and B of the 106th Pennsylvania regiments, back to the wall against the charging Rebels. A small portion of that brigade had fallen back from the wall moments earlier, and now the advancing enemy, led by General Armistead, was determined to crush the right of the 69th Pennsylvania. Moving quickly, Webb positioned himself and his troops in the hottest fire immediately behind the stone wall, near the angle, and sometimes it is inaccurately reported that he was wounded there. For his heroics that day, Webb would win the

Medal of Honor. As an indicator of all the efficient killing and maiming on that field at that moment, Webb's brigade suffered 451 casualties, in a mere matter of minutes.[95]

Standing near General Stannard were two of his aides, Lieutenants George W. Hooker and George C. Benedict. As Hancock approached, the latter noted that his own "eyes were upon Hancock's striking figure—I thought him the most striking man I ever saw on horseback, and magnificent in the flush and excitement of battle..." According to Benedict, while he was gazing upon the general, Hancock was hit.[96] In his small volume, *Vermont at Gettysburg*, Benedict continues: "Major General Hancock rode down to speak to Gen. Stannard, and fell, while addressing him, close to the front line, just after the flank attack had been ordered."[97] According to Almira Hancock, who undoubtedly got her information from the general, she basically agrees with Benedict's details though the comment about the precise timing of the flank attack order and execution are subject to some serious debate. In her *Reminiscences* Almira noted, "Turning away [from Stannard] toward the clump of bushes in Webb's front, he was shot from his horse."[98] This author feels that there is an excellent chance that General Hancock was brought down by "friendly fire," very possibly from those Vermont volleys. Note that according to Benedict, Hancock would have been riding south when he was wounded, making him an unlikely candidate for a Rebel bullet. It is also interesting to note the silence of the Confederate units. This author knows of no Rebel body that claimed the honor of bringing down the prize that General Hancock represented.

Apparently, when Hancock was hit, his horse also went down, though it is not clear if the beast was mortally wounded. The general himself later recalled that shortly after he was hit, he was "carried a few yards to the spot which I lay down, by the Officers of the Vermont troops..." In fact, it was Lieutenants Benedict and Hooker of the 13th Vermont who took Hancock off his mount.[99] Several days after the battle, Benedict wrote:

> Hooker and I with a common impulse sprang toward him, and caught him as he toppled from his horse into our outstretched arms. General Stannard bent over him as we laid him upon the ground, and opened his clothing where he indicated by a movement of his hand that he was hurt, a ragged hole, an inch or more in diameter, from which the blood was pouring profusely, was disclosed in the upper part and on the

side of his thigh. He was naturally in some alarm for his life.[100]

Hancock personally noted that he was lying on his back looking "through the remains of a very low, disintegrated stone wall [and he] could observe the operations of the enemy and give directions..."[101] Captain Bingham recalled that the ball that hit the general "passed through the front of the saddle and carried into the wound...a large nail from the saddle tree. The bullet and nail entered near the groin, the ball passing back through the thigh, and lodging near the socket of the thigh bone which it slightly splintered."[102]

Lying on the ground with his head to the raging battle, Hancock reportedly could also watch the unfolding contest by "raising himself on his elbow." Though he was in severe pain, he refused to be removed from the field until he knew the outcome of the contest in his front.[103] It is possible that while Hancock was in that prone position, portions of the Vermont regiments were still responding to General Stannard's order to move upon Kemper's flanks and as they passed the fallen Hancock, he called out to Colonel Veazey, "Go in, Colonel, and give it to them on the flank."[104] Again, the sequential timing of the Vermont moves, in relationship to the timing of Hancock's wounding, is not perfectly clear.

Whenever Randall maneuvered his lines, Captain John Lonegran of Company A, 13th Vermont, anchored by the right guide, Sergeant James B. Scully, swung the balance of his line northward. All other companies followed and now the Green Mountain boys were only 60 yards away from the Rebels. As all the Vermont lines moved into position, they soon heard the command, "Fire," and they let fly a horrible killing wall of lead. According to one eyewitness, "The effect upon the rebel lines was instantaneous...For a moment they crowded together in bewilderment, falling like wheat before a reaper..."[105] In a few moments, General Stannard, who had narrowly missed at least two other wounds that afternoon, was finally felled by flying shrapnel to his leg.[106]

Of those intense and confusing minutes, the Rebel commander, General John Brown Gordon, leaves this unobserved but appropriate description of conditions at the wall:

> The Confederates rally under the impulse, and rush onward. At one instant their gray jackets and flashing bayonets are plainly seen in the July sun. At the next they disappear, hid-

den from view as the hundreds of belching cannon conceal and envelop them in sulfurous smoke. The brisk west wind lifts and drives the smoke from the field, revealing the Confederate banners close to the rock wall.[107]

At about the same time that Hancock was hit, General Armistead had been leading his band of Rebel soldiers over the wall into the Yankee ranks. With his black felt hat held aloft by his sword, that proud Virginia product of a long line of American military heroes yelled out, "Boys, give them the cold steel." Over went Armistead and his followers and they seized the silent muzzles of the remaining two abandoned guns that moments before belonged to the dead Lieutenant Alonzo H. Cushing. According to General Howard, who was not an eyewitness, when Armistead began to mount the wall, "most of that part of Webb's Brigade posted here abandoned their position, but fortunately did not retreat entirely."[108] This was the restorative action Webb was leading and, with no small effort, he and his staff were able to rally his men and lead them forward again. According to Webb, Armistead mounted the wall "with about 150 of his men," and about 42 of them were promptly killed. Webb further states that he took six flags and approximately 1,000 prisoners at the wall.[109] Some historians question the count of prisoners that Webb reported.

Mounting the wall near General Armistead was Lieutenant John A. I. Lee, of the 28th Virginia, who proudly carried the shredded Confederate colors but was promptly brought down by a hail of flying Yankee lead.[110] Another poignant incident was occurring just beyond the wall that perhaps became all too common that day, certainly in that war. An unidentified soldier who had worn the Union blue told of an equally unidentified Confederate private who simply decided that, despite the desperate and hopeless nature of the critical moments at the wall, he must continue the fight. The Union man sadly noted: "I tried to save him, but he would not give up, so I had to kill him to save my own life."[111] Those bloody minutes were the legendary pinnacle for the Confederacy and those brave attacking Rebels simply lacked the physical tenacity to hold on against the impregnable Yankee position.

Within five to ten minutes of his being wounded, Hancock sent his aide, Major William G. Mitchell, to locate General Meade and advise him that he was down and that "we had gained a great victory."[112] The II Corps commander was completely unaware of Armistead's penetration and that his own line had literally blown away another of his former companions, Brigadier-

General Richard B. Garnett, as he approached the wall on his horse. Such are the sad dictates of civil war!

Meanwhile, Armistead continued his brief move inside the Yankee territory by approximately thirty yards when he was met by two Yankee balls which came from a volley fired by either the 71st or the 72nd Pennsylvania. One of those balls hit him in an arm while the second grazed him just below the opposite knee. Tradition tells us that as he fell onto one of Cushing's cannon, Armistead gave the verbal Masonic sign for distress though he undoubtedly also gave the hand sign as well. Ironically, when he went down, his mortal wounding seemed to act as a relief valve that allowed the steam to run out of the entire Rebel thrust.[113] But, his distress signal was heard, or seen, by members of General Webb's ranks and they promptly threw aside sectional bitterness and went to his aid. At the same time, Captain Bingham, also a Mason, was passing the area and while unaware that Hancock was down, inquired about the wounded Confederate officer near the wall. He was erroneously told that the man was General Longstreet. Bingham ordered the Keystone men back to their posts as he would care for the wounded man, who soon told him that his correct name was "General Armistead of the Confederate Army."[114]

At the same time, back near the Vermont troops, Hancock was receiving a lot of attention. The first reaction of the men around him was to apply a tourniquet to his wound and Lieutenant S. S. Morey of the 13th Vermont asked a comrade, Private Clark H. Butterfield, for the one he normally carried. But, when Morey returned to Hancock with the life-saving device, much to his dismay, he found that the wound was too high in the groin for any tourniquet application. That discovery only heightened Hancock's concern and Benedict noted that the general cried out:

> "Don't let me bleed to death, Get something around it quick." Stannard had whipped out his handkerchief, and as I helped to pass it around General Hancock's legs I saw that the blood, being of dark color and not coming in jets, could not be from an artery, and I said to him: "This is not arterial blood, General; you will not bleed to death." From my use of the surgical term he took me for a surgeon, and replied, with a sigh of relief: "That's good; thank you for that Doctor." We tightened the ligature by twisting it with the barrel of a pistol, and soon stopped the flow of blood.[115]

But everyone realized that the wound required the attention of a surgeon, and Major Mitchell set out for one and soon returned with Dr. Alexander N. Dougherty, Medical Director for the II Corps. Dougherty recalled that he found the general "lying on the hill slope, under a tree, and facing the enemy. There was a deep, wide gash in his leg, near the groin."[116] Since Dougherty was more rushed then normal owing to the raging battle only yards away, he made a quick and cursory inspection of the wound. He placed his forefinger into the hole and extracted some pieces of wood and a "severely bent ten-penny nail." Perhaps believing that he had removed the major problem, Dougherty held the nail aloft and told his patient: "This is what hit you, General, and you are not so badly hurt as you think."[117] Dougherty apparently threw the nail away but his words must have allayed some of Hancock's mounting fears. Still, one onlooker viewed the wound as "ugly...and ghastly" and compared it to "the stab of a butcher's knife."[118]

Meanwhile, Bingham had introduced himself to General Armistead and told him he was a member of General Hancock's staff and asked: "if you have anything valuable in your possession which you desire to be taken care of—I will take care of it for you." Armistead might have brightened for a moment when he asked Bingham to confirm if he was indeed attached to *The General Winfield Scott Hancock*. When Bingham responded in the affirmative, he later noted, Armistead told him that he and Hancock were old and valued friends. Then, Armistead reportedly said to Bingham: "Tell General Hancock for me that I shall <u>regret</u> or <u>repent</u> (I forgot the exact word [These clarifying statements made by Bingham]) the longest day I live." [Emphasis in original] Then, Armistead gave his "host" his spurs, watch, chain, seal and pocketbook for safekeeping.[119] Despite current popular impressions, to date, there is absolutely no known record of Hancock's interest in Armistead's wounding.

But, General Hancock did record his impressions about the cost of his and General Gibbon's woundings, which resulted in their both being removed from the field. In little less than one year later, Hancock reported:

> I think it was probably an unfortunate thing that I was wounded at the time I was, and equally unfortunate that Genl Gibbon was also wounded; because the absence of a prominent commander who knew the circumstances & thought at such a movement as that was a great disadvantage. *I think that our lines should have advanced immediately, and I believe we should have won a great victory.* I was very confi-

dent that the advance would be made...And the rule is, and it is natural, that when you repulse or defeat an enemy you should pursue him...we shall never reach the just fruits of a victory until we do follow it up promptly.[120] [Emphasis added]

Despite his warm feelings for General Gibbon, just over a year later, he would sadly be at odds with his trusted subordinate over some confusion that he, Hancock, probably caused at the battle of the Wilderness.[121] But, in addition to his view about the loss of prominent commanders, Hancock also offered his critical thoughts on Meade's soft pursuit of Lee and his army, after the battle, when he was asked: "In your opinion as a military man, I will ask, whether or not our Army should have attacked the enemy before he crossed the Potomac at Williamsport?" To that, Hancock replied: "I was not there; but my impression is that I should have voted for an attack. My military opinion may not be good for much, because I have not seen the ground, but my impression is that the enemy should have been attacked there."[122] However, it should be noted that according to D. Scott Hartwig, "...every [other] Union commander, except for Howard, voted against attacking Lee on that position."

But all of that was for the future! Bingham had Armistead sent back to the home of George Spangler, which was being used for a field hospital by the XI Corps. There, surgeon Henry C. Hendrick of the 157th New York and Dr. Daniel G. Brinton treated him and they noted: "His prospects of recovery seemed good..." Fate dictated otherwise and about 9:00 a.m. on the 5th, Lewis Armistead died at the age of 46.[123]

Once Armistead was on his way to receiving medical care, Bingham went looking for his own commander. He recalled that he found Hancock "about fifteen minutes after I got Armistead's message and effects...I rode up to you in company with General [then Major William] Mitchell," who was just returning from delivering Hancock's message to General Meade. Also with Captain Bingham at that time was Lieutenant J. B. Parker.[124]

When the three arrived in front of their wounded general, the High Watermark of the Confederacy had already crested, and they found a number of others in Hancock's company who were also wounded, including his color-bearer, Private Wells. Undaunted, and still very much in charge, Hancock instructed Bingham to find General Caldwell and tell him that he was now in command of the II Corps.[125] Hancock was also eager to hear Meade's response to Mitchell, who was instructed to tell the army commander: "the troops under my command have repulsed the enemy's assault, and that we have gained a great victory. The enemy is now flying in all directions in my front." When Mitchell found Meade, the army commander was so preoccupied that he was completely unaware that his son, Captain George Meade, who accompanied him, had just narrowly missed being severely wounded or killed. Instead, General Meade was intent on listening carefully to Mitchell's report. As they stood near the crest of Cemetery Hill, Meade instructed Mitchell: "Say to General Hancock that I regret exceedingly that he is wounded and that I thank him in the name of the Country and for myself for the service he has rendered today."[126] After his return and report to Hancock, Mitchell went in search of an ambulance for his commander. Later, when Meade wrote home to his wife Margaret, he lamented that one of his great problems of the battle had been the want of competent subordinate commanders, but he quickly added: "The loss of Reynolds and Hancock is most serious; their places are not to be supplied."[127] Still, Meade soon directed that the mediocre Brigadier-General William Hays assume command of the II Corps.

There are many quotations that might be inserted here that would further the image of General Hancock. But, of all the possibilities, the following unsophisticated note, from an unknown foot soldier of the 140th Pennsylvania is, perhaps, the best. Writing home to his family, the unidentified warrior told his kin: "Hancock is the best fighting man in this army. He fights to whip and isn't afraid of anything."[128] Soldierly comments of that nature, coming from the ranks, are to be savored.

Finally, Mitchell returned with a wagon and after Hancock was placed inside, Dr. Dougherty crawled next to his charge. Once aboard, the ambulance started to carry the general back beyond Taneytown Road to the field hospital thought to be located at the juncture of Rock and White Creeks. The path was described as being amidst a "hot fire," but Hancock dictated another message to Dr. Dougherty, who described his patient as "calm, patient and heroic."[129] That message was a second, more detailed note for General Meade:

HEADQUARTERS SECOND CORPS, July 3, 1863

Although I repulsed a tremendous attack, yet on seeing it from my left and advancing to the right, much to my sorrow, I found that the twelve guns on my salient had been removed by some one, whom I call upon you to hold accountable, as without them, with worse troops, I should certainly have lost the day. I arrived just in time to put a small battalion of infantry in the place occupied by those two batteries. I have never seen a more formidable attack, and if the Sixth and Fifth Corps have pressed up, the enemy will be destroyed. The enemy must be short of ammunition, as I was shot with a tenpenny nail. I did not leave the field till the victory was entirely secured and the enemy no longer in sight. I had to break the line to attack the enemy in flank on my right, where the enemy was most persistent after the front attack was repelled. Not a rebel [sic] was in sight upright when I left. The line should be immediately restored and perfected. General Caldwell is in command of the corps, and I have directed him to restore the line.

      Your obedient servant,
         WINF'D S. HANCOCK
          Major-General

     By A. N. Dougherty
  Surgeon, and Medical Director Second Corps
General Meade[130]

  By the time that note was completed, Hancock's younger brother, Colonel John, who served as Assistant Adjutant for General John Caldwell, joined the growing curious party so he might see his wounded kin. After speaking a few private words with his brother, Hancock sent John with his new message, in search of General Meade.[131] It may have been at this time that he also wired Almira of his wounding for she reports that "he sent me the second dispatch, while lying upon the battle-field desperately—and presumably fatally—wounded. 'I am, severely wounded, not mortally. Join me at once in Philadelphia. Parker and Miller, I fear, are gone up.'"[132]

  The ambulance came to a rest stop in an area that brought it into potential peril, owing to the sporadic Confederate cannon fire that was effectively harassing the area. Captain Thomas L. Livermore, Chief of Ambulances for the II Corps, warned the group to move to safer ground. He told General Hancock that the enemy was attempting to enfilade that part of the Union line, which sent Hancock's adrenaline flowing and ignited his verbal afterburners, causing him to bark, "We've enfiladed them, God damn them."[133] Then, the wagon moved forward to a greater area of safety!

  Apparently, Hancock was first taken to a II Corps hospital, perhaps the

"Tell General Hancock..." 149

Courtesy; The Pennsylvania Historical and Museum Commission.

Pickett's Charge

Taken from the painting, *Battle of Gettysburg: Pickett's Charge*, by Peter F. Rothermel.

150 Hancock at Gettysburg...*and beyond.*

General Hancock During Pickett's Charge

General Hancock, far right, during the Confederate attack on July 3, 1863. Taken from the painting, *Battle of Gettysburg*, by Paul Philippoteaux.

Courtesy; Albert H. Wunsch, III and Son Collection.

"Tell General Hancock..."

General Hancock Wounded

General Hancock shortly after he received his wound on July 3, 1863 at Gettysburg.

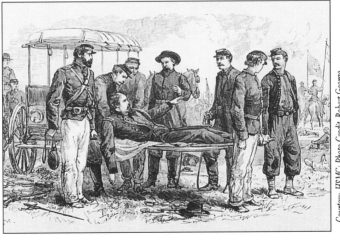

General Hancock Removed From the Field

General Hancock being removed from the field at Gettysburg on July 3, 1863.

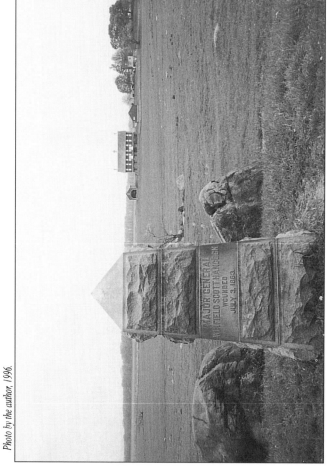

Monument Marking Spot of Hancock's Wounding

Monument marking the spot where General Hancock was wounded on July 3, 1863. In the background is the Codori farm.

Brevet Major-General Alexander S. Webb

Surgeon, Major Alexander N. Dougherty

This is the doctor that treated Hancock on the field at Gettysburg.

Captain Henry H. Bingham

Henry Bingham, an important aide to General Hancock, assisted General Armistead when he was mortally wounded during Pickett's Charge.

Major-General George E. Pickett, CSA

Brigadier-General Lewis A. Armistead, CSA

Where Armistead Fell

This monument is located near the angle on Cemetery Ridge and marks the spot where Confederate General Lewis Armistead fell on July 3, 1863 during Pickett's Charge.

John Hancock Taken in 1896

The author believes this is a photo of General Hancock's brother John. Unfortunately, the identification is not certain.

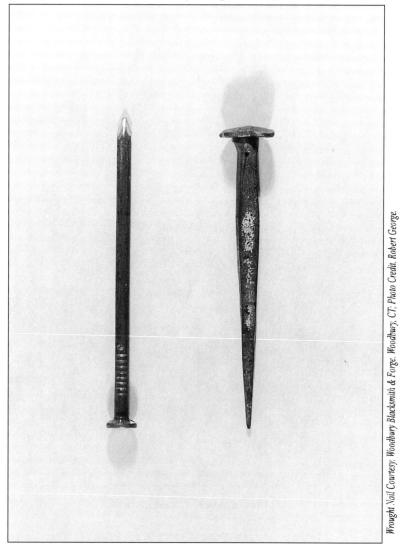

Wrought Nail Courtesy, Woodbury Blacksmith & Forge, Woodbury, CT; Photo Credit: Robert George.

A Modern Wire and a Hand Wrought 10d-Nail.

The wrought nail is the type used in some Civil War saddles with their point peened to act as rivets.

"Tell General Hancock..."

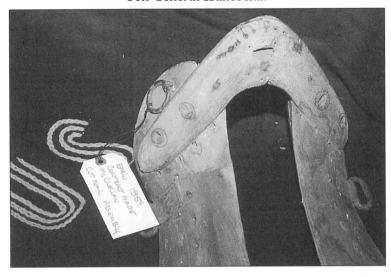

An 1859 McClellan Saddle Pommel

These two photographs were taken of an 1859 McClellan saddle pommel. The circled areas highlight the heads of large cut nails.

162 Hancock at Gettysburg...*and beyond.*

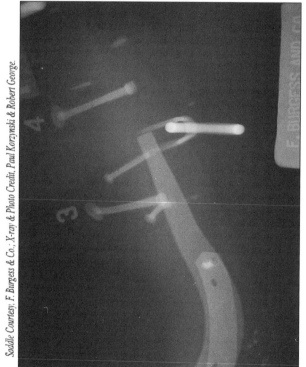

Saddle Courtesy: F. Burgess & Co.; X-ray & Photo Credit, Paul Korzynski & Robert George.

X-Ray of an 1859 McClellan Saddle

This photo was produced by an X-ray of the 1859 McClellan saddle shown on page 161. Note the elongated ghosts of the large cut nails in the pommel marked 3 and 4. Nail 3 measures 1 7/8" while nail 4 measures 2 7/16". A modern 10d wire measure 3".

one situated on the Jacob Schwartz Farm, located between the Taneytown Road and the Baltimore Pike. Unfortunately, precise details are lacking and certainly confused, though upon his arrival at the field hospital, word of his presence spread quickly and physicians and soldiers alike sought to see him. In the process, with his large loss of blood and the shock of the wound being fully appreciated, Hancock fell exhausted and faint into the arms of nearby aides. One eyewitness at the hospital noted that he "saw the blood from his wound as it dripped from the wagon to the ground."[134] Another wrote that the hospital was overcrowded and contained "about 4,500 wounded, of whom 1,000 were rebels."[135]

After receiving some very basic medical attention, he was supposedly taken to the Wills Home in downtown Gettysburg where he reportedly spent the night of the third, though this report is highly suspect. That home, where President Lincoln would stay the night before he delivered his momentous speech that November, was owned by the lawyer and future judge, David Wills, and his wife Jennie Smyser Wills, who was a native of Norristown. More likely on the morning of the 4th, Hancock was moved again to another, unidentified position in Westminster, Maryland, located about 22 miles south of Gettysburg. Perhaps the only remaining piece of evidence is a passing reference in a Christian Commission report that informs us: "At Westminster, meeting hundreds of the wounded...Among those to whom they ministered were Major-General Hancock and his aid [sic], General Miller."[136] After Westminster, Hancock was transported to Baltimore and then to the LaPierre House in Philadelphia, where he arrived on July 6th. During all of those travels, he was always attended by a physician known only as Dr. Taylor, perhaps a resident of Gettysburg.[137]

With the monumental three-day battle concluded, the ghastly task of counting the dead and wounded was begun. The largest battle ever fought on the North American continent also proved to be the costliest with approximately 53,000 combined casualties. The II Corps count was indeed frightful as the official records show 12,744 men and officers present for duty on June 30th. At the end of July 3rd, the cost was an incredible 34.3% or 4,369 casualties of which 797 men were killed, 3,212 were wounded and 378 were captured or missing. The only other corps to surpass the II was the I Corps, which had an incredible casualty rate of 51.7%. Reynolds entered the battle with 11,719 men present and Newton counted a total of 6,059 casualties.[138]

As might be imagined, no sooner was the epic battle of Gettysburg over when the news reports began to flow along with a host of misinformation, charges and countercharges that continue to this day. *The New York Times* cried out that General Longstreet had been killed on the third along with his comrade, General William Barksdale. The *Times* went so far to claim that "...prisoners captured yesterday [July 3] confirmed the [Longstreet–Barksdale] report." That same newspaper also claimed that Lee's III Corps commander, General A. P. Hill, had also been killed.[139] With such a "rush-to-judgment" mentality, is there any wonder that out of the great Union victory would emerge a host of lasting arguments, controversies, debates and distortions? Another of the lasting debates is the challenge that General Meade should have been far more aggressive in pursuing Lee's army when it withdrew from the field on July 4th. Even General Hancock felt this way. Perhaps, with the valuable asset of hindsight, this thought is true, especially since it is now known that Lee's army had been crippled. But, as a small indicator of what was perceived *at the time*, on July 18, Brigadier-General Horatio G. Wright wrote home to his wife and told her what the Union high command had *thought* confronted them: "A common estimate of his [Lee's] whole strength after crossing into Maryland, was 120,000-counting his losses in the [Gettysburg] campaign at 30,000, which is a large figure, and it would leave him 90,000. My own estimate is from 75 to 80,000."[140] If this is indicative of the type of information that General Meade was dealing with, perhaps we can better understand his actions. Looking back with hindsight and judging events accordingly can be a luring but costly mistake!

All of this is exemplified by a comment ascribed to General Robert E. Lee, who responded to some classic Monday morning hindsight. Perhaps we should all ponder this: "Young man, why did you not tell me that *before* the battle?...even as stupid a man as I am can see it all *now*..."[141] [Emphasis added]

———————————— ◆ ————————————

"War hath no fury like a non-combatant."
                                    C. E. Montague, 1922.

CHAPTER FIVE

"...I may never see you again."

The battle of Gettysburg essentially ended on July 3rd and many might believe that through some magical formula, everything and everybody immediately returned to something close to normal. The fact is that any such battleground never really returns to its former placid status. There is a certain solemnity that soon develops upon ground that has been soaked with the life-vehicle of human existence. One pretty 23-year-old woman from Salem, New Jersey, Miss Cornelia Hancock, no relative to the general, arrived on the field July 6th, the same day the general arrived in Philadelphia to begin his convalescence. As a nineteenth century nurse, she had answered the cry for help and in her eagerness and innocence, Miss Hancock immediately recoiled at the horror and gore she found. She saw that near the hospitals, doctors and orderlies were already practicing the unidentified but early stages of triage. The wounded had been categorized and those deemed close to death and hopeless were afforded the least, if any, consideration so that others with a better chance of living might be given some succor. Many years later, speaking to a reporter, Miss Hancock clearly remembered the ghastly scene that greeted her upon arrival at Gettysburg:

> There was a tiny brook running down from where the surgeons were working, and the blood of the soldiers mingled with the water of the brook until it was all red, and was a vertable river of blood. Oh! if we had only known about carbolic acid in those days! We knew nothing about antiseptics, and the gangrene and rotting came so quickly. I spent hours with a spoon scooping out from the wounds [The correspondent continued]—but it was too horrible to print, albeit she was not trying to tell a tale of horror.[1]

For others, the ghoulish detail of burying the dead had been a sad soldier's duty since time immemorial. But even such horrible quantities of death could have its moment of levity as reported by a volunteer woman, who came from across the river from Hancock's hometown of Norristown, to assist the seemingly endless numbers of needy men. In 1866, Mrs. Anna M. Holstein, of Upper Merion, Pennsylvania, after noting that the green sod of Gettysburg was everywhere stained with the lifeblood of dying men, reported the following incident about Luther White, a member of the 20th Massachusetts:

> One afternoon...the stretcher bearers came trampling wearily, bearing three bodies...as the last reached the place, the men dropped with a rough, jolting motion the army couch whereupon he rested. The impatient effort to be rid of their burden was probably the means of saving a precious life; for the man –dead as they supposed–raising his head, called in a clear voice: "Boys, what are you doing?" The response as prompt: "We came to bury you, Whitey." His calm response was: "I don't see it, boys; give me a drink of water, and carry me back."[2]

To the utter amazement of everyone involved, White was carried back to his regiment and sent to a hospital in Chestnut Hill, then a suburb of Philadelphia. Unfortunately, despite his miraculous recovery on the field, the soldier was to die of his wounds, which had torn away part of an ear, shattered his jaw and laid bare a portion of his throat.

For General Hancock, matters were gratefully better though it took until July 27th before he returned to Norristown. He first convalesced in the City of Brotherly Love, which was not impressive. All the frequent and fruitless probing for a bullet by the well-meaning surgeons only intensified his agony. During his stay in Philadelphia, Hancock undoubtedly lost much weight while under the direct charge of a physician known only as Dr. D. Agnew.[3] Perhaps, because of the lack of medical success combined with the extreme heat in the city, it was decided that the general would be better-off at his father's home in Norristown, where he might be more comfortable.

When it became known that he was to leave the LaPierre House, which was located on the west side of Broad Street, between Chestnut and Sansom Streets, a contingent of local firemen respectfully turned out in dress uniform to carry and escort Hancock to the train station. According to Almira, "They presented themselves in full regalia at the time appointed for the journey, and in a tender, impressive manner, conveyed him, worn and shattered, but without fatigue, to the Philadelphia depot."[4] They placed Hancock's stretcher upon the backs of several seats in an ordinary passenger coach for the difficult 18-mile ride.

When the *Philadelphia, Norristown and Germantown* train arrived at the Mill and Washington Streets Station in Norristown, it was met by a contingent of the Invalid Corps under the direction of an officer known only as Lieutenant Burns, plus a "large concourse of people."[5] While such a reception might normally have been flattering, the general's escort did not linger. Hancock was still in far too much pain to even stand the trial of a brief wagon ride over the few short blocks between the depot and his father's home on the east side of Swede Street, let alone the trials of happily addressing a crowd. So, the men arranged to carry him carefully over a number of streets, including Lafayette, DeKalb, and Swede, where they reached the neat three-story brick home of Benjamin and Elizabeth Hancock.[6]

It is not exactly clear where they placed Hancock during the early stages of his recovery, but it appears logical that they initially placed him into one of the rooms on the main floor to avoid the difficulty of climbing steps. In anticipation of his arrival back in Norristown, and unaware of the gravity of his wound, the local citizenry had decided to provide him with a grand reception to demonstrate their appreciation. When they learned the precariousness of his health, they prudently postponed the event.[7] Through it all, the general's wound kept him in constant pain while it continued to drain and simply refused to improve or heal.

Shortly after his arrival in Norristown, a local newspaper stated that while he was severely wounded, "he is in good spirits" and, optimistically stated that he was "recovering as fast as could be expected." A few day later, another local paper erroneously noted that "he is getting along very well..."[8]

In early August, Hancock unexpectedly received a warm note from Secretary of War Edwin M. Stanton, which certainly pleased him. Rather uncharacteristically, Stanton wrote:

>   Washington City, August 5, 1863
>   War Department
> Dear General:
>   I hope you are recovering from your severe wound.

> Of the many gallant officers wounded on the great field of Gettysburg, no one has more sincerely my sympathy, confidence and respect than yourself. We felt that the blow that struck you down was a heavy and disastrous one to the country, but rejoice that your life will be spared, and that you were not among the list of those whose loss we deplore.
>
> Yours truly,
>
> Edwin M. Stanton[9]

As August began to pass, the constant diet of severe pain persisted and the wound still showed no signs of healing. Hancock realized that he was failing and, perhaps, on the verge of death. After his arrival at his father's home, other Norristown doctors also made attempts to ease his condition but none was the least bit successful.[10] Most, if not all, of those doctors who attended to Hancock were convinced that some sort of a foreign body, probably a "Minie ball," still resided deep within his groin wound, which prevented its healing. All attempts to find and remove the intruder simply failed and left the general in deeper, excruciating pain. Each added session must have lowered his confidence and patience with all those well-meaning physicians.

Then, late in August, General Meade granted Dr. Louis Wernwag Read, another Norristown resident, a ten-day leave specifically to attend to Hancock's surgical needs. Read was the Medical Director of the Pennsylvania Reserves and was also in charge of the McKim United States Hospital in Baltimore.[11] According to Read's own written testimony, when he returned to Norristown, he called upon the general and was shown into the room where Hancock lay. Read was stunned at what he saw:

> I found him [Hancock] much disheartened. He had grown thin, and looked pale and emaciated. He said he felt as if he was going to die, and that he had been probed and tortured to such an extent that death would be a relief. I endeavored to cheer him up, and as I was about bidding him farewell he said: "Goodbye, Doctor: I may never see you again."
> I had my hand on the door knob of his chamber, when he said: "See here, Doctor, why don't you try to get this ball out.

I have had all the reputation[s] in the country at it; now let's have some of the practical."[12]

Dr. Read was a sensitive individual and one with some significant medical accomplishments for his day. Born July 5, 1828, young Read "read" medicine with his maternal uncle, Dr. William Corson of Norristown, who was affectionately known as "Uncle Billy." In 1849, when he was only 21, Read received his M.D. from the University of Pennsylvania and he began his medical practice in Norristown. At age 27, he offered his services to Czar Nicholas I during the Crimean War and was soon serving in Sebastopol. No doubt, his experience in that war offered him important insight into the gruesome wounds inflicted by shot and saber. During his stay in Sebastopol, Read became a surgeon of some renown and also introduced some new, but regrettably unidentified, techniques for wound treatment. With the outbreak of the Civil War, he was appointed a major and made surgeon for the 30th Pennsylvania Infantry, First Reserves. Read's experience in the Crimea would serve him well in the Great Rebellion. By the time he visited Hancock, he was a Surgeon of U.S. Volunteers in addition to his other noted duties. Later, in 1866, Read won a brevet to lieutenant-colonel, U.S. Volunteers, and in 1874 fellow Norristownian, comrade-in-arms and Pennsylvania Governor, John Frederick Hartranft, appointed him brigadier-general and Surgeon General of the National Guard of Pennsylvania.[13] Obviously, Read was not the typical Civil War battlefield surgeon!

When Hancock made his feeble request, Read must have looked back and studied the patient for a moment. What he actually saw was the solution to the general's problem. According to Read, "He was lying in the bed with his wounded limb actually flexed, and all the probing had been done with his leg at right angles. The ball had hit him just below the right groin, within an inch of the femoral artery, while he was sitting in the saddle with his legs distended."[14] This brief observation was to prove itself most important.

There must have been something of a poignant lament in Hancock's voice because Read apparently decided to make his initial attempt immediately. He was keenly aware that a number of other clumsy attempts had been made in both Philadelphia and Norristown, but he soon resolved to do his best as long as the general was a willing patient. Unfortunately, history has not left a complete and clear record of Read's precise activities and list of medical assistants. While Read himself acknowledges that he was aided by his maternal uncle, Dr.

William "Uncle Billy" Corson, other records indicate that Doctors Smyser, Cooper and Edgar Buyers were also in attendance.[15]

After giving the matter some quick thought, Read concluded that all of the other attempts to remove any remaining foreign bodies failed because they were attempted while Hancock's leg was at a right angle to his torso. Logically, Read felt that body geometry prevented any success of a probe. As a result, he felt that advancement could only be met if Hancock were in a position similar to that when he was seated in the saddle when hit. This would straighten his leg and make the groin area far more accessible.

Read noted that he had gone into his office to obtain "a probe with a concealed blade..." Then, he and Cooper assisted Hancock into a chair, "on top of the dining room table..." Read felt that this elevation would provide a better path for his probe. According to Read: "I inserted the probe and dropped [penetrated] fully eight inches into the channel and struck the ball, which was imbedded in the sharp bone which you sit upon." This probing session, according to the general, took place on Friday, August 21st, and after making contact with the bullet, Read decided that no further work would be concluded that day.[16] The results of Dr. Read's procedure could only have provided Hancock with new hope while it certainly must have encouraged the physician as well.

On Saturday the 22nd, Read then had to surgically extract the ball which "was located posterior to the femur." When finished, Read recalled, "I forget the caliber of the bullet but it was a big Minie ball." Hancock himself described the bullet as weighing "one ounce and ninety grains."[17] Some modern reports indicate that Read never gave Hancock any anesthesia but there is no record to prove or disprove such claims. In either case, the entire proceeding could not have been pleasant for the general and his cooperative spirit can only be seen as a testimony to the agony he sustained prior to Read's attention. When the ball had finally been removed, Read apparently gave it to one of his assistants, Dr. Corson, who misplaced it for years among his private papers. Please refer to the drawings on pages 172 and 173 for a better understanding of Hancock's wound.[18]

Read's records leave us little doubt that the extraction of the ball accelerated Hancock's improvement, and he noted that "In a week's time the General was out on crutches, and in two weeks more, the general even attended a Masonic gathering at Odd Fellows' Hall."[19] Another progress report stated that the doctors "extracted an ugly-looking customer a minie bullet...The General bore the operation very well and is now able to come down stairs, for a few hours each day."[20]

While Hancock was recuperating in Norristown, he was visited by a

"...I may never see you again."

Major-General Winfield Scott Hancock

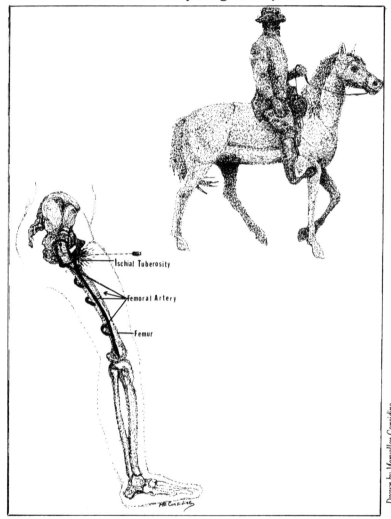

Bullet Trajectory

The approximate trajectory of the bullet that hit General Hancock on July 3, 1863.

"...I may never see you again."

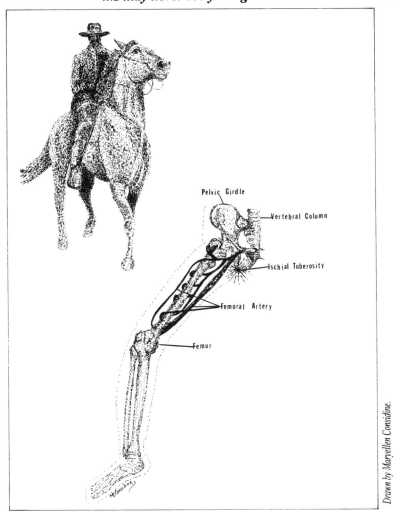

Hancock's Wound

Location of the wound General Hancock received on July 3, 1863.

174 Hancock at Gettysburg...*and beyond.*

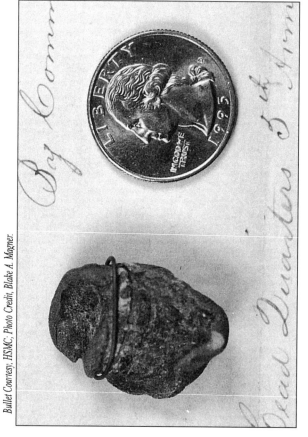

Bullet Courtesy: HSMC; Photo Credit; Blake A. Magner.

The Bullet That Hit Hancock

This is the bullet that Dr. Read extracted from General Hancock. The paper it rests upon is General Meade's Special Order sending Read back to Norristown to attend the general. The bullet belongs to HSMC, which made this photo possible in conjunction with the CWLM. The photograph was taken by Mr. Blake Magner and the coin provides some perspective.

"...I may never see you again."

Home of General Hancock's Parents

This is the home of General Hancock's parents, located on East Swede Street, between Main and Lafayette Streets, in Norristown, Pennsylvania. This is where Dr. Read removed the bullet that hit Hancock on July 3, 1863 at Gettysburg. The home was torn down in 1992.

Dr. Louis W. Read

Dr. Louis W. Read, the surgeon who removed the bullet from General Hancock's groin, from a painting.

"...I may never see you again."

Courtesy: HSMC; Photo Credit: Joseph F. Morsello.

Hancock in Norristown

This undated photo is taken from Main Street in Norristown, looking south on Swede Street. The Schulykill River is clearly visible at the bottom of the street. General Hancock is the taller of the two men on the right corner. The home of the general's father was just left of the trees on the left.

Modern Site of the Home of General Hancock's Parents

This empty lot on Swede Street in Norristown, Pennsylvania, is all that remains of the home belonging to Hancock's father. It was this home where the general was moved to recuperate from the wound received on July 3, 1863.

number of comrades, including Brigadier-General Alexander Hays, commander of his Third Division. Hays later recounted this story to Colonel Clinton D. MacDougall, commander of the 111th New York, part of the Third. During that visit, the two men talked about various aspects of the battle of Gettysburg and more specifically about matters on the second day. In the process, the issue of Hancock's arrest of Colonel Eliakim Sherrill came up and, perhaps realizing he had been a little too hasty that day, Hancock sheepishly asked Hays, "What has become of the Col. of your Division I put in arrest at Gettysburg[?]" Probably finding it difficult not to explode in front of his superior, Hays nonetheless erupted with, "That's just like all your d—d apologies Hancock... They come too late. He's dead."[21] Colonel Sherrill had died on July 4th of mortal wounds received on July 3rd while repulsing the advance of Confederate Brigadier-General James Lane's North Carolina brigade. Oddly enough, he was brought down about the same time that Hancock was wounded. Hancock made no further comment.

There is something of a sequel to the Read-Hancock relationship that is little known outside of a few local Norristown newspaper articles. While on recruiting duty in Auburn, New York, probably in 1864, Hancock met a soldier of his command, W. E. Webster, who was part of the Independent Battery of Captain Andrew Cowan. Webster was on crutches and suffering from a wound very similar to the general's. Hancock informed Webster of his own experience and suggested that he go see Dr. Read at the earliest possible moment. Encouraged by Hancock's remarks, Webster went to Baltimore where he found Dr. Read around midnight.[22]

After a brief discussion and subsequent inspection, Read agreed to attempt an extraction there and then and asked the gunner if he "wanted to take anything." Webster replied, "No, go ahead!" According to Webster, "bracing myself by grasping the back of the sofa the tug-of-war commenced. In a much shorter time than it takes to write this, a part of the Southern Confederacy was in my hand, a small piece of bone sticking to the ball."[23]

Dr. Read's operation on Webster parallels the general's wounding because they are similar in nature and Webster leaves us more detail. While it is impractical to be absolutely certain, we can better appreciate some of Hancock's problems by Webster's descriptions of himself. Having gone through no less than two deep probes, up to "11 inches," Webster states: "Abscesses formed, my left hip swelling to twice its size. These were opened but others soon followed and the discharge of pus was very large. When wounded I weighed 150 pounds, now I weighed [sic] 80 pounds."[24]

The very next day, as Webster was lying in the hospital recuperating, General Hancock came in to visit and, according to Webster, he "acted like a school boy." So pleased with Read's success, Hancock told the patient: "Why Webster, that man could take a body out of the grave and make him live!" Dr. Read, who was witness to this event, must have smiled at the general's exuberance and Hancock turned to the surgeon and said: "Doctor, this is one of my boys. I want you to give him everything he wants and get him on his feet again."[25]

With Read's success, Hancock began to make rapid healing strides and remained extremely grateful for the balance of his life.[26] As for Dr. Read, he lived through the rest of the war, and afterward, he went back to the practice of medicine in the Norristown area. On November 1, 1900, at the age of 72, Dr. Read was laid to rest in Montgomery Cemetery, not far from the general whose life he certainly saved.[27]

With the generosity of hindsight, Hancock became too anxious to rejoin his command and it is clear today that a longer recuperative period would have undoubtedly rendered a much more repaired and effective battlefield general. But, he was too impatient and not a man to be argued with when it came to such matters. There is plenty of record that clearly demonstrates that while his zeal remained constant, his stamina was sharply impaired by the wound. His aide Bingham noted that on long marches, he frequently rode in an ambulance and mounted only at the battle site. When he rode for extended periods, the painful wound suppurated causing the general to forfeit his command. Following a fight near Petersburg, Bingham noted that Hancock found some relief only when "a large piece of bone [discharged] from the wound."[28]

Nonetheless, for the moment, Hancock improved rapidly and by September 11, the following article appeared in a Norristown newspaper:

> At the close of the [local] Republican ratification meeting held at the League Room on last Thursday evening, the Band serenaded General W. S. Hancock, at the residence of his father. Three cheers were given for the Hero, when he hobbled to the window and excused himself from saying anything further than thanking them for the compliment. The General is now able to get along out doors on two crutches. Some two weeks ago, a flattened minnie [sic] ball was taken out of the wound; it had sunk some four or five inches into the flesh, and had remained there ever since the battle of Gettysburg. It

now seems that the ball in its flight struck a fence and a nail, and carried the nail along with it into the wound, for the nail was bent as though twisted around the ball. The pieces of lead that have been taken out from time to time, were probably only portions of the ball shelling off.[29]

By the middle of September Hancock thought he felt well enough to visit New York City and West Point. Then, he made up his mind to go to St. Louis to meet up with Almira and the children, whom he had sent earlier.[30] After his arrival there, Hancock wrote to his father on October 12th:

> I threw away my crutches a few days after my arrival, and now walk with a cane. I am improving, but do not yet walk without a little "role." My wound is still unhealed, though the doctors say it is closing rapidly. I find some uneasiness in sitting long on a chair, and cannot ride yet. The bone appears to be injured, and may give me trouble for a long time. I hope, however, I may be well enough in two weeks to join my Corps.
>
> I am busy in trimming up the forest trees in the lawn of "Longwood," which covers nearly eleven acres. I know it is not the best time; but still it will do.
>
> Allie and the children send their best love to you and mother. Please give my best love to mother, and I remain, as ever,
>
> Your affectionate son,
>
> Winfield S. Hancock[31]

Hancock's impatience drove him back to his command on December 27, 1863. When he reported for duty, however, it was quickly determined that he was not really physically fit for active field service so he was sent on recruiting duty. One of his major objectives was to raise 50,000 troops of which some would fill out the thinning ranks of his II Corps. He established his headquarters in Harrisburg and sent out a plea to his fellow Pennsylvanians to assist in his efforts.[32]

During the winter of 1864, Hancock was to receive several important and gracious honors from cities in the Northeast. Foremost was Philadelphia, where the city fathers passed a special resolution and held a reception on his behalf in Independence Hall. There, in the sanctuary of American freedom, Hancock occupied the desk and chair utilized by George Washington when he presided over the Constitutional Convention.[33]

New York City also honored him and gave him the governor's room at City Hall wherein a reception was held. Boston too hailed him as the Legislature invited him to speak on the floor. In Albany, the State of New York passed an official resolution of its appreciation for his valor.[34]

The people from his hometown also sought out opportunities to demonstrate their admiration for his heroics. Accordingly, on July 4, 1864, several of his schoolmates began a drive to raise funds for a suitable testimonial for the general. Under the leadership of his friend and sometime financial counselor, Benjamin C. Chain, the group raised $1600, an enormous sum for the period, and purchased a nine-piece gold and silver plate tea service which was engraved with the badge of the II Corps and inscribed with:

> TO
> MAJOR GENERAL WINFIELD SCOTT HANCOCK,
> FROM
> CITIZENS OF HIS BIRTH-PLACE
> NORRISTOWN
> MONTGOMERY COUNTY, PENNSYLVANIA
> JULY 4th,
> 1864[35]

But testimonials and mementos become forgotten and lost. In 1911, a family member of Dr. William Corson, Miss Katherine Corson, was going through some papers of her father, Dr. Ellwood M. Corson—a nephew of "Uncle Billy." During her search, Miss Corson came upon a strangely shaped bullet. An attached note identified the ball as being the one extracted from General Hancock. It was proposed at that time to present the missile to the Valley Forge Museum to be placed on display.[36] However, through an undefined route, the bullet finally came into the possession of the HSMC, where it remains on public display. Regrettably, it, like the general himself, is of little interest to the public today.

"...I may never see you again."

Hancock finally returned to active field service on March 23, 1864 though his wound was to plague him for the rest of his life. That January, however, Congress issued its resolution of thanks to Generals Hooker, Meade and Howard for the "skill, energy, and endurance which first covered Washington and Baltimore...[and the] skill and heroic valor which, at Gettysburg, repulsed, defeated, and drove back...the veteran army of the rebellion."[37] That resolution wounded Hancock's pride because of its obvious omission of his efforts. The entire matter brought quick responses from Hancock supporters and when General Howard responded to one pro-Hancock newspaper article, Hancock wrote directly to Howard:

> My temperament is such that the fact that Congress chose to thank you for services in a battle where I had a like command, and did not do the same for me, could not cause me to cease speaking of your gallantry, nor would I consider it a matter personal between ourselves, should I think my services had been overlooked by any tribunal having the authority to judge, and that yours had not been.[38]

With Hancock back with his command, the wound continued to plague him. His aide, Captain Bingham, noted: "He continued to suffer from his wound during all the remaining time of the war, and indeed feels serious effects from it to this time, March 1874...[during the remainder of the war] he was obliged to travel in an ambulance a great portion of the time...until in the vicinity of the enemy, when he mounted his horse, and so remained until the fighting was over.... During the whole of the summer of 1864 he was daily attended by a [unknown] Surgeon on account of his wound, which at that time was much irritated and discharging more or less all the time, Small portions of the bone at time passing from it."[39] From another eyewitness, we are afforded this account of the wound's impact upon the general's activities: "Hancock lay, at full length, in a covered wagon...He lies down as much as he can, to give his wounded leg rest...Hancock is a very great and vehement talker but always says something worth hearing."[40]

During 1864, Hancock led the II Corps at the Wilderness, Spotsylvania, Cold Harbor, Ream's Station and Boydton Plank Road. In November of that same year, his wound drove him to accept positions that were mainly administrative, which is how he then served out the balance of the war, except for a very brief stint as commander of the Department of West Virginia and the Middle Military Division. Immediately following the war, in concert with another Norristownian, Major-General John F. Hartranft, Hancock played a key role in the Lincoln Conspiracy Trial and the hangings of George A. Atzerodt, Lewis Paine, David E. Herold and the first woman to be put to death in this country by the Federal Government, Mary E. Surratt. In his later political life, the execution of Mrs. Surratt was to earn him the vile sobriquet of "Woman Killer;" as if he personally made the decision.

Hancock then went back onto the plains, and on April 21, 1866 he belatedly received the Thanks of Congress for his contributions at Gettysburg.[41] On July 26, he was promoted to the full rank of major-general of regulars. In February of 1867, Hancock's father, who suffered from diabetes, died in Norristown. In August of that same year, President Johnson appointed him military governor to succeed "Little Phil" Sheridan, in the Fifth Military District, which included Louisiana and Texas.[42] During his brief, three-month service there, Hancock shocked the nation when he restored civil rule to those two states, which won him lasting praise of the natives and disdain of many in the North. In 1872, he was appointed to command the Military Division of the Atlantic and he took up headquarters at Governor's Island off New York City. In 1880, while still in the military, and one year after his mother's death, Hancock was the Democratic Presidential contender and his Vice Presidential running mate was William H. English of Indiana. While that race was very close, Hancock lost to James A. Garfield by fewer than 7,100 popular votes. Typical Hancock, at 5:00 a.m. on the morning following the election, he rolled over in bed and asked his wife about the election results. Undoubtedly, attempting to minimize any disappointment to her husband, Almira quietly told him, "It has been a complete Waterloo for you." Without a pause, he replied, "I can stand it." Then, according to his spouse, he rolled over again and immediately went back to sleep.[43]

At that time, Hancock was 56 years old and less than six years away from his death. He had grown to a position of national recognition and he certainly matured in his mental and philosophical ways. He was far more pragmatic and tolerant as witnessed by his ability to accept the defeat of the presidency with an air of resignation. He found solace in the fact that he was secure with his position on Governor's Island but he harbored inner struggles. Perhaps, for the first time in his life, Hancock was ready to truly dedicate his full time and attention to his beloved wife, their only remaining child, Russell, his wife and their grandchildren, including the general's namesake. The Hancocks already knew the terrible sting of the nineteenth century when their daughter

"...I may never see you again."

Winfield Scott Hancock

A rare photograph of General Hancock in civilian clothes. While the date of the photograph is not known, it may have been taken during his 1880 presidential bid.

186   Hancock at Gettysburg...*and beyond.*

ENGRAVING OF HANCOCK IN *HARPER'S WEEKLY*

This engraving appeared in the *Harper's Weekly* shortly after Hancock lost the 1880 presidential election. It was drawn by his friend, Thomas Nast. The drawing shows a defeated Hancock being comforted by Lady Liberty. The caption states: "No change is necessary, General Hancock; we are too well satisfied with your brave record as a Union soldier."

"...I may never see you again."

Ada died on March 28, 1875, at the tender age of eighteen. In addition, it *appears* that the general himself knew that he was not in the greatest health, though there is no record that he ever shared that with anyone, including Almira. Indications suggest that the hero of Gettysburg was something of a coward when it came to dealing with his own well-being and with diabetes, a disease that was silently looming as his feared and final enemy.

———————————— ◆ ————————————

"Death is a punishment to some, to some a gift, and to many a favor."
Seneca

Chapter Six

"The citizens of Louisiana...cherish the memory..."

The death of General Hancock really came as a surprise to the public and undoubtedly to some within his family circle as well. While medical science in 1886 was certainly a far cry from today, his physicians were competent for the time though it is difficult to appreciate fully how they remained ignorant about his major physical crisis. Nonetheless, the responsibility for Hancock's terminal medical problem appears to rest principally with himself. He did not take proper care of himself and he failed to heed his body's warnings and his doctor's repeated requests for necessary, thorough examinations. The fatal, but undiagnosed medical problem for Hancock was advanced diabetes, which he certainly suspected but, out of fear, ignored. It became his last battle. Indeed, his father's demise in 1867 was brought about by diabetes so there was every logical reason for the general, and his doctors, to be concerned about a potential inheritance factor. Hancock was not alone in his reluctance to confront such problems, for conditions strongly indicate that Almira also refused to deal with such a serious potential. In the end, all of that denial did not serve either very well.

According to Almira, "Hancock was last seen for the last time in public, in his official capacity, commanding the grandiose funeral pageant which escorted the remains of General Grant...," in August of 1885.[1] While this may be something of a slight exaggeration, it does convey the vastly diminished public nature of Hancock's last six months, though in November of 1885, he eagerly went to Gettysburg where he had not visited for nearly 20 years. The purpose of that visit was to clarify some "historical points with regard to the movements of Second Corps troops" during the three-day epic battle. No doubt, Hancock relished that visit, for he was accompanied by many old comrades and past subordinates, including General Francis A. Walker, historian for the II Corps, and the bewhiskered Colonel John B. Bachelder, one of the more significant historians of the Gettysburg battlefield. Another participant was Hancock's dear friend, Colonel John P. Nicholson, of the Military Order of Loyal

Legion, of which Hancock was then commander-in-chief, plus members of the local G.A.R. Post IX. One other veteran on that team was Thomas B. Musgrave, whom the general had personally invited. In his invitation, Hancock very considerately asked Musgrave to bring along his young son, Percy, who joined the entourage on the battlefield trip. When the visit was over, Hancock prophetically said to Musgrave, "Your boy will remember what has been said when we have passed away."[2]

Whatever health problems he may have had, Hancock was still pragmatic in other areas and he was constantly concerned about inadequate family finances. Those wanting conditions always kept him hopeful of another promotion during his final months, which would have meant a sorely needed pay and retirement increase. Perhaps, in an attempt to mask those fiscal concerns, he told Almira, "I consider that I am well paid for my services, and am satisfied, particularly so that I am indebted to no one but myself for the rank that I hold and the privileges that belong to it."[3] Perhaps he was attempting to convince himself, as opposed to convincing Almira, since the reality was that the Hancocks owned little property and had only the most meager financial resources. Much of their paucity was caused by the general's personal extended generosity, which compelled him to give funds to virtually any veteran down on his luck. In addition, he was faced with the financially draining effects of his twin brother Hilary, who was in constant need owing to his dubious life-style in Minneapolis.

Still, despite those problems, the last several months for Almira and the general had some idyllic qualities and, according to one newspaper report:

> In his home life Gen. Hancock was a high minded, noble-hearted affable gentleman. His old fashioned wooden two-story home on the top of the hill overlooked the boat landing at Governor's Island, and often in Summer evenings he would be seen chatting with his wife or a visitor on the wide piazza...The devotion of Gen. and Mrs. Hancock to each other and the charming amenities of their home life were little less than domestic proverbs to many of their friends.[4]

An important indicator of Hancock's rapidly failing physical and depressed mental status was his refusal to most social invitations, while sharply curbing his home entertainment, which his doctors strongly encouraged. Those

A Corpulent General Hancock

This photo is undated though it is well after the war.

"The citizens of Louisiana...cherish the memory..." 191

Major-General Winfield Scott Hancock

This photo and the prior photograph were undoubtedly taken during the same sitting.

192   Hancock at Gettysburg...*and beyond.*

General Hancock and Family

Photograph taken from *The Life of Winfield Scott Hancock*, by D. X. Junkin, D. Appleton and Company, pub. This stylized drawing shows the General with Almira to his right. Russell, his wife May, and their two children are to the General's left. The scene is depicted from Governor's Island overlooking Manhattan.

Commandant's Residence, Governor's Island

Photograph taken from *The Life of Winfield Scott Hancock*, by D. X. Junkin, D. Appleton and Company, pub.

"The citizens of Louisiana...cherish the memory..." 193

Hancock at the Head of Grant's Funeral Procession

General Hancock at the head of General Grant's funeral procession in New York City, August 8, 1885.

194   **Hancock at Gettysburg...*and beyond.***

Hancock at Gettysburg

This photo was taken during Hancock's last visit to Gettysburg on November 19, 1885. Hancock is seventh from the left in a top hat. A number of these men served with the general during the war and the gentleman to his left with the muttonchop sideburns is John B. Bachelder.

curtailments were made despite the fact that he and Almira were in great social demand throughout the nation. His failing physical health had finally coupled with his internal mental grief which was sparked by immediate family losses. According to one newspaper article, following the untimely death of his daughter Ada on March 28, 1875, "social parties at the [Hancock] house became more rare...and...somewhat restricted."[5] However, he did continue to attend the meetings of the Military Service Institution on Governor's Island, of which he was the president. In fact, as recently as a month before his death he was at such a meeting where he refused to allow any recognition for himself.[6]

Several deaths had occurred within his immediate family over the past decade and Hancock never really got over any of them. The sad loss of his 18-year-old daughter Ada was followed on July 13, 1880 by the death of his four-month-old namesake grandson, which was then followed by the death of the child's father, Russell, on December 21, 1884. Russell was only 33 when he died and he left behind a wife and three small children. It was Russell, who as a young man of 20, ran off and married May Gwyn of Louisville, Kentucky, the daughter of an ex-Confederate. The Southern family was strongly opposed to that union and the entire event must have been difficult for the Hancocks as well.[7] More important, however, all of that mortality was almost more than the hearts of Almira and the general could bear.[8]

When Ada died, the Hancocks had her laid to rest in the tomb of a friend, Christian Meeh, at Montgomery Cemetery in Norristown, because she had such an aversion to being buried. No doubt, that sad event, followed by the interment of his grandson at Montgomery, crystallized for General Hancock that his own final resting place would be in that same ground. Consequently, he abandoned his idea of a mausoleum in New York's Woodlawn Cemetery, or any other place, which was estimated at a costly $3,000. Instead, he asked his Norristown boyhood friend, Benjamin E. Chain, to investigate the possibilities of constructing a tomb in Montgomery Cemetery and, owing to family finances, he implored Chain, "You know my purposes and necessities of the hour...Please look into it for me and bend your energies in the direction of progress so that by Autumn of this year we shall have performed our manifest intentions." Then, remembering that his heart was larger than his wallet, Hancock chided his friend, "bring it within the range of possibility as to finances...."[9]

According to a local newspaper report, the Hancock vault was finally completed at a cost of only $700 and the "stone came from the Templin Quarry in lower Norristown." But, cheaper was not better and within two years of its completed construction, the tomb was already in need of significant repairs. Unfortunately, necessary restorations were destined to become a chronic prob-

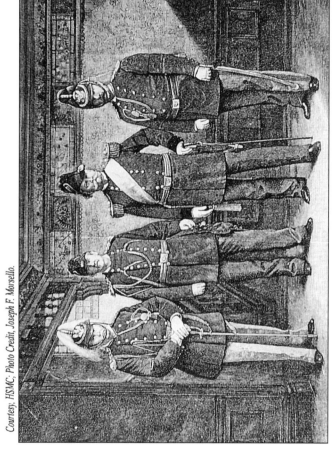

Courtesy, HSMC; Photo Credit, Joseph F. Morsello.

General Hancock and Staff

Left to right, Captain John S. Wharton, General William G. Mitchell, Hancock, and Lieutenant T. H. Barber. (Circa 1883)

lem with the crypt and as early as 1895, Dr. L. W. Read, the physician who removed the bullet from the general, personally paid to have the crumbling, outer sandstone walls replaced with durable bluestone.[10]

With the death of Ada and Russell, the Hancocks had lost both of their children, with Russell preceding the general's death by a mere 14 months. Clearly, the resulting intermittent lethargic attitude of his last days, combined with his growing diabetic menace, had to have an ever-growing negative impact on the general.[11]

On January 27, 1886, just two weeks before his death, Hancock left Governor's Island with Lieutenant John A. DaPray for a quick visit to Washington, to attend to some military business.[12] He planned to see President Grover Cleveland, Secretary of War William C. Endicott and, finally, General Philip H. Sheridan about an appointment for one of his old brigade commanders, John Rutter Brooke, of Montgomery County, Pennsylvania, which turned out to be unsuccessful. While in Washington, it was quickly noted that Hancock's health was rapidly failing, though he was making every effort to ignore and disprove such rumors. He registered at the popular Wormley Hotel but scarcely left his room. One of the reasons that did drive him from that hotel was a rapidly growing and painful boil that had developed on the back of his neck. By the 29th, the boil made him so uncomfortable that he went to see a military physician, Doctor O'Reilly, who naturally proceeded to lance the growth. That surgical procedure may have provided Hancock with some immediate relief, but, at best, that alleviation was destined to be very temporary.

Nonetheless, when the surgeon finished, Hancock returned to the Wormley and as he entered the lobby, he was greeted by an old friend and former member of his staff, George A. Armes. Eager to see his former commander, Armes was shocked to see blood running down Hancock's neck. Instinctively, Armes reached out and took Hancock's silk handkerchief from his coat pocket and tied it around the general's neck to prevent the blood from creeping onto his omnipresent white shirt. Hancock attempted to pass the matter off and he told Armes, "That is nothing; it is just a little lancing of a carbuncle." Soon after, Hancock departed from the Wormley and Armes accompanied him to a carriage and pleaded that he should be careful not to aggravate the boil by catching cold. With that, someone, perhaps DaPray, retorted that Hancock was "too old a soldier to pay any attention to a little scratch of that kind."[13]

On their way to the railroad station, DaPray recalled that President Cleveland was planning a reception that afternoon and mentioned to Hancock they had been invited. In a disappointed tone the general said, "I wish you had told me that before. I would have gone there. I am feeling so much better."[14] In retrospect, Hancock probably did not feel "much better" and it is doubtful that he was even comfortable with the effects of his "little scratch."

Upon his return to Governor's Island on the 30th, the boil began to grow again and the pain drove Hancock to see his personal physician, Doctor John H. Janeway. That physician concluded that the boil was only one source of the general's problems, so he decided to watch and monitor developments, suspecting other complications. One of Janeway's concerns was that Hancock had lost quite a bit of blood from the Washington lancing which substantially reduced his natural robust nature.[15] Too, Janeway had long been concerned about the general's health and even two years before, he was alarmed when Hancock sustained a leg injury while aboard a steamer, resulting in an abscess. At that time, Janeway suggested a complete physical but Hancock refused, which caused the doctor to suspect that Hancock probably knew he was not in the best of health. Janeway speculated that Hancock was probably fearful about contracting diabetes owing to his family history. But, in spite of those concerns, the general refused this and at least one other later suggested examination, which might have extended his life.[16] Regardless of all those worries, no one really thought the general was in imminent, mortal danger and Almira was even proceeding with plans to visit Florida with Hancock's niece, Mrs. Eugene Griffin.[17]

Meanwhile, the boil simply continued to grow, and three days after his initial meeting with Janeway, Hancock was in unbearable agony because the boil had developed into a hard carbuncle, which painfully restricted the movement of his head.[18] Still, even with that discomfort, Janeway again concluded that the carbuncle still posed no serious threat to his patient's life, and he simply continued to watch developments, which only grew worse.

Over the next few days, Hancock showed brief signs of improvement, though Saturday evening, February 6, he began to fail quickly. Sometime during that night, he alarmed Almira when he entered her bedroom fully dressed, looking for a traveling bag.[19] By then, the general was obviously delirious and Dr. Janeway was called and was joined by Colonel Charles Sutherland, the Department Medical Director stationed on the Island. Apparently, Hancock was soon brought down by a sudden hemorrhaging of the carbuncle, and the two physicians decided upon periodic injections of "brandy, ether, and whiskey and carbonate of ammonia," which "produce[d] a good effect."[20] We can only wonder if the "good effect" was the sole result of the alcohol or if the patient realized any real therapeutic effect from that potent elixir. We will simply never know!

All the while, Almira kept a constant vigil upon her husband. During those final hours, Hancock made a few occasional bursts of improvement, which offered some false hope to the doctors though Almira always remained vitally concerned. As the general's devoted wife, Almira had always been the orchestrator and center of their highly touted social life. A very talented woman, she was once described as "queen of the community at the island, dispensing its hospitality with the utmost grace...." Almira was also an accomplished organist, and she served in that position at the Chapel of St. Cornelius on the Island. During her tenure, she composed and published a lovely *Te Deum*, which won her significant praise.[21]

Perhaps in an attempt to improve the general's spirits during his lucid moments, Almira allowed their grandson, Gwyn, the son of their own late son Russell, to play and visit in his grandfather's sickroom. It appears that the youngster was actually living with his grandparents and the mere presence of the tot must have buoyed the general, who lovingly allowed him to fill a good portion of his bedroom with his precious toys. According to one newspaper report, when their son Russell died, the general and Almira made their three grandchildren a large factor in their lives; "and the boy [Gwyn] especially...was the very apple of his [Hancock's] eye."[22] Gwyn would attend West Point like his grandfather and unveiled the general's equestrian statue in Washington, D.C., on May 12, 1896.[23]

The room where Hancock rested was on the second floor in the southwest portion of the two-story, gingerbread style wooden home. He was lying on a plain black walnut bedstead, while in the fireplace a warming glow gave some comfort against the cold and raw, early February air. In one corner of the room stood a number of flags which acted as silent sentinels, while the mantle held a tiny locomotive and other toys utilized to occupy his grandson.[24] But none of those mementos, or anything else, would be able to restore good health to the ailing general.

During the night and early morning of Sunday and Monday, February 7-8, Hancock began to fail even further, causing great fear in Almira. Despite the adequate number of nurses there to attend the general, Almira steadfastly remained by his bedside, speaking softly to her gravely ill husband. She insisted on personally administering all of his medicines and sadly, when she spoke to him, he could only respond in staccato-like monosyllables. All during the night of the 7th, Almira remained by his bedside and by early morning on Monday, she was exhausted and thought it best to catch a little sleep. About 6:15, as she picked herself up to leave the bedside, Hancock opened his weary eyes and poignantly, silently watched her move across the floor. Perhaps "feeling" his stare upon her back, when she reached the doorway, Almira looked back at her husband of 36 years and could see that his once bright, flashing blue eyes were now sad and misted. Yet, Hancock looked directly at his wife and pathetically attempted to call to her his favorite and affectionate diminutives,

> "O, Allie, Allie! Myra! Good——"

The emotional strain of the moment was too great for Almira, and she broke down into a hail of tears and had to be led away. For the general, those were his last coherent words, and within one hour he slipped into unconsciousness.[25]

For the balance of that day and evening of the 8th, Doctor Janeway and Colonel Sutherland kept their vigil and attempted to diagnose Hancock's problems, Janeway now confident that the difficulties were somehow kidney-related. Finally, the two men concluded that Hancock's accelerated decline had to be caused by some "hidden disease" and at 8:30 on the evening of the 8th, they sent for Dr. Daniel M. Stimson, who arrived just before 10 o'clock Tuesday morning. Stimson immediately performed a urine analysis which promptly confirmed his suspicion that Hancock was suffering from a severe, and now fatal, case of diabetes. That diagnosis shocked both Sutherland and Janeway and the latter then admitted to the family, "with tears in his eyes, that there was no hope of the General's recovery." That announcement sent Almira back into the sickroom where she made one last futile attempt to speak to her dying husband. Overcome with grief, she had to be led off again into an adjacent room, which signaled to the other occupants of the house that the end was very near.[26] According to a newspaper account:

> Soon after 1 o'clock all pretense of work in the house stopped, and all waited in silence for the end. General J[ames] B. Fry went into the sick room, and sat on a chair near the bed, speaking at intervals to Oliver Russell, Mrs. Hancock's brother. Col. Sutherland moved about doing such little acts as he thought would ease the General's last moments; Hospital Steward D. Robinson stood near a window, and Messenger Ward walked slowly in and out of the doorway. Lieut. Eugene Griffin, who married a niece of General Hancock, moved at intervals from the bedside to the couch in another

room where Mrs. Griffin, Mrs. Emma Bouvier, and Dr. Janeway were in attendance upon Mrs. Hancock.

From that time until 2:30 o'clock the house was still. Then the General's breathing grew labored, and the muscles of his face twitched with symptoms of convulsions. It was feared that death would be accompanied with convulsions, but after a short time the General lay as if asleep. The increasing difficulty of his breathing, however, warned the watchers that the end was very near, and the entire household broke into murmurs of grief. Col. Sutherland, Steward Robinson, Messenger Ward, Mr. Russell, and Lieut. Griffin gathered silently about the bed. Gen. Fry sat opposite the west window and near the General's pillow. The little group remained without moving for several minutes. Then Gen. Hancock drew a long, deep breath, his body quivered slightly, and then lay still. "He is dead." said Col. Sutherland.[27]

It was 2:35 p.m. and General Winfield Scott Hancock was just five days away from his 62nd birthday. Shortly after he died, the ticker-tape machines in New York City carried the following message into the hotels and offices:

"Gen. Hancock died at 3 o'clock."[28]

As an added coincidence, that day also marked the last day for the six months of official mourning over the death of General Grant, who died on July 23, 1885. Later, during an interview, Dr. Janeway described Hancock's acceptance of death as one who simply "went down to the close of his life like a person descending a flight of stairs."[29] Another, unidentified report noted that Hancock's remains "presented an exceedingly emaciated appearance and his face was so sunken that he was scarcely recognizable."[30] Whatever the description, the nation, and the North in particular, had known a heavy toll in 1885–1886 since Hancock's name could now be added to that of Generals Grant, McClellan and Irvin McDowell, all who died during that period. That night, the general's body would remain in the same room, while Colonel W. B. Beck and Lieutenant A. D. Vogel kept the vigil.[31]

The funeral arrangements would reflect Almira's spartan wishes and were handled by her brother, Colonel Russell, Lieutenant Eugene Griffin, and Hancock's close friend, Colonel Nicholson, from the Philadelphia Loyal Legion. Despite the fact that Almira acquiesced to friends and Dr. Janeway's request that she not attend the funeral services, she steadfastly insisted that her husband "not be buried with the military honors to which his rank entitle him, but that the obsequies should be as simple and unostentatious as possible."[32] While Mrs. Hancock was certainly entitled to such consideration, it is well to remember that Hancock was a national figure and words like "simple and unostentatious" were subject to a vast degree of interpretation and execution. For example, her request has led some to believe that the general was buried in civilian clothes. In fact, Hancock was buried in the full uniform of a major-general, which was duly noted by several sources during the funeral.[33] In the end though, every effort was made to accommodate Almira's desire for a modest funeral with a minimum of pageantry, while affording honor to the general's memory.

It didn't take long before news of his untimely death spread across Governor's Island, New York City and the nation. The soldiers and staff on the Island were deeply moved and Ann Lee, the 70-year-old black female servant, who had been with the Hancocks since 1850, moaned quietly to herself as she rocked alone on the front porch in disbelief. In front of the main doorway to the house lay the general's prize pet, a large Cuban mastiff, who simply did not understand the historic moment and patiently waited in vain for his master to come and pet him.[34]

When Dr. Janeway took a final look upon Hancock's body, he noted that it did indeed appear emaciated even though the general had attained a portly status prior to his last days. Officially, Janeway first indicated that the cause of death was either related to uremia or diabetes.[35] He ruled out the carbuncle as the primary source, believing that it could have only created a minor problem. Unfortunately for historical accuracy, Janeway decided that no autopsy would be required and, for unknown reasons, he soon changed his mind about the official cause of death. On the 12th, the following appeared in a New York newspaper: "The formal certificate of Gen. Hancock's death was recorded at Sanitary Headquarters yesterday. It was signed by John H. Janeway, M.D.... It stated that the primary cause of death was *malignant carbuncle* [Emphasis added] and the second immediate cause diabetes."[36] Unfortunately, Janeway's fateful decision does nothing to assist modern historians.

Telegrams and statements of condolence, from across the nation, were soon being received on Governor's Island. Regrets soon came from Washington, where officials had been briefed about Hancock's impending death, and President Cleveland was officially informed of his passing. While the Chief Executive would be unable to attend the funeral, he immediately ordered the flags over the White House and all executive departments flown at half mast until after the interment. He then issued the following statement:

> Tidings of the death of Winfield Scott Hancock, the senior Major-General of the army of the United States, have just been received. A patriotic and valiant defender of his country; an able and heroic soldier; a spotless and accomplished gentleman-crowned alike with the laurels of military-renown and the highest tribute of his fellow-countrymen...It is fitting that every mark of public respect should be paid to his memory.

Then, President Cleveland sent the following personal telegram to Almira:

> Accept my heartfelt sympathy and condolence in your terrible bereavement. The heroism and worth of your late husband have gathered to your side in this hour of your affliction a nation of mourners.[37]

General Sherman was beginning a trip to Cincinnati when he stopped and sent a telegram, asking his former aide and now Hancock's second in command, Major-General W. D. Whipple, "Can I do anything to manifest my love for him and his widow?" Soon afterward Sherman was approached by a reporter and asked to give his estimate of Hancock. After telling the journalist, "It would hardly be fair to others to give it," the general continued:

> I regarded Hancock as one of the greatest soldiers in history. In my mind he was always a knight, a large man, with a great large forehead and most commanding presence. I know of no General in all of the war who in the saddle and before his

troops presented a more magnificent appearance than Gen. Hancock, and then he was a man of great brain power and huge resources. As a military commander he had in his lifetime few, if any, superiors.[38]

General Sherman was then off to eulogize Hancock before the Ohio Commandery of MOLLUS, which he did extemporaneously. When his speech appeared in the newspapers, Almira was touched by his sincerity.[39]

Below the Mason-Dixon line, Fitzhugh Lee, the nephew-general of General Robert E. Lee, who was Governor of Virginia, wired Almira: "The country mourns the loss of a superb soldier and noble citizen." Shortly thereafter, Governor Lee also stated during an interview:

> I was very fond of Gen. Hancock. He was a noble, gallant fellow and a soldier of undoubted merit and great ability...He fought so well on his side during the war that when it was over he was satisfied, and sheathed his sword and believed that there must be fraternity between both sections to make the whole Republic prosperous. Virginia and the South will deeply regret the death of a generous soldier, a courteous gentleman, and a strong, firm and constant friend.[40]

From Cincinnati, ex-President and General Rutherford B. Hayes wired Almira that "The sad intelligence of the death of your noble husband fills with grief the companions of the Ohio Commandery of the Loyal Legion...We tender you our heartfelt sympathy...."[41] Shortly after, Hayes, who was a Republican and political adversary, gave what became his well-known personal opinion of the dead general while addressing the Legion in Cincinnati:

> ...If, when we make up our estimate of a public man, conspicuous as a soldier and in civil life, we are to think first and chiefly of his manhood, his integrity, his purity, his singleness of purpose, and his unselfish devotion to duty, we can say truthfully of Hancock that he was through and through

pure gold.[42]

Perhaps no other Union soldier was to receive as many Southern laurels as those gathered by General Hancock. One of the most touching Southern messages was a telegram from Louisiana Governor Samuel D. McEnery, who attempted to convey the deep regrets and long admiration felt by the people of his state. Those warm feelings stemmed from Hancock's General Order Number 40, issued during the Reconstruction period. On his first day as Military Governor of Texas and Louisiana, November 29, 1867, Hancock restored civilian rule against the suggestion of many, including General Ulysses S. Grant. According to one of his biographers, "This simple order was a sensation. It was like a breath of fresh air...." Mrs. Hancock was lavished with gifts, which she prudently returned, and with numerous effusive messages saying, "Thank God we are at peace again," or "Thank God for sending us this great and good man."[43] In the end, however, that sensitive act probably cost Hancock the 1880 Presidential election, even though some influential people thought he was even more popular than Grant.[44] But, the people of Louisiana, and most throughout the South, who voted solidly for Hancock in 1880, had never forgotten his healing ways and Governor McEnery's message meant to convey their warm emotions when he stated: "The citizens of Louisiana have reason to honor the character and cherish the memory of the humane and magnanimous Hancock. They deplore his death, and in their name I tender you their heartfelt sympathy."[45]

Another voice of Southern praise was offered by the *Charleston News and Courier*:

> The South has changed little in some respects since the day when the men who recoiled from Hancock's line at Gettysburg began the retreat which ended at Appomattox. But the men who stood with him on the summit of the hill that day, and who cheered him in triumph as he rode along their lines, scarcely mourn his loss today more sincerely than do those whom he opposed. A mighty man has fallen....[46]

As with the death of many high profile individuals, Hancock's passing saw many friends, comrades and even past foes eager to express their sincere regrets and condolences. Of the many expressions and recollections, one New York State newspaper offered the following story which exemplified Hancock's mental agility: Following the battle of Antietam, when Hancock's very close friend, General McClellan, was relieved by President Lincoln, a group of officers came to him to "express...our sense of wrong and our indignation at the removal of Gen. McClellan." Quickly understanding the tenor of the group's complaint, Hancock interrupted them and said, "Stop one moment, gentlemen." Then, with the articulate capacity of a true executive, he told those officers, "Return to your commands at once and remember always that we are here not to serve the interests of any one man. We are here to serve our country." With that sobering statement, the group went back to their own commands with a better understanding of why he was their leader.[47] Another newspaper article reported an added dramatic moment, when a prominent politician, noticing Hancock dashing off into the heat of combat, exclaimed, "There goes the impersonation of war."[48]

Woven into all the funeral fabric came the sensitive social problem of the general's at-arms-length posture with religion. While he had come out of a Quaker heritage, Hancock had never professed any particular religious affiliation and never belonged to any specific church.[49] In all probability, while he had paid a modest homage to the Baptist Church, Hancock probably vacillated somewhere between being a Deist and an Agnostic. Undoubtedly, for the sake of social propriety, it was decided that the general's remains would be afforded the "graces" of a Christian burial. But, the final sparse specifics of those ceremonies would leave no doubt that even in death, "Hancock was Hancock," including matters of religion.[50]

But, as fastidious as the general might be about his dress, correspondence and all other matters, he had always been in a state of total disarray when it came to financial matters. He made no real attempts to amass anything even approaching a fortune and, in fact, the Hancocks had little in the way of equity. One of his close associates noted that when it came to money, "he was laughably thoughtless." To emphasize his point, the friend recalled:

> He frequently came over to the [New York] city without a cent in his pocket. On discovering his moneyless condition a look of helpless surprise would come over his face, and winking his eye in that peculiar manner usual with him when he was puzzled, he would say: "Well I declare! I haven't got a cent. Will you lend me some money?"...he would only accept

a quarter or at most a half a dollar and go up town as happy as a school boy.[51]

Because Hancock had little or no financial resources to fall upon, his friends quickly began a campaign to raise funds for Almira's welfare. While the Hancocks owned a little property near St. Louis, they had no appreciable savings owing to the general's generous nature.[52] According to one report, General Hancock carried one life insurance policy for $9,000 but even with that and any other assets, "the balance of the General's estate is on the debit side."[53] To assist Almira, the internationally famous financier, J. P. Morgan, became the Treasurer and overseer of collected funds which ultimately reached a total of about $55,000. To assist in the fund-raising effort, MOLLUS appointed a committee of 15 to solicit the entire nation and by the 27th of February, just 18 days after his death, almost $35,000 had already been gathered. Certainly, the national plea made by Generals William F. Smith, James B. Fry and Thomas L. Crittenden spurred contributions along.[54]

Almost simultaneously, friends decided to acquire a home in Washington, D.C., for Almira and as early as March 6th, over $5,000 had been collected in Boston alone.[55] Those friends managed to give Almira a home "reportedly worth another $22,000." The move to purchase that home for Mrs. Hancock involved the general's former aide, George A. Armes, who wrote that Mr. W. W. Corcoran gave $3,000 with the stipulation that Almira make Washington her home. Then, Armes noted that he also received $5,000 from Mr. B. H. Warder, $2,500 from Mr. H. G. Dulaney of Virginia and $3,000 from U.S. Senator James G. Fair, a Democrat from Nevada, who was a wealthy friend and businessman. In fact, Armes noted that within ten days of his starting efforts, he had already collected $45,700.[56] The final disposition of all those funds remains unknown though it is likely that any excess monies, beyond the cost of the home, were given to Almira. Consequently, while the Hancocks had no equity, their friends graciously saw to Almira's well-being out of love and respect for both.

With regard to the trust that Morgan headed, in addition to himself, other large contributors to Almira's fund read like a veritable who's-who and included: John Jacob Astor, August Belmont, Andrew Carnegie, George W. Childs, A. J. Drexel, Joseph W. Drexel, William R. Grace, John W. MacKay, Joseph Pulitzer, Samuel J. Tilden, Cornelius Vanderbilt, F. W. Vanderbilt, G. W. Vanderbilt, W. K. Vanderbilt and John Lowber Welsh, each of whom gave $1,000 except Grace, who gave $500.[57] One final political attempt at addressing the general's poor financial condition occurred when a congressional bill had been introduced to promote and then retire Hancock with the rank of lieutenant-general. That would have increased his pay and pension while Lieutenant-General Philip Sheridan would have been promoted to the rank of General of the Army. Unfortunately, for Almira in particular, Hancock's promotion never materialized.[58]

In reality, Almira was to realize relatively independent financial means soon after the general's death. In addition to the home and funds raised, within two months, she was given a generous pension of $2,000 a year. While this may appear modest by current standards, it should be noted that Mrs. Grant received the highest annual pension of any military spouse at $5,000 per year, which equaled that of a President. The families of many other generals had to be content with only $600 per year and that list included Generals Robert Anderson, Edward D. Baker, George Armstrong Custer, Samuel P. Heintzelman, James B. McPherson, George H. Thomas, Gouverneur K. Warren, plus numerous others including admirals and commodores. At $2,000 per year, Mrs. Hancock received the second highest pension paid to any soldier up to that time with the exception of Grant.[59]

While the final funeral plans were being made, the wartime governor of New York State, Horatio Seymour, died on the evening of February 12. Seymour had been the state's chief executive during the so-called New York City draft riots, immediately following the battle of Gettysburg. Many felt that the governor's death, combined with Hancock's, dealt the national Democratic Party a hard blow. Both would have their final New York City services at Trinity Church.[60]

Some early reports stated that Hancock would be buried in Saint Louis, in Almira's family plot. But, his wife ultimately decided to respect his wishes and after the New York City services, his remains would be sent back to Norristown and interred in the vault which he had built at Montgomery Cemetery in 1883.[61] That news led many G.A.R. members to request that his remains first lie in state at Independence Hall since he was such an honored son of the Keystone State.[62] For whatever personal reasons, Almira would not agree to such pomp and the plans for a direct route to Montgomery Cemetery prevailed.

After the body had been prepared, it was placed in a cloth-covered steel casket, which was placed in the parlor on the ground floor of the Island home. For future identification, a simple gold plate had been mounted on the top of the casket with the inscription:

"The citizens of Louisiana...cherish the memory..."

MAJOR-GENERAL
WINFIELD SCOTT HANCOCK
BORN
FEBRUARY 14, 1824
DIED
FEBRUARY 9, 1886

During the 72 hours between his death and final church services, Almira was the recipient of many kind messages plus a large number of people who personally called to express sorrow and offer their assistance. Understandably, she begged her regrets to most of those visitors though she did afford ample time for her good friend, Mary Ellen McClellan, who had buried her own husband-general only 100 days earlier. Perhaps the two widows commiserated about how, just a short while ago, Generals Hancock, Franklin and Confederate General Joseph E. Johnston all stood together at General McClellan's gravesite at Riverview Cemetery in Trenton, New Jersey.[63] No matter how the two women may have assuaged one another, Dr. Janeway still found it necessary to give Almira a sedative elixir of "chloral and bromine" to allow her the comfort of some sleep and escape.

Until Friday the 12th, the body, with a proper guard, had remained in the bedroom where the general had died. Sometime during the 10th, Hospital Steward Robinson had embalmed the cadaver and while few other details survive, some early newspaper reports claimed that there would be no chemical preservatives made on the remains.[64] At 7:30 Friday evening, the military personnel on the Island were permitted a private viewing. In line with Almira's wishes, that private sitting, along with the entire funeral, was kept very modest and austere in comparison to other recent military funerals for generals. According to a newspaper account, the entire funeral was "a simple one in its cemonial features, but memorable on account of the number of distinguished persons who attended it...."[65] Regrettably, the general's closest living sibling, his brother John, was in Florida when he died and was unable to return in time for the obsequies.[66] Hilary's name does not appear in any of the profiles as attending his brother's funeral.

On Saturday morning, the 13th, the weather proved to be very uncooperative as a moderating thermometer caused a drizzling rain, which fell through a thick blanket of fog. By 8:30, three batteries of the Fifth Artillery posted 114 men outside Hancock's home with polished, reversed rifles, to serve as the military escort. Overall command belonged to Brevet Brigadier-General

Richard H. Jackson, commandant of Fort Columbus on the Island. Lieutenant Anthony W. Vogdes led Battery A, while Captain J. A. Fessenden led Battery H, and Battery K was led by a Captain Brewerton. The casket was closed that morning at 7:45 sharp, and when the doors of the home swung open, eight precision sergeants, bearing the coffin upon their shoulders, moved behind the large escort toward the dock. Another eight sergeants stood close by as relief and the silence was deafening. No martial music or muffled drums annoyed the solemn moment; only the steady fall of the cold rain plus the soft shuffling of heavy military shoes on wet winter grass created any audible funeral accompaniment. By 9:00 a.m., the casket had been placed on the port side of the steamer *Chester A. Arthur*, and draped with two American flags. Hancock's sword and chapeau were also taken down to the steamer and placed on the top of the casket. As the lines of the boat were cast off, a low rumbling boom split the haze as a minute gun from Castle Williams announced the start of the 15-minute trip to Manhattan.[67]

Along with the booming minute gun and the foghorns on the steamer constantly blaring, the bells of Trinity Church and those atop the Barge Office began their grim toll. When the steamer docked, the casket was carried inside the Barge Office where it was met by the distinguished honorary pallbearers: The Honorable Thomas A. Bayard, President Cleveland's Secretary of State and personal representative; General Sherman, who would die five years later, almost to the day; General Sheridan, whom Hancock called "the whirlwind with spurs," and who would himself be dead in 18 months,[68] plus Generals John M. Schofield, William B. Franklin, William F. [Baldy] Smith, Alfred H. Terry, Nelson A. Miles, James B. Fry, Orlando B. Willcox, Francis A. Walker, plus Colonel Finley Anderson, Major D. W. Miller of Hancock's staff during the war, and Mr. B. M. Hartshorne, an old personal friend. All of those men wore heavy white sashes with black rosettes and rode in six horse-drawn carriages. Behind that line came the hearse bearing Hancock's body, which was accompanied by the guard of honor. Following the hearse and guard came at least another dozen carriages carrying family, friends and other dignitaries, including Secretary of War Endicott and the Reverend E. H. C. Goodwin, Post Chaplain of Governor's Island, who would assist the Reverend Morgan Dix in the church service. Also following were five posts from the Grand Army of the Republic, including the new W. S. Hancock Post, a detachment of the Legion of Honor, plus a delegation from Tammany Hall, led by General Daniel E. Sickles, who always remained grateful for Hancock's assistance at Gettysburg.[69] While Hancock and the irascible, Republican Sickles frequently held different views on matters, Sickles always held his colleague in high esteem. During the 1880 election, the former III Corps commander publicly declared he would vote for Hancock because "he believed that the country would be entirely safe under an administration of which he was the head."[70]

The short route to Trinity Church would take the procession over State Street to Broadway and up Broadway to the church. Despite the cold, penetrating rain, about 900 police officers had to be employed to hold back the curious crowds that had gathered upon the sidewalks to pay their last respects. Flags had been lowered to half mast, business had been essentially suspended in the entire area and the Stock Exchange adjourned between 10:30 and 11:00 a.m. as a token of respect.[71] Despite all of the attending notables, one newspaper commented, "It was probably the least pretentious funeral ever given a great soldier."[72]

Inside Trinity Church, only three hundred seats had been reserved for Hancock's family, honored guests, funeral service participants, and, of course, the aging Ann Lee. Those remaining were made available to the public, who made use of all the seats plus the available standing room. In front of the chancel rail were a number of floral tributes including a special piece from the Hancock Legion. This was a "large star of roses and immortelles, surmounted by a dove with spread wings" and bore the inscription, "The Hancock Legion Mourns the Nation's Loss." Among the many well-known citizens who attended the service were William M. Evarts, Joseph H. Choate, John Jacob Astor, William W. Astor and Hamilton Fish.[73]

Before the coffin entered the church, the organist, A. H. Messiter, played Chopin's *Funeral March*. When he finished, the boys choir entered from the southwest door and stationed themselves on both sides of the chancel, which started the tolling chimes and signaled everyone to rise. With that, Messiter began Beethoven's *Funeral March* in C flat minor.

Led by a "pretty mild-faced blonde boy," the white-robed Reverends Dix and Goodwin moved up the center aisle where they met the incoming procession and led it back toward the chancel, reciting, "I am the Resurrection and the Life."[74] Immediately behind the clergy were General Sherman and Secretary Bayard, who were followed by the eight sergeants bearing the coffin, which they rested in front of the rail. Then, "The funeral service was the simple ceremony of the Episcopal Church." Following the music of Croft's burial service, the ageless lesson set down by Saint Paul was heard:

> But as it is, Christ is now raised from the dead, the first fruits
> of those who have fallen asleep. Death came through a man;

hence the resurrection of the dead comes through a man also. Just as in Adam all die, so in Christ all will come to life again...[75]

Then, the congregation sang the hymn,

"Rock of Ages" and the anthem "I Heard a Voice." Chaplain Goodwin read the selections from the Scriptures. After the hymn the boy [sic] [the boys choir] went down from the chancel, surrounded the coffin, and sang "Man that is born of a woman," from the burial service. Chaplain Goodwin pronounced the committal [here, Goodwin "dropped the ashes on the lid."] and Dr. Dix recited the Lord's Prayer and the ensuing petitions of the service. [When Dix finished, the choir "responded with a beautifully chorded 'Amen.'"] Then the boy bearing the cross faced the main entrance and the procession moved slowly to the door to the music of the Dead March in Saul.[76]

It was nearly 11:00 a.m. when the procession left the church, and it had absorbed an additional 2,000–3,000 people who followed as the relatively spartan cortege made its way back to the Barge Office. Once there, the coffin was again transferred to the *Chester A. Arthur*, while most of the bells in the area pealed a solemn toll. The moment everyone was aboard, the steamer got under way and reached Pier D at Jersey City at 11:40 a.m. There, the entourage was met by 80 local police officers who had no problems controlling the curious crowd that had gathered there. Efficiently, the funeral group made its way to the special train at Pennsylvania Railroad Station, which waited to take them to Philadelphia and then to Norristown, where the weather proved to be just as dismal.[77] That special train consisted of four cars, plus the same locomotive that pulled the remains of General McClellan to Trenton less than four short months ago. The coffin rested in the front car, draped with an American flag, plus the general's sword, chapeau and a laurel wreath from the Pennsylvania Loyal Legion, which were all placed on the cover. Around the casket sat the ever-present eight sergeants while the remaining eight waited their turn for

"The citizens of Louisiana...cherish the memory..." 213

duty in the rear car. The VIPs took their seats within the two middle cars, and at noon the small train began to roll.

> The fence that encloses the track within the limits of Jersey City was lined on both sides with people for fully a half mile beyond the station, and at every crossing was a crowd, all standing bared to the rain while the train passed. At Newark this scene was reproduced on a smaller scale. There were gatherings all along the line, at Elizabeth, New Brunswick, Princeton, and Trenton. Flags hung at half mast at every settlement...Toward Philadelphia the demonstrations became more marked. At Germantown festoons of crepe were displayed on many of the factories...and great crowds of people turned out to see the train pass.[78]

As the "sable-draped" train rolled into Philadelphia, it stopped at 52nd Street where three more cars were added to carry Pennsylvania Governor Robert E. Pattison and his staff. In addition, a host of other dignitaries, including another Norristown notable, past governor and Brevet Major-General John F. Hartranft, plus 140 members of the Pennsylvania Loyal Legion, climbed aboard. Then, engine number 466 was added and the quick trip to Norristown got under way. As the train journeyed west along the Schuylkill River, it came into the milltown of Manayunk. There, respect and admiration for Hancock were very evident as "mill hands crowded into the upper stories of the big brick factories. Here and there along the grimy walls hung streamers of black. Their very poverty showed these decorations to be the work, not of masters, but the men." The train continued and passed through Roxborough, Shawmont, Miquon and Conshohocken. Finally, at 2:48 p.m. the train pulled into Norristown at the DeKalb Street Station, where it was met by a "waiting multitude."[79]

One report noted, "All Norristown came out to witness the soldier's final return home." Because of the persistent rain, the funeral party wasted little time and the coffin was soon lifted into a waiting hearse while 16 carriages stood by to carry the VIPs. All of the local obsequies were being handled by some very impressive residents, including Dr. L. W. Read, who had removed the Gettysburg bullet from the general; Professor Thaddeus S. C. Lowe, who had introduced aerial reconnaissance with tethered balloons during the war; Benjamin E. Chain, banker and long-time personal friend of the general, who

Hancock's Funeral Procession

The Hancock funeral cortege in New York City. From Frank Leslie's *Illustrated Newspaper*, February 20, 1886.

Hancock Family Gravesite

This is the vandalized Hancock family gravesite in Montgomery Cemetery. Here lies his parents, twin brother Hilary and his namesake grandson. The general's tomb lies approximately 100 yards off the point of the fallen obelisk.

"The citizens of Louisiana...cherish the memory..."

The Hancock Tomb

Top: The Hancock tomb shortly after his funeral services.
Bottom: The Hancock tomb several years later, showing the rapid erosion of the soft stone.

216 **Hancock at Gettysburg...*and beyond.***

Interior of the Hancock Tomb

Interior of the Hancock tomb in Montgomery Cemetery, West Norriton Township, Pennsylvania. This photo was taken during the rededication ceremonies held by the Historical Society of Montgomery County on October 7, 1995. Hancock's remains are in the left center crypt while those of his daughter Ada are in the upper right. Note the inscription on the lintel, "W. S. Hancock".

"The citizens of Louisiana...cherish the memory..."

***Harpers Weekly* Salutes the Fallen Hancock**

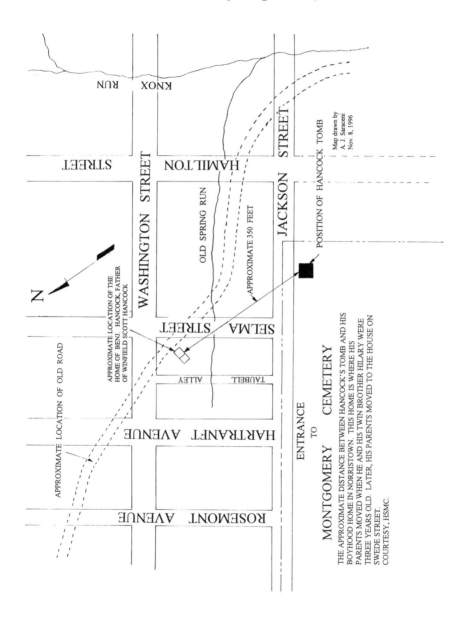

"The citizens of Louisiana...cherish the memory..."

Hancock's Boyhood Home

The above two photographs are the home generally considered to be where the general grew up. See map on p. 218 for precise location. His parents later moved to the home on Swede Street and neither structure stands today. These photographs were taken in 1952.

Hancock's Bust in "Hancock Park"

Bust of General Hancock in "Hancock Park" which is located at the juncture of Manhattan Avenue, St. Nicholas Avenue and 123rd Street in northern Manhattan's Harlem Section. The park is located due east of the Grant Tomb by a few blocks. The bust was completed by artist Wilson MacDonald and was dedicated on December 30, 1893.

"The citizens of Louisiana...cherish the memory..."

also lent Hancock the money to pay for his tomb; Irving P. Wagner, a district attorney; Joseph K. Gotwalz, one of the founding members of the HSMC; and Charles Hunsicker, a county judge. After the services, Professor Lowe had made arrangements to host the entire body at his laboratory at Main and Arch Streets.[80]

Moving along without any martial music, the procession slowly made its way up DeKalb to Main Street, where it turned west toward the cemetery, about one and one half miles away. The rain continued to fall, but the crowds defiantly huddled under umbrellas or, out of deep respect, bravely bared their heads to the raw elements. "Nearly every building was draped-some of them most ornately." As the march began its entrance into the cemetery, members of the local Zook Post No. 11, named for General Samuel K. Zook, who was killed at Gettysburg while serving under Hancock, forced back the pressing crowd so the funeral procession might continue. During the entire march, church bells tolled and cannon boomed.[81]

Of the many mourners in his hometown, an aged 90-year-old former schoolmaster of Hancock, Eliphalet Roberts, fondly and clearly recalled his young pupil who could always rapidly raise a military company. Hancock had only recently assisted Roberts's daughter in securing a job at the Philadelphia mint and, as a token of his respect, whenever he came to Norristown, the general attempted to visit his aging instructor. When Roberts learned of the general's death a day or two before, he exclaimed: "Winfield came to my school in Norristown when he was only seven years old...I won't flatter him. He was just like other boys about studying his lessons...he has always been more than kind to me." But then a twinkle must have appeared in Roberts's clouding eyes when he told how young Winfield once had to quit playing soldier to help his ailing mother with the dishes. Once inside, his youthful "command" taunted him endlessly until he furiously chased them "several blocks."[82] We are left with only the endless possible variants that might have passed through the master's mind as he contemplated the sad death of his pupil and junior of nearly 30 years.

The rain and moderating temperature had turned the ground at Montgomery Cemetery into a veritable mud hole. According to one eyewitness, "Rain and thaw had made the ground soft. As the throngs spread about over, the turf the surface was churned into a sea of mud."[83]

It was into this slippery, thick, muddy mess that the funeral cortege entered at approximately 4:00 p.m. The pale steely daylight was already beginning to fade, and the ominous cloud cover only enhanced the growing gray emotional strain of the crowd. Planks had been laid in front of the tomb to allow for better footing, and the lack of any colorful flowers only accentuated the dreariness of the surrealistic tableau.[84] Finally, General Sherman and Secretary Bayard approached the opening of the mausoleum with the eight sergeants carrying the coffin immediately behind them. On top of the metal box, Hancock's sword and chapeau still rested and, as the casket was guided into the mouth of the vault, Sergeant Sill removed those two personal emblems. In their stead, he placed a wreath of white immortelles with the word "Husband" fashioned with red flowers on its top. Then, as 5,000 spectators looked on, four loud field guns from Griffin's Battery F of the Frankford Arsenal fired a salute, which brought instant silence and a sense of impending finality. Immediately following, Sergeant Sill went back into the tomb and placed another, similar wreath with the word "Daughter" on its top, into Ada's upper vault, which the undertaker had already opened. Sill had been personally presented both wreaths by Mrs. Hancock for this purpose, the day before.[85]

At about that same time, approximately 1,200 air miles to the south, in New Orleans, Battery B of the Washington Artillery, under the command of Sergeant Arthur Costi, fired a memorial 13-gun salute of its own. Positioned at the head of Canal Street, that famous and oldest artillery command of the Crescent City honored their one-time foe, who probably sacrificed his political career in his attempt to restore civil law in their state. As their loud salvos boomed, the noise caught the attention of Admiral LaCombe, Commander of the North Atlantic squadron of the French Navy, who happened to be anchored in the bay. When he learned the purpose of those fiery guns, LaCombe ordered the French flag on his own frigate, *La Flore*, to be lowered to half mast and the American flag to be placed on the fore. Then, with all the majesty she could muster, the *La Flore* fired a salvo of 13 guns in her own gracious martial salute to General Hancock.[86]

Virtually simultaneously and unplanned, matters at Montgomery Cemetery were just about complete, and when Sergeant Sill had placed the wreath for Ada, the undertaker stepped forward and closed the two crypts. With that, the aging Major Wallace F. Randolph, commander of the Germantown battery, raised his cap, which was the signal for Richard Frank to raise his bugle and begin the lamenting wail of taps. While standing on the muddy mound adjacent the stone-covered tomb, with the red cord from his bugle falling over the blue sleeve of his coat, Frank carefully chose his mournful notes, which he had played a thousand times before. As he exhaled his last breath for that aching strain, 13 minute guns suddenly sounded four salvos, which roared across those Pennsylvania valleys like August thunder. Those repeated concussions were intensified by the thick fog and they shocked the sensibilities of all the moist eyes and burning throats in the cemetery. When those guns suddenly fell silent, the undertaker moved forward and secured the iron gate on the front of the tomb. Major-General Winfield Scott Hancock had joined the countless legions belonging to the ages.[87]

APPENDIX — A

THANKS OF CONGRESS

The joint resolution was officially approved on April 21, 1866. However, it was introduced on March 13th and entered into the *Congressional Globe* on April 10, 1866. The following is an exact copy of that entry:

Mr. Ancona, from the Committee of Military Affairs, reported back joint resolution of the House No. 88, expressive of the thanks of Congress to Major General W. S. Hancock, with a substitute, recommending its passage. The substitute for the joint resolution was read, as follows:

*Be it resolved by the Senate and House of Representatives, &c...*That in addition to the thanks heretofore voted by joint resolution, approved January 28, 1866 to Major General George G. Meade, Major General Oliver O. Howard, and to the officers and soldiers of the army of the Potomac, for the skill and heroic valor which, at Gettysburg repulsed, defeated, and drove back, broken and dispirited, the veteran army of the rebellion, the gratitude of the American people and the thanks of their representatives in Congress, are likewise due and are hereby tendered to Major General Winfield S. Hancock for his gallant, meritorious and conspicuous share in that great and decisive victory.

Source: *The Congressional Globe*, The First Session, The Thirty-Ninth Congress, 1866, pp. 1375 & 1869.

APPENDIX — B

HEADQUARTERS, FIFTH MILITARY DISTRICT,
New Orleans, La., November 29, 1867.

General Order, No. 40.

I. In accordance with General Orders No. 81, Headquarters of the Army, Adjutant-General's Office Washington, D.C., August 27, 1867, Major-General W. S. Hancock hereby assumes command of the Fifth Military District, and of the Department composed of the States of Louisiana and Texas.

II. The General Commanding is gratified to learn that peace and quiet reign in this Department. It will be his purpose to preserve this condition of things. As a means to this great end, he requires the maintenance of the civil authorities, and the faithful execution of the laws, as the most efficient under existing circumstances. In war it is indispensable to repel force by force, to overthrow and destroy opposition to lawful authority, but when insurrectionary forces have been overthrown and peace established, and the civil authorities are ready and willing to perform their duties, the military power should cease to lead, and the civil administration resume its natural and rightful dominion. Solemnly impressed with these views, the General announces that the great principles of American liberty are still the inheritance of this people, and ever should be. The right of trial by jury, the *habeas corpus*, the liberty of the press, the freedom of speech, the natural rights of person, and the rights of property must be preserved. Free institutions, while they are essential to the prosperity and happiness of the people, always furnish the strongest inducements to peace and order. Crimes and offenses committed in this district must be left to the consideration and judgement of the regular civil tribunals, and those tribunals will be supported in their lawful jurisdiction. Should there be violation of existing laws which are not inquired into by the civil magistrates, or should failure in the administration of justice be complained of, the cases will be reported to these Headquarters, when such orders will be made as may be deemed necessary. While the General thus indicates his purpose to respect the liberties of the people, he wishes all to understand that armed insurrection or forcible resistance to the law will be instantly suppressed by arms.

By command of Maj.-Gen. W. S. Hancock.

ENDNOTES

Preface

[1] *Report of the Joint Committee on the Conduct of the War*, 2nd Session, 38th Congress, General W. S. Hancock, March 1, 1864, vol. I, p. 409, courtesy, USAMHI. Note, the author frequently refers to the transcripts of the testimony offered by several Gettysburg participants who were called before the Committee. Each is identified as *Joint Committee Report*, the name and date of the person testifying. When General Hancock testified before this committee, he told them that he believed that if the V and VI Corps had promptly attacked Lee's disorganized troops following Pickett's Charge, as Meade had promised and he had requested: "I think we would have won a greater victory had the advance been promptly made and with spirit...we shall never reap the just fruits of a victory until we follow it up promptly."

[2] *Letters and Addresses, In Memory of Winfield Scott Hancock*, New York: G. P. Putnam's Sons, For The Military Service Institute, 1886, p. 20. This comment was made by Brevet Major-General John F. Hartranft, who served with Hancock during the Lincoln Conspiracy trials and after the war was twice Governor of Pennsylvania.

[3] *Norristown Times Herald*, August 12, 1929. One credible report claims that "General Hancock had never been a member of any church." *See also*,
Edward W. Hocker, "Hancock Landmarks," *Historical Sketches, Historical Society of Montgomery County*, vol. V [1925]: 19. *See also*,
Henry H. Bingham, *An Oration at the Unveiling of the Equestrian Statue of Major-General Winfield Scott Hancock on the Battlefield of Gettysburg*, June 5, 1896, p. 5, courtesy, USAMHI.

[4] *Encyclopedia Britannica*, vol. 2, 15th Edition, 1986, pp. 263–264.

[5] *Official Register of the Officers and Cadets of the U.S. Military Academy, June 1841–1844*, courtesy, United States Military Academy, West Point, New York.

[6] *Norristown Times Herald*, May 17, 1940.

Preface Endnotes

[7] *Army and Navy Journal*, February 27, 1886.

[8] *Hamilton Fish to Mrs. Griffin*, October 31, 1893, The Winfield Scott Hancock Papers, Hancock Correspondence, 1887–1893, courtesy, USAMHI.

[9] The author has discussed the popular Hancock–Armistead relationship with Armistead biographer, Wayne Motts, a historian and Gettysburg battlefield guide. Mr. Motts readily agrees that the depth of that fraternal bond has probably been overstated, or at least, there is little or no documentation to substantiate the near passionate association created by some. Accentuating some of the Hancock fantasy, Mr. George R. Stammerjohan, State Historian for California, wrote the author on August 31, 1995, claiming that "...everything in print concerning Hancock and Armistead in California, especially the farewell party, is not the most accurate. In fact, most of Hancock's assignment in Los Angeles is wrong."

[10] Robert V. Bruce, **Lincoln and the Tools of War**, Indianapolis, Indiana: Bobbs-Merrill, 1956, reprint; Chicago: University Press of Illinois, 1989, pp. 290–291. *See also,*

George R. Stammerjohan, "The Camel Experiment in California," ***Dogtown Territorial Quarterly***, Number 18 [Summer 1994]: 48.

[11] Glen Tucker, "A Personality Profile," *Civil War Times Illustrated* [August, 1968]: 7. *See also,*

WSH to Francis A. Walker, May 1, 1884, The Winfield Scott Hancock Papers of MOLLUS, folder of W. S. Hancock Correspondence, courtesy, USAMHI.

[12] Jubal A. Early, **General Jubal A. Early**, Philadelphia: J. B. Lippincott Company, 1912, reprint; Wilmington, North Carolina: Broadfoot Publishing Company, 1989, pp. 72–73. In his book, Early, not surprisingly, does not agree with McClellan's report about Hancock's bayonet charge and he states that "This statement is entirely devoid of truth...This charging with bayonets was one of the myths of this as well as all other wars. Military commanders sometimes saw the charges, after the fighting was over..." It is true that Civil War soldiers had an aversion to stabbing their opponents with the bayonet except as a last, dire measure. Author's note. *See also,*

Millard Kessler Bushong, **Old Jube**, Shippensburg, Pennsylvania: White Mane Publishing Co., Inc., 1955, p. 56.

[13] Clarence C. Buell and Robert U. Johnson, eds., **Battles and Leaders of the Civil War**, 4 vols., New York: The Century Company, 1888, reprint;

Preface Endnotes

Secaucus, New Jersey: Castle, 1989, vol. II, p. 199. Hereafter, referred to as *Battles and Leaders*. *See also*,
O. R., I, vol. XI, part I, p. 448. In his telegram to Washington on May 5, 1862, General McClellan reported, "Hancock has...repulsed Early's brigade by a real charge with the bayonet...His conduct was brilliant in the extreme."

[14] Hancock file, misc. clippings, courtesy, USAMHI. This particular reference came from the *Evening Star* newspaper dated May 12, 1896.

[15] *Army and Navy Journal*, February 27, 1886. These comments were made by General William [Baldy] Smith.

[16] *Ecclesiastes*, 3: 1–8.

[17] *Evening Star*, May 12, 1896.

[18] Glen Tucker, *Hancock the Superb*, Indianapolis, Indiana: Bobbs-Merrill Company, Inc., 1960, reprint; Dayton, Ohio: Morningside Bookshop, 1980, p. 263.

[19] Henry H. Bingham, *Anecdotes Concerning Gen. Hancock and Other Officers at Gettysburg and Elsewhere*, 1874, courtesy, GNMP. Vertical file #5-45. Hereafter, referred to as *Anecdotes Concerning Gen. Hancock*.

[20] Tucker, "A Personality Profile," p. 9.

[21] D. X. Junkin and Frank H. Norton, *The Life of Winfield Scott Hancock: Personal, Military, and Political*, New York: D. Appleton and Company, 1880, p. 385. Hereafter, referred to as *Winfield Scott Hancock*.

[22] *Mary Todd Lincoln to WSH*, undated, The Winfield Scott Hancock Papers, Correspondence, 1863–1865, courtesy, USAMHI. *See also*, Justin G. and Linda L. Turner, eds., *Mary Todd Lincoln, Her Life and Letters*, New York: Alfred A. Knopf, Inc., 1972, reprint; New York: Fromm International Publishing Corporation, 1987, p. 201. Mrs. Lincoln frequently sought favors from military men of high position and General Hancock was no exception. On February 12, 1865, Mrs. Lincoln sent the following request to General Hancock:

My Dear Sir:
My estimable friend Mrs. Hughes [unidentified], understanding from me, that if possible, you would grant her request, relative to her son, entrusts me, with a note to you. She supplicates, in a very ardent *& motherly* style, for the promotion of her son, who is considered very promising; any favor granted in the case, will be truly appreciated, by

Preface Endnotes

yours very respectfully. [Emphasis in original]

Mary Lincoln

[23] *The Gettysburg Compiler*, August 26 and October 21, 1880. The author readily acknowledges that *The Compiler* was a newspaper dedicated to the ideals of the Democratic party and therefore strongly supported Hancock in every way possible. *The Compiler* actually published this Lincoln quote a few times during the election year of 1880.

[24] Bingham, *Anecdotes Concerning Gen. Hancock*. "Genl. Hancock's personal appearance." Some reports indicate that Hancock was as tall as six foot two or three inches. Unfortunately, the author does not know of any completely accurate measurement. *See also*,

The New York Times, February 12, 1886.

[25] Almira Hancock, *Reminiscences of Winfield Scott Hancock*, New York: Charles L. Webster & Company, 1887, p. 332. Hereafter, referred to as *Reminiscences*.

[26] Bingham, *Anecdotes Concerning Gen. Hancock*.

[27] *Army and Navy Journal*, February 27, 1886. Before leaving for West Point, Hancock prophetically wrote the following in an album belonging to Miss Sarah Woodman, later, Mrs. William B. Hahn:

> Wreath thy garlands, fairest one,
> Ere the beams of day are done.
> Soon will close each fragrant flower
> Blooming in the garden's bower,
> While the midnight dews are shed
> O'er each sleeping floweret's head.
>
> Wreath thy garlands, fairest one,
> Soon will summer's reign be gone;
> Tempests come with chilling breath,
> Sweeping o'er the barren heath;
> So stern winter's fearless band
> Stalks in fierceness o'er the land.
>
> Wreath thy garlands, fairest one,
> Soon will set life's glowing sun;
> Youth's gay dreams too quickly fade,
> Loving hearts are soon betrayed;

Wreath thy garlands ere their bloom
Fade around thy earthly tomb.

[28] William Corby, *Memoirs of Chaplain Life*, New York: Fordham University Press, 1993, p. 174.

[29] David T. Hedrick and Gordon Barry Davis, Jr., eds., *I'm Surrounded by Methodists...Diary of John H. W. Stuckenberg Chaplain of the 145th Pennsylvania Volunteer Infantry*, Gettysburg: Thomas Publications, 1995, pp. 30–31. Hereafter, referred to as *Diary of John H. W. Stuckenberg*.

[30] J. W. Muffly, ed., *The Story of Our Regiment, A History of the 148th Pennsylvania Volunteers*, Des Moines, Iowa: The Kenyon Printing and Mfg. Co., 1904, reprint; Baltimore, Maryland: Butternut and Blue, 1994, p. 581. Hereafter, referred to as *A History of the 148th Pennsylvania*.

[31] **Ibid.**, pp. 654–655.

[32] Glen Tucker, *Hancock at Gettysburg*, p. 9. This is a manuscript, courtesy, GNMP.

[33] Courtesy, HSMC. *See also,*
Register of Applications to Charity Lodge, No. 190, AYM, Norristown, PA. According to this record, Hancock was the 267th individual to petition this lodge, which was done in 1859.

[34] July 3, 1991 was declared "Major-General Winfield Scott Hancock Day" by Louisiana Governor Buddy Roemer. In his proclamation, Governor Roemer declared: "Foremost in Hancock's administration was the return of the basic rights of the citizen guaranteed by the Constitution of the United States...citizens of Louisiana applauded General Hancock's fair and enlightened administration...[In return] the State of Louisiana voted almost unanimously for him." Copy of Governor Roemer's proclamation, courtesy, Marsha Rader.

[35] *New Orleans Times*, March 17, 1868.

[36] *Concurrent Resolution*, State of Louisiana, February 11, 1878. The Winfield Scott Hancock Papers, Hancock Correspondence file, 1868–1878, courtesy, USAMHI.

[37] *U. S. Grant to Abraham Lincoln*, July 25, 1864, courtesy, CWLM.

[38] Ulysses S. Grant, *Personal Memoirs*, 2 vols., New York: Charles L. Webster & Company, 1886, vol. II, p. 539.

[39] John Y. Simon, ed., *The Papers of Ulysses S. Grant*, vol. 16, Carbondale, Illinois: Southern Illinois University Press, 1936, pp. 223–224.

Preface Endnotes

[40] Courtesy, National Rifle Association.

[41] *The Times Herald*, July 30, 1960. *See also,*

Theodore W. Bean, ed., *History of Montgomery County, Pennsylvania*, Philadelphia: Everts & Peck, 1884, reprint: Mt. Vernon, Indiana: Windmill Publications, 1990, p. 528. *See also,*

Frederick E. Goodrich, *The Life and Public Services of Winfield Scott Hancock, Major-General, USA*, Boston: Lee and Shepard, 1880, p. 329. *See also,*

Norristown Daily Herald, November 9, 1880. The reader should know that irrespective of whatever may have happened with the 1880 vote in New York City, Hancock was not even afforded the courtesy of carrying his home state of Pennsylvania nor his home area of Montgomery County, nor his hometown of Norristown. The records show that of the total 22,051 votes cast in that county, James A. Garfield received 11,026 while General Hancock received 11,025. From the Norristown residents, Garfield received 1,680 votes to Hancock's 1,296, while the Keystone State gave Garfield a total of 444,704 votes to Hancock's 407,428. Consequently, if Hancock's home state had given him the same national consideration, or vote, they afforded Garfield, he would have won a plurality of 37,276 votes. *See also,*

The Times Herald, July 30, 1960. *See also,*

Hancock, *Reminiscences*, pp. 243 and 314. *See also,*

Hancock File, untitled, undated newspaper clipping, courtesy, HSMC. In a local newspaper, there appeared a correction that demonstrates Hancock's difficulties within his own hometown area: "Engineer Riegel, of the Perkiomen R. R., denies a report published in the *Register* that he has hoisted a Hancock rooster on his engine, and says he is for Garfield. He sent a request for a correction to the *Register* but it was not complied with." *See also,*

Allen Johnson and Dumas Malone, eds., *Dictionary of American Biography*, 22 vols., New York: Charles Scribner's Sons, 1931–1936, reprint; New York: Charles Scribner's Sons, 10 vols, 1958, vol. 4, p. 222.

[42] John M. Taylor, "General Hancock: Soldier of the Gilded Age," *Pennsylvania History*, vol. XXXII, No. 2 [April, 1965]: 195–196.

[43] *The Gettysburg Compiler*, September 23, 1880.

[44] Taylor, "General Hancock: Soldier of the Gilded Age."

[45] *Norristown Daily Herald*, May, 1896. Commentary from Mr. Frank Derr, courtesy, HSMC.

Preface Endnotes

[46] Courtesy, HSMC. N.B. Conditions at Montgomery Cemetery are currently deplorable though Hancock's gravesite has recently been restored, and in the past, it received modest attention from the Old Baldy CWRT in Philadelphia and some members of the HSMC, which owns the site. However, Hancock's gravesite, plus those of many other Civil War veterans there, have had a long history of neglect. As early as May 20, 1896, only ten years after the general's death, a veteran of Hancock's command wrote to the *Norristown Weekly Herald* and complained that "it has been reported to me that his [Hancock's] resting-place ...is in a sad state of neglect..." The writer, identified only as E. F. J., concluded with the following lament which still rings true today, "It is to be hoped that the land of Penn, hallowed by the memories of the martyrs...may not blush at her ingratitude to one of the foremost of her many glorious sons." Unfortunately, these are lofty words that have been lost upon the desecrated graves of many who fought to sustain the continuity of the Union, including Winfield Scott Hancock.

Chapter One

A Changing Order and tense moments

[1] St. Clair A. Mulholland, *The Story of the 116th Regiment, Pennsylvania Infantry*, reprint; Gaithersburg, Maryland: Olde Soldier Books, Inc., n.d., p. 368.

[2] Among the list of other general officers who were openly opposed to Hooker were O. O. Howard, John Reynolds, John Sedgwick, and George Stoneman.

[3] William F. Hanna, "Major General Darius N. Couch: A Civil War Profile," *Lincoln Herald*, 86 No. 1 [Spring 1984]: 25-31. Hereafter, referred to as "General Darius N. Couch."

[4] Carl Sandburg, *Abraham Lincoln: The War Years*, 4 vols., New York: Harcourt, Brace & Company, 1936-1939, vol. 2, p. 334.

[5] Hancock, *Reminiscences*, pp. 94-95. *See also,*

Edwin B. Coddington, *The Gettysburg Campaign*, New York: Charles Scribner's Sons, 1958, reprint; Dayton, Ohio: Morningside Bookshop, 1983, p. 37. *See also,*

Tucker, *Hancock the Superb*, p. 124. *See also,*

Chapter One Endnotes

David M. Jordan, *Winfield Scott Hancock, A Soldier's Life*, Indianapolis, Indiana: Indiana University Press, 1988, p. 75. Hereafter, referred to as *Winfield Scott Hancock*. Despite the numerous references made about Hancock's being approached as a possible successor to General Hooker, this author has not found an official record of that nature. Mrs. Hancock appears to be the sole source of that consideration. Author's note.

6. Walter H. Hebert, *Fighting Joe Hooker*, New York: Bobbs-Merrill Company, 1944, reprint; Gaithersburg, Maryland: Butternut Press, Inc., 1987, pp. 229-230.
7. Hancock, *Reminiscences*, p. 94.
8. Freeman Cleaves, *Meade of Gettysburg*, Norman, Oklahoma: University of Oklahoma Press, 1960, reprint; Dayton, Ohio: Morningside Bookshop, 1980, p. 117. *See also*,
   Meade, *The Life and Letters of General George Gordon Meade*, vol. I, p. 372.
9. Hanna, "General Darius N. Couch," p. 29.
10. Francis A. Walker, *History of the Second Army Corps in the Army of the Potomac*, New York: Charles Scribner's Sons, 1887, reprint; Gaithersburg, Maryland: Olde Soldier Books, Inc., 1990, p. 254. Hereafter, referred to as *History of the Second Army Corps*.
11. *O. R.*, I., vol. XXV, part I, p. 4. *See also*,
    O. R., I., vol. XXVII, part I, p. 57.
12. Gilbert C. Moore, Jr., ed., *Cornie*, Chattanooga, Tennessee: By the Editor, 1989, p. 151. *See also*,
    Ezra J. Warner, *Generals in Blue*, Baton Rouge, Louisiana: Louisiana State University Press, 1964, p. 63.
13. John Gibbon, *Personal Recollections of the Civil War*, New York: G. P. Putnam's Sons, 1928, reprint; Dayton, Ohio: Morningside House, Inc., 1988, p. 126.
14. *O. R.*, I., vol. XXVII, part III, p. 247.
15. Courtesy, Albert H. Wunsch, III and Son collection. After the war, Dr. William D. Hall had some correspondence with General Doubleday regarding the latter's volume, *Chancellorsville and Gettysburg*. In his copy of Doubleday's volume, on p. 97, Dr. Hall noted this story about Corporal Rihl. The author readily acknowledges that such claims of being "first" are not always reliable.
16. *The New York Times*, June 27, 1863.
17. *O. R.*, I., vol. XXVII, part III, p. 269.

Chapter One Endnotes

[18] **Ibid.**, p. 270.
[19] *O. R.*, I., vol. XXVII, part III, p. 306.
[20] David L. and Audrey J. Ladd, eds., and Richard Allen Sauers, Publisher's Consultant, *The Bachelder Papers*, 3 vols., Dayton, Ohio: Morningside House, Inc., 1994–1995, vol. III, p. 1347. Hereafter, referred to as *The Bachelder Papers*. See also,
O. R., I., vol. XXVII, part II, pp. 692-693. See also,
Ibid., part III, p. 309.
[21] *O. R.*, I., vol. XXVII, part III, p. 309. See also,
Emory M. Thomas, *Bold Dragoon, The Life of J.E.B. Stuart*, New York: Harper and Row, Publishers, 1986, p. 241.
[22] Tucker, *Hancock the Superb*, pp. 125-126.
[23] **Ibid.**, pp. 127-128. See also,
Walker, *History of the Second Army Corps*, pp. 260-261. See also,
Gibbon, *Personal Recollections of the Civil War*. On the matter of the arrest of General Owen, General Gibbon is silent in his volume. Author's note.
[24] Josiah Marshall Favill, *Diary of a Young Officer*, Chicago: R. R. Donnelly & Sons Company, 1909, p. 240.
[25] *O. R.*, I., vol. XXVII, part III, p. 354.
[26] George Gordon Meade, ed., *The Life and Letters of General George Gordon Meade*, 2 vols., New York: Charles Scribner's Sons, 1913, vol. II, p. 11. Hereafter, referred to as *George Gordon Meade*. See also,
A. M. Gambone, *The Life of General Samuel K. Zook*, Baltimore, Maryland: Butternut and Blue, 1995, pp. 163-164.
[27] Walter H. Hebert, *Fighting Joe Hooker*, New York: The Bobbs-Merrill Company, 1944, reprint; Gaithersburg, Maryland: Butternut Press, Inc., 1987, pp. 245, 269-270.
[28] *Battles and Leaders*, vol. III, p. 243.
[29] Horace Greeley, *The American Conflict*, 2 vols., Hartford, Connecticut: O. D. Case & Company, 1864 & 1866. Vol. II, p. 375. See also,
Hebert, *Fighting Joe Hooker*, p. 247.
[30] *Joint Committee Report*, General George G. Meade, March 5, 1864, p. 329.
[31] *Alexander S. Webb to his Father*, July 17, 1863, courtesy, USAMHI.
[32] Gambone, *The Life of General Samuel K. Zook*, p. 164.
[33] Corby, *Memoirs of Chaplain Life*, pp. 172-173.

Chapter One Endnotes

[34] *Joint Committee Report*, General George G. Meade, March 5, 1864, p. 329.

[35] Gibbon, *Personal Recollections of the Civil War*, pp. 128-129.

[36] Johnson and Dumas, ed., *Dictionary of American Biography*, vol. IV, pp. 236-237.

[37] James Longstreet, *From Manassas to Appomattox, Memoirs of the Civil War in America*, Philadelphia, Pennsylvania: 1896, reprint; Secaucus, New Jersey: The Blue and Grey Press, 1984, pp. 346-348. Hereafter, referred to as *From Manassas to Appomattox*. See also,

Douglas Southall Freeman, *Robert E. Lee*, 4 vols., New York: Charles Scribner's Sons, 1934, reprint; Charles Scribner's Sons, 1962, vol. III, pp. 60-61. See also,

Jeffry D. Wert, *General James Longstreet*, New York: Simon and Schuster, 1993, pp. 254-255.

[38] Freeman, *R. E. Lee*, vol. III, p. 62.

[39] Corby, *Memoirs of Chaplain Life*, pp. 173-174.

[40] *O. R.*, I., vol. XXVII, part III, p.395. See also,
The Bachelder Papers, vol. III, p. 1348.

[41] *O. R.*, I., vol. XXVII, part III, p. 396. See also,
Harry W. Pfanz, *Gettysburg, The Second Day*, Chapel Hill, North Carolina: The University of North Carolina Press, 1987, p. 17.

[42] Coddington, *The Gettysburg Campaign*, p. 228. See also,
Joint Committee Report, General W. S. Hancock, March 22, 1864, p. 403.

[43] Gilbert Frederick, *The Story of a Regiment*, Chicago: The Fifty-Seventh [N.Y.] Veterans Association, 1895, p. 164.

[44] Favill, *Diary of a Young Officer*, p. 241.

[45] *O. R.*, I., vol. XXVII, part I, p. 267.

[46] Emory M. Thomas, *Bold Dragoon, The Life of J.E.B. Stuart*, New York: Harper & Row, Publishers, 1986, pp. 242-244. See also,
Wilbur Sturtevant Nye, *Here Come the Rebels!*, Dayton, Ohio: Press of Morningside Bookshop, 1988, p. 320.

[47] *The Bachedler Papers*, vol. III, p. 1348.

[48] **Ibid.**, pp. 11-12.

[49] Favill, *Diary of a Young Officer*, p. 242.

[50] Frederick, *The Story of a Regiment*, p. 163.

[51] Jacob H. Cole, *Under Five Commanders*, Paterson, New Jersey: News Printing Company, 1906, p. 164. See also,

Chapter One Endnotes

Michael Phipps & John S. Peterson, *"The Devil's to Pay," Gen. John Buford, USA*, Gettysburg: Farnsworth Military Impressions, 1995, p. 37.

52 *The Bachelder Papers*, vol. II, p. 961. *See also*,
Mulholland, *The Story of the 116th Regiment, Pennsylvania Infantry*, p. 130.

53 Millard K. Bushong, *Old Jube*, Shippensburg, Pennsylvania: White Mane Publishing Co., Inc., 1955, p. 138.

54 *O. R.*, I, vol. XXVII, part III, p. 435.

55 **Ibid.**, p. 436.

56 **Ibid.**

57 *The New York Times*, June 30, 1863.

58 **Ibid.**

59 **Ibid.**, June 29, 1863.

60 *O. R.*, I., vol. XXVII, part III, p. 416.

61 *O. R.*, I., vol. XXVII, part III, p. 415.

62 Walker, *General Hancock*, p. 102.

63 *The New York Times*, July 1, 1863.

Chapter Two

"Terminological Inexactitude"

1 Rev. Dr. Jacobs, *Meteorology of the Battle*, courtesy, GNMP. The weather conditions given by Dr. Jacobs are for Gettysburg proper. The author believes that while conditions might have varied slightly between the 13 miles separating Gettysburg and Taneytown, any differences would be slight.

2 Mulholland, *The Story of the 116th Regiment, Pennsylvania Infantry*, p. 369. *See also*,
Frederick E. Goodrich, *The Life and Public Service of Winfield Scott Hancock, Major-General, U.S.A.*, Boston: Lee & Shepard, 1880, p. 133.

3 *Joint Committee Report*, General W. S. Hancock, March 22, 1864, pp. 403–404. *See also*,
Ibid., General George G. Meade, March 5, 1864, p. 330.

Chapter Two Endnotes

[4] Meade, *The Life and Letters of General George Gordon Meade*, vol. II, pp. 35–36.

[5] *O. R.*, I., vol. XXVII, part I, pp. 924–925. *See also*,
Phipps & Peterson, *"The Devil's To Pay"*, p. 44. The author recommends this brief volume for those who wish an introduction to General Buford.

[6] Edward J. Nichols, *Toward Gettysburg, A Biography of General John F. Reynolds*, The Pennsylvania State University, 1958, reprint; Gaithersburg, Maryland: Olde Soldier Books, Inc., 1987, p. 194.

[7] *Charles H. Veil to D. McConaughy*, April 7, 1864, p. 1, courtesy, Pennsylvania Historical and Museum Commission and USAMHI, The Robert L. Brake Collection, General John F. Reynolds folder.

[8] Meade, *The Life and Letters of General George Gordon Meade*, vol. II, p. 35. Note, in this volume, Captain Stephen Weld is erroneously referred to as Captain Stephen H. Weed, who was a brigadier-general commanding the Third Brigade, Second Division, V Corps. This correction was brought to the author's attention by Dr. Harry Pfanz, author of *Gettysburg, The Second Day*.

[9] Some reports of Reynolds's death state that he was shot by the bullet of a sharpshooter. After a critical review of an early draft of this chapter, Dr. Harry Pfanz and Gettysburg Battlefield Guide, Tim Smith, both challenged the sharpshooter theory. Specifically, Dr. Pfanz stated: "With all of the bullets flying who can say that Reynolds was shot by a sharpshooter?" However, while the author agrees with both historians, that doesn't end the issue for everyone. *See also*,

Nichols, *Toward Gettysburg, A Biography of General John F. Reynolds*, p. 205. *See also*,

George H. Otis, *The Second Wisconsin Infantry*, Alan D. Gaff, ed., Dayton, Ohio: Press of Morningside Bookshop, 1984, p. 290. In this volume, Dr. Pfanz appears to receive some support from one of the members of the "Iron Brigade," who wrote: "He [Reynolds] was struck by a *stray ball* immediately after the volley the Second Wisconsin received as it charged over the top of the ridge where Archer's Brigade was lying." [Emphasis added] *See also*,

O. O. Howard to Jacobs, March 23, 1864, courtesy, Bowdoin College. The precise answer to Dr. Pfanz's question is uncertain, but it is easy to appreciate how casual statements become tradition, which have a way of becoming "historical facts." In the above letter, General How-

Chapter Two Endnotes

ard noted that Reynolds was shot "by that said to have been from a 'sharpshooter'." [Emphasis in original] *See also,*

Charles S. Wainwright, *A Diary of Battle*, Allan Nevins, ed., New York: Harcourt, Brace & World, Inc., 1962, p. 232. In this volume, Colonel Wainwright, commander of the artillery brigade for the First Corps, noted: "In the midst of the battle Reynolds fell from his horse dead, with a sharpshooter's bullet through his brain." *See also,*

Aaron Brainard Jerome, *Buford in the Battle of Oak Ridge, The 1st Day's Fight at Gettysburg A.M. Wednesday, 1st July, 1863*, courtesy, Michael Phipps. This undated letter/report was written by Lieutenant Jerome, an aide to General Buford. It was written after he had sent a prior letter to General Hancock on October 18, 1865. Hereafter, referred to as *Buford in the Battle.*

10 *Charles H. Veil to D. McConaughy*, April 7, 1866, pp. 3 and 4.
11 *The National Tribune*, April 14, 1910.
12 Stephen Minot Weld, *War Diary and Letters*, Boston: 1912, pp. 231–232.
13 Meade, *The Life and Letters of General George Gordon Meade*, vol. II, p. 35.
14 Daniel Alexander Skelly, *A Boy's Experiences During the Battles of Gettysburg*, Gettysburg: By the Author, 1932, pp. 11–12. *See also,*

Charles H. Howard, "First Day at Gettysburg," *War Papers*, vol. IV, Military Essays and Recollections, Illinois MOLLUS, read on October 1, 1903, p. 244.

15 Oliver Otis Howard, "Campaign and Battle of Gettysburg, June and July, 1863," *Atlantic Monthly*, vol. XXXVIII, no. 225 [July, 1876]: 54. Hereafter, referred to as "Campaign and Battle of Gettysburg." In this article, General Howard provides an excellent reminder, "All the time[s] I give was by my own watch. I notice variations in the time from a half to three quarters of an hour, as different officers have recorded the same event." *See also,*

A. Wilson Greene, *The First Day at Gettysburg*, Gary W. Gallagher, ed., "From Chancellorsville to Cemetery Hill, O. O. Howard and the Eleventh Corps Leadership," Kent, Ohio: The Kent State University Press, 1992, p. 71. Hereafter, referred to as Greene, "Howard and the Eleventh Corps Leadership." Note: Some reports vary regarding the names of the aides who approached General Howard with the news that General Reynolds was wounded and, later, killed. *See also,*

Skelly, *A Boy's Experiences During the Battles of Gettysburg*, p. 12. In his volume, Skelly claims that the messenger was a George Guinn, a member of Cole's Maryland Cavalry and a person well-known by Skelly.

[16] Cleaves, *Meade of Gettysburg*, p. 135. See also,
O. R., I., vol. XXVII, part I, p. 702.

[17] Meade, *The Life and Letters of General George Gordon Meade*, vol. II, p. 34.

[18] Hancock, *Reminiscences*, pp. 185–186.

[19] *Joint Committee Report*, General W. S. Hancock, March 22, 1864, pp. 404–405.

[20] Hancock, *Reminiscences*, pp. 290–291. After General Hancock's death, the former Captain George Gordon Meade, son of the major-general, wrote that the first time he met Hancock was at Fredericksburg. Hancock had come to speak to Meade's father and the young officer found himself impressed with Hancock's striking demeanor. When Hancock left the senior Meade, the youthful officer asked his father who the visiting commander was and General Meade replied: "Why, don't you know who that is? Why, that's Hancock." See also,

Cleaves, *Meade of Gettysburg*, pp. 300–302. Despite these warm feelings that Meade expressed for Hancock, their relationship does not end on a good basis. Author's note: All the reason for Meade remaining in Taneytown, as opposed to his going to Gettysburg immediately, are not clear. It appears that he felt that battle at Pipe Creek was still a possibility, so he remained in nearby Taneytown.

[21] Meade, *The Life and Letters of General George Gordon Meade*, vol. I, p. 349. See also,

Cleaves, *Meade of Gettysburg*, p. 143.

[22] WSH, "Gettysburg Reply to General Howard," *The Galaxy* [December, 1876]: 822. According to Hancock: "The commissions of Generals Howard and Sickles, as Major-Generals of Volunteers, bore the same date as my own, but their commissions as Brigadier antedated mine, and that determined our relative ranks as Major-Generals of Volunteers." *See also,*

Joint Committee Report, General W. S. Hancock, March 22, 1864. In his testimony on p. 492, Hancock stated that while Meade showed or told him of the authority Washington granted him, in his own opinion: "That did not make it legal, because it was contrary to law to place a junior officer over a senior. At the same time it was one of those emergencies in which Genl Meade was authorized as before stated, to exercise that power."

Chapter Two Endnotes 241

[23] WSH, "Gettysburg Reply to General Howard," p. 821. *See also*,
Joint Committee Report, General W. S. Hancock, March 22, 1864, pp. 404–405. *See also*,
Gibbon, *Personal Recollections of the War*, pp. 389–411. While Generals Hancock and Gibbon shared a warm relationship, even they became embroiled in a controversy of sorts following the battle of the Wilderness.

[24] Richard Elliot Winslow III, *General John Sedgwick, The Story of a Union Commander*, Novato, California: Presidio Press, 1982, pp. 103–104.

[25] Michael A. Cavanaugh, Compiler, "Field Operations—First Day of Gettysburg," by J. William Hofmann, *Military Essays and Recollections of the Philadelphia Commandery MOLLUS*, Wilmington, North Carolina: Broadfoot Publishing Company, vol. 1, February 22, 1866–May 6, 1903, 1995, p. 294.

[26] WSH, "Gettysburg Reply to General Howard," p. 826.

[27] *O. R.*, I., vol. XXVII, part III, p. 461.

[28] *Joint Committee Report*, General W. S. Hancock, March 22, 1864, p. 492. Hancock's comment about being an "older soldier" is directed at his military longevity. He graduated from West Point in 1844 while Howard graduated in 1854. Dan Sickles was not a professional soldier though, chronologically, he was the oldest of the three men.

[29] Coddington, *The Gettysburg Campaign*, pp. 284–285. *See also*,
Tucker, *Hancock the Superb*, p. 130. *See also*,
O. R., I., vol. XXVII, part I, pp. 367–368.

[30] L. A. Smith, "Recollections of Gettysburg," *War Papers*, Michigan MOLLUS, From December 7, 1893 to May 5, 1898, reprint; Wilmington, North Carolina: Broadfoot Publishing Company, 1993, p. 298.

[31] Jordan, *Winfield Scott Hancock, A Soldier's Life*, p. 81. *See also*,
The Bachelder Papers, vol. III, p. 1350.

[32] *O. R.*, I., vol. XXVII, part I, pp. 924–925. *See also*,
Coddington, *The Gettysburg Campaign*, p. 303. Understandably, General Howard did not share General Buford's feeling here.

[33] *O. O. Howard to D. H. Davis and Company*, September 14, 1875. The Robert L. Brake Collection, courtesy, USAMHI.

[34] WSH, "Gettysburg Reply to General Howard," p. 827. *See also*,
The Bachelder Papers, vol. I, pp. 200–202. This letter is dated October 18, 1865, from Lieutenant Aaron Brainard Jerome, an aide to General Buford, to General Hancock. The author is unable to locate any such

Chapter Two Endnotes

written message from Buford and while he questions the validity of such a communiqué, Jerome's letter is considered to be highly reliable by others. Jerome does state that he is uncertain if the message was written or verbal. For others who have cited Jerome's message as factual, *see also,*

Tucker, ***Hancock the Superb***, p. 132. *See also,*

Phipps & Peterson, *"The Devil's To Pay"*, p. 52. *See also,*

Jerome, ***Buford in the Battle***. In this letter/report, Jerome states that Buford urgently pleaded with General Meade: "For God's sake send up Hancock, Everything at odds. Reynolds is killed, and we need a controlling spirit."

[35] Coddington, ***The Gettysburg Campaign***, p. 700. Professor Coddington also concluded that Hancock's arrival was between 4:00 and 4:30 p.m.

[36] William C. Oates, ***The War Between the Union and the Confederacy, and Its Lost Opportunities; The History of the 15th Alabama***, New York: The Neale Publishing Company, 1905. Hereafter, referred to as ***The History of the 15th Alabama***. *See also,*

James H. Cooper to "Mac", June 14, 1886, courtesy, USAMHI and GNMP. Cooper was in command of Battery B, 1st Pennsylvania Light Artillery, under General Doubleday. In his letter, Cooper indicates that Hancock might have arrived on the field as late as 5:30 p.m. Unfortunately, the letter is incomplete.

[37] Francis Wiggins, "Sixteenth Maine Regiment at Gettysburg," ***War Papers***, vol. IV, Portland: Lefavor-Tower Company, 1915, reprint; Wilmington, North Carolina: Broadfoot Publishing Company, 1992, pp. 161–162.

[38] Edward Whittier, 5th Maine Battery, a private note, courtesy, Brian C. Pohanka.

[39] John G. Nicolay and John Hay, ***Abraham Lincoln, A History***, 10 vols., New York: The Century Company, 1890, vol. VII, p. 243.

[40] Allan Nevins, ***Ordeal of the Union, The War for the Union***, 8 vols., New York: Charles Scribner's Sons, 1971, vol. IV, p. 457.

[41] **Ibid**.

[42] Carl Sanburg, ***Abraham Lincoln, The War Years***, 4 vols., New York: Harcourt, Brace & Company, 1939, vol. II, p. 355.

[43] Larry M. Strayer & Richard A. Baumgartner, eds., ***Echoes of Battle, The Atlanta Campaign***, Blue Acorn Press, 1991, pp. 116–120.

Chapter Two Endnotes 243

[44] Stewart Sifakis, *Who Was Who in the Civil War*, New York: Facts on File Publications, 1988, p. 321. *See also,*
Warner, *Generals in Blue*, pp. 237–238. *See also,*
Mark Boatner III, *The Civil War Dictionary*, New York: David McKay Company, Inc., pp. 413–414. *See also,*
W. F. Beyer and O. F. Keydel, eds., *Deeds of Valor*, Detroit, Michigan: Perrien-Keydel Co., 1903, reprint; Stamford, Connecticut: Longmeadow Press, 1992, pp. 38–39. *See also,*
Dumas Malone, ed., *Dictionary of American Biography*, vol. V, New York: Charles Scribner's Sons, 1960–1961, pp. 279–281.

[45] Coddington, *The Gettysburg Campaign*, p. 282.

[46] *O. R.*, I., vol. XXVII, part I, p. 702.

[47] **Ibid.**, pp. 702 and 727.

[48] Howard, "Campaign and Battle of Gettysburg," pp. 55–56. *See also,*
O. R., I., vol. XXVII, part I., p. 721.

[49] Bushong, *Old Jube*, pp. 145 and 289. General Early remained an ardent unreconstructed Rebel for the rest of his life. One of his many inaccurate irritants was that as soon as Grant was sworn in as President, one of the new chief executive's first acts was to remove General Hancock as military governor of Louisiana and Texas.

[50] *O. R.*, I., vol. XXVII, part I, p. 292.

[51] Coddington, *The Gettysburg Campaign*, p. 292.

[52] Howard, "First Day at Gettysburg," pp. 260–261.

[53] *O. R.*, I., vol. XXVII, part I., p. 151. *See also,*
Ibid., part III, p. 1065. *See also,*
Joint Committee Report, March 1, 1864, General Abner Doubleday, p. 309. Note that General Doubleday estimated the total strength of the I and XI Corps to be approximately 14,000 men with 3–4,000 in reserve. He also estimated the total strength of the Confederate troops at 60,000 men. However, Doubleday is quick to add: "I do not mean that 60,000 of the enemy were in the front line opposed to us, but that there were 60,000 including the reserves of the two rebel corps..." It is more likely that the combined forces in Richard Ewell's and A. P. Hill's Second and Third Corps were about 30,000 men.

[54] *O. R.*, I., vol. XXVII, part I, pp. 250 and 729.

[55] Timothy H. Smith, *The Story of Lee's Headquarters, Gettysburg, Pennsylvania*, Gettysburg: Thomas Publications, 1995, pp. 27–28.

Chapter Two Endnotes

[56] *Francis C. Barlow to His Mother*, July 7, 1863. The Robert L. Brake collection, courtesy, USAMHI.

[57] *O. R.*, I., vol. XXVII, part I, pp. 250 and 704

[58] Greene, "Howard and Eleventh Corps Leadership," p. 83.

[59] *The Bachelder Papers*, vol. III, p. 1350.

[60] *Joint Committee Report*, General W. S. Hancock, March 22, 1864, p. 405.

[61] Edward C. Culp, *The 25th Ohio Veteran Volunteer Infantry in the War for the Union*, Topeka, Kansas: Geo. W. Crane & Co., 1885, p. 77.

[62] *O. R.*, I., vol. XXVII, part I, p. 368. *See also,*
Jerome, *Buford in the Battle*.

[63] Hartwell Osborn, *Trials and Triumphs, The Record of the Fifty-fifth Ohio Volunteer Infantry*, Chicago: A. C. McClurg & Co., 1904, p. 97.

[64] *Joint Committee Report*, General W. S. Hancock, March 22, 1864, p. 405.

[65] *Battles and Leaders*, vol. III, p. 285. The reader should know that Captain Halstead claimed, after the war, that he was the only other person on the spot when Hancock and Howard had their discussion. That claim is at odds with reports from Captain J. O. Kerby and Captain William G. Mitchell of Hancock's staff. *See also,*
E. P. Halstead, "The First Day of the Battle of Gettysburg." This was a paper prepared by Halstead and delivered to the Washington, D.C. MOLLUS Commandery on March 2, 1887, courtesy, USAMHI.

[66] **Ibid**. *See also,*
Abner Doubleday, *Chancellorsville and Gettysburg*, New York: Charles Scribner's Sons, 1881, reprint; Harrisburg, Pennsylvania: The Archive Society, 1992, p. 151. Note that General Doubleday is considered by some historians as a very unreliable source. *See also,*
John A. Carpenter, "Doubleday's Chancellorsville and Gettysburg," *Military Affairs*, vol. 27 [Summer, 1963]: 84–88. In this article, Dr. Carpenter critiqued portions of Doubleday's book, *Chancellorsville and Gettysburg*, and its contribution toward improving the understanding of the war. In part, Dr. Carpenter stated that Doubleday "...felt a personal animosity toward two of the major participants in those battles, Generals Meade and Howard, and the result is a book which turns out to be a polemic of little literary or historical value." See pp. 87-88 of Dr. Carpenter's article for other Doubleday critics that he cites. While this author acknowledges that Doubleday's work contains some flaws, it is not as bad as Dr. Carpenter presents. To dis-

card his work would be tantamount to "throwing out the baby with the bath water."
[67] *O. R.*, I., vol. XXVII, part I, p. 252.
[68] *Philadelphia Weekly Press*, July 14, 1887.
[69] *S.H.S.P.*, vol. V, p. 169.
[70] *Philadelphia Weekly Press*, August 3, 1887.
[71] Carpenter, "Doubleday's Chancellorsville and Gettysburg," p. 85. See also, Doubleday, *Chancellorsville and Gettysburg*, p. 137.
[72] *Joint Committee Report*, March 1, 1864, General Abner Doubleday, p. 308.
[73] **Ibid.**, pp. 32, 34 and 72.
[74] Bruce Catton, *The Army of the Potomac, Mr. Lincoln's Army*, New York: Doubleday & Company, 1951, p. 203.
[75] William K. Winkler, ed., *Letters of Frederick C. Winkler 1862 to 1865*, By the family, 1963, pp. 43, 52 and 153.
[76] Isaac Jones Wistar, *Autobiography of Isaac Jones Wistar*, Philadelphia: The Wistar Institute of Anatomy and Biology, 1937, p. 398, courtesy, GNMP.
[77] Albert Castel, *Decision in the West, The Atlanta Campaign of 1864*, Lawrence, Kansas: University of Kansas Press, 1992, p. 98.
[78] *Battles and Leaders*, vol. III, pp. 196 and 220. On p. 196, Howard claims that he never received an important message from General Hooker. On p. 220, Major-General Carl Schurz, Howard's second-in-command, claims that his superior *did* indeed receive Hooker's message. *See also,*
O. R., I., vol. XXV, part I, pp. 647–660.
[79] **Ibid.**, vol. XXVII, part I, p. 261. Note: General Newton did not assume command of the I Corps until either very late in the evening of the first or very early on the morning of the second. Doubleday wrote in his report: "...on the evening [no specific time] of July 1, I resumed command of the Third Division of the First Corps..."
[80] The author is unable to locate any report or record of a report, from Howard to Meade, regarding the fleeing of the I Corps. This charge by Doubleday appears to be wholly unfounded and General Hancock agrees. *See also,*
Carpenter, "Doubleday's Chancellorsville and Gettysburg," p. 85. In his article, Dr. Carpenter states: "It is most unlikely that Howard ever sent such a message to Meade."

Chapter Two Endnotes

[81] Author's note: On p. 101 of this journal, the publisher noted: "We publish in this issue, in facsimile, some extracts from Doubleday's *Chancellorsville and Gettysburg*, with the notes thereon made by General Hancock in the copy recently found in the Adjutant-General's Office, Headquarters Department of the East, on Governor's Island."

[82] Sidney G. Cooke, "The First Day of Gettysburg," *War Talk in Kansas*, Kansas City, Missouri: Franklin Hudson Publishing Company, 1906, reprint; Wilmington, North Carolina: Broadfoot Publishing Company, 1992, p. 284.

[83] *O. R.*, I., vol. XXVII, part I, pp. 712–713. *See also*,
The Bachelder Papers, vol. III, pp. 1351–1352.

[84] *O. O. Howard to Mr. M. S. O'Donnell*, March 9, 1891, courtesy, Northwest Corner [Conn.] CWRT and USAMHI.

[85] WSH, "Gettysburg Reply to General Howard," p. 825. *See also*,
John Purifoy, "The Battle of Gettysburg, July 2," *Confederate Veteran*, vol. XXXI, No. 7 [July, 1923]: 252. According to Colonel William C. Oates, of the 15th Alabama, late in the day of the second "Ewell received a message from General Lee to attack it [Cemetery Hill] if he could do so with advantage. He could not bring artillery to bear on it..."

[86] Doubleday, *Chancellorsville and Gettysburg*, p. 149.

[87] R. K. Beecham, *Gettysburg, The Pivotal Battle of the Civil War*, Chicago: A. C. McClurg & Co., 1911, pp. 93–94.

[88] Abner Doubleday, "Gettysburg Thirty Years After," *North American Review*, No. CCCCXI [February, 1891]: 146. Note, this work also contains articles by Generals Howard and Slocum plus the Count of Paris.

[89] *S.H.S.P.*, vol. V, pp. 168–169.

[90] Lance J. Herdegen and William J. K. Beaudot, *In the Bloody Railroad Cut at Gettysburg*, Dayton, Ohio: Morningside House, Inc., 1990, p. 228.

[91] **Ibid.**, p. 172. *See also*,
Gary W. Gallagher, *The First Day at Gettysburg*, Gary W. Gallagher, ed., "Confederate Corps Leadership on the First Day at Gettysburg; A. P. Hill and Richard S. Ewell in a Difficult Debut," p. 40.

[92] *Philadelphia Weekly Times*, November 3, 1877.

[93] John B. Gordon, *Reminiscences of the Civil War*, New York: Charles Scribner's Sons, 1903, reprint; Alexandria, Virginia: Time-Life Books, Inc., 1981, p. 156.

Chapter Two Endnotes

[94] Edward P. Alexander, *Fighting For the Confederacy, The Personal Recollections of General Edward Porter Alexander*, Gary W. Gallagher, ed., Chapel Hill, North Carolina: The University of North Carolina Press, 1989, p. 233. Hereafter, referred to as *Fighting For the Confederacy*.

[95] Johnson and Dumas, eds., *Dictionary of American Biography*, vol. IV, p. 230.

[96] *Abner Doubleday to Mr. S. O. Donnell*, February 26, 1891. Courtesy, Northwest Corner [Conn.] CWRT and USAMHI.

[97] *S.H.S.P.*, vol. V, p. 173.

[98] *O. R.*, I., vol. XXVII, part II, p. 445. See also,
Ibid., part I, p. 368. See also,
S.H.S.P., vol. V, p. 168. See also,
Ralph Lowell Eckert, *John Brown Gordon, Soldier–Southerner–American*, Baton Rouge, Louisiana: Louisiana State University Press, 1989, pp. 54–55. Hereafter, referred to as *John Brown Gordon*.

[99] Doubleday, "Thiry Years After," p. 147.

[100] *Army and Navy Journal*, August 14, 1886.

[101] *WSH to Francis A. Walker*, December 12, 1885, courtesy, CWLM. See also,
Joint Committee Report, March 22, 1864, General W. S. Hancock, p. 405. See also,
O. R., I., vol. XXVII, part I, pp. 266–267, 825. See also,
William H. Powell, *The Fifth Army Corps*, New York: G. P. Putnam's Sons, 1896, pp. 521 and 556.

[102] Tucker, *Hancock at Gettysburg*, p. 10.

[103] Powell, *The Fifth Army Corps*, p. 368. See also,
John D. S. Cook, "Personal Reminiscences of Gettysburg," *War Talk in Kansas*, p. 284.

[104] *The Putnam Ledger*, May 16, 1978. Relations and trust between Generals Meade and Butterfield were not exactly the best. In this report, written about local Generals Butterfield, Couch and Warren, the author contends that Butterfield "...was in the center of controversies. He was roundly despised by many of his fellow officers—Meade was warned of his possible treachery."

[105] *O. R.*, I., vol. XXVII, part I, p. 927.

[106] WSH, "Gettysburg Reply to General Howard," p. 828. See also,
Joint Committee Report, March 9, 1864, General G. K. Warren, p. 377.

Chapter Two Endnotes

[107] *O. R.*, I., vol. XXVII, part I, pp. 712–713.
[108] Walker, *General Hancock*, p. 112. See also,
O. R., I., vol. XXVII, part I, p. 361. See also,
Edward N. Whittier, "The Left Attack (Ewell's) At Gettysburg," Massachusetts MOLLUS *War Papers*, Volume I, pp. 77 and 86.
[109] Carl Schurz, "The Battle of Gettysburg," *McClure's Magazine* [July, 1907]: 277.
[110] *The Bachelder Papers*, vol. III, p. 1352.
[111] Coddington, *The Gettysburg Campaign*, p. 313.
[112] *Henry W. Slocum to T. H. Davis & Co.*, September 8, 1875, courtesy, GNMP. The author strongly suggests that interested parties should consult this letter for General Slocum's explanation of what transpired on July 1, 1863 and beyond. The data contained in this letter seriously challenge the conclusions drawn by General Howard and Pennsylvania historian Samuel P. Bates. See also,
Charles Elihu Slocum, *The Life and Services of Major-General Henry Warner Slocum*, Toledo, Ohio: The Slocum Publishing Company, 1913, pp 101–102. See also,
O. R., I., vol. XXVII, part I, p. 825. See also,
The National Tribune, April 14, 1910.
[113] *O. R.*, I., vol. XXVII, part I, p. 368.
[114] John A. Carpenter, "General O. O. Howard at Gettysburg," *Civil War History*, vol. 9, no. 3, Kent, Ohio: The Kent State University Press [September, 1963]: 261–276. Note: When this article was written, Dr. Carpenter was associate professor at Washington and Jefferson College. See also,
John A. Carpenter, *Sword and Olive Branch*, Pittsburgh: University of Pittsburgh Press, 1964, p. 53.
[115] Charles S. Wainwright, *A Diary of Battle, The Personal Journals of Charles S. Wainwright*, Allan Nevins, ed., New York: Harcourt, Brace & World, Inc., 1962, p. 23–240.
[116] *O. R.*, I., vol. XXVII, part I, p. 704.
[117] **Ibid.**, p. 368. See also,
The Bachelder Papers, vol. III, pp. 1350–1351. This is an account from Hancock's aide, Lieutenant-Colonel Charles H. Morgan, who states that Hancock said to Howard, when they met at the cemetery gate: "General, I have been ordered here to take command of all troops on the field, until General Slocum arrives."

Chapter Two Endnotes

[118] WSH, "Gettysburg Reply to General Howard," p. 825.
[119] *Battles and Leaders*, vol. III, pp. 283–284.
[120] *WSH to Joseph Hooker*, July 27, 1876, courtesy, Pennsylvania State Archives.
[121] Howard, "Campaign and Battle of Gettysburg," pp. 58–60.
[122] WSH, "Gettysburg Reply to General Howard," p. 830.
[123] Howard, "Campaign and Battle of Gettysburg," pp. 58–60.
[124] Emerson Gifford Taylor, *Gouverneur Kemble Warren*, Boston: Houghton Mifflin Company, 1932, reprint; Gaithersburg, Maryland: Ron. R. Van Sickle Military Books, 1988, pp. 120–121. *See also*,
Cleaves, *Meade of Gettysburg*, p. 175.
[125] *O. R.*, I., vol. XXVII, part III, p. 466. *See also*,
Ibid., part I, pp. 71–72.
[126] Howard, "Campaign and Battle of Gettysburg," p. 60.
[127] Cleaves, *Meade of Gettysburg*, pp. 140–141. *See also*,
Meade, *The Life and Letters of General George Gordon Meade*, vol. II, pp. 62–63. *See also*,
O. R., I., vol. XXVII, part I, p. 115.
[128] *WSH to Joseph Hooker*, July 27, 1876, courtesy USAMHI.
[129] WSH, "Gettysburg Reply to General Howard," pp. 825 and 830.
[130] *WSH to Joseph Hooker*, July 23, 1876.
[131] WSH, "Gettysburg Reply to General Howard," pp. 821–831.
[132] *Oliver Otis Howard Papers*, letter written by General Howard dated July 10, 1888 and marked, "Not to be sent." Courtesy, Special Collections, Bowdoin College.
[133] **Ibid**.
[134] Oliver Otis Howard, address to the graduating class, Syracuse University, June 10, 1903. Courtesy, Bowdoin College.
[135] Oliver Otis Howard, *Autobiography of Oliver Otis Howard*, 2 vols., New York: The Baker & Taylor Company, 1907, vol. I, p. 418.
[136] *O. R.*, I., vol. XXVII, part I, p. 696. The reference to General Slocum relates to those who believe he was reluctant to assume command and that he delayed deliberately. Today, some historians seriously question that school of thought.
[137] *The National Tribune*, November 29, 1888.
[138] *WSH to O. O. Howard*, March 14, 1864, courtesy, Pennsylvania State Archives and Bowdoin College.

Chapter Two Endnotes

[139] *O. R.*, I., vol. XXVII, part I, p. 366. Certainly, logic dictates that if there was *any* doubt that Hancock was in command, he would not have told Meade that he would "transfer the command" to General Slocum.

[140] *Joint Committee Report*, General George G. Meade, March 5, 1864, p. 330.

[141] Meade, *The Life and Letters of General George Gordon Meade*, vol. II, pp. 40–41.

[142] *O. R.*, I., vol. XXVII, part III, p. 466.

[143] **Ibid.**, part I, pp. 696–697. *See also,*
WSH, "Gettysburg Reply to General Howard," p. 89. Relative to Howard's first learning of his appointment at 7:00 that evening, Hancock expresses serious doubt when he noted: "The apparent intention of that sentence is to convey the impression that he had no knowledge of the existence of that order until that time."

[144] *O. R.*, I., vol. XXVII, part III, pp. 824–825.

[145] *O. R.*, I., vol. XXVII, part I, p. 115.

[146] *Joint Committee Report*, General George G. Meade, March 5, 1864, p. 330.

[147] *Abner Doubleday to Samuel P. Bates*, April 4, 1874. Samuel P. Bates Collection, courtesy, Pennsylvania Historical and Museum Commission and USAMHI.

[148] *O. R.*, I., vol. XXVII, part III, p. 368. *See also,*
Hancock, **Reminiscences**, p. 191. For some further insight into the precise timing and decision details relating to Meade's "ordering up the troops," the reader might want to consult pp. 192–194 of Mrs. Hancock's book. *See also,*
WSH, "Gettysburg Reply to General Howard," p. 830. Note: This statement by Meade about sending up the troops is also subject to some debate.

[149] *The New York Times*, July 1, 1863.

[150] *O. R.*, I., vol. XXVII, part III, p. 480.

[151] Walker, *General Hancock*, p. 113.

[152] Gary Lash, *The Gibraltar Brigade on East Cemetery Hill*, Baltimore, Maryland: Butternut and Blue, 1995, p. 28.

[153] *O. R.*, I., vol. XXVII, part I, pp. 115 and 169. *See also,*
Cleaves, *Meade of Gettysburg*, p. 138. *See also,*
Thomas W. Hyde, *Civil War Letters of General Thomas W. Hyde*, John Hyde, 1933, p. 96. In this volume, Thomas Hyde, who was then on

Chapter Two Endnotes 251

the staff of Major-General John Sedgwick, noted that he passed Hancock on his way to see Meade and the time was "about 11 p.m." *See also,*
Joint Committee Report, General W. S. Hancock, March 22, 1864, p. 496.

[154] *S.H.S.P.*, vol. V, p. 168. *See also,*
Doubleday, "Gettysburg, Thirty Years After," p. 145. In this article, General Doubleday agrees with Hancock that a Rebel attack before 4 p.m. would have been successful.

[155] *The Bachelder Papers*, vol. III, p. 1353.

[156] *Gettysburg Compiler*, July 29, 1889, July 26, 1906 and July 9, 1932, courtesy, ACHS. *See also,*
Oliver Otis Howard, "Gettysburg Thirty Years After," *North American Review*, No. CCCCXI [February, 1891]: 138.

[157] *General Howard's Eulogy to General Slocum*, April 24, 1894, at Plymouth Church in Brooklyn, courtesy, Bowdoin College and Pennsylvania State Archives. *See also,*
Howard, "First Day at Gettysburg," p. 264. Note: No mention is made here of General Sickles joining Howard and Slocum in the gatehouse to catch some sleep. It appears that Sickles may have joined the two generals because he is present whenever General Meade arrives on Cemetery Hill.

[158] Henry W. Slocum, "Gettysburg Thirty Years After," *North American Review*, No. CCCCXI [February, 1891]: 141.

[159] *A. S. Webb Papers*, No. 007-110, p. 2, courtesy, Yale University Library. *See also,*
General Howard's Eulogy to General Slocum, April 24, 1894.

[160] Meade, *The Life and Letters of General George Gordon Meade*, vol. II, pp. 62–63. *See also,*
General Howard's Eulogy to General Slocum, April 24, 1894. *See also,*
Howard, "First Day at Gettysburg," p. 264. *See also,*
Cleaves, *Meade of Gettysburg*, p. 140.

[161] *The New York Times*, October 16, 1880.

[162] *The Bachelder Papers*, vol. III, p. 1952.

[163] Greene, "Howard and Eleventh Corps Leadership," in Gallagher, ed., *The First Day at Gettysburg*, p. 91.

[164] *S.H.S.P.*, vol. II, pp. 33–39. Robert E. Lee, "Final and Full Report of the Pennsylvania Campaign and Battle of Gettysburg."

[165] John W. Forny, *Life and Military Career of Winfield Scott Hancock*, Philadelphia: Hubbard Bros., 1880, p. 101.

Chapter Two Endnotes

[166] WSH, "Gettysburg Reply to General Howard," p. 831.
[167] *WSH to Joseph Hooker*, July 23, 1876.

Chapter Three

"I'd be God Damned"

[1] *Army and Navy Journal*, December 31, 1881.
[2] *Joint Committee Report*, General W. S. Hancock, March 22, 1864, p. 496. Author's note: Hancock is undoubtedly wrong about the time he left Taneytown. This type of error, even by the participants, is a good example of the confusion that time factors can create.
[3] Frank L. Byrne and Andrew T. Weaver, eds., *Haskell of Gettysburg*, Madison, Wisconsin: State Historical Society of Wisconsin, 1970, p. 103. *See also,*

Meade, *The Life and Letters of General George Gordon Meade*, vol. II, p. 63. According to a report in this volume, "between six and seven o'clock in the morning," General Gibbon reported to General Meade that the II Corps was approaching Gettysburg. Shortly thereafter, "General Hancock...arrived on the field and assumed command of his corps." *See also,*

Gibbon, *Personal Recollections of the Civil War*, p. 133.
[4] *Battles and Leaders*, vol. III, p. 294.
[5] *O. R.*, I., vol. XXVII, part I, p. 369. It is the opinion of this author that General Meade's changing concerns reflect the uncertainty of the moment rather than an indecisive posture on his part. Author's note.
[6] Byrne and Weaver, *Haskell of Gettysburg*, p. 108.
[7] *Joint Committee Report*, General W. S. Hancock, March 22, 1864, p. 497.
[8] *O. R.*, I., vol. XXVII, part I, p. 369.
[9] *Joint Committee Report*, General W. S. Hancock, March 22, 1864, p. 497.
[10] *Ibid.*, General George Gordon Meade, March 5, 1864, p. 331.
[11] Cleaves, *Meade of Gettysburg*, p. 143.
[12] Allen Johnson, ed., *Dictionary of American Biography*, vol. I, pp. 290–291. *See also,*

Richard A. Sauers, *A Caspian Sea of Ink: The Meade–Sickles Controversy*, Baltimore, Maryland: Butternut and Blue, 1989, p. 142.

Chapter Three Endnotes 253

[13] George Gordon Meade, ed., *The Battle of Gettysburg*, Ambler, Pennsylvania: By the editor, 1924, reprint; Gettysburg: Farnsworth House Military Impressions, 1988, p. 65.

[14] W. A. Swanberg, *Sickles the Incredible*, New York: Charles Scribner's Sons, 1956, reprint; Gettysburg: Stan Clark Military Books, 1991, p. 208.

[15] Edward G. Longacre, *The Man Behind the Guns*, New York: A. S. Barnes and Company, 1977, pp. 162–163.

[16] *The Bachelder Papers*, vol. III, p. 1389. N.B. Lieutenant-Colonel Harris was released from arrest on July 7, 1863.

[17] Richard Elliott Winslow III, *General John Sedgwick, The Story of a Union Corps Commander*, Novato, California: Presidio Press, 1982, p. 99. See also,

Penrose G. Mark, *Red: White: and Blue Badge, A History of the 93rd Regiment Pennsylvania Veteran Volunteers*, Harrisburg, Pennsylvania: The Aughinbaugh Press, 1911, pp. 213–214. Hereafter, referred to as *93rd Regiment Pennsylvania Volunteers*. See also,

George T. Stevens, *Three Years in the Sixth Corps*, Albany: S. R. Gray, Publisher, 1866, reprint; Alexandria, Virginia: Time-Life Books, Inc., 1984, p. 239.

[18] *O. R.*, I., vol. XXVII, part I, p. 665.

[19] Pfanz, *Gettysburg, The Second Day*, p. 267.

[20] Meade, *The Life and Letters of General George Gordon Meade*, vol. II, p. 78.

[21] Mulholland, *The Story of the 116th Regiment, Pennsylvania Infantry*, p. 371.

[22] *Joint Committee Report*, General W. S. Hancock, March 22, 1864, p. 497.

[23] *The Bachelder Papers*, vol. II, p. 1194 and vol. III, p. 1354.

[24] *O. R.*, I., vol. XXVII, part I, p. 416. See also,
Gibbon, *Personal Recollections of the Civil War*, p. 136.

[25] Byrne and Weaver, eds., *Haskell of Gettysburg*, p. 117.

[26] *O. R.*, I., vol. XXVII, part I, pp. 482–483.

[27] Longacre, *The Man Behind the Guns*, p. 162. See also,
Swanberg, *Sickles the Incredible*, pp. 208–209. See also,
Joint Committee Report, General W. S. Hancock, March 22, 1864, p. 406.

[28] *O. R.*, I., vol. XXVII, part I, pp. 112 and 151.

[29] Henry Edwin Tremain, *Two Days of War, A Gettysburg Narrative and Other Excursions*, New York: Bonnell, Silver and Bowers, 1905, p. 63. Hereafter, referred to as *Two Days of War*.

Chapter Three Endnotes

[30] Pfanz, *Gettysburg, The Second Day*, p. 406.
[31] Benjamin H. Child, "From Fredericksburg to Gettysburg," Rhode Island MOLLUS *War Papers*, vol. 8, p. 170.
[32] Tremain, *Two Days of War*, pp. 64–65.
[33] *WSH to Francis Walker*, December 12, 1885, courtesy, CWLM.
[34] Malone, *Dictionary of American Biography*, vol. IX, p. 255.
[35] Pfanz, *Gettysburg, The Second Day*, p. 268.
[36] *Joint Committee Report*, General W. S. Hancock, March 22, 1864, p. 406.
[37] *The Bachelder Papers*, vol. III, pp. 2000–2002.
[38] Gambone, *The Life of General Samuel K. Zook*, p. 6. *See also*, Corby, *Memoirs of Chaplain Life*, p. 184.
[39] Mulholland, *The Story of the 116th Regiment, Pennsylvania Infantry*, p. 372.
[40] D. Scott Hartwig, "Caldwell's Division in the Wheatfield," Gary Gallagher, ed., *The Second Day at Gettysburg*, Kent, Ohio: The Kent State University Press, 1993, p. 149.
[41] William Child, *A History of the Fifth Regiment, New Hampshire Volunteers in the American Civil War, 1861–1865*, Bristol, New Hampshire: R. W. Musgrove, 1893, reprint; Gaithersburg, Maryland: Ron R. Van Sickle Military Books, 1988, p. 217.
[42] Charles A. Hale, "With Colonel Cross at the Wheatfield," *Civil War Times Illustrated* [August, 1974]: pp. 30–38, courtesy, USAMHI.
[43] Gambone, *The Life of General Samuel K. Zook*, pp. 3–4.
[44] **Ibid.**, pp. 9 and 23. *See also*,
Hale, "With Colonel Cross at the Wheatfield," p. 38.
[45] Byrne and Weaver, eds., *Haskell of Gettysburg*, p. 125.
[46] Isaac R. Pennypacker, *General Meade*, New York: D. Appleton and Company, 1901, reprint; Gaithersburg, Maryland: Olde Soldier Books Inc., 1987, p. 176.
[47] Frank D. Sloat, *History of the Twenty-Seventh Regiment Connecticut Volunteer Infantry*, p. 6, courtesy, 27th Connecticut Volunteers, A Uniformed Historical Society.
[48] Kevin E. O'Brien, ed., *My Life in the Irish Brigade*, San Jose, California: Savas/Woodbury Publishers, 1996, p. 87.
[49] **Ibid.**, p. 88.
[50] *O. R.*, I., vol. XXVII, part I, p. 378.
[51] *Gettysburg Compiler*, June 6, 1899. *See also*,

Chapter Three Endnotes

Mark Boatner III, *The Civil War Dictionary*, New York: David McKay Company, Inc., 1959, p. 760.
[52] *Spanish Proverb.*
[53] *Joint Committee Report*, General W. S. Hancock, March 1, 1864, p. 407, March 22, 1864, p. 502. See also,
O. R., I., vol. XXVII, part I, p. 370.
[54] Gibbon, *Personal Recollections of the Civil War*, p. 137.
[55] *O. R.*, I., vol. XXVII, part I, pp. 483–484.
[56] **Ibid.**, p. 370. See also,
Louis P. A. d'Orleans, *History of the Civil War in America*, 7 vols., reprint; Philadelphia: Porter & Coates, 1888, vol. III, p. 645.
[57] *A. A. Humphreys to WSH*, October 2, 1863, courtesy, Historical Society of Pennsylvania. See also,
WSH to A. A. Humphreys, October 10, 1863, courtesy, Historical Society of Pennsylvania. See also,
Joint Committee Report, General W. S. Hancock, March 22, 1864, pp. 501–502. See also,
WSH to Francis A. Walker, November 7, 1865, courtesy, CWLM. According to Hancock, he encountered General Humphreys shortly after the episode with the 1st Minnesota.
[58] Eric A. Campbell, "Remember Harper's Ferry! The Degradation, Humiliation, and Redemption of Col. George L. Willard's Brigade," Part 2, *The Gettysburg Magazine*, Issue Number Eight [January, 1993]: 97. Hereafter, referred to as "Remember Harper's Ferry!" See also,
Pfanz, *Gettysburg, The Second Day*, pp. 404–406. See also,
The Bachelder Papers, vol. II, p. 1134. See also,
O. R., I., vol. XXVII, part I, pp. 370–371.
[59] **Ibid.**, pp. 474–475.
[60] William Barksdale, Participants File, courtesy, GNMP. Like so many Gettysburg claims, no one is exactly certain about the Union regiment that brought down General Barksdale. Author's note.
[61] Richard Moe, *The Last Full Measure, The Life and Death of the First Minnesota Volunteers*, New York: Henry Holt and Company, Inc., 1993, reprint; New York: Avon Books, 1993, pp. 269–272. Hereafter, referred to as *The Last Full Measure*. See also,
The Bachelder Papers, vol. I, pp. 256–259. See also,
Ezra J. Warner, *Generals in Gray*, Baton Rouge, Louisiana: Louisiana State University Press, 1959, pp. 16–17. See also,

Chapter Three Endnotes

Charles E. Hooker, *Confederate Military History*, vol. VII, part II, Chapter X, Atlanta, Georgia: Confederate Publishing Company, 1899, reprint; Harrisburg, Pennsylvania: The Archive Society, 1994, p. 180.

[62] Allen Johnson and Dumas Malone, eds., *Dictionary of American Biography*, vol. I, New York: Charles Scribner's Sons, 1957, pp. 607–608. *See also*,

Warner, *Generals in Gray*, pp. 16–17.

[63] *O. R.*, I., vol. XXVII, part I, pp. 472–473.

[64] Campbell, "Remember Harper's Ferry!," p. 97. *See also*,

Pfanz, *Gettysburg, The Second Day*, pp. 404–406.

[65] "Minnesota at Gettysburg," The Winfield Scott Hancock Papers, Scrapbook on his death and obituaries, courtesy, USAMHI.

[66] *WSH to Francis A. Walker*, November 5, 1885. *See also*,

Moe, *The Last Full Measure*, p. 268.

[67] *WSH to ?*, November 16, 1885, courtesy, CWLM. While this letter does not identify the addressee, it appears to have been written to General Francis A. Walker, *See also*,

Hancock, *Reminiscences*, p. 199.

[68] Moe, *The Last Full Measure*, p. 272.

[69] **Ibid.**, p. 275.

[70] *WSH to ?*, November 16, 1885. *See also*,

Bachelder to WSH, November 13, 1885, courtesy, CWLM. In his research, Bachelder concluded that the 1st Minnesota did not take any colors during their fight on July 1, 1863. Hancock was adamant that they did, and noted: "Mr. Bachelder must be mistaken about the colors...I saw the colors very close (from 50 to 100 paces), pointed them out to the Colonel [Colvill] and told him to take them." The matter has never been confidently concluded.

[71] *WSH to Francis A. Walker*, November 7, 1885.

[72] William Lochren, "The First Minnesota at Gettysburg," Minnesota MOLLUS *War Papers*, vol. 3, pp. 45–47. *See also*,

Moe, *The Last Full Measure*, p. 262.

[73] "Minnesota at Gettysburg," The Winfield Scott Hancock Papers, Scrapbook on his death and obituaries, courtesy, USAMHI.

[74] *The National Tribune*, February 12, 1885.

[75] Shakespeare, *I Henry IV*, IV, 1.

Chapter Three Endnotes

[76] *WSH to Francis A. Walker*, December 12, 1885, courtesy, CWLM. In this letter, General Hancock states that he supposed the regiment in question was the 19th Maine, which appears to be incorrect. See also,
O. R., I., vol. XXVII, part I, p. 422. In his battlefield report, Colonel Francis E. Heath, of the 19th Maine, states that he was sent to support "Brown's Rhode Island battery." However, Heath also states: "I also retook four Napoleon guns that had been abandoned by some of our forces that had been posted to my left and front." See also,
John B. Bachelder to WSH, November 13, 1885, courtesy, CWLM. Bachelder initially thought that the infantry sent to protect Weir's battery was the 13th Vermont under Lieutenant-Colonel William D. Munson.

[77] **Ibid**. Bachelder later confirms that it was Colonel Randall and a portion of the 13th Vermont which pulled off those guns. See also,
WSH to Francis A. Walker, January 2, 1886, courtesy, CWLM. See also,
Ibid., November 5, 1885, courtesy, CWLM. See also,
The Bachelder Papers, vol. I, pp. 54–55. See also,
O. R., I., vol. XXVII, part I, pp. 351–352. See also,
Coffin, *Full Duty*, p. 187.

[78] *The Bachelder Papers*, vol. II, p. 1058.

[79] *WSH to Francis A. Walker*, November 5, 1885.

[80] Pfanz, *Gettysburg, The Second Day*, p. 378.

[81] John Purifoy, "Battle of Gettysburg, July 2, 1863," *Confederate Veteran*, vol. XXXI, No. 11 [November, 1923]: p. 417.

[82] *The Bachelder Papers*, vol. III, p. 1651.

[83] *O. R.*, I., vol. XXVII, part I, p. 533. See also,
The Bachelder Papers, vol. II, p. 1135.

[84] **Ibid**., vol. III, p. 1356. See also,
Hartwig, "No Troops on the Field Had Done Better," *The Second Day at Gettysburg*, p. 170. According to Hartwig, Hancock ordered an investigation into Sykes's accusations and found that "no troops on the field had done better." However, Hartwig continues that "Hancock may have harbored a seed of doubt about his lieutenant," because Caldwell lost his command in 1864.

[85] *O. R.*, I., vol. XXVII, part I, pp. 379–380.

[86] Walker, *History of the Second Army Corps*, pp. 286–287. Hereafter, referred to as *History of the Second Army Corps*. See also,

Chapter Three Endnotes

O. R., I., vol. XXVII, part I, pp. 372. Soon after Hancock ordered Carroll's brigade to assist Howard, he also ordered the 71st and 106th Pennsylvania regiments to assist "General Slocum's front..."

[87] Gibbon, *Personal Recollections of the Civil War*, p. 138.

[88] *WSH to Francis A. Walker*, November 5, 1885. *See also*,
O. R., I., vol. XXVII, part I, p. 372.

[89] *The National Tribune*, April 6, 1893.

[90] Lash, *The Gibraltar Brigade on East Cemetery Hill*, p. 87. The author recommends this volume for those wishing to know more about the attack of the Gibraltar Brigade and its own controversy.

[91] *O. R.*, I., vol. XXVII, part I, p. 457.

[92] **Ibid.**, p. 894.

[93] *WSH to Joseph Hooker*, July 27, 1876, courtesy, Pennsylvania State Archives.

[94] *Samuel S. Carroll to WSH*, July 23, 1876, Robert L. Brake Collection, courtesy, USAMHI.

[95] **Ibid.** *See also*,
Lash, *The Gibraltar Brigade on East Cemetery Hill*, pp. 110–119. Before and after the end of the war, General Howard became embroiled in another controversy involving Carroll's brigade and their assistance on the night of July 2, 1863. *See also*,
Samuel S. Carroll to WSH, July 23, 1876.

[96] *O. R.*, I., vol. XXVII, part I, p. 457.

[97] W. S. Hancock, *Official Reports of Military Operations of Troops Commanded by Major General W. S. Hancock, During the War, 1861–1865*. This volume appears to have been privately printed and it is a compilation of his reports during the war. Unfortunately, the date is obliterated though he dated the copy to General Carroll, August 3, 1882. The volume was graciously provided by Matt and Heather Philbin of Lake Zurich, Illinois.

[98] Gibbon, *Personal Recollections of the Civil War*, pp. 199–200 and 206.

[99] Lash, *The Gibraltar Brigade on East Cemetery Hill*, p. 98.

[100] *The National Tribune*, October 14, 1915.

[101] *Joint Committee Report*, General W. S. Hancock, March 22, 1864, p. 406.

[102] Bruce, *The Twentieth Regiment of Massachusetts Volunteer Infantry 1861–1865*, pp. 283–284.

[103] Isaac R. Pennypacker, *General Meade*, New York: D Appleton and Company, 1901, p. 182.

Chapter Three Endnotes

[104] Byrne and Weaver, eds., *Haskell of Gettysburg*, p. 133.
[105] *Battles and Leaders*, vol. III, p. 313. Author's note: Visitors to the Gettysburg battlefield can still visit and view the restored Leister home.
[106] **Ibid.** *See also*,
Gibbon, *Personal Recollections of the Civil War*, p. 140.
[107] *Joint Committee Report*, March 9, 1864, General G. K. Warren, p. 379.
[108] Gibbon, *Personal Recollections of the Civil War*, p. 140.
[109] Slocum, "Gettysburg Thirty Years After," p. 142.
[110] *O. R.*, I., vol. XXVII, part I, p. 73.
[111] Gibbon, *Personal Recollections of the Civil War*, pp. 142–143.
[112] *O. R.*, I., vol. XXVII, part I, p. 73. *See also*,
Battles and Leaders, vol. III, p. 313.
[113] Gibbon, *Personal Recollections of the Civil War*, p. 144.
[114] *Battles and Leaders*, vol. III, p. 314.
[115] *Army and Navy Journal*, August 14, 1886.
[116] Gibbon, *Personal Recollections of the Civil War*, p. 145.
[117] Arabella M. Willson, *Disaster, Struggle, Triumph. The Adventures of 1000 "Boys in Blue," August, 1862, to June 1865*, Albany, New York: The Argus Company, Printers, 1870, p. 178.
[118] Gregory A. Coco, *A Vast Sea of Misery*, Gettysburg, Pennsylvania: Thomas Publications, 1988, p. 65.

Chapter Four

"Tell General Hancock"

[1] H. E. Jacobs, "Meteorology of the Battle," courtesy, GNMP.
[2] *Joint Committee Report*, General W. S. Hancock, March 22, 1864, p. 407. Author's note: There is some debate on the precise scope of Hancock's authority on July 3, 1863.
[3] *WSH to Peter F. Rothermel*, December 31, 1868.
[4] Hancock, *Reminiscences*, p. 97.
[5] Coddington, *The Gettysburg Campaigns*, p. 469.
[6] Muffly, ed., *A History of the 148th Pennsylvania*, p. 463 and, p. 10 of Introduction. *See also*,
Pfanz, *Gettysburg, The Second Day*, p. 74.
[7] Alexander, *Fighting for the Confederacy*, Gallagher, ed., pp. 244–245.

Chapter Four Endnotes

[8] E. P. Alexander, *Military Memoirs of a Confederate*, New York: Charles Scribner's Sons, 1907, reprint; Dayton, Ohio: Morningside Bookshop, 1977, pp. 418–419. *See also,*

Meade, *The Life and Letters of General George Gordon Meade*, vol.II, p. 104. In this compilation of Meade's papers, it is confirmed that "By ten o'clock in the morning of the 3d it could be plainly seen, from the Union lines, that the enemy were massing their artillery along Seminary Ridge..."

[9] Sloat, *History of the Twenty-Seventh Regiment Connecticut Volunteer Infantry*, p. 6.

[10] Henry W. Bingham, "Memoirs of Hancock," 1872, courtesy, Western Reserve Historical Society, Cleveland, Ohio, and GNMP, vertical file #5-45. Transcribed by John Stoudt, December, 1992. It is very possible that this was a Vermont regiment belonging to General George J. Stannard.

[11] **Ibid**.

[12] Jordan, *Winfield Scott Hancock*, p. 95. *See also,*

Charles P. Hamblen, *Connecticut Yankees at Gettysburg*, Walter L. Powell, ed., Kent, Ohio: The Kent State University Press, 1993, pp. 93–96. It is only fair to inform the reader that this episode at the Bliss Barn is the source of another Gettysburg controversy that exists between the 14th Connecticut and the 12th New Jersey. *See also,*

The Bachelder Papers, vol. I, pp. 397–407. *See also,*

Ibid., vol. II, p. 872. *See also,*

Bingham, "Memoirs of Hancock." Note that Hays improperly refers to Captain Bingham as major.

[13] *The Bachelder Papers*, vol. III, p. 1612. *See also,*

Beyer and Keydel, eds., *Deeds of Valor*, p. 552.

[14] *Joint Committee Report*, General W. S. Hancock, March 22, 1864, p. 408.

[15] Byrne and Weaver, eds., *Haskell of Gettysburg*, pp. 145–147.

[16] Muffly, ed., *A History of the 148th Pennsylvania*, p. 439.

[17] *WSH to Peter F. Rothermel*, December 31, 1868, p. 2. *See also,*

The Bachelder Papers, vol. III, p. 1360.

[18] *Battles and Leaders*, vol. III, p. 362.

[19] Kathleen Georg Harrison, "Gettysburg—The Third Day," *Blue & Gray Magazine*, Vol. V, Issue 6 [July, 1988]: 35. Note that some reports indicate that there were three initial cannon shots to mark the start of the cannonade. *See also,*

Chapter Four Endnotes 261

Alexander, *Military Memoirs of a Confederate*, p. 422. *See also,*
William Miller Owen, *In Camp and Battle With the Washington Artillery of New Orleans*, Boston: Ticknor and Company, 1885, p. 253.

[20] Bingham, "Memoirs of Hancock." *See also,*
Hancock, *Reminiscences*, p. 207.

[21] Gibbon, *Personal Recollections of the War*, p. 149. *See also,*
John G. Waugh, *The Class of 1846*, New York: Warner Books, 1994, p. 468.

[22] Walker, *History of the Second Army Corps*, p. 292.

[23] Harrison, "Gettysburg—The Third Day," pp. 36–38.

[24] *Henry H. Bingham to WSH*, January 5, 1869, courtesy, GNMP and Pennsylvania State Archives. *See also,*
The Bachelder Papers, vol. I, p. 358.

[25] *WSH to Peter F. Rothermel*, December 31, 1868, Note that on p. 209, Hancock's wife, Almira, writes in her *Reminiscences* that her husband was initially riding his own horse, which became unmanageable during the cannonade, and he then requested the loan from Captain Brownson. Also note that Rothermel is the artist who painted the enormous portrait of the battle for the State of Pennsylvania. See p. 152 for a photograph of Rothermel's painting. *See also,*
D. X. Junkin, *The Life of Winfield Scott Hancock*, New York: D. Appleton and Company, 1880, p. 105. *See also,*
WSH to Peter F. Rothermel, December 31, 1868. In this note, Hancock states that he took the horse from Captain Brownson "...just as the assault commenced." The author emphasizes this point because it is impractical to determine exactly when Hancock took the borrowed animal. It appears that he rode his own sorrel during the morning but at some point during the cannonade, he was forced to change his mount.

[26] Tucker, *Hancock the Superb*, p. 328. It should be noted here that according to Tucker, Private Wells was not carrying a flag with a trefoil, which is commonly assumed. Instead, Tucker states, "...that flag was swallow-tailed, of blue silk, bearing a white Maltese cross in the center on which the corps designation appeared in a red figure in the center." *See also,*
Forney, *Life and Military Career of Winfield Scott Hancock*, p. 129.

[27] **Ibid.**, p. 151.

[28] Bingham, "Memoirs of Hancock," p. 1.

Chapter Four Endnotes

[29] *Rutherford B. Hayes Papers*, courtesy, GNMP, pp. 63–64.

[30] Shakespeare, *Othello*, III, 1604.

[31] James Ford Rhodes, *History of the Civil War, 1861–1865*, New York: The MacMillan Company, 1917, p. 238. Rhodes acknowledges that he received this quote from Captain Thomas L. Livermore on March 30, 1914. On July 3, 1863, Livermore was on detached service from the 5th New Hampshire Infantry as the II Corps Chief of Ambulances. The author seriously doubts that Hancock made such a statement. While it is rather poetic and memorable, Livermore makes no mention of such a statement in his own volume, *Days and Events*. It is also very difficult to reconcile that Livermore was even near Hancock when the general was riding down the line during the cannonade. Livermore states, on p. 263 of his volume, "I was with General Hancock during the cannonade at General Meade's headquarters, but whether I went with him away from that place I cannot tell." In his December 31, 1868 letter to artist Peter F. Rothermel, Hancock himself noted that during that ride, "I had of my own people only an orderly [Wells] with me..." *See also,*

James Ford Rhodes., *History of the United States*, vol. IV. 1862–1864, Norwood, Massachusetts: Berwick & Smith, 1899, reprint; New York: The MacMillan Company, 1907, p. 287. In this earlier work on Gettysburg, Rhodes makes no similar comment by Hancock.

[32] Douglas R. Harper, "*If Thee Must Fight*," West Chester, Pennsylvania: Chester County Historical Society, 1990, p. 252. *See also,*

Joint Committee Report, General W. S. Hancock, March 22, 1864, p. 409.

[33] George R. Stewart, *Pickett's Charge*, Boston: Houghton Mifflin Co., reprint; Dayton, Ohio: Morningside Bookshop, 1983, pp. 127–128.

[34] Edward G. Longacre, *The Man Behind the Guns*, New York: A. S. Barnes and Company, 1977, p. 173. *See also,*

Meade, *The Life and Letters of General George Gordon Meade*, vol. II, p. 108.

[35] Bingham, "Memoirs of Hancock," p. 1.

[36] G. G. Benedict, *Vermont at Gettysburg*, Burlington, Vermont: The Free Press Association, 1870, p. 14.

[37] Longstreet, *From Manassas to Appomattox*, p. 392. *See also,*

Arthur J. L. Fremantle, *Three Months In the Southern States*, London: William Blackwood and Sons, 1863, reprint; Alexandria, Virginia: Time-Life Books, Inc., 1981, p. 270.

Chapter Four Endnotes

[38] Howard Coffin, *Full Duty, Vermonters In the Civil War*, Woodstock, Vermont: The Countryman Press, Inc., 1993, p. 192. Hereafter, referred to as *Full Duty*.

[39] *O. R.*, I., vol. XXVII, part I, p. 239. *See also,*
Alexander, *Military Memoirs of a Confederate*, p. 423.

[40] Freeman Cleaves, *Meade of Gettysburg*, Norman, Oklahoma: University of Oklahoma Press, 1960, reprint; Dayton, Ohio: Morningside Bookshop, 1980, p. 161.

[41] *The Bachelder Papers*, vol. I, p. 245. *See also,*
H. R. Report No. 592, 43rd Congress, 1st Session, May 13, 1874, p. 8.

[42] **Ibid.**, p. 433. *See also,*
Battles and Leaders, vol. III, p. 375.

[43] Longacre, *The Man Behind the Guns*, pp. 174–175. While Hunt's biographer makes a valid point here, it must be remembered that Hancock's decision was made during the heat of battle. Nonetheless, Hunt later claimed that "Had my instructions been followed here, as they were by McGilvery, I do not believe that Pickett's division would have reached our line. We lost not only the fire of one-third of our guns, but the resulting crossfire, which would have doubled its value." Hunt goes on to argue rather convincingly that "Had my orders been fully carried out [to cease fire], I think their whole line would have been—as half of it was—driven back before reaching our position, and this would have given us our only chance for a successful counter-attack." In January 1887, in defense of his superior, General Francis A. Walker rejoined that "Hancock had full authority over that line of battle; he used that authority according to his own best judgement, *and he beat off the enemy.*" Rather emphatically and pragmatically Walker concluded, "That is the substance of it." [Emphasis added] *See also,*
Battles and Leaders, vol. III, pp. 385–387.

[44] **Ibid.**, vol. III, p. 386. The reader should note that General Hunt is not always as agreeable as he is in this particular statement. It is very obvious that in other instances, Hunt believed that General Hancock did not have command over the Reserve Artillery on his own line.

[45] **Ibid.**, vol. II, pp. 810–811. *See also,*
The Bachelder Papers, vol. I, pp. 425–435, 439–442, 443–444, 502–504, 647–651 and 674–676. For good examples of Hunt's endless whining and haranguing, see these accounts dated Janury 20, 1873, August 22, 1874, May 8, 1875, December 29, 1876, June 18, 1879 and July 27,

Chapter Four Endnotes

1880 respectively. Let the reader understand that this is only a *partial* listing of Hunt's multitudinous, laborious, plaintive writings. Also note that within the records of the entire debate, at times, distinction between corps and Reserve Artillery is frequently lost. Author's note.

46. Stewart, *Pickett's Charge*, p. 71.
47. Warner, *Generals in Blue*, p. 242. *See also*,
    Mark M. Boatner III, *The Civil War Dictionary*, New York: David McKay Company, 1988, reprint; New York: Vintage Books, 1991, p. 418. *See also*,
    Malone, ed., *Dictionary of American Biography*, vol. V, pp. 386–387.
48. *Stanley H. Ford Papers*, Letter of Henry J. Hunt, July 28, 1863, courtesy, USAMHI.
49. *Battles and Leaders*, vol. III, p. 374.
50. *The Bachelder Papers*, vol. I, pp. 353–354. This is a January 5, 1869 letter from Bingham to Hancock wherein the aide stated that he was stopped by an aide of General Meade and given a hand-written message for Generals Hancock and Hunt. Acccording to Bingham's memory, that message directed "that the batteries should observe great care with their ammunition and endeavor to preserve it and not fire so rapidly or extravagantly." Bingham noted: "These were not the exact words but they convey the proper meaning."
51. *Henry J. Hunt Papers, General Miscellaneous, Number 14*, p. 15, courtesy, Library of Congress.
52. *O. R.*, I., vol. XXVII, part I, pp. 159, 480–481.
53. *O. R.*, I., vol. XXV, part I, p. 252. *See also*,
    Hebert, *Fighting Joe Hooker*, p. 259.
54. Longacre, *The Man Behind the Guns*, pp. 155, 179–180. *See also*,
    Henry J. Hunt to A. A. Humphreys, July 26, 1863, courtesy, Library of Congress.
55. Longacre, *The Man Behind the Guns*, pp. 150, 158, 160 and 180. *See also*,
    Henry J. Hunt to A. A. Humphreys, July 26, 1863. In this letter, Hunt requested that he "be relieved...as soon as...arrangements will permit. Under existing orders and practices the position is not one that I can hold with any advantage to the service, and, consistently with self-respect." Courtesy, Library of Congress. *See also*,
    The Bachelder Papers, vol. II, p. 811. Here, Hunt disagrees with General Hancock's statement, "...nor did he [Hunt] come into command of it

Chapter Four Endnotes

[the artillery] for more than a month afterwards, [not true]..." Comments in brackets belong to Hunt.

[56] Powell, *The Fifth Army Corps*, p. 558.

[57] *Joint Committee Report*, General Henry J. Hunt, March 1, 1864, pp. 456–457. In this transcript, note the ambiguous answers that General Hunt affords Mr. Loan when examined:

> Q. Were you on General Meade's staff as chief of artillery?
> A. Yes, sir.
> Q. At what time were you assigned to duty as chief of artillery on General Meade's staff?
> A. On assuming command he found me chief of artillery of the army. I continued chief of artillery of the army; no order was necessary to confirm it, *and none was issued.* [Emphasis added]
> Q. At what time did General Hooker appoint you as chief of artillery of his staff?
> A. I will not say now that he appointed me at all; he found me there, and I continued so...
> Q. At what time did he [Hooker] issue an order assigning you to that duty?
> A. I cannot remember positively that I was ever announced in orders; I would continue on duty as chief of artillery until relieved.
> Q. Did General Meade, on assuming command, assign to duty the staff officers of General Hooker, in the positions they occupied on General Hooker's staff at the time General Meade took command?
> A. I have seen no orders from General Meade about the staff. He brought his personal staff with him. He recognized or continued the chiefs of "the staff" of artillery and of engineering as they stood when he took command. *At least he did not relieve me from my duties.* [Emphasis added]

Certainly, this is not a scenario of absolutes. If readers feel that too much attention is being paid to Hunt linguistics, it is suggested they refer to *The Bachelder Papers*, vol. II, pp. 790–829.

[58] *Joint Committee Report*, General Henry J. Hunt, March 1, 1864, pp. 457–458.

[59] *Henry J. Hunt Papers*, Container Number 14, Subject File, *Miscellaneous–General Miscellaneous*, courtesy, Library of Congress. This is

Chapter Four Endnotes

a handwritten report made by General Hunt which is twenty-one pages in length. The document is not dated but he signed it, "Maj. Genl. Late Chief of Artillery Army of the Potomac." It is believed that Hunt wrote this between the late 1860s and 1870s. Hereafter, referred to as *Hunt Papers, Container Number 14.*

60 Ibid.
61 *O. R.*, I., vol. XXVII, part I, p. 167.
62 *Hunt Papers, Container Number 14.*
63 *O. R.*, I., vol. XXVII, part I, pp. 373 and 375. See also,
   Henry J. Hunt to William T. Sherman, February, 1882. See also,
   The Bachelder Papers, vol. II, pp. 790–829. In this acidic, lengthy letter, Hunt invokes the name of General Hancock more than 95 times. Further, while he refers casually to *General* Meade, *General* Sherman or *General* Newton, his references to Hancock are always an acerbic *Major General* Hancock.
64 Joseph C. Mayo, "Pickett's Charge at Gettysburg," *S.H.S.P.*, vol. 34, p. 330.
65 Byrne and Weaver, eds., *Haskell of Gettysburg*, p. 151. N.B. It is interesting to note that in his lengthy battlefield report on Gettysburg, General Hancock never mentions General Hunt. See also,
   O. R., I, vol. XXVII, pp. 367–377.
66 Longacre, *The Man Behind the Guns*, p. 159.
67 James Stewart, "Battery F Fourth United States Artillery at Gettysburg," *Sketches of War History, 1861–1865*, vol. IV, Cincinnati: The Robert Clarke Comnpany, 1896, reprint; Wilmington, North Carolina: Broadfoot Publishing Company, 1993, p. 192.
68 Edwin E. Bryant, "The Battle of Gettysburg," *War Papers*, Wisconsin MOLLUS, vol. II, reprint; Wilmington, North Carolina: Broadfoot Publishing Company, 1993, p. 265.
69 Allan Nevins, ed., *A Diary of Battle*, New York: Harcourt, Brace & World, Inc., 1962, pp. 252–253.
70 Alexander, *Military Memoirs of a Confederate*, p. 423.
71 *H. R. Report No. 592*, p. 8. See also,
   The Bachelder Papers, vol. II, p. 827. Note that despite indications otherwise, even portions of McGilvery's command reopened fire upon order from General Hancock. See also,
   O. R., I., vol. XXVII, part I., pp. 884–885.

Chapter Four Endnotes

[72] *Henry J. Hunt Papers, Container Number 2, General Correspondence, 1846–1879* [11 folders], courtesy, Library of Congress. Hereafter, referred to as *Hunt Papers, Container Number 2*. Note that in a letter to General Hunt dated August 16, 1879, Hart also stated that "...my view of General Hancock's interference with the *arty* on the 3rd at Gettysburg should have caused him to be tried by a General Court Martial." *See also*,
The Bachelder Papers, vol. II and III, pp. 827 and 1798. *See also*,
Patrick Hart to Henry J. Hunt, August 27, 1879.

[73] *John Bigelow to Henry J. Hunt*, November 4, 1875.

[74] *O. R.*, I., vol. XXVII, part I., p. 885. *See also*,
The Bachelder Papers, vol. I, pp. 170–171.

[75] James I. Robertson, Jr., ed., *The Medical and Surgical History of the Civil War*, 15 vols., vol. XII, Wilmington, North Carolina: Broadfoot Publishing Company, 1991, p. 891.

[76] **Ibid.**, p. 884.

[77] Longacre, *The Man Behind the Guns*, p. 174. N.B. The author has serious doubt about such a comment being made.

[78] "Longstreet's Report of the Pennsylvania Campaign," *S.H.S.P.*, vol. X, p. 341.

[79] *Joint Committee Report*, General W. S. Hancock, March 22, 1864, pp. 409–410.

[80] *Brian C. Pohanka* collection.

[81] *The Bachelder Papers*, vol. II, pp, 804–805.

[82] Alexander, *Fighting For the Confederacy*, Gallagher, ed., p. 260.

[83] *H. R. Report No. 592*, p. 8.

[84] Fred Fuger, "Battle of Gettysburg and Personal Recollections of that Battle," pp. 25–26, *S. Webb Papers*, courtesy, Yale University Library.

[85] Kathleen Georg Harrison, "Ridges of Grim War," *Blue & Gray Magazine*, vol. V, Issue VI [July, 1988]: 39.

[86] *National Tribune*, November 28, 1886.

[87] Willson, *Disaster, Struggle, Triumph, The Adventures of 1000 "Boys in Blue," From August, 1862 to June, 1865*, pp. 184–185.

[88] *Battles and Leaders*, vol. III, p. 387.

[89] *O. R.*, I., vol. XXVII, part I, p. 374. *See also*,
Coddington, *The Gettysburg Campaign*, p. 799. General Stannard wrote to General Doubleday on September 3, 1865, and he recounted a slightly different version of this story.

Chapter Four Endnotes

[90] Stewart, *Pickett's Charge*, pp. 204–205.
[91] John Edward Pierce, "The Civil War Career of Richard Brooke Garnett: A Quest for Vindication," Master of Arts diss., Virginia Polytechnic Institute, 1969, courtesy, Andy De Cusati.
[92] *Battles and Leaders*, vol. III, p. 388.
[93] *The Bachelder Papers*, vol. III, Dayton, Ohio: Morningside House, Inc., 1995, pp. 1609–1610, 1879. *See also,*
Gary G. Lash, "The Philadelphia Brigade at Gettysburg," *The Gettysburg Magazine*, Issue Number Seven [July/1992]: 108.
[94] Gibbon, *Personal Recollections of the Civil War*, p. 152. *See also,*
Byrne and Weaver, eds., *Haskell of Gettysburg*, p. 192. *See also,*
WSH to Peter F. Rothermel, December 31, 1868.
[95] Beyet and Keydel, eds, *Deeds of Valor*, pp. 224–225. *See also,*
Warner, *Generals in Blue*, p. 545.
[96] Steven J. Wright, "Don't Let Me Bleed to Death," *Gettysburg*, Issue Number Six [January 1, 1992]: 89.
[97] George G. Benedict, *Vermont At Gettysburg*, Burlington, Vermont: The Free Press Association, 1870, p. 21. N.B. The matter of General Hancock's wounding is most confusing. It is generally assumed, and Hancock himself assumed, that he was hit by Rebel fire. However, when we look closely at his reported position and southerly vector, it becomes increasingly possible that he was hit by one of the volleys fired by the Vermont regiments or some other unidentified Union soldier. The precise timing of those volleys is not exactly clear. This possibility is furthered when we consider that the bullet which hit the general had to penetrate his wooden saddle tree, remove a hand wrought nail that had been peened into rivet form, exit the saddle tree while carrying the bullet, and enter Hancock's groin. All of that demanded energy indicates a missile fired from a close range with a direct northerly path. Shots from the attacking Rebels would have been to Hancock's right flank, most likely. Unfortunately, we will probably never know for certain.
[98] Hancock, *Reminiscences*, p. 214. *See also,*
Benedict, *Vermont At Gettysburg*, p. 21. Hancock felt that the description of his wounding in this volume was accurate. *See also,*
WSH to Peter F. Rothermel, December 31, 1868.
[99] *WSH to Francis A. Walker*, December 12, 1885, courtesy, CWLM.
[100] Wright, "Don't Let Me Bleed To Death," p. 91.
[101] *WSH to Francis A. Walker*, December 12, 1885.

Chapter Four Endnotes 269

[102] Bingham, *Anecdotes Concerning Gen. Hancock*. See also, *Norristown Times Herald*, February 11, 1924.

[103] Walker, *History of the Second Army Corps*, p. 300. See also, *O. R.*, I, vol. XXVII, part I, p. 375. Note: There have been several attempts to credit Hancock with a much more gradiose statement about not being moved from the field. This author is unable to find any such record.

[104] Jordan, *Winfield Scott Hancock*, pp. 98–99. Some historians claim that Hancock ordered the Vermonters to fall upon the Rebel flank. Stannard claimed that he alone gave the order. Unfortunately, like so many other Gettysburg events, it is not perfectly clear. See also, Coffin, *Full Duty*, p. 194.

[105] Ralph Orson Sturtevand and Carmi Lathrop Marsh, *History of the 13th Regiment, Vermont Volunteers*, Burlington: Regimental Association, 1910, p. 305. See also,

WSH to Francis A. Walker, April 16, 1864, courtesy CWLM. After the battle, there were a number of attempts to expand the importance played by the Vermont regiments. Perhaps the most disturbing claim was made in the small volume, *Vermont At Gettysburg*. There, on p. 23, the author states, "*the flank of the 2d Vermont Brigade decided the fate of the great rebel charge on Friday afternoon [July 3, 1863], and with it the issue of the battle.*" [Emphasis in original] In his April 16th letter, Hancock stated that "Any attempt at this date to enhance the service of the Vermont Brigade, (at the expense of the other troops) over that accorded to them in the past histories, would not in my opinion be entitled to consideration." Courtesy, CWLM. See also,

O. R., I, vol. XXVII, part I, pp. 367–377. In his official report, Hancock always felt he had given the Vermont Brigade all the credit they were due. See also,

John Gibbon to Francis A. Walker, March 14, 1886. In this note, General Gibbon comments to Walker that he had recently read his Gettysburg article in a March 5, 1886 edition of the *Boston Herald*, and commented: "[I] think you attach more importance to the part played by Stannard's Brig. so far as concerns the repulse of Pickett's assault then the facts warrant." [Emphasis in original] Courtesy, The Sessler Collection, CWLM.

[106] Benedict, *Vermont At Gettysburg*, p. 20. See also,

Coffin, *Full Duty*, p. 196. In his work, Coffin is a bit more detailed about Stannard's wounding and states that "a small iron ball took the Vermont general in a thigh and dug deep."

[107] Gordon, *Reminiscences of the Civil War*, p. 165.

[108] *National Tribune*, Janury 15, 1885.

[109] *Alexander S. Webb to His Father*, July 17, 1863, courtesy, USAMHI. It should be noted that it is not clear if Hancock was wounded before or after Armistead. Author's note.

[110] Ida Lee Johnston, "Over the Stone Wall at Gettysburg," *Confederate Veteran*, vol. XXXI, No. 7 [July, 1923]: 249.

[111] Joseph C. Mayo, "Pickett's Charge at Gettysburg," *S.H.S.P.*, vol. 3, pp. 334–335.

[112] *WSH to Peter F. Rothermel*, December 31, 1868. *See also*, *The Bachelder Papers*, vol. I, pp. 231, 378–380.

[113] Wayne E. Motts, *Trust In God and Fear Nothing, Gen. Lewis A. Armistead, CSA*, Gettysburg, Pennsylvania: Farnsworth House Military Impressions, 1994, p. 46. Hereafter, referred to as *Lewis A. Armistead*. When this author discussed Armistead's wounding with Mr. Motts, that author made it clear that the facts *indicate* that Armistead was hit in the right arm but he stressed that it is not certain. Also, it is the opinion of this author that with all the noise on that field, it is far more probable that Armistead gave the hand sign for distress and that was seen rather than his being heard. *See also*,

Allen E. Roberts, *House Divided, The Story of Freemasonry and the Civil War*, Macoy Publishing & Masonic Supply Co., Inc., Richmond, Virginia: 1990, p. 163. While the Masonic signs for distress are held to be secret, this volume, written by a Mason, describes Armistead's moment of wounding: "At this moment, Armistead was struck by a ball. As he fell, he called out *'I am a widow's son...'*" Since Mr. Roberts offers no reference for this statement, the reader is left to his own decision on the validity of this comment. *See also*,

Lash, "The Philadelphia Brigade at Gettysburg," p. 110. *See also*, *The Bachelder Papers*, vol. III, pp. 1495–1496.

[114] *Henry H. Bingham to WSH*, January 5, 1869. It is interesting to note that despite popular thought, there is no known record that Bingham ever knew that Armistead was a Mason.

[115] Wright, "Don't Let Me Bleed to Death," p. 91.

[116] *The Sunday Herald*, July 4, 1880.

Chapter Four Endnotes

[117] Wright, "Don't Let Me Bleed to Death," Also note: The reader should know that this author *assumes* that Hancock was seated upon a McClellan saddle, undoubtedly an officer's variety, when he was shot. This assumption applies if he was still riding Captain Brownson's mount or if he had returned to his own horse. While there is no known record of the saddle type he had that day, the McClellan, custom or Regulation issue, was the most common. Regarding the nail that hit Hancock, Dr. Dougherty stated it to be a 10d variety, which, if that were not technically or exactly correct, it undoubtedly demonstrates the general size of the nail. It appears that Dougherty simply, and naturally, threw the nail away after he showed it to General Hancock. Some reports indicate that the nail came from the pommel of his saddle and there is at least one report claiming that it came from a fence post. Any fences in that general area were probably destroyed by the Vermont boys for modest breastworks before Hancock was wounded. Another theory offers that perhaps the nail came from one of the Rebel guns, meaning canister fire, which is impractical in view of their position and that of the Confederate ranks. Consequently, we are left to conclude that the ball did indeed come from his saddle. Note the photographs on page 160 which show the actual size of a modern wire 10d nail vs. a wrought [or handmade] 10d nail that would have been used at that time period. The wrought nail was made by a modern blacksmith who specializes in reproductions. The author sought the assistance of saddle maker-experts, and while most of the initial reaction was that 10d size nails were not used in McClellan saddles, that position is definitely incorrect. Mr. Nick Nichols, a saddle expert, of Virginia, reports that "the pommel of the M1859 McClellan saddle is fitted with an iron reinforcing plate which was intended to be mounted with two large wood screws and two machine-made iron 'wire' rivets. But...contractors typically substitued cut nails for rivets." With further research assistance from Mr. Paul Korzynski, Mr. Hank Kluin and the National Archives, the author was able to obtain a copy of a Federal Ordnance Office contract dated October 18, 1864. This contract for horse equipment was issued to Moores & Company in Cincinnatti, Ohio, and states: "The use of rivets made from cut nails will not be permitted." It appears that the change was affected, at least in part, by D. Demarest & Son in Newark, New Jersey. This means that Hancock's wound was undoubtedly aggravated by a large nail, whatever its precise size. See photos on page 161. *See also,*

Chapter Four Endnotes

The Bachelder Papers, vol. III, p. 1364. In this report by Hancock aide, Lieutenant-Colonel Charles H. Morgan, it is stated that "saddlers say no nails of that size are used in the construction of saddles..." This erroneous position is in harmony with the initial reaction the author encountered.

[118] Walker, *General Hancock*, pp. 144–145.

[119] *Henry H. Bingham to WSH*, January 5, 1869, courtesy GNMP. The comments made by General Armistead have been debated almost from the time immediately following the close of the battle. Writers from both the North and South have attempted to place their own sectional emphasis on his comments. Bingham's quote here is undoubtedly the best that history currently has to offer. *See also,*

James E. Poindexter, "Gen. Lewis Addison Armistead," *Confederate Veteran*, vol. XXII, No. 11 [November, 1914]: 504. The reader should know that Poindexter was a captain in the 38th Virginia, belonging to Armistead's Brigade. In his article, Poindexter tells that Hancock and Armistead met on the field at Gettysburg as the Confederate general was being carried to the rear. Poindexter also stated that Hancock grabbed Armistead's hand and "told him with a soldier's sympathy how sorry he was to see him wounded and promised to send mementos and messages to his loved ones in Virginia..." The author finds no factual basis for this description and he again consulted with Armistead's biographer, Mr. Wayne Motts, who concurs. *See also,*

S.H.S.P., vol. X, p. 428. Here, Hancock refused to comment on Bingham's quotation of Armistead comments of July 3, 1863. When Hancock was later confronted by an official of the Southern Historical Society, he prudently responded: "He [Bingham] is the officer to whom the message was delivered and [he] is the best witness in the case." *See also,*

The Bachelder Papers, vol. III, pp. 1494–1497. This is yet another version of assistance afforded to General Armistead by Captain John C. Brown, Company K, 20th Indiana. In his 1887 letter to Bachelder, Brown claims that that he came upon Armistead, a "brother," who identified himself as a Mason but not by name. Brown claims to have employed the help of two soldiers, who placed the unknown wounded soldier [Armistead] on a litter and carried him back to a hospital. The author again discussed this version with Armistead's biographer, Wayne Motts, and, candidly, it is not entirely possible to either confirm or dismiss Brown's story. Sadly, we are simply left with the reali-

Chapter Four Endnotes 273

zation that it only increases the scope of unknowns about the battle of Gettysburg.

[120] *Joint Committee Report*, General W. S. Hancock, March 22, 1864, p. 408.
[121] Gibbon, *Personal Recollections of the Civil War*, pp. 386–411.
[122] *Joint Committee Report*, General W. S. Hancock, March 22, 1864, p. 412.
[123] Gary Gallagher, ed., *The Third Day At Gettysburg and Beyond*, Chapel Hill, North Carolina: The University of North Carolina Press, 1994, pp. 121–122. See also,
Motts, *Lewis A. Armistead*, p. 49.
[124] *Henry H. Bingham to WSH*, January 5, 1869. See also,
WSH to Peter F. Rothermel, December 31, 1868.
[125] *Henry H. Bingham to WSH*, January 5, 1869. See also,
Meade, *The Life and Letters of General George Gordon Meade*, vol. II, p. 134.
[126] Junkin, *The Life of Winfield Scott Hancock*, p. 110. See also,
The Bachelder Papers, vol. I, pp. 231, 321 and 380.
[127] Junkin, *The Life of Winfield Scott Hancock*, p. 110. See also,
Meade, *The Life and Letters of General George Gordon Meade*, vol. 2, p. 136.
[128] *Timothy Brooks Collection*, Unknown Soldier of the 140th Pennsylvania Volunteers, courtesy, USAMHI.
[129] *The Sunday Herald*, July 4, 1880. Note: It appears that when Dr. Dougherty wrote this article, 17 years after the battle, he too suffered from some inability to accurately place events in their sequential order. *See also,*
Hedrick & Davis, eds., *Diary of John H. W. Stuckenberg*, p. 80. *See also,*
Gregory A. Coco, *A Vast Sea of Misery*, Gettysburg, Pennsylvania: Thomas Publications, 1988, p. 94.
[130] *O. R.*, I., vol. XXVII, part I, p. 366. The requested pursuit of the V and VI Corps did not materialize in the timely manner that Hancock had desired and Meade had intended. Consequently, Hancock felt that their delay, for whatever the reasons, failed to follow through on the Union victory and destroy the Rebel army.
[131] *WHS to Peter F. Rothermel*, December 31, 1868. *See also,*
Tucker, *Hancock the Superb*, p. 158. Note, if sequential matters begin to become somewhat confusing, that is perfectly normal. It is almost impossible to establish every detail in its precise order of occurrence. This problem was aptly addressed by author Glen Tucker and John B. Bachelder, the noted Gettysburg historian. In Tucker's book, *Hancock*

Chapter Four Endnotes

the Superb, p. 163, he wrote that when Bachelder was doing his research on Gettysburg, that historian noted: "...I believe I have discovered how Joshua made the sun stand still." Bachelder continues that he had interviewed various regiments about specific times and positions and found that they invariably disagreed with each other and all claimed that "We were there...and we ought to know, I guess." Tucker rightly concludes that "no one can ever be sure of the precise time of events on Cemetery Hill on the afternoon of July 3." **Nothing has changed!**

[132] Hancock, *Reminiscences*, p. 97.

[133] Thomas L. Livermore, *Days and Events*, Boston: Houghton Mifflin Company, 1920, p. 264.

[134] Coddington, *The Gettysburg Campaign*, p. 528. *See also,* Muffly, ed., *A History of the 148th Pennsylvania*, p. 332.

[135] Willson, *Disaster, Struggle, Triumph, The Adventures of 1000 "Boys in Blue," From August, 1862 to June, 1865*, p. 193.

[136] Coco, *A Vast Sea of Misery*, pp. 33–34, 91–92, and 164.

[137] *Philadelphia Public Ledger*, July 6, 1863. On the front page of this newspaper, the following brief message appeared regarding Hancock's arrival in the city: "Arrival of Major General Hancock. On Saturday, Major-General Hancock, who was wounded in the fight at Gettysburg, reached Philadelphia, accompanied by several of his staff. He was taken to the LaPierre House." *See also,*

M. G. Mitchell to L. W. Read, September 20, 1880, courtesy, GNMP. *See also,*

Norristown Times Herald, February 11, 1924.

[138] *O. R.*, I., vol. XXVII, part I, pp. 151, 174 and 177.

[139] *The New York Times*, July 4 & 6, 1863. General Barksdale was indeed mortally wounded on July 2nd and he died on the 3rd. Neither Longstreet nor Hill were even wounded at Gettysburg.

[140] *Horatio G. Wright to His Wife*, July 18, 1863, Charles Bednar Collection, courtesy, USAMHI.

[141] *S.H.S.P.*, vol. V, p. 175.

Chapter Five Endnotes
Chapter Five

"I may never see you again"

1. *The National Tribune*, August 16, 1934.
2. Anna M. Holstein, *Three Years in Field Hospitals of the Army of the Potomac*, Philadelphia: J. B. Lippincott & Co., 1867, pp. 41–42.
3. *William G. Mitchell to L. W. Read*, September 20, 1880.
4. Hancock, *Reminiscences*, p. 99.
5. **Ibid**. *See also*,
   Norristown Times Herald, February 11, 1924.
6. *Norristown Republican*, July 31, 1863. *See also*,
   Herald and Free Press, July 28, 1863. The reader should note that on November 5, 1992, this home, which belonged to Hancock's father, was torn down to make way for the "reconstruction of Norristown..." According to one local newspaper, the area where the home was located had become "a hangout for drunks and beggars...one of Norristown's worst." *See also*,
   The Times Herald, November 5, 1992. As late as June 19, 1995, a local newspaper article noted that the fate of the empty lot resulting from the demolition of Hancock's father's home has still not been decided. The article noted that "The Hancock Square redevelopment project in Norristown has hit another snag, with the Montgomery County Redevelopment Authority and would-be developers disagreeing on the next step." *See also*,
   The Times Herald, June 19, 1995. *See also*,
   Norristown Weekly Herald, October 10, 1867. In this edition, most, if not all, of the properties belonging to the general's late father were put up to auction by the general's mother, Elizabeth. Those holdings had grown to a substantial portion.
7. *Norristown Times Herald*, February 11, 1924.
8. *Herald and Free Press*, July 28, 1863. *See also*,
   National Defender, August 4, 1863.
9. *Edwin Stanton to WSH*, August 5, 1863, The Winfield Scott Hancock Papers, Hancock Correspondence, 1863–1865, courtesy, USAMHI.
10. The names of the other Norristown doctors have been lost to history. Author's note.

Chapter Five Endnotes

[11] *Philadelphia Times*, undated clippings courtesy, HSMC. This clipping, in its transcribed form, is undoubtedly in error since it states that Dr. Read was on leave, "just before the 1st of November, 1865." However, there is some doubt about the precise date that Read actually went home even though one report, which is probably correct, in the *Norristown Republican* dated Friday, August 28, 1863, announces the success of his medical attention. Part of the reason for this confusion is Special Order Number 235 [courtesy, HSMC] issued by General Meade, dated "Sept 1st 1863." In part, that order states, "Leave of absence is granted to Surgeon L. W. Read 3d Div. 5th Army Corps, to enable him to attend professionally Major Genl. W. S. Hancock at Norristown, Pa. If Genl. Hancock can sooner dispense with his services Surgeon Read will promptly return to this Army. By Command of Major-General Meade." It is certainly possible that the date [September 1, 1863] of the formal leave was delayed simply due to its voyage through the "system." However, and more important, it is clear that Dr. Read's visit to General Hancock was predetermined and *not* coincidental as previously thought. *See also*,

Joseph T. Riemer, "General Hancock and Dr. Read," *The Bulletin of the Historical Society of Montgomery County Pennsylvania*, Vol. XVIII, No. 2 [Spring, 1972]: 173. N.B. Sometimes, the improper spelling of *Reed* is utilized in written works.

[12] *Philadelphia Times*, undated clipping, courtesy, HSMC.

[13] Riemer, "General Hancock and Dr. Read," pp. 174–178.

[14] *Philadelphia Times*, undated clipping, courtesy, HSMC.

[15] *Norristown Republican*, August 28, 1863. *See also*,

Untitled newspaper clipping dated September 26, 1911, courtesy, HSMC. *See also*,

Riemer, "General Hancock and Dr. Read," p. 174. *See also*,

William G. Mitchell to Dr. L. W. Read, dated September 20, 1880, courtesy, GNMP. Mitchell was Hancock's senior aide-de-camp and whoever transcribed his letter mistakenly gave him the first initial of "M." In some of the Hancock-related letters, the name of a Doctor-Surgeon Cooper is mentioned as being present as well. Dr. Cooper remains a mystery today because he is not traceable in the Hancock papers at the HSMC. The author has not been able to locate any positive identification or data on Dr. Cooper. *See also*,

Judith A. Meier to author, November 28, 1995.

Chapter Five Endnotes

[16] *WSH to Major William G. Mitchell*, August 24, 1863, courtesy, Hartzell collection.

[17] *Philadelphia Times*, undated clipping, courtesy, HSMC. *See also*, Riemer, "General Hancock and Dr. Read," p. 174. *See also*, *Norristown Times Herald*, February 11, 1924. *See also*, *William G. Mitchell to Dr. L. W. Read*, September 20, 1880, courtesy, GNMP. In this letter, Mitchell notes that Dr. Read "performed the operation of extracting the ball by cutting open the wound from the point in front at which..it..had entered the body." This is the only reference the author has found of any kind of incision being made on Hancock and it is entirely possible that any such cut was made by the "concealed blade" before mentioned. *See also*, *WSH to Major William G. Mitchell*, August 24, 1863, courtesy, Hartzell collection.

[18] *Times Herald*, September, 1911, courtesy HSMC. Also note that the drawings on pages 172 and 173, prepared by Ms. Maryellen Considine, are the results of the combined efforts of Doctor C. G. Mesologites, a pulmonologist, Ms. Jonna Racela a certified physician's assistant, plus Mr. and Mrs. Thomas and Jane Brown, a respiratory care practioner and Registered Nurse respectively. All of the members of this medical team are actively on the staff at the noted Gaylord Hospital in Wallingford, Connecticut, and Dr. Mesologites is also part of the staff at Bradley Memorial Hospital in Southington, Connecticut.

[19] *Philadelphia Times*, undated clipping, courtesy, HSMC. *See also*, Riemer, "General Hancock and Dr. Read," p. 174. *See also*, *Norristown Times Herald*, February 11, 1924.

[20] *Norristown Republican*, August 28, 1863, courtesy, HSMC.

[21] Eric A. Campbell, "'Remember Harper's Ferry!' The Degradation, Humiliation, and Redemption of Col. George L. Willard's Brigade." *The Gettysburg Magazine*, Issue Number Eight [January/1993]: 110.

[22] *Norristown Republican*, August 28, 1863, courtesy, HSMC.

[23] Untitled, undated newspaper clipping titled, "W. E. Webster, Cowan's Battery," Hancock File, courtesy, HSMC.

[24] Untitled, undated newspapers clipping, Scrap Book, Dr. L. W. Read, H-1, courtesy HSMC.

[25] **Ibid**.

[26] Maria Randall Allen, *My Darling Wife*, Watertown, Connecticut: By the author, 1994, pp. 220–221. In February, 1864, Dr. Washington

Chapter Five Endnotes

George Nugent, a friend of General Hancock and Dr. Read, wrote home to his wife Sarah that "Dr. Read might now with a very good grace *merely signify* [Emphasis in original] his desire of being in his [Hancock's] command on his staff as medical director or any other little corner not already occupied over which the General would exercise a controlling voice, think you not?"

27 Untitled newspaper clipping, Scrap Book, Dr. L. W. Read, courtesy HSMC.
28 Bingham, *Anecdotes Concerning Gen. Hancock*.
29 *National Defender*, September 8, 1863, courtesy, HSMC.
30 Jordan, *Winfield Scott Hancock*, p. 102.
31 John W. Forney, *Life and Military Career of Winfield Scott Hancock*, Philadelphia: Hubbard Bros., 1880, p. 151.
32 Goodrich, *The Life and Public Service of Winfield Scott Hancock*, pp. 161–162.
33 Augustus T. Reed, *The Life and Services of Winfield Scott Hancock, Major General U.S. Army*, Chicago: Henry A. Sumner & Company, 1880, pp. 45–46.
34 Goodrich, *The Life and Public Service of Winfield Scott Hancock*, pp. 162–163.
35 Ibid., pp. 149–150. *See also,*
C. W. Denison, *Winfield the Lawyer's Son*, Philadelphia: Ashmead & Evans, 1865, pp. 211–212. The current whereabouts of this silver service are unknown to this author.
36 *Times Herald*, September, 1911.
37 *O. R.*, I., vol. XXVII, part I, p. 140.
38 Jordan, *Winfield Scott Hancock*, p. 106.
39 Bingham, *Anecdotes Concerning Gen. Hancock*.
40 Theodore Lyman, *With Grant and Meade, From the Wilderness to Appomattox*, Boston: Atlantic Monthly Press, 1922, reprint; Lincoln, Nebraska: University of Nebraska Press, 1994, p. 189.
41 Ibid., p. 183.
42 Vivian Taylor, comp., *Memorials in Stone, Tombstone Inscriptions, Montgomery County, Pennsylvania*, Norristown, Pennsylvania: HSMC, p. 136. Hereafter, referred to as *Memorials in Stone*. *See also,*
Jordan, *Winfield Scott Hancock*, p. 315.
43 Hancock, *Reminiscences*, p. 172.

Chapter Six Endnotes
Chapter Six

"The citizens of Louisiana...cherish the memory"

[1] Hancock, *Reminiscences*, p. 178.
[2] *Gettysburg Compiler*, November 24, 1885, "Hancock Again At Gettysburg," courtesy, GNMP. *See also,*
Jordan, *Winfield Scott Hancock*, p. 313.
[3] Hancock, *Reminiscences*, pp. 179 & 328. Note that throughout most of the war, the rank of major-general was the highest possible in the Union Army. President Lincoln reinstituted the rank of lieutenant-general, when he appointed General Grant to command all of the Union Armies in 1864. Prior to Grant's appointment, that rank had been retired in deference to George Washington though General Winfield Scott was honored as a brevet lieutenant-general. In May of 1866, Congress promoted Grant to the rank of full general, four stars, which made him surpass the rank of George Washington. Thus, Hancock, as a major-general, had two possible added promotions and potential pay increases. *See also,*
The Bachelder Papers, vol. I, p. 414. This is a rare Hancock letter wherein he makes public his tight financial means.
[4] *The New York Times*, February 11, 1886. The author notes that the home the Hancocks lived in on Governor's Island was rather substantial as witnessed by the photographs in this volume. See p. 192.
[5] Ibid.
[6] *Army and Navy Journal*, February 20, 1886.
[7] Untitled and undated newspaper clipping in the *Hancock File*, courtesy, HSMC.
[8] Ada was born on February 24, 1857. To emphasize how confusing matters can be, on p. 166 of her volume, *Reminiscences*, Almira notes the age of her daughter, at death, as 28, when it was really 18. *See also,*
Taylor, comp., *Memorials in Stone*, pp. 136, 220–221.
[9] *WSH to B. E. Chain*, June 18, 1883 and April 7, 1884, courtesy, HSMC.
[10] *Norristown Daily Herald*, May, 1896.
[11] *The New York Times*, February 11, 1886. Ada died on March 28, 1875, the grandson died on July 13, 1880 and Russell died on December 30, 1884.

Chapter Six Endnotes

[12] Tucker, *Hancock the Superb*, p. 309. *See also*,
The Sun, February 10, 1886.

[13] George A. Armes, *Ups and Downs of an Army Officer*, Washington, D.C.: By the Author, 1900, p. 551.

[14] *The Sun*, February 10, 1886.

[15] *The New York Times*, February 11, 1886.

[16] Jordan, *Winfield Scott Hancock*, p. 314.

[17] *The Philadelphia Inquirer*, February 10, 1886.

[18] Charles B. Clayman, ed., *The American Medical Association Encyclopedia of Medicine*, New York: Random House, 1989, p. 233. Hereafter referred to as *Encyclopedia of Medicine*. According to this reference volume, a carbuncle is described as "A cluster of interconnected boils (painful, pus-filled, inflamed hair roots). Carbuncles are usually caused by the bacterium *Staphylococcus Aureus*; they generally begin as single boils, then spread. Common sites are the back of the neck and the buttocks...They mainly affect people who have a lowered resistance to infection, in particular, *diabetics*." [Emphasis added]

[19] *The Sun*, February 10, 1886.

[20] *The New York Times*, February 10, 1886. *See also*,
Army and Navy Journal, February 13, 1886.

[21] Goodrich, *The Life and Public Services of Winfield S. Hancock*, p. 334. *See also*,
The Norristown Times Herald, May 17, 1940.

[22] *The Sun*, February 10, 1886.

[23] Untitled and undated newspaper clippings in *Hancock File*, courtesy, HSMC.

[24] *The New York Times*, February 10, 1886.

[25] **Ibid**.

[26] **Ibid**.

[27] **Ibid**., and February 14, 1886. Note that when Mrs. Hancock was assisted away from the dying general, she was taken to her bedroom, where she stayed until the funeral was over. Reportedly, Almira never looked upon Hancock's face in death, owing to the strong urging of her friends and Dr. Janeway. However, Almira clearly had a hand in the selection of the pallbearers and other key funeral decisions.

[28] *New York World*, February 10, 1886.

[29] Tucker, *Hancock the Superb*, p. 310.

Chapter Six Endnotes

[30] *New York World*, February 10, 1886.
[31] *The Philadelphia Inquirer*, February 11, 1886.
[32] *The New York Times*, February 10, 11, & 12, 1886. The author is not aware of any record indicating why Mrs. Hancock requested a low-profile funeral for her husband. His personal opinion is that the Hancocks found the enormous size and pageantry of Grant's funeral procession, which Hancock directed, very garish and distasteful.
[33] Ibid., February 13, 1886. *The New York Times* noted that day, "The body is attired according to the rank of the dead soldier." *See also*,

New York Post, February 13, 1886 which noted, "The body of the General, clothed in full uniform..." *See also*,

The Sun, February 12, 1886, which states, "In the afternoon, clothed in the full uniform of his rank, with epaulets and yellow sash, it [the body] was laid in the cloth-covered steel coffin." *See also*,

The Philadelphia Inquirer, February 12, 1886, which states, "Dressed in the uniform of a major-general..."
[34] *The New York Times*, February 10 & 11, 1886. *See also*,

The Sun, February 14, 1886.
[35] Clayman, ed., *Encyclopedia of Medicine*, pp. 860–861, 1023. This modern volume defines Uremia as "The presence of excess urea and other chemical waste products in the blood. Uremia develops as a result of kidney failure (see renal failure)." Renal failure is defined as "The reduction in the ability of the *kidneys* to filter waste products from the blood and excrete them in the urine...Chronic renal failure can result from any disease that causes progressive damage to the kidneys, such as...Well *diabetes mellitus*...In the end-stage [of] renal failure, long-term dialysis or, ideally, *kidney transplant* is the only satisfactory form of treatment."
[36] *The New York Times*, February 12, 1886. This conclusion does not appear to be a correct diagnosis. The deadly potential of a carbuncle was identified in the February 10, 1886 edition of *The Sun* when it reported that a carbuncle had been the cause of death to Newark Alderman George S. Smith. In part, that report stated: "On Thursday morning a small pimple appeared on his upper lip...before night it assumed a very angry appearance. On Friday it was observed to increase rapidly... Saturday his whole lip and the cheek adjoining became so much swollen that he could not take food...On Sunday...[his] neck and chest were involved...the bronchial tubes and lungs became congested. At the

Chapter Six Endnotes

time of death his neck had swollen...much larger around than his head." None of these conditions were ever reported for Hancock.

37 *The New York Times*, February 12, 1886. For both messages from President Cleveland.
38 **Ibid.** *See also*,
The Philadelphia Inquirer, February 10, 1886.
39 Rachel Sherman Thorndike, ed., *The Sherman Letters*, New York: Da Capo Press, 1969, p. 370.
40 *The New York Times*, February 10, 1886.
41 **Ibid.**
42 *New York World*, February 11, 1886.
43 Tucker, *Hancock the Superb*, pp. 279–280. *See also*,
H. M. Lovett, "Hancock the Superb," *Confederate Veteran*, vol. XXVI, No. I [January, February, 1918], reprint; Harrisburg, Pennsylvania: The National Historical Society, pp. 14–16, 93. In addition to his November proclamation, on March 9, 1868, Hancock also addressed the Governor of Texas, E. M. Pease, and chastised him for complaining about his movement toward civil rule. His rebuking posture with that inept politician won him added Southern respect and as late as 1918, Mr. Lovett wrote that Hancock "...is a just man—a simple, massive, and heroic character, as calm and dispassionate in the formation of his opinions as he is firm and inflexible in his adherence to them. He is not to be driven from his convictions of right..." These sentiments were echoed again that year in the February issue of *Confederate Veteran* when the Honorable Pat Henry of Mississippi was quoted as saying: "I note with pride the very interesting January number. The orders of Hancock are resonant of his grand character and read well beside the miserable little orders of Sheridan, Sherman, Hunter..."
44 Gideon Welles, *Diary of Gideon Welles*, 3 vols., Boston: Houghton Mifflin, 1911, vol. II, p. 394. Gideon Welles was Secretary of the Navy for Presidents Lincoln and Johnson. Again, it is interesting to note that during the 1880 Presidential election, Hancock *did not* carry his home state, county or town.
45 *The New York Times*, February 11, 1886.
46 Courtesy, Brian C. Pohanka collection.
47 *Utica Observer*, February 11, 1886.
48 *The New York Times*, February 10, 1886.

Chapter Six Endnotes

[49] Hocker, "Hancock Landmarks," p. 19.
[50] *The New York Times*, May 1, 1893. Note that when Mrs. Hancock was buried at the Bellefontaine Cemetery in St. Louis, Missouri, in April, 1893, "There were no [religious] ceremonies whatsoever at the interment..." Bellefontaine Cemetery, established in 1849, was destined to become the final resting place for over 70 Civil War notables [North and South] including, Lincoln's Attorney General, Edward Bates, USA Major-General Don Carlos Buell, CSA Major-General Sterling Price, USA Major-General John Pope, John Buchanan Eads, who built the river-going ironclads, Rosell Martin Field, Dred Scott's attorney, and at least eight men who won the Medal of Honor during the conflict.
[51] *State Sentinel*, July 13, 1896.
[52] *The Philadelphia Inquirer*, February 10, 1886.
[53] *Army and Navy Journal*, March 20, 1886.
[54] **Ibid.**, February 13, 27 and March 6, 1886.
[55] **Ibid.**, March 6, 1886.
[56] Armes, *Ups and Downs of an Army Officer*, p. 553.
[57] Jordan, *Winfield Scott Hancock*, p. 316. See also,
John M. Taylor, "General Hancock: Soldier of the Gilded Age," *Pennsylvania History*, vol. XXXI, Number 2 [April, 1965]: 195. See also,
The New York Times, February 13 & 16, 1886. See also,
The Philadelphia Public Ledger, February 11, 1886. See also,
The Philadelphia Inquirer, February 15, 1886. See also,
Untitled newspaper clipping in *Hancock File*, courtesy, HSMC. According to a clipping dated July 29, 1913 and datelined New York, the total amount raised for Almira was about $47,000, which was wisely invested into bonds, and the income was paid to Almira until her death, and the funds then went to the grandson, Gwyn. According to another unidentified newspaper clipping in the *Hancock File*, dated May 7, 1911, datelined Memphis, Tennessee, Mrs. Hancock was erroneously reported as remarried to a Ellerton Dorr from Boston.
[58] *The New York Times*, February 10, 1886.
[59] *Army and Navy Journal*, April 10, 1886.
[60] **Ibid.**, February 13 & 16, 1886. See also,
Stewart Sifakis, *Who Was Who in the Civil War*, New York: Facts on File Publications, 1988, p. 582.

Chapter Six Endnotes

[61] *The New York Times*, February 10, 1886. This edition incorrectly reported that Hancock's parents were buried in his tomb. In fact, they, and other family members, are indeed buried in Montgomery Cemetery but approximately 100 yards to the south of the general's tomb, in a family plot purchased by the general and his twin brother Hilary. *See also,*
The Philadelphia Inquirer, February 11, 1886. It was recently confirmed that only two of the six crypts in the general's tomb, which now belongs to the HSMC, are occupied. According to HSMC officials, Mr. Edward T. Addison, Jr., President, Mr. Paul Koons and Ms. Karin Jones, Co-Chairpersons of the Hancock Tomb Restoration Committee, the vault was entered on June 28, 1995, to determine the extent of needed repairs. As part of the inspection, a monument builder-expert also entered the tomb and, without any invasive methods, ascertained that the top crypt on the right [Ada's] and the middle crypt on the left [the general's] are the only two occupied. *See also,*
New York Post, February 13, 1886. Almira, understandably, wanted her husband to be buried in St. Louis where their son Russell was buried and where Almira would be buried. According to this newspaper report, when Hancock's father and namesake grandson died and were both buried at Montgomery Cemetery, he decided that was to be his own resting place as well. Accounts vary. *See also,*
The Philadelphia Inquirer, February 11, 1886. *See also,*
Hancock File–Death, courtesy, HSMC. In a letter written after 1911 by Mr. Joseph Fornance, President of the HSMC, he noted the following: "While General Hancock was stationed at Governor's Island, not long before his death, he and his wife agreed, in the presence of Rev. Mr. Goodwin the Chaplain there, that he should be buried in his vault at Norristown, and she should be buried in her father's vault in St. Louis, Mo. They were afterwards interred as they had arranged."

[62] *The Philadelphia Inquirer*, February 11, 1886.

[63] *New York Post*, February 10, 1886. *See also,*
Waugh, *The Class of 1846*, p. 524.

[64] *The Sun*, February 11, 1886. *See also,*
New York World, February 10, 1886.

[65] *Frank Leslie's Illustrated Newspaper*, February 20, 1886.

[66] *The Sun*, February 12, 1886.

[67] *The New York Times*, February 14, 1886.

[68] Corby, *Memoirs of Chaplain Life*, p. 352.

Chapter Six Endnotes 285

[69] *Daniel E. Sickles to WSH*, undated letter, courtesy, Albert Henry Wunsch, III and Son collection.
[70] *The Gettysburg Compiler*, September 30, 1880.
[71] *The New York Times*, February 20, 1886. *See also,*
Frank Leslie's Illustrated Newspaper, February 20, 1886. *See also,*
New York Post, February 13, 1886.
[72] *The Philadelphia Inquirer*, February 15, 1886.
[73] *The New York Times*, February 14, 1886. *See also,*
New York Post, February 13, 1886.
[74] *The Philadelphia Inquirer*, February 15, 1886.
[75] *I Corinthians*, 15: 20–23.
[76] *The New York Times*, February 14, 1886. *See also,*
The Sun, February 14, 1886. *See also,*
The Philadelphia Inquirer, February 15, 1886.
[77] **Ibid**.
[78] **Ibid**.
[79] **Ibid**. *See also,*
The Times Herald, February 13, 1924. *See also,*
Untitled and undated news clippings *Hancock File*, courtesy, HSMC. [N.B. This particular reference is undoubtedly from a Philadelphia newspaper.]
[80] *New York Post*, February 13, 1886.
[81] *The Times Herald*, February 13, 1924. Note: One newspaper estimated that "...the [Norristown] people on the street numbering fully 10,000..." When the Civil War broke out in 1861, the entire population of Norristown was approximately 8,000 souls.
[82] *The Philadelphia Inquirer*, February 11, 1886.
[83] *The Times Herald*, February 13, 1924. *See also,*
Untitled and undated news clippings in *Hancock File*, courtesy, HSMC. *See also,*
Hocker, "Hancock Landmarks," p. 20. *See also,*
Philadelphia Press, undated clipping, *The Winfield Scott Hancock Papers*, Misc. clippings 1839–1885, courtesy, USAMHI.
[84] *New York Post*, February 13, 1886.
[85] *The New York Times*, February 14, 1886.
[86] **Ibid**.
[87] **Ibid**. *See also,*
New York Post, February 13, 1886.

SELECTED BIBLIOGRAPHY

Books, Articles and Pamphlets
Works Consulted and Cited

Alexander, Edward P., *Military Memoirs of a Confederate*, New York: Charles Scribner's Sons, 1907, reprint; Dayton, Ohio: Morningside Bookshop, 1977.

Allen, Maria Randall, *My Darling Wife*, Watertown, Connecticut: By the author, 1994.

Andrew, Michael J., *The Brooke, Fauquier, Loudoun and Alexandria Artillery*, Lynchburg, Virginia: H. E. Howard, Inc., 1990.

Armes, George A., *Ups and Downs of an Army Officer*, Washington, D.C.: By the author, 1900.

Bandy, Ken, Florence Freeland and Margie Riddle Bearss, eds., *The Gettysburg Papers*, 2 vols., Dayton, Ohio: Press of Morningside Bookshop, 1978.

Banes, Charles H., *History of the Philadelphia Brigade*, Philadelphia: J. B. Lippincott & Co., 1876, reprint; Gaithersburg, Maryland: Butternut Press, 1984.

Bean, Theodore W., ed., *History of Montgomery County Pennsylvania*, Philadelphia: Everts & Peck, 1884, reprint; Mt. Vernon, Indiana: Windmill Publications, 1990.

Beecham, R. K., *Gettysburg, The Pivotal Battle of the Civil War*, Chicago: A. C. McClurg & Co., 1911.

Benedict, G. G., *Vermont at Gettysburg*, Burlington, Vermont: The Free Press Association, 1870.

Beyer, W. F. and O. F. Keydel, eds., *Deeds of Valor*, Detroit, Michigan: Perrien-Keydel Company, 1903, reprint; Stamford, Connecticut: Longmeadow Press, 1992.

Bingham, Henry H., "Memoirs of Hancock," 1872.

_____., *Anecdotes Concerning Gen. Hancock and Other Officers at Gettysburg and Elsewhere*, 1874.

Selected Bibliography

_____., *An Oration by Brevet Brigadier-General Henry H. Bingham at the Unveiling of the Equestrian Statue of Major-General Winfield Scott Hancock on the Battlefield of Gettysburg*, June 5, 1896.

Black, John D., "Reminiscences of the Bloody Angle," *Glimpses of the Nation's Struggle*, Fourth Series, Saint Paul: H. L. Collins Co., 1898, reprint; Wilmington, North Carolina: Broadfoot Publishing Company, 1992.

Boatner, Mark M. III, *The Civil War Dictionary*, New York: Vintage Books, 1991.

Brown, Kent Masterson, *Cushing at Gettysburg*, Lexington, Kentucky: The University Press of Kentucky, 1993.

Bruce, George A., *The Twentieth Regiment of Massachusetts Volunteer Infantry, 1861–1865*. Boston: Houghton, Mifflin and Company, 1906, reprint; Baltimore, Maryland: Butternut and Blue, 1988.

Bruce, Robert V., *Lincoln and the Tools of War*, Indianapolis, Indiana: Bobbs-Merrill, 1956, reprint; Chicago: University of Illinois Press, 1989.

Bryant, Edwin E., "The Battle of Gettysburg," *War Papers*, Being Read Before the Commandery of the State of Wisconsin, MOLLUS, vol. II, Read October 4, 1893, reprint; Wilmington, North Carolina: Broadfoot Publishing, 1993.

Buel, Clarence C. and Robert U. Johnson, eds., *Battles and Leaders of the Civil War*, 4 vols., New York: The Century Company, 1888, reprint; Secaucus, New Jersey: Castle, 1989.

Bushong, Millard K., *Old Jube*, Shippensburg, Pennsylvania: White Mane Publishing Co., Inc., 1955.

Byrne, Frank L. and Andrew T. Weaver, eds., *Haskell of Gettysburg, His Life and Civil War Papers*, Madison, Wisconsin: State Historical Society of Wisconsin, 1970.

Campbell, Eric, "'Remember Harper's Ferry': The Degradation, Humiliation, and Redemption of Col. George L. Willard's Brigade, Part 2," *The Gettysburg Magazine*, Issue Number Eight, [January, 1993]: 95–110.

Carpenter, John A., "General O. O. Howard at Gettysburg," *Civil War History*, vol. 9, Number 3 [September, 1963].

_____., *Sword and Olive Branch, Oliver Otis Howard*, Pittsburgh: University of Pittsburgh Press, 1964.

_____., "Doubleday's Chancellorsville and Gettysburg," *Military Affairs*, vol. 27 [Summer, 1963].

Selected Bibliography

Castel, Albert, *Decisions in the West, The Atlanta Campaign of 1864*, Lawrence, Kansas: University of Kansas, 1992.

Catton, Bruce, *The Army of the Potomac: Mr. Lincoln's Army*, New York: Doubleday & Company, Inc., 1951.

Cavanaugh, Michael A., compiler, *Military Essays and Recollections of the Pennsylvania Commandery Military Order of the Loyal Legion of the United States*, vol. I, February 22, 1866–May 6, 1903, Wilmington, North Carolina: Broadfoot Publishing Company, 1995.

Child, Benjamin H., "From Fredericksburg to Gettysburg," Rhode Island MOLLUS *War Papers*, vol. 8.

Child, William, *A History of the Fifth Regiment, New Hampshire Volunteers in the American Civil War, 1861–1865*, Bristol, New Hampshire: R. W. Musgrove, 1893, reprint; Gaithersburg, Maryland: Ron R. Van Sickle Military Books, 1988.

Clayman, Charles B., ed., *The American Medical Association Encyclopedia of Medicine*, New York: Random House, 1989.

Cleaves, Freeman, *Meade of Gettysburg*, Norman, Oklahoma: University of Oklahoma Press, 1960, reprint; Dayton, Ohio: Morningside Bookshop, 1980.

Coco, Gregory A., *A Vast Sea of Misery*, Gettysburg, Pennsylvania: Thomas Publications, 1988.

Coddington, Edwin B., *The Gettysburg Campaign*, New York: Charles Scribner's Sons, 1968, reprint; Dayton, Ohio: Morningside Bookshop, 1983.

Coffin, Howard, *Full Duty, Vermonters in the Civil War*, Woodstock, Vermont: The Countryman Press, Inc., 1993.

Cole, Jacob H., *Under Five Commanders*, Paterson, New Jersey: News Printing Company, 1906.

Confederate Veteran, Nashville, Tennessee, 1893–1932, reprint; 35 vols., Wilmington, North Carolina: Broadfoot Publishing Company, 1990.

Cook, John D. S., "Personal Reminiscences of Gettysburg," *War Talk in Kansas*, Kansas City, Missouri: Franklin Hudson Publishing Company, 1906, reprint; Wilmington, North Carolina: Broadfoot Publishing Company, 1992, pp. 325–341.

Cooke, Sidney G., "The First Day of Gettysburg," *War Talk in Kansas*, Kansas City, Missouri: Franklin Hudson Publishing Company, 1906, reprint; Wilmington, North Carolina: Broadfoot Publishing Company, 1992, pp. 277–287.

Selected Bibliography

Corby, William, *Memoirs of Chaplain Life*, New York: Fordham University Press, 1992.
Culp, Edward C., *The 25th Ohio Veteran Volunteer Infantry in the War for the Union*, Topeka, Kansas: Geo. W. Crane & Co., 1885.
Curtis, Greely S., Gettysburg, "Report of Committee," *Papers of the Military Historical Society of Massachusetts*, vol., III, March 13, 1876.
d'Orleans, Louis P.A., *History of the Civil War in America*, 7 vols., reprint; Philadelphia: Porter & Coates, 1888.
Denison, C. W., *Winfield the Lawyer's Son*, Philadelphia: Ashmead & Evans, 1865.
Dornbusch, Charles E., *Military Bibliography of the Civil War*, 3 vols., New York: New York Public Library, 1961–1972, reprint; 1994.
Doubleday, Abner, *Chancellorsville and Gettysburg*, New York: Charles Scribner's Sons, 1881, reprint; Harrisburg, Pennsylvania: The Archive Society, 1992.
_____., "Chancellorsville and Gettysburg," *Journal of the Military Service Institution of the United States*, vol. XLVIII, Governor's Island, New York: Military Service Institution [1911]: 105–108.
_____., "Gettysburg Thirty Years After," *North American Review*, No. CCCCXI [February, 1891]: 146.
Early, Jubal A., *General Jubal A. Early*, Philadelphia: J. B. Lippincott Company, 1912, reprint; Wilmington, North Carolina: Broadfoot Publishing Company, 1989.
Eckert, Ralph Lowell, *John Brown Gordon, Soldier—Southerner—American*, Baton Rouge, Louisiana: Louisiana State University Press, 1989.
Encyclopaedia Britannica, 15th Edition, 1986.
Evans, Clement A., ed., et al., *Confederate Military History*, 12 vols., 16 parts, Atlanta Georgia: Confederate Publishing Company, 1899, reprint; Harrisburg, Pennsylvania: The Archive Society, 1994.
Favill, Josiah Marshall, *The Diary of a Young Officer*, Chicago: R. R. Donnelley & Sons Company, 1909.
Forney, John W., *Life and Military Career of Winfield Scott Hancock*, Philadelphia: Hubbard Bros., 1880.
Freed, Augustus T., *The Life and Public Services of Winfield Scott Hancock, Major General U. S. Army*, Chicago: Henry A. Sumner & Company, 1880.
Frederick, Gilbert, *The Story of a Regiment, Being a Record of the Military Services of the Fifty-Seventh New York State Volunteer Infantry in*

Selected Bibliography

the War of the Rebellion 1861–1865, Chicago: The Fifty-Seventh Veteran Association, 1895.

Fremantle, Arthur J. L., *Three Months in the Southern States*, London: William Blackwood and Sons, 1863, reprint; Alexandria, Virginia: Time-Life Books, Inc., 1981.

Fuger, Fred, "Battle of Gettysburg and Personal Recollections of that Battle," *S. Web Papers*, courtesy, Yale University Library.

Gallagher, Gary W., ed., *The First Day at Gettysburg, Essays on Confederate and Union Leadership*, Kent, Ohio: The Kent State University Press, 1992.

_____., *The Second Day at Gettysburg, Essays on Confederate and Union Leadership*, Kent, Ohio: The Kent State University Press, 1993.

_____., *The Third Day at Gettysburg and Beyond*, Chapel Hill, North Carolina: The University of North Carolina Press, 1994.

_____., *Fighting for the Confederacy, The Personal Recollections of General Edward Porter Alexander*, Chapel Hill, North Carolina: The University of North Carolina Press, 1989.

Gambone, A. M., *The Life of General Samuel K. Zook*, Baltimore, Maryland: Butternut and Blue, 1996.

Gibbon, John, *Personal Recollections of the Civil War*, New York: G. P. Putnam's Sons, 1928, reprint; Dayton, Ohio: Morningside Bookshop, 1988.

Goodrich, F. E., *The Life and Public Services of Winfield Scott Hancock, Major-General, U. S. A.*, Boston: Lee & Shepard, 1880.

Gordon, John B., *Reminiscences of the Civil War*, New York: Charles Scribner's Sons, 1903, reprint; Alexandria, Virginia: Time-Life Books, Inc., 1981.

Grant, Ulysses S., *Personal Memoirs*, 2 vols., New York: Charles L. Webster & Company, 1886.

Greeley, Horace, *The American Conflict*, 2 vols., Hartford, Connecticut: O. D. Case & Company, 1864–1866.

Hale, Charles A., "With Colonel Cross at the Wheatfield," *Civil War Times Illustrated* [August, 1974]: 30–38.

Halstead, E. P., "The First Day of the Battle of Gettysburg," A paper delivered by Brevet Major Halstead to the Washington D.C. MOLLUS Commandery, March 2, 1887. Courtesy, USAMHI.

Hamblen, Charles P., *Connecticut Yankees at Gettysburg*, Walter L. Powell, ed., Kent, Ohio: The Kent State University Press, 1993.

Selected Bibliography

Hancock, Almira R., *Reminiscences of Winfield Scott Hancock*, New York: Charles L. Webster & Company, 1887.

Hancock, Winfield Scott, "Gettysburg Reply to General Howard," *The Galaxy*, [December, 1876].

Hancock, Winfield Scott, *Official Reports of Military Operations of Troops Commanded by Major General W. S. Hancock, During the Civil War, 1861–65*, n.p., n.d.

Hanna, William F., "Major General Darius N. Couch: A Civil War Profile," *Lincoln Herald*, 86 No. 1 [Spring 1984].

Harper, Douglas R., *"If Thee Must Fight,"* West Chester, Pennsylvania: Chester County Historical Society, 1990.

Harrison, Kathleen Georg, "Ridges of Grim War," *Blue & Gray Magazine*, Volume V, Issue 6 [July, 1988].

Hassler, Warren W., *Crisis at the Crossroads, The First Day at Gettysburg*, Birmingham, Alabama: University of Alabama Press, 1970, reprint; Gettysburg, Pennsylvania: Stan Clark Military Books, 1991.

Hebert, Walter H., *Fighting Joe Hooker*, New York: Bobbs-Merrill Company, 1944, reprint; Gaithersburg, Maryland: Butternut Press, Inc., 1987.

Hedrick, David T. & Gordon Barry Davis, Jr., eds, *I'm Surrounded by Methodists...Diary of John H. W. Stuckenberg, Chaplain of the 145th Pennsylvania Volunteer Infantry*, Gettysburg: Thomas Publications, 1995.

Herdegen, Lance J., and William J. K. Beaudot, *In the Bloody Railroad Cut at Gettysburg*, Dayton, Ohio: Morningside House, Inc., 1990.

Hocker, Edward W., "Hancock Landmarks," *The Sketches of the Historical Society of Montgomery County*, vol. V [1925].

Holstein, Anna M., *Three Years in Field Hospitals of the Army of the Potomac*, Philadelphia: J. B. Lippincott & Co., 1867.

Hooker, Charles E., *Confederate Military History*, Vol. VII, part II, Chapter X, Atlanta, Georgia: Confederate Publishing Company, 1899, reprint; Harrisburg, Pennsylvania: The Archive Society, 1994, p. 180.

Howard, Charles H., "First Day at Gettysburg," *War Papers*, vol. IV, Military Essays and Recollections, Illinois MOLLUS, Read October 1, 1903.

Howard, Oliver Otis, *Autobiography of Oliver Otis Howard*, 2 vols., New York: The Baker & Taylor Company, 1907.

_____., "Campaign and Battle of Gettysburg, June and July, 1863," *Atlantic Monthly Magazine*, vol. 38 [July–November]: 1876.

Selected Bibliography

_____., Henry W. Slocum, Abner Doubleday and The Count of Paris, "Gettysburg Thirty Years After," *North American Review*, No. CCCCXI [February, 1891].

Hyde, Thomas W., *Civil War Letters by General Thomas W. Hyde*, John H. Hyde, 1933.

Jacobs, H. E., "Meteorology of the Battle," 1885. Courtesy, GNMP.

Johnson, Allen and Dumas Malone, *Dictionary of American Biography*, 22 vols., New York: Charles Scribner's Sons, 1931, reprint; 10 vols., 1958.

Johnston, Ida Lee, "Over the Stonewall at Gettysburg," *Confederate Veteran*, vol. XXXI, No. 7 [July, 1923].

Jordan, David M., *Winfield Scott Hancock, A Soldier's Life*, Indianapolis, Indiana: Indiana University Press, 1988.

Junkin, D. X. and Frank H. Norton, *The Life of Winfield Scott Hancock: Personal, Military, and Political*, New York: D. Appleton and Company, 1880.

Ladd, David L., Audrey J. Ladd, eds., and Richard Allen Sauers, Publisher's Consultant, *The Bachelder Papers*, 3 vols., Dayton, Ohio: Morningside House, Inc., 1994–1995.

Lash, Gary, *The Gibraltar Brigade on East Cemetery Hill*, Baltimore, Maryland: Butternut and Blue, 1995.

_____., "The Philadelphia Brigade at Gettysburg," *The Gettysburg Magazine*, Issue Number Seven [July, 1992].

Letters and Addresses, In Memory of Winfield Scott Hancock, New York: G. P. Putnam's Sons, For The Military Service Institute, 1886.

Livermore, Thomas L., *Days and Events*, Boston: Houghton Mifflin Company, 1920.

Lochren, William, "The First Minnesota at Gettysburg," Minnesota MOLLUS *War Papers*, vol. 3.

Longacre, Edward G., *The Man Behind the Guns*, New York: A. S. Barnes and Company, 1977.

_____., *To Gettysburg and Beyond*, Highstown, New Jersey: Longstreet House, 1988.

Longstreet, James, *From Manassas to Appomattox, Memoirs of the Civil War in America*, Philadelphia: 1896, reprint; Secaucus, New Jersey: The Blue and Grey Press, 1984.

_____., "Longstreet's Report of the Pennsylvania Campaign," *S.H.S.P.*, Vol. X.

Selected Bibliography

Lovett, H. M., "Hancock the Superb," *Confederate Veteran*, vol. XXVI, No. 1 [January, 1918].

Lyman, Theodore, *Meade's Headquarters, 1863–1865*, Boston: Atlantic Monthly Press, 1922, reprint; *With Grant and Meade, From the Wilderness to Appomattox*, Lincoln, Nebraska: University of Nebraska Press, 1994.

Lynch, Louis, "The Generals, Three Major Figures Linked to Putnam," *The Putnam Ledger*, May 16, 1978.

Malone, Dumas, ed., *Dictionary of American Biography*, vol. V, Charles Scribner's Sons, 1960–1961.

Mark, Penrose G., *Red: White: and Blue Badge, A History of the 93rd Regiment Pennsylvania Veteran Volunteers*, Harrisburg, Pennsylvania: Aughinbaugh Press, 1911.

Mayo, Joseph C., "Pickett's Charge at Gettysburg," *S.H.S.P.*, vol. 34, [May, 1906].

Meade, George Gordon, ed., *The Battle of Gettysburg*, New York: Charles Scribner's Sons, 1913, reprint; Gettysburg, Pennsylvania: Farnsworth House Military Impressions, 1988.

_____., *The Life and Letters of General George Gordon Meade*, 2 vols., New York: Charles Scribner's Sons, 1913, reprint; Baltimore, Maryland: Butternut and Blue, 1994.

Moe, Richard, *The Last Full Measure, The Life and Death of the First Minnesota Volunteers*, New York: Henry Holt and Company, 1993, reprint; New York: Avon Books, 1994.

Moore, Gilbert C. Jr., ed., *Cornie*, Chattanooga, Tennessee: By the Editor, 1989.

Motts, Wayne E., *"Trust In God and Fear Nothing"*, Gettysburg, Pennsylvania: Farnsworth House Military Impressions, 1994.

Muffly, J. W., ed., *The Story of Our Regiment, A History of the 148th Pennsylvania Volunteers*, Des Moines, Iowa: The Kenyon Printing & Mfg. Co., 1904, reprint; Baltimore, Maryland: Butternut and Blue, 1994.

Mulholland, St. Clair A., *The Story of the 116th Regiment, Pennsylvania Infantry*, reprint; Gaitherburg, Maryland: Olde Soldier Books, Inc., n.d.

Nelson, Lee H., *Nail Chronology As An Aide to Dating Old Buildings*, Nashville, Tennessee: American Association for State and Local History, 1968.

Nevins, Allan, *Ordeal of the Union*, 8 vols., New York: Charles Scribner's Sons, 1971.

Selected Bibliography

Nichols, Edward J., *Toward Gettysburg, A Biography of General John F. Reynolds*, The Pennsylvania State University Press, 1958, reprint; Gaithersburg, Maryland: Olde Soldier Books, Inc., 1987.

Nicolay, John G. and John Hay, *Abraham Lincoln, A History*, 10 vols., New York: The Century Co., 1890.

Nye, Wilbur Sturtevant, *Here Come the Rebels!*, Dayton, Ohio: Press of the Morningside Bookshop, 1988.

O'Brien, Kevin E., ed., *My Life in the Irish Brigade: The Civil War Memoirs of Private William McCarter, 116th Pennsylvania Infantry*, San Jose, California: Savas/Woodbury Publishers, 1996.

Oates, William C., *The War Between the Union and the Confederacy, and Its Lost Opportunities; The History of the 15th Alabama*, New York: The Neale Publishing Company, 1905.

Osborn, Hartwell, *Trials and Triumphs, The Record of the Fifty-fifth Ohio Volunteer Infantry*, Chicago: A. C. McClurg & Co., 1904.

Otis, George H., *The Second Wisconsin Infantry*, Alan D. Gaff, ed., Dayton, Ohio: Press of Morningside Bookshop, 1984.

Owen, William Miller, *In Camp and Battle With the Washington Artillery of New Orleans*, Boston: Ticknor and Company, 1885.

Paine, Albert Bigelow, *TH. NAST, His Period and His Pictures*, New York: The Macmillan Company, 1904, reprint; Princeton, New Jersey: The Pyne Press, 1974.

Pennypacker, Isaac R., *General Meade*, New York: D. Appleton and Company, 1901, reprint; Gaithersburg, Maryland: Olde Soldier Books Inc., 1987.

Pfanz, Harry W., *Gettysburg, The Second Day*, Chapel Hill, North Carolina: The University of North Carolina Press, 1987.

Phipps, Michael & John S. Peterson, *"The Devil's to Pay"*, Gettysburg, Pennsylvania: Farnsworth Military Impressions, 1995.

Poindexter, James E., "Gen. Lewis Addison Armistead," *Confederate Veteran*, vol. XXII, No. 11 [November, 1914].

Powell, William H., *The Fifth Army Corps*, New York: G. P. Putnam's Sons, 1896.

Purifoy, John, "The Battle of Gettysburg, July 2," *Confederate Veteran*, vol. XXXI, No. 7 [July, 1923].

Reed, Augustus T., *The Life and Services of Winfield Scott Hancock, Major General U.S. Army*, Chicago: Henry A. Sumner & Company, 1880.

Rhea, Gordon C., *The Battle of the Wilderness, May 5–6, 1864*, Baton Rouge: Louisiana State University Press, 1994.

Selected Bibliography

Rhodes, James Ford, *History of the Civil War, 1861–1865*, New York: The MacMillan Company, 1917.

_____., *History of the United States*, vol. IV, 1862–1864, Norwood, Massachusetts: Berwick & Smith, 1899, reprint; New York: The MacMillan Company, 1907.

Riemer, Joseph T., "General Hancock and Dr. Read," *The Bulletin of the Historical Society of Montgomery County Pennsylvania*, vol. XVIII, No. 2 [Spring, 1972]: 173–179.

Roberts, Allen E., *House Divided, The Story of Freemasonry and the Civil War*, Richmond, Virginia: Macoy Publishing & Masonic Supply Co., Inc., 1990.

Robertson, James I. Jr., ed., *Medical and Surgical History of the Civil War*, 15 vols., Wilmington, North Carolina: Broadfoot Publishing Com-pany, 1991.

Rollins, Richard, ed., *Pickett's Charge, Eyewitness Accounts*, Redondo Beach, California: Rank and File Publications, 1994.

Sandburg, Carl, *Abraham Lincoln, The War Years*, 4 vols., New York: Harcourt, Brace & Company, 1936–1939.

Sauers, Richard A., *A Caspian Sea of Ink: The Meade–Sickles Controversy*, Baltimore, Maryland: Butternut and Blue, 1989.

_____., *The Gettysburg Campaign, June 3–August 1, 1863, A Comprehensive, Selectively Annotated Bibliography*, Westport, Connecticut: Greenwood Press, 1982.

Scott, Robert Garth, ed., *Fallen Leaves, The Civil War Letters of Major Henry Livermore Abbott*, Kent, Ohio: The Kent State University Press, 1991.

Schurz, Carl, "The Battle of Gettysburg," *McClure's Magazine* [July, 1907].

Sifakis, Stewart, *Who Was Who in the Civil War*, New York: Facts on File Publications, 1988.

Simon, John Y., ed., *The Papers of Ulysses S. Grant*, 16 vols., Carbondale, Illinois: Southern Illinois University Press, n.d.

Simpson, Harold B., *Hood's Texas Brigade, Lee's Grenadier Guard*, Waco, Texas: Texian Press, 1970.

Skelly, Daniel Alexander, *A Boy's Experiences During the Battles of Gettysburg*, Gettysburg: By the Author, 1932.

Sloath, Frank D., *History of the Twenty-Seventh Regiment Connecticut Volunteer Infantry*, courtesy, 27th Connecticut Volunteers, A Uniformed Historical Society.

Selected Bibliography

Slocum, Charles Elihu, *The Life and Services of Major-General Henry Warner Slocum*, Toledo, Ohio: Slocum Publishing Company, 1913.

Smith, L. A., "Recollections of Gettysburg," *War Papers Being Read Before the Commandery of the State of Michigan MOLLUS*, vol. II, from December 7, 1893 to May 5, 1898, Read May 3, 1894, reprint; Wilmington, North Carolina: Broadfoot Publishing Company, 1993.

Smith, Timothy H., *The Story of Lee's Headquarters, Gettysburg, Pennsylvania*, Gettysburg, Pennsylvania: Thomas Publications, 1995.

Sorrel, G. Moxley, *Recollections of a Confederate Staff Officer*, Neale Publishing Company, 1915, reprint; New York: W. S. Konecky Associates, Inc., 1994.

Southern Historical Society Papers [S.H.S.P.], 55 vols., Richmond, Virginia: 1876, reprint; Wilmington, North Carolina: Broadfoot Publishing Company, 1991–1993.

Stammerjohan, George R., "The Camel Experiment in California," *Dogtown Territorial Quarterly*, Number 18 [Summer 1994]: pp. 10–63.

Stewart, George R., *Pickett's Charge, A Microhistory of the Final Attack at Gettysburg*, Boston: Houghton Mifflin Company, 1959 reprint; 1987.

Stewart, James, "Battery B Fourth United States Artillery at Gettysburg," *Sketches of War History 1861–1865*, vol. IV, Cincinnati: The Robert Clarke Company, 1896, reprint; Wilmington, North Carolina: Broadfoot Publishing Company, n.d.

Stevens, George T., *Three Years With the Sixth Corps*, Albany, New York: S. R. Gray, Publishers, 1866, reprint; Alexandria, Virginia: Time-Life Books, Inc., 1984.

Stiles, Robert, *Four Years Under Marse Robert*, New York: Neale Publishing Company, 1903, reprint; Dayton, Ohio: Press of Morningside Bookshop, 1977.

Storrick, W. C., *The Battle of Gettysburg*, Gettysburg, Pennsylvania: Stan Clark Military Books, 1991.

Strayer, Larry M., & Richard A. Baumgartner, eds., *Echoes of Battle, The Atlanta Campaign*, Huntington, West Virginia: Blue Acorn Press, 1991.

Sturtevand, Ralph Orson and Carmi Lathrop Marsh, *History of the 13th Regiment, Vermont Volunteers*, Burlington, Vermont, 1910.

Swanberg, W. A., *Sickles the Incredible*, Charles Scribner's Sons, 1956, reprint; Gettysburg, Stan Clark Military Books, 1991.

Taylor, Emerson Gifford, *Gouverneur Kemble Warren*, Boston: Houghton Mifflin Company, 1932, reprint; Gaithersburg, Maryland: Ron. R. Van Sickle Military Books, 1988.

Selected Bibliography

Taylor, John M., "General Hancock: Soldier of the Gilded Age," *Pennsylvania History*, vol. XXXI, Number 2 [April, 1965].
Taylor, Vivian, comp., *Memorials in Stone, Tombstone Inscriptions, Montgomery County, Pennsylvania*, Norristown, Pennsylvania: HSMC, 1985.
Thomas, Emory M., *Bold Dragoon, The Life of J. E. B. Stuart*, New York: Harper & Row, Publishers, 1986.
Thorndike, Rachel Sherman, *The Sherman Letters*, New York: DaCapo Press, 1969.
Trask, Benjamin H., *9th Virginia Infantry*, Lynchburg, Virginia: H. E. Howard, Inc., 1984.
Tremain, Henry Edwin, *Two Days of War, A Gettysburg Narrative and Other Excursions*, New York: Bonnell, Silver and Bowers, 1905.
Tucker, Glenn, "Hancock at Gettysburg," *The Bulletin of the Historical Society of Montgomery County Pennsylvania*, vol. XIII, No. 4 [Spring, 1961].
_____., *Hancock the Superb*, Indianapolis, Indiana: Bobbs-Merrill Company, Inc., 1960, reprint; Dayton, Ohio: Morningside Bookshop, 1980.
_____., *High Tide at Gettysburg*, Indianapolis, Indiana: Bobbs-Merrill Company, Inc., 1958, reprint; Dayton, Ohio: Morningside House, 1983.
_____., *Lee and Longstreet at Gettysburg*, 1968, reprint; Dayton, Ohio: Morningside House, Inc., 1982.
_____., "A Personality Profile," *Civil War Times Illustrated* [August, 1968].
_____., *Hancock at Gettysburg*, a manuscript.
Turner, Justin G. and Lind L., eds., *Mary Todd Lincoln, Her Life and Letters*, New York: Alfred A. Knopf, Inc., 1972.
Wainwright, Charles A., *A Diary of Battle*, Allan Nevins, ed., New York: Harcourt, Brace & World, Inc., 1962.
Walker, Francis, *General Hancock*, New York: D. Appleton and Company, 1894, reprint; Gaithersburg, Maryland: Olde Soldier Books Inc., 1987.
_____., *History of the Second Corps in the Army of the Potomac*, New York: Charles Scribner's Sons, 1887, reprint; Gaithersburg, Maryland: Olde Soldier Books, Inc., n.d.
Wallace, Lee A. Jr., *1st Virginia Infantry*, Lynchburg, Virginia: H. E. Howard, Inc., 1984.

Selected Bibliography

Wallber, Albert, "From Gettysburg to Libby Prison," *War Papers* Being Read before the Commandery of the State of Wisconsin, MOLLUS, vol. IV, October 6, 1906, reprint; Wilmington, North Carolina: Broadfoot Publishing Company, 1993.

Warner, Ezra J., *Generals in Blue*, Baton Rouge, Louisiana: Louisiana State University Press, 1984.

_____., *Generals in Gray*, Baton Rouge, Louisiana: Louisiana State University Press, 1983.

Waugh, John G., *The Class of 1846*, New York: Warner Books, 1994.

Weld, Stephen Minot, *War Diary and Letters*, Boston: 1912.

Welles, Gideon, *Diary of Gideon Welles*, 3 vols., Boston: Houghton Mifflin, 1911.

Wheeler, Richard, *Witness to Gettysburg*, New York: Meridian, 1987.

Whittier, Edward N., "The Left Attack (Ewell's) At Gettysburg," Massachusetts MOLLUS *War Papers*, vol. 1.

Wiggin, Francis, "Sixteenth Maine Regiment at Gettysburg," *War Papers*, vol. IV, Read before the Commandery of the State of Maine, MOLLUS, Portland: Lefavor-Tower Company, 1915, reprint; Wilmington, North Carolina: Broadfoot Publishing Company, 1992.

Willson, Arabella M., *Disaster, Struggle, Triumph, The Adventures of 1000 "Boys in Blue," from August, 1862, to June, 1865*, Albany, New York: The Argus Company, Printers, 1870.

Winkler, William K., ed., *Letters of Frederick C. Winkler 1862 to 1865*, By the family, 1963.

Winslow, Richard Elliot III, *General John Sedgwick, The Story of a Union Corps Commander*, Novato, California: Presidio Press, 1982.

Wistar, Isaac Jones, *Autobiography of Isaac Jones Wistar*, Philadelphia: The Wistar Institute of Anatomy and Biology, 1937.

Wright, Steven J., "Don't Let Me Bleed to Death," *The Gettysburg Magazine*, Issue Number Six [January 1, 1992]: pp. 87–92.

Magazines and Bulletins

Atlantic Monthly, Boston, Massachusetts.
Blue & Gray Magazine, Columbus, Ohio.
Century Magazine, New York.

Selected Bibliography

Civil War Times Illustrated, Harrisburg, Pennsylvania.
Confederate Veteran, Nashville, Tennessee.
Dogtown Territorial Quarterly, Paradise, California.
Lincoln Herald, Harrogate, Tennessee.
McClure's Magazine, New York, New York
Military Affairs, Kansas State University.
North American Review, Boston, Massachusetts.
Pennsylvania History, Gettysburg, Pennsylvania.
The Bulletin of the Historical Society of Montgomery County, Norristown, Pennsylvania.
The Galaxy, New York, New York.
The Gettysburg Magazine, Dayton, Ohio.

Newspapers

Army and Naval Journal, Philadelphia, Pennsylvania.
Boston Herald, Boston, Massachusetts.
Charleston News and Courier, Charleston, South Carolina.
Frank Leslie's Illustrated Newspaper, New York, New York.
Gettysburg Compiler, Gettysburg, Pennsylvania.
Herald and Free Press, Norristown, Pennsylvania.
National Defender, Norristown, Pennsylvania.
New Orleans Times, New Orleans, Louisiana.
New York Post, New York, New York.
New York World, New York, New York.
Norristown Daily Herald, Norristown, Pennsylvania.
Norristown Republican, Norristown, Pennsylvania.
Norristown Times Herald, Norristown, Pennsylvania.
Norristown Weekly Herald, Norristown, Pennsylvania.
Philadelphia Public Ledger, Philadelphia, Pennsylvania.
Philadelphia Times, Philadelphia, Pennsylvania.
Philadelphia Weekly Press, Philadelphia, Pennsylvania.
Pittsburgh Gazette, Pittsburgh, Pennsylvania.
State Sentinel, New York, New York.
The Evening Post, New York, New York.
The National Tribune, Washington, D.C.

Selected Bibliography

The New York Times, New York, New York.
The Philadelphia Inquirer, Philadelphia, Pennsylvania.
The Putnam Ledger, Putnam, New York.
The Sun, New York, New York.
The Sunday Herald, Washington, D.C.
The Times Herald, Norristown, Pennsylvania.
The World, New York, New York.
Utica Observer, Utica, New York.
Washington Times, Washington, D.C.

Manuscripts and Government Documents

William Barksdale, Participants File, courtesy, GNMP.
The Samuel P. Bates Collection, courtesy, Pennsylvania Historical and Museum Commission and USAMHI.
The Charles Bednar Collection, letters of Horatio G. Wright, courtesy, USAMHI.
The Robert L. Brake Collection, Box: Northern Commanders and Staff Officers, Folders for: Generals Francis Channing Barlow, Abner Doubleday, Winfield Scott Hancock, O. O. Howard, John F. Reynolds, Alexander S. Webb, and Colonel E. E. Cross, courtesy, USAMHI.
The Timothy Brooks Collection, Letter of unknown soldiers of the 140th Pennsylvania, courtesy, USAMHI.
Charity Lodge No. 190 records, AYM, Norristown, Pennsylvania.
James H. Cooper to "Mac", June 14, 1886, courtesy USAMHI and GNMP.
Abner Doubleday Letter, February 26, 1891, courtesy, Northwest CWRT and USAMHI.
Stanley H. Ford Papers, courtesy, USAMHI.
William D. Hall to Abner Doubleday, n.d., courtesy, Albert H. Wunsch, III and Son Collection.
U. S. Grant to Abraham Lincoln, July 25, 1864, courtesy, CWLM.
H. R. Report No. 592, Promulgation of Army Regulations, 43rd Congress, 1st Session, May 13, 1874.
Winfield Scott Hancock Papers, Special Collections, courtesy, Bowdoin College Library.
Winfield Scott Hancock Papers, courtesy, CWLM.

Selected Bibliography

Winfield Scott Hancock Papers, courtesy, GNMP.
Winfield Scott Hancock Papers, courtesy, HSMC.
Winfield Scott Hancock Papers, courtesy, USAMHI.
Winfield Scott Hancock to Peter Frederick Rothermel, December 31, 1868, courtesy, Pennsylvania State Archives.
Winfield Scott Hancock to Joseph Hooker, July 23 and 17, 1876, courtesy, Pennsylvania State Archives.
D. Scott Hartzell Collection. This private collection contains several original Hancock letters to his aide, Major William G. Mitchell, courtesy, USAMHI.
Rutherford B. Hayes Papers, courtesy, GNMP.
Oliver Otis Howard Papers, Special Collections, Bowdoin College Library.
Oliver Otis Howard Letter, March 9, 1891, courtesy, Northwest [Conn.] CWRT and USAMHI.
Andrew Atkinson Humphreys Papers, courtesy, Historical Society of Pennsylvania.
Henry J. Hunt Papers, Undated, 21-page report, believed to have been written in the late 1860's or the 1870's, by Henry J. Hunt. Courtesy, Library of Congress, Misc.–General Misc., Container No. 14. *See also*, Container No. 2.
Aaron Brainard Jerome, *Buford in the Battle of Oak Ridge The 1st Day's Fight at Gettysburg A.M. Wednesday 1st July, 1863*, undated, courtesy, Michael Phipps.
William G. Mitchell to Dr. L. W. Read, September 20, 1880, courtesy, GNMP. Note that the individual who transcribed this letter transposed Mitchell's first initial as "M" and not "W."
Official Register of the Officers and Cadets of the U.S. Military Academy, June 1841–1844.
John Edward Pierce, "The Civil War Career of Richard Brooke Garnett: A Quest for Vindication," Master of Arts diss., Virginia Poltechnic Institute, 1969, courtesy, Mr. Andy DeCusati.
Dr. L. W. Read Papers, courtesy, HSMC.
Report of the Joint Committee on the Conduct of the War, 2nd Session, 38th Congress, vol. I.
Sessler Collection, courtesy, CWLM.
Daniel E. Sickles to WSH, undated letter, courtesy, Albert H. Wunsch, III and Son Collection.
Henry W. Slocum to T. H. Davis & Co., September 8, 1875, courtesy, GNMP.

U. S. Department of War, *The War of the Rebellion: A Compilation of the Official Records of the Union and Confederate Armies*, 128 vols., Washington: Government Printing Office, 1880–1901.

A. S. Webb Papers, Folder numbers 007-0100 and 007-0111, courtesy, Yale University Library.

Edward Whittier, 5th Maine Battery, courtesy, Brian C. Pohanka.

INDEX

Adam 22
Adams, Charles 97
Agnew, D. 166
Agnostic 206
Alabama,
    Montgomery County xix
Albany, New York 71, 182
Alexander, Edward Porter 55
    at Gettysburg 114, 116, 117, 133
    ponders Union lack of deterrent 114
    agrees with Hancock about artillery authority 137
America vii
American .... xiii, xv, 3, 5, 21, 95, 119, 182
American Flag 210, 212, 222
Ames, Adelbert 57, 102, 104
Anderson, Finley 210
Anderson, Robert 208
Andover College 79
Ann Lee, *Miss* 202, 211
Antietam,
    battle of .... xiii, 40, 95, 123, 128, 129, 206
Anti-Slavery Party 79
Apache Indians 40
Appomattox Courthouse, Virginia 205
Arkansas 124
Armes, George A. 197, 207
Armistead, Lewis A. .... viii, 157
    during Pickett's charge 139, 143
    mortally wounded 144, 145, 155, 158
    death of 146
    romanticized relationship with Hancock viii
Army of Northern Virginia 1, 138

Index

Army of the Potomac .... xix, 1, 3, 4, 8, 13, 16, 19, 57, 97, 102
Arnold, William A. 78, 128
Astor, John Jacob 207, 211
Astor, William W. 211
Atlanta, Georgia 48
Atlantic Monthly 61, 63
Atzerodt, George 184
Auburn, New York 179
Avery, Isaac E. 101
Aztec Club of 1846 xix

Bachelder, John B. 54, 56, 188, 194
Baker, Edward D. 208
Balaklava 82
Balls Bluff 7
Baltimore, Maryland 71, 163, 168, 179, 183
Baltimore Pike 58, 60, 64, 65, 163
Bannock Indians 41
Baptist Church 206
Barber, T. H. 196
Barksdale, William 92, 94, 95
    biography 95
    wounded at Gettysburg on July 2nd 92
    death of 110, 164
Barlow, Francis C. 41, 42, 57
    wounded at Gettysburg 57
    evaluation of troops on July 1 42
Battle of Gettysburg 150
Bayard, Thomas F. .... xix, 210, 211, 222
Beck, W. B. 202
Beecham, R. K. 53
Beethoven,
    Funeral March 211
Bellefontaine Cemetery xx
Belmont, August 207
Benedict, George C. 141
Benner's Hill 57
Berdan, Hiram 81
Bigelow, John 131, 134

Index 305

Bingham, Henry H.	xv, 118, 124, 146, 180, 183
aide to Hancock	115, 116
describes Hancock	119, 142
wounded at Gettysburg	118
renders aid to General Armistead	144, 145
wins Medal of Honor	116
Birney, David B.	79, 83, 91
attends council of war	105, 107, 109
III Corps destroyed	92, 97
unhappy about Hancock's appointment	109
Birney, James G. [father]	79
Black Hat Brigade [*see* Iron Brigade],	
Blackstone, Sir William	vii
Commentaries	vii
Bliss Home and Barn	81
burned	115
Boston, Massachusetts	182, 207
Bouvier, Emma	201
Bowdoin College	40
Boyd, *Captain*	5
Boydton Plank Road	183
Brady, L.	81
Brady, Mathew	96
Brandy Station, Virginia	55
Brewerton, *Captain*	210
Brinton, Daniel G.	146
Brooke, John Rutter	197
speaks to Hancock	114, 120
Brooks, Preston	95
Brown, T. Fred	78, 128
Brownson, Edward P.,	
exchanges horses with Hancock	118
Bryan House	95
Bryant, Edwin E.	133
Buckner, Simon Bolivar	vii
Buell, Don Carlos	vii
Buford, John	15, 22, 24, 27, 35, 41, 43, 53
opening moments at Gettysburg	22, 74
opinion of Hancock	27, 43, 57

Index

Bull, James M. 95
Bull, Octavius 120
Bull Run, First 40, 123
Burgoyne, John 21
Burnside, Ambrose E. 128
    president of the National Rifle Association xix
Butterfield, Clark H. 144
Butterfield, Daniel 62, 107
    chief-of-staff for General Meade 24
Butternut and Blue v
Buyers, Edgar 170

Caldwell, John C. 4, 25, 82, 87, 120, 146, 148
    leads Hancock's First Division 78, 85, 87, 92, 101
California viii
"Campaign and Battle of Gettysburg" 61
Canadian 124
Carnegie, Andrew 207
Carpenter, John A. 59
Carlisle, Pennsylvania 8
Carroll, Samuel S. 72, 103, 104
    sent to aid General Howard on July 2nd 102
        explanation of what he saw 102
        upset with portions of the XI Corps 104
        prevents disaster to General Howard's line 102, 105
    corresponds with Hancock 102
    corresponds with General Gibbon 104
    General Howard's treatment of 104
Cashtown, Pennsylvania 13, 27
Castel, Albert 48
Castle Williams 210
Catton, Bruce 48
Centreville, Maryland 7
Century Company 61
Cemetery Hill 24, 27, 28, 36, 43, 44, 46, 48, 50, 54–57, 59–61, 64–66, 72–74, 76, 102, 104, 105, 139
    East Cemetery Hill 57, 101
Cemetery Ridge 76, 82, 92, 100, 112, 114–116, 120, 122, 127, 133, 138, 158
Chain, Benjamin E. 213

    friend and financial advisor to Hancock 182
        builds tomb for 195
Chamberlain, Joshua 84, 102
    praised by Hancock 84
Chambersburg, Pennsylvania 5, 9, 13
Chambersburg Pike 22, 23, 53
Chancellorsville and Gettysburg 47, 48, 51
Chancellorsville, Virginia 2, 4, 85
    battle of .... xiii, xvii, 1, 3, 5, 15, 40, 47, 48, 58, 67, 95, 128–130
Chantilly 79
Charge of the Light Brigade 82
Charleston News and Courier 205
Charlotte, North Carolina 13
Chattanooga, Tennessee 48
Chestnut Hill, Pennsylvania 166
Chester A. Arthur 210, 212
Child, William 87
Childs, George W. 207
Choate, Joseph H. 211, 212
Chopin,
    Funeral March 211
Christ 211
Christian 206
Christian Commission 163
Cincinnati, Ohio 79, 203, 204
Cleveland, Grover .... xix, 197, 203, 210
Cochise, Indian Chief 40
Coddington, Edwin B. 42, 58
Codori Farm 152
Cold Harbor 183
Columbia, Pennsylvania 8
Columbus, Ohio 71
Congregational Church 40
Connecticut 88
Connecticut Regiments,
    14th Connecticut Infantry 115
    27th Connecticut Infantry 88, 89, 114
Conshohocken, Pennsylvania 213
Constitutional Convention 182

Index

Cooke, Sidney G. 50
Cooper, *Dr.* 170
Corby, William, Reverend 13, 14, 85
   grants absolution at Gettysburg 85, 87
   on Hancock's profanity .... xvii, 14
Corcoran, W. W. 207
Corn Exchange of Philadelphia 18
Corps, Confederate,
   I 83
   II 40, 41
   III 115, 184
Corps, Union,
   I 22, 23, 25, 41–43, 49, 50, 53, 59, 62, 68, 78, 100, 112, 115, 139, 163
      First Division 50, 53, 59
         First Brigade 53
      Third Division 23, 129
         Third Brigade 100, 139
   II ... vii, viii, xiii, xv, xvi, 1, 2, 4, 6, 7, 9, 13, 15, 21, 24–26, 40, 45, 48, 60, 63, 76, 78, 81–83, 85, 91, 97, 101, 102, 104, 112, 114, 115, 117, 121, 122, 124, 129, 131, 133–135, 138, 139, 143, 145, 147, 148, 163, 181–183, 188
      First Division .... xiii, 3, 4, 5, 9, 25, 78, 85, 87, 92, 114
         First Brigade 87
         Third Brigade 9, 14, 87
         Fourth Brigade 114
      Second Division 7, 25, 40, 78, 100, 139
         First Brigade 97
         Second Brigade 7
      Third Division 7, 72, 78, 92, 102, 115, 139, 179
         First Brigade 72, 102
         Third Brigade 92
   III ... 22, 25, 62, 68, 69, 71, 79, 79, 81, 82, 84, 87, 91, 92, 97, 101, 109, 112, 115
      First Division 79
         First Brigade 79, 83
         Second Brigade 79, 83
         Third Brigade 79, 83
      Second Division 92

Index

IV	48
V	2, 25, 68, 78, 82, 83, 101, 109, 116, 148
Third Division	78
VI	xiii, 49, 78, 82, 83, 101, 109, 116, 148
XI	22, 23, 25, 40–43, 46, 47, 55, 57–59, 61, 62, 64, 68, 73, 78, 102, 146
First Division	41, 42, 102
Second Brigade	41, 43, 102
Second Division	73
Third Division	41, 48
XII	56, 58, 59, 68, 78, 101, 105
First Division	101
Second Brigade	101
Second Division	56
Corson, Ellwood M.	182
Corson, John P.	23
Corson, Katherine	182
Corson, William	169, 170, 183
Costi, Arthur	222
Couch, Darius N.	xii, xiii, 2, 6, 12, 16
commands II Corps	2, 3
disdain for Hooker	2
suffers from dysentery	2
visits Washington after Chancellorsville	2
has meetings with Lincoln	2
refuses offer to command Union army	2
recommends General Meade for that position	2
resigns in disgust	4
appointed commander of Department of the Susquehanna	4
Covill, William Jr.	97, 100
arrested by Hancock's aide	98
leads 1st Minnesota	97
Hancock orders suicide attack	97
is wounded	97
released from arrest	98
Cowan, Andrew	179
Crimean War	169
Crittenden, Thomas L.	107
Croft	211

Index

Cross, Edward E. 101
    premonition of death 87
    death of 87
Cross, Richard 87
Culp's Hill 28, 45, 50, 57, 61, 112, 114
Cumberland Valley 8
Cushing, Alonzo H. 128, 143, 144
Custer, George A. .... xiii, 13, 15, 208
Czar Nicholas I 169

DaPray, John A. 197
Daily Morning Chronicle 3
Davis, Jefferson viii
Dead March in Saul 212
Decisions in the West 48
de Trobriand, P. Regis 79, 83
Deep Bottom, battle of 134
Delaware and Hudson Canal Company, The 18
Delaware troops,
    1st Delaware Infantry 81
    Delaware Cavalry 14
Democratic Party .... xviii, xix, 3, 184, 207, 208
Department of the South 124
Department of the Susquehanna 4, 6
Department of West Virginia 184
Detroit, Michigan 123
Devereaux, Arthur F.,
    ordered to charge by Hancock 140
Devil's Den 85, 87
Diest 206
Division of the Atlantic xix
Division of the East 41
Dix, Morgan 210–212
Doles, George,
    Brigade 42
Doubleday, Abner .... vii, 23, 24, 34, 41–46, 53, 59, 69, 71, 78, 100
    inaccurate article in *Journal of Military Service Institution* 49–52
    authors *Chancellorsville and Gettysburg* 47
    describes Hancock during the cannonade 118, 119

Index

disdain for Howard 47
    probable cause for Hancock-Howard controversy 45, 46, 66, 68
    version of the Hancock-Howard meeting on Cemetery Hill, 45, 46
irritates Hancock 50
supports Hancock 56
takes command at Gettysburg 23
Dougherty, Alexander N. 154
    attends to Hancock at Gettysburg 145
    throws away nail that hit Hancock 145
    accompanies Hancock back to hospital 147
Drexel, A. J. 207
Drexel, Joseph W. 207
Dulaney, H. G. 207

Early, Jubal A. .... xiii, 9, 16, 17, 41, 42, 101
Edwards's Ferry 67
Elizabeth, New Jersey 213
Ellis, Theodore G. 115
Emmitsburg, Maryland 41, 69, 83
Emmitsburg Road 23, 76, 78, 114, 116
Endicott, William C. 197, 216
Enfield rifles 26
England .... vii, 1
English .... vii, xviii
English, William H. .... xix, 184
Episcopal Church .... xviii, 211
Evarts, William M. 211
Evening Bulletin [Philadelphia] 67
Evergreen Cemetery 24
Ewell, Richard S. 8
    at Gettysburg 27, 41, 42, 55, 101, 112
    as a fighter 54, 55
    reasons for not attacking Cemetery Hill 50, 54–56, 74

Fair Oaks, Virginia,
    battle of 40, 41
Fair, James G. 207

Index

Fairfield Road.. 42
Fahnestock's Observatory.. 23
Falmouth, Virginia.. 3, 4
Farnsworth, Elon John... 15
Favill, Josiah.. 14
Fazende, P. O. 117
Fenians... 124
Fessenden, J. A. 210
Fifth Artillery... 209
    Battery A.. 210
    Battery H.. 210
    Battery K.. 210
Fifth Military District.. 184
First Union Cavalry Division... 15
Fish, Hamilton.. viii, 211
Florida.. vii, 198, 209
Foote, Andrew Hull... 20
Fort Columbus... 210
Fort Donelson.. 20
Fort Henry.. 20
Fort Leavenworth... vii
Fort Smith.. 124
France... 1
Frank, Richard... 222
Frankford Arsenal.. 222
    Griffin's Battery F.. 222
Franklin, *General*... 17
Franklin, William B. 209, 210
Frederick, Gilbert... 15
Frederick, Maryland... 7–9, 13, 68
Fredericksburg, Virginia.. 1, 88
    battle of................................... xiii, 40, 95, 123, 128, 136
Freedman's Bureau,
    headed by Howard... 40
French, William H. 6
Frizzelburg, Maryland... 14
Fry, James B. 200, 207, 210

Galaxy, The 63, 64

Index

Garfield, James A., xix, 184
Garnett, Richard B., vii, viii, 140
    killed at Gettysburg, 143, 144
Gatling guns viii
Geary, John W. 56
George, *Mr.* 22
Georgia 114
German 40, 41
Germantown, Pennsylvania 213
Germantown Battery [*see* Frankford Arsenal],
Gettysburg Address 3
Gettysburg, Pennsylvania... v, vii, viii, 13, 15, 18, 22–26, 28, 42, 43, 48, 50, 54,
                                                              55, 183, 184, 187, 210
    battle of .... v, vi, xiv, 1, 8, 40, 57, 124, 129–131, 208
    Baltimore and Middle Streets 23
    Hancock's last visit 186, 187, 194
    July 1, 1863 .... 58–62, 64–75, 114
    July 2, 1863 .... 76, 82, 87, 88, 98, 106, 110, 179
    July 3, 1863 ..... 112, 119, 122, 124, 129, 134–137, 151, 154, 163, 165,
                                                                       168, 205
"Gettysburg Reply to General Howard" 63
Gibraltar Brigade 102
Gibbon, John .... vii, xviii, 7, 13, 68, 72, 76, 78, 82, 97, 102, 115, 117, 139
    takes command of the II Corps 25, 26
    comments on Sickles's move 82
    changes name 13
    difficulties with Hancock 13, 146
    attends council of war 105–107, 109
    General Meade's like of 109
    wounded 140, 145
    supports Colonel Covill 102, 104
God 85
Goodwin, E. H. C. 210–212
Gordon, John Brown 42, 55, 142
    denied permission to attack Cemetery Hill 55, 56
Gotwaltz, Joseph K. 221
Governor's Island, New York 104, 184, 189, 195, 197, 198, 202, 203, 210
    Chapel of St. Cornelius 199
    Hancock stationed there xix

Index

home of 192
Grace, William R. 207, 208
Graham, Charles K. 83
Grand Army of the Republic [G.A.R.] 208, 210
    Post IX 189
Grant, Julia 208
Grant, Ulysses S. .... vii, xix, 48, 208
    death of 201
    tomb of 220
        Hancock in charge of funeral 189, 193
        opinion of Hancock xix
        opposition to Hancock's General Order No. 40 .... xix, 205
        as President 40
Greeley, Horace 3
"Green Mountain" 100, 140, 142
Greencastle, Pennsylvania 5
Griffin's Battery F 222
Griffin, Eugene 200–202
Griffin, Eugene, Mrs. [niece of General Hancock] 198, 201
Grover's Theater xvii
Gum Springs, Virginia 6

Hagerstown, Maryland 8
Hagerstown Pike 41
Hale, Charles A. 87
Hall, James S. 26
Hall, William D. 5
Halleck, Henry W. 3, 4, 8, 62, 68
    "Old Brains" 8
Halstead, Eminel P. 44, 45, 49, 66
Hamilton, Alfred Thornley 95
Hamlin, Hannibal 62–64
Hancock, Ada [the general's daughter] .... viii, x, 216, 222
    death of .... xx, 184, 187, 195, 197
Hancock, Almira Russell [the general's wife] ..... viii, ix, xx, 3, 4, 112, 141, 148, 167, 184, 188, 189, 192, 195, 198, 200, 201, 203–205, 208, 209, 222
    authors book on the general 141
    accomplished organist .... viii, 199
        writes a *Te Deum* 199

Index

diminutive names for 3, 200
influence on Hancock's funeral 202, 208, 209
help of friends 207
wants to be buried in St. Louis 208
death watch over the general 199
Hancock, Benjamin Franklin [the general's father] .... vii, 167, 184, 214
Hancock, Cornelia 165
Hancock, Elizabeth Hoxworth [the general's mother] .... vii, 167, 184, 214
Hancock, Gwyn [the general's grandson] 199
Hancock, Hilary B. [the general's twin brother] .... vii, 209, 214
    dubious lifestyle of 189
Hancock, John [the general's younger brother] .... vii, 148, 159, 209
    serves in II Corps vii
Hancock, May Gwyn [the general's daughter-in-law] 192, 195
Hancock Park in New York City 220
Hancock, Russell [the general's son] .... viii, xi, 184, 192
    death of .... xx, 195, 197
Hancock, Winfield Scott .. v, vi, viii, xi–xiv, xvi, 3, 4, 6, 7, 9, 10, 13–16, 19–21,
        30, 43, 49–51, 58, 59, 73, 79, 82, 84, 96, 124, 125, 129, 154, 155,
        166, 171–174
    ancestry of vii
    appointed brigadier-general xiii
    appointed commander of II Corps 4, 5
    attitude toward money 189, 206–208
    birth of vii
        named for vii
    children of .... x, xi
    death of .... xx, 195, 199
        final hours 199, 200
        cause of .... xx, 188, 200
        wake and funeral processions 209–213, 221–223
        service at Trinity Church 210–212
        interred in Montgomery Cemetery .... xx, 221–223
    descriptions of .... xiv–xviii
        as a disciplinarian .... xiii, xiv, 14
    difficulties with General Doubleday 50
        refutes General Doubleday's article in *Journal of Military
        Service Institution* 49, 51, 52
    use of profanity .... xvii, 14, 90

Index

felt General Lee's army should have been destroyed .... v, 164

July 1

briefed by General Meade.. 21–23
    ordered to *assume command*. 24, 25, 45, 53, 60–63, 66, 68–70
    reasons for his selection... 24
    feelings about 25, 26, 45
ride to Gettysburg.. 26
    encounters body of General Reynolds 26
    arrival at.. 27, 43
    impressions of 27, 28
    meets General Howard 43, 60
        corresponds with.. 183
        reports of 44, 45
        Hancock-Howard controversy defined................... 44
            turns command to Hancock 59
            claims made by 58, 60–62
            refutes General Howard's claims..49, 50, 62, 63, 70
            comments to Vice President Hamlin........ 64
orders troops into positions 44, 50, 56, 57
problems with General Doubleday... 50
    opinion of General Howard... 59
    version of Hancock's meeting with General Howard 44–46
    Hancock's view of General Doubleday's version........49, 51, 52
    accusations of General Doubleday 47
    supports Hancock's authority 53
issues with General Ewell 54, 55
creates fish hook configuration... 56
views field with General Warren 57
turns command over to General Slocum 58, 68, 71
praised by General Hunt... 61
command confusion aided by General Meade............................ 62, 63
    changes his position on Hancock's appointment................. 69
returns to Taneytown to report to General Meade 72
    encounters his II Corps... 72
    reports to General Meade... 72

Index

remains in Taneytown on night of July 1 72
final opinion of General Howard 64, 75

July 2

leaves Taneytown for Gettysburg................................. 72, 76
    joins the II Corps.. 76
arranges his line at Gettysburg.................................. 76, 78
orders Lieutenant-Colonel Edward P. Harris arrested 81, 82
watches unauthorized movement of the III Corps 82
    comments on III Corps move.. 82
sends Caldwell's division to aide General Sykes 85
watches Father Corby grant absolution 85
    described by a member of the Irish Brigade 90
speaks with Colonel Cross... 87
incident with "Richmond Dick".................................... 90, 91
orders the attack of the 1st Minnesota 97
    described by a member of the 1st Minnesota 98
    the arrest of Colonel Covill...................................... 98
    conversation with Senator Wilkinson of Minnesota 98
    addresses a reunion of the 1st Minnesota.......................... 98
incident with Lieutenant Gulian V. Weir and lost battery.............. 100
    request's 13th Vermont to retrieve those guns 100
placed in command of the III Corps 91
    displeased with that assignment................................... 91
    turns command of II Corps to General Gibbon....................... 91
leads Colonel Willard and his brigade to aide General Birney 92
    encounters General Birney on the field 92
views General Humphreys's lines being pushed back 92
orders 111th New York into line 92
orders the arrest of Colonel Eliakim Sherrill 95, 97
    appoints Colonel Clinton D. MacDougall to command 97
incident between the 19th Maine and artillery battery.............100, 101
learns true fate of his First Division................................ 101
sends Colonel Samuel S. Carroll and his First Brigade to aid General
    Howard 102
    correspondence with Carroll...................................... 104
evaluates the results of the day 105

Index

attends council of war 105, 107
    described by Lieutenant Frank Haskell 106
    his recommendations at 107
General Birney displeased with Hancock's appointment 109
spends the night in an ambulance 109

July 3

defines his scope of responsibility 112
    describes his dress 112
wires Almira 112
learns of Colonel Merwins's death 114
orders burning of Bliss buildings 115
accepts General Gibbon's luncheon invitation 115
    speculates on Lee's probable attack 116
    relieves the 16th Vermont 116
cannonade begins 116, 117
    exchanges horses with Captain Brownson 118
rides along his line 118–120
    described at 118, 119
    speaks to Colonel Brooke and Major Bull 120
realizes that his artillery is shutting down 121
    orders the guns to reopen fire 121, 123
definition of the Hancock-Hunt controversy 122
    General Hunt offers endless justification 122, 123, 130, 131
    General Meade agrees with Hunt 121
praises the artillery 136
fails to bring up half of his artillery train 132
opinion of Colonel Wainwright 133
opinions of,
    Captain Patrick Hart 134
    Captain John Bigelow 134, 135
    Captain Charles A. Phillips 135
    Lieutenant-Colonel Freeman McGilvery 135
        allegedly tells Hancock to "go to hell" 136
    Colonel E. P. Alexander 133
Pickett's charge begins 138, 139, 150
    directs General Stannard 139

Index

    orders Colonel Devereaux forward.................................. 140
    is wounded 141, 143, 151, 152
        perhaps hit by "friendly fire"........................141, 268
    aided by Vermont men 141, 144
    description of wound 142, 144
advises General Meade that a great victory had been gained...143, 146, 147
becomes concerned for his life...142, 144
is aided by Dr. Alexander N. Dougherty...................................... 145
Hancock's comments [or lack of] on the wounding of:
    General Lewis Armistead 145
    General John Gibbon.. 13, 145
        difficulties with... 13, 146
General Meade sends his regrets to 147
is removed to hospital 147, 151, 163
    dictates message to Meade...147, 148
    visited by his brother John 148
    advises wife he is wounded.. 148

taken to Westminster, Maryland.. 163
taken to La Pierre House in Philadelphia................................163, 165
    removed to Norristown 167
relationship with Ulysses S. Grant... xix
    appraised by xix
    recommended by to take command of the Army of the Potomac... xix
    leads funeral of... 188
Hancock clubs.. xix
views of General Joseph Hooker at Chancellorsville.................. 3, 4, 15
    corresponds with 61, 63
incident with Private David H. Young.................................. xvii, xviii
relationship with President and Mrs. Lincoln xvi
Masonic Brother xviii
marriage of... viii
military governor of Louisiana and Texas .... xviii, 184
    issues General Order No. 40 ....xviii, xix, 184, 205
parents of.. vii
on the Peninsula,
    wins sobriquet, *Hancock the Superb* xiii

Index

    writes poetry xvii
    presidential candidate in 1880................................. xix, 184
        William H. English, running mate........................... xix, 184
        lost bid for office .... xix, 184
    relationship with Lewis Armistead................................viii
    religious affiliations .... xviii, 206
    replies to Howard's media attack 64
    given Thanks of Congress 184
    at West Point..vii
    his white shirts...xviii
    willingness to try new tools and methods.................viii, xiii
Hancock, Winfield Scott [the general's grandson] 195, 214
Hancock, Winfield Scott G.A.R. Post..210, 211
Hardie, James A. 78
Hardi, W. T. 117
Harpers Ferry, West Virginia.. 8, 123
Harper's Magazine 47, 186, 217
Harris, Edward P. 81
Harrisburg, Pennsylvania......................... 4, 6, 8, 9, 14, 18, 71, 181
Harrisburg Road 41
Harrison, Henry Thomas... 13
Harrows, William 140
Hart, Patrick 131, 134, 137
Hartranft, John F. 169, 184, 213
Hartshorne, B. M. 210
Hartwig, D. Scott.. 146
Haskell, Frank A. 76, 78, 82, 87, 105
    describes Hancock.. 106
Hay, John,
    describes Hancock.. 28
Haymarket, Virginia... 6
Hays, Alexander 78, 97
    absorbed into II Corps 7
    upset with Hancock's command.. 7
    burns Bliss buildings... 115
    visits Hancock in Norristown 179
Hays, Harry T. 101
Hays, William... 147
Hayes, Rutherford B. 119, 204

Index

Hazard, John G. 78, 121, 124, 134, 135
Hazlett, Charles E. 85, 120
Heath, Francis E. 100, 101
Heidlersburg Road 41, 42
Heintzelman, Samuel P. 208
Hendrick, Henry C. 146
Herbst Woods 23
Herold, David E. 184
Heth, Henry 22, 41, 42, 74
Hill, A. P. .... vii, 23, 88, 115, 164, 181
Historical Society of Montgomery County [HSMC] 182, 216, 221
Hofmann, J. William xviii
Honesdale, Pennsylvania 18
Hood, John Bell 87
Hooker, George W. 141
Hooker, Joseph .... xiii, 1, 3, 4, 6, 7, 9, 11, 13, 25, 48, 128–131, 137
    "Fighting Joe" 1
    defeat at Chancellorsville 1, 2, 15
    Hancock's dismay over 34
    "Hooker's retreat" 3
    resigns command of the Union army 8
    correspondence with Hancock 61, 63, 64
    given Thanks of Congress 183
Holstein, Anna M. 166
Howard, Oliver Otis ..... xv, 23, 25–27, 32, 49, 50, 53, 54, 57, 58, 60, 67, 68, 72, 73, 143, 146
    ability to lie 48, 59
    assumes command of the field at Gettysburg 24, 41
    biography 40, 41
    defended by Hancock 52, 59, 65, 74
    endless justifications 58, 61–63
    comments to Hannibal Hamlin 62, 64
    problems at Chancellorsville 47
        version challenged by Schurz 48
    prolific writer 40, 41, 65
    "Old Prayer Book Howard" 40, 48
    "Christian General" 40
        in the West 40, 48
        under Sherman 40, 48

Index

    established headquarters on Cemetery Hill 43, 59
    meets Hancock at Gettysburg 43, 45
    reports of same 43–46
    claims that he and Hancock shared command ... 58, 60, 61, 64, 65, 69
    laments to General Meade 66, 69, 70
    rationale 62, 71
    problems on July 2 .... 101, 102, 104
    attends council of war 105, 107
Howard University,
    Howard as president 40
Hummelbaugh, Jacob 110
Humphreys, Andrew Atkinson 82, 91, 101
Hungarian 6
Hunsicker, Charles 221
Hunt, Henry J. .... xii, 73, 76, 79, 81, 120, 126, 127, 131, 133, 135
    ambiguities of title, Chief of Artillery 129
    assumes too much about his authority 136, 137
    biography 123, 124
    censured by General Meade 129
        admits that he was no favorite of Meade's 129, 130
    concedes that II Corps artillery is under Hancock 122, 124
    demoted at Chancellorsville by General Hooker 128, 129
    endless written justifications 122–124, 130, 131
    Hancock-Hunt Controversy .... xv, 122, 132
    as a *prima donna* 124
        threatens to resign 124, 129
    makes provisions for extra ammunition wagons 132
    becomes concerned about use of long range ordnance 121
        General Meade agrees with 121
        General Warren agrees with 124
        General Howard agrees with 124
        Hunt was right 136, 137
    orders artillery to cease fire on July 3rd 121, 133
    praise for 61
    supports Hancock 122
    support from subordinates 134, 135
    testifies before the *Joint Committee on the Conduct of the War* 265
Huntington, James F. 102

Index

Huntsville, Alabama 79
Hutchins, Waldo 17

I Heard a Voice 212
Illinois troops,
    8th Cavalry 22
Independence Hall 182, 208
Indiana xix
Invalid Corps 167
Irish Brigade .... xvii, 85, 90
    estimate of Hancock from a member of 90
Iron Brigade 23, 53, 54

Jackson, Richard H. 210
Jackson, Thomas J. [Stonewall] 27, 40, 47
Janeway, John H. 202, 209
    physcian to Hancock 198, 201
    surprised by Hancock's diabetes 200
    announces Hancock's death 200
Janus 44, 66
Jenkins, A. G. 5
Jerome, Aaron B. 22
Jersey City, New Jersey 213
    Pier D 212
Johnson, Andrew 184
Johnson, Edward 56, 74, 101
    "Old Allegheny" 41
Johnston, Joseph E. 209
Jones, Marcellus 22
Joint Committee on the Conduct of the War 27, 57, 59, 63, 70, 71, 88, 106
Journal of Military Service Institution 49, 51, 52
Junkin, D. X. 192

Kansas vii
Kearny, Philip 79
Kelly, Patrick 85
Kentucky 27, 71
Key, Barton,
    shot and killed by Dan Sickles 83

Index

Key, Francis Scott... 83
Kemper, James L. 139, 140, 142
    wounded at Gettysburg... 140
Kerby, J. O. 40, 46
Kilpatrick, Judson... 14

LaCombe, *Admiral* 222
LaFlore 222
LaPierre House 163, 166
Lane, James... 179
Latin.. 85
Lee, Fitzhugh 58
    sends regrets over Hancock's death... 204
Lee, John A. I. 143
Lee, Robert E. ... v, xv, 1, 2, 5, 8, 9, 13, 21, 55, 56, 72, 74, 76, 78, 95, 116, 131, 138, 164, 204
Leeds, Maine 40
Leister House... 76, 82, 105, 108, 109, 112, 116
"Leppin's" Old Battery.. 57
Leslie's *Illustrated Newspaper*.. 214
Lincoln, Abraham.. xix, 1, 3, 4, 8, 16, 17, 28, 40, 53, 163, 206
    conspiracy trial 184
    opinion of Hancock xvi
Lincoln, Mary Todd,
    invites Hancock to visit at the theater xvi
Little Big Horn 13
Livermore, Thomas,
    responsible for alleged Hancock statement 262
    warns Hancock on July 3.. 148
Lockwood, Henry H. 101
Lone Ranger... xvi
Lonegran, John... 142
Longstreet, James 13, 54, 55, 74, 83
    orders attack on July 2... 84, 85
    orders artillery duel on July 3 116
        rested during the cannonade 121
        thought to have been wounded on Cemetery Ridge, 144
        thought to have been killed 163

Index

    urges Lee to move on the Federal left 76
Longwood 181
Louisiana .... xviii, 184, 205
    Hancock as military governor of .... xviii, 184
    Hancock Day 231
    Concurrent Resolution to Hancock xviii
Louisville, Kentucky 195
Lowe, Thaddeus S. C. 213, 221
    Civil War balloonist 213
    at Hancock's funeral 213
Lowell, Vermont 4
Lupercus vii
Lutheran Seminary 22

McCarter, William 90
McClellan, George B. .... vii, xiii, 16, 17, 128, 206
    creates the sobriquet, *Hancock the Superb* xiii
    death of 201, 212
    saddle 161, 162
McClellan, Mary Ellen xiii
    visit with Mrs. Hancock 209
McClure, A. K. 17
McDowell, Irvin 201
McEnery, Samuel D. 205
McGilvery, Freeman 121, 131, 133–135
    allegedly tells Hancock to "go to hell" 136
McKim United States Hospital 168
McLaws, Lafayette vii
McLean, Jim .... xiv, v
McPherson, James B. 208
McPherson's Ridge 42

MacDonald, Wilson 220
MacDougall, Clinton D.,
    Hancock appoints to command 97
Mackay, John W. 207
Madeira, *Captain* 44
Maine 62, 63, 100, 135
Maine troops,

Index

1st Maine Cavalry 23
3rd Maine Infantry 81
16th Maine Infantry 28
19th Maine Infantry 100
20th Maine Infantry 84
5th Maine Battery 28, 57
Malvern Hill 95, 123
Manayunk, Pennsylvania 213
Manchester, Maryland 82
Man that is born of a woman 212
Manhattan [*see* New York City],
Maryland 164
Mason-Dixon Line .... vii, 204
Masons, Masonic .... xviii, 144, 170
    Charity Lodge Chapter #190 xviii
    Norristown Royal Arch Chapter #190 xviii
Massachusetts Troops,
    19th Massachusetts Infantry 140
    20th Massachusetts Infantry 166
    28th Massachusetts Infantry 85
    Massachusetts Light Artillery, Battery #5 ...... 131, 135
    Massachusetts Light Artillery, Battery #9 ...... 131, 134
Mayo, Joseph C. 132
Meade, George Gordon [General] ..... xv, 2–4, 14, 15, 18–20, 26, 27, 29, 40, 46, 48, 49, 56, 58, 60, 62, 64, 74, 78, 79, 81, 82, 85, 100–102, 108, 115, 121, 124, 129–132, 136, 140, 143, 146
    appointed commander of Union Army 7–9, 13
    disdain for Dan Butterfield 62
    explains plans to Hancock 21–23
    receives word that General Reynolds is dead 24
    orders Hancock to Gettysburg to *assume command* 24, 45, 53, 60, 61
        orders Hancock to determine if Gettysburg is a good place to fight 25
    shows poor regard for General Doubleday 25, 47
    receives field report from Hancock 67
    sends wire to General Halleck about battle of Gettysburg 62, 68
    send 6 p. m. wire to Hancock and General Doubleday 68, 69
    received plaintive message from General Howard 69, 70
    Hancock reports to at Taneytown 72

Index 327

    arrives at Gettysburg 73
        changes his position on Hancock's assignment from *assume command* to *represent me* 65, 70
    sends his son, Captain George, to see General Sickles 79
    sends Hunt to view General Sickles's position 79
    he personally rides to speak with General Sickles 83, 84
        Longstreet begins his attack 84
    instructs Hancock to send aid to General Sykes 85
    orders Hancock to command III Corps 91
    calls for council of war at Leister House 105, 106
        poses three critical questions 107
        notes that Hancock was "puzzled" 107
        concluding statement 109
        speaks with General Gibbon 109
    potential reflection on Sickles's unauthorized move 109
    accepts luncheon invitation from General Gibbon 115
        expresses thoughts on possible attack from General Lee .. 109, 116
    agrees with General Hunt about conserving long-range ammunition, 121
    sends Captain Bingham to instruct Hunt to "observe great care with their ammunition" 124
    fails to recognize General Hunt as Chief of Artillery 129, 130
    expresses regrets over Hancock's wounding 147
    Hancock request that the V and VI Corps be sent to the front on July 3rd 148
    has faulty information on the size of Lee's army 164
    given Thanks of Congress 183
    sends Dr. Read to tend to the wounded Hancock 168
Meade, George Gordon [son] 79
    first introduction to General Hancock 240
    views Sickles's position 79
    almost killed 147
Meade, Margaret [wife of general] 15, 147
Medal of Honor 41, 85, 91, 116
Meeh, Christian 195
Merritt, Wesley 15
Merwin, Henry C.,
    killed at Gettysburg 88, 89

Index

Messiter, A. H. 211
Mexican War .... vii, xix, 2, 95
Michigan 123
Middle Military Division 184
Middletown, Maryland 8
Miles, Nelson A. 210
Miller, D. W. 97, 148, 163, 210
Miller, Merrit B. 116
Military Division of the Atlantic 184
Military Order of Loyal Legion [MOLLUS] .... xix, 188, 207, 210
    Hancock as commander-in-chief 189
    Ohio Commandery 204
    Pennsylvania Commandery 212, 213
    Philadelphia Commandery 202
Military Service Institution 195
Minneapolis, Minnesota 189
Minnesota 98
Minnesota Troops,
    1st Minnesota Infantry .... xv, 16, 97, 99, 100
Miquon, Pennsylvania 213
Mississippi 95
Mississippi troops,
    13th Mississippi Infantry 95
Mitchell, William G. 27, 38, 118, 146, 147, 196
    aide to Hancock 26, 143
Montgomery Cemetery .... xx, 180, 195, 214, 221, 222
    condition of 233
    location of 216
    final resting place for Hancock 208, 216
Montgomery County, Alabama xix
Montgomery County, Pennsylvania 182, 197
    does not vote for Hancock 232
Morey, S. S. 144
Morgan, Charles H. 37, 58
    aide to Hancock 26, 50, 116
Morgan, J. P. 207
Muffly, J. W. 110
Mulholland, St. Clair 21, 85
Musgrave, Percy 185

Index

Musgrave, Thomas B. 189

Napoleons 114
Napoleonic vii
Napoleonic Wars 138
Nast, Thomas 186
National Guard xix
National Guard of Pennsylvania 169
National Intelligencer [Washington D. C.] 3
National Rifle Association,
    Hancock president of xix
Nevada 107
Newark, New Jersey 213
New Brunswick, New Jersey 213
New England 114
New Hampshire troops,
    2nd New Hampshire Infantry 73
New Haven, Connecticut 20
New Jersey troops 18
    11th New Jersey Infantry 95
New Orleans, Louisiana .... xviii, 222
    Canal Street 222
    Concurrent Resolution to Hancock xvii
    Crescent City 222
New York .... viii, 2, 17, 58, 79, 83, 208
New York City .... xix, xx, 181, 182, 184, 193, 195, 201, 202, 206, 208, 214
    City Hall 182
    Harbor xix
    Manhattan 192
        Barge Office 210, 212
        Broadway 211
        Harlem Section 220
        123rd Street 220
        St. Nicholas Avenue 220
        State Street 211
New York Times, The 64, 163, 164
New York Troops,
    42nd New York Infantry 140
    57th New York Infantry 5, 14, 15

Index

63rd New York Infantry 85
69th New York Infantry 85
88th New York Infantry 85
111th New York Infantry 92, 179
126th New York Infantry 95, 109
147th New York Infantry 50
157th New York Infantry 146
1st New York Cavalry 5
6th New York Cavalry 118
1st New York Light, Battery B 78, 128
15th New York Light Battery 131, 134
Nevins, Allan 60
Newton, John 79, 109, 115, 163
   appointed to command I Corps 49, 71, 78
   attends council of war 105–107
Nez Percé, Indians 41
Nichols, William T. 140
Nicholson, John P. 188, 202
Nicolay, John,
   describes Hancock 28
Norristown, Pennsylvana .... vii, xiv, xx, 18, 24, 133, 163, 166, 168–170, 179, 180, 182, 184, 195, 208, 212, 213, 221
   Arch Street 221
   DeKalb Street 167, 221
   DeKalb Street Station 213
   does not vote for Hancock 232
   Lafayette Street 167
   Main Street 221
   Mill and Washington Streets Station 167
   Swede Street 167
North American Continent 5
North Atlantic Squadron, French Navy 222
North Carolina Brigade 179
Notre Dame University 85
Nutmeg 114

O'Reilly, *Dr.* 197
Odd Fellows Hall 170
Official Reports, by General Hancock 104

Index

Ohio Commandery of the Loyal Legion 204
Old Baldy, General Meade's horse 84
Owen, Joshua T. [Paddy] 7

Paine, Lewis 184
Paiute Indians 41
Parker, Isaac 118
Parker, I. B. 67
Parker, J. B. 146, 148
Parker, Joel 18
Parrots 114
Pattison, Robert E. 213
Peach Orchard 81, 95, 116, 224
Pender, William Dorsey 42
Peninsula Campaign xiii
Pennsylvania 5, 7, 16, 18, 116, 120, 213, 222
    does not vote for Hancock 232
    Keystone State 144, 208
Pennsylvania Monument at Gettysburg 85
Pennsylvania Railroad Station 212
Pennsylvania Troops 168
    30th Pennsylvania Infantry, First Reserves 169
    53rd Pennsylvania Infantry 26, 120
    56th Pennsylvania Infantry xviii
    69th Pennsylvania Infantry 140
    71st Pennsylvania Infantry 48, 140, 144
    72nd Pennsylvania Infantry 140, 144
    106th Pennsylvania Infantry 140
    116th Pennsylvania Infantry 21, 85, 90
    140th Pennsylvania Infantry 115, 147
    145th Pennsylvania Infantry xvii
    148th Pennsylvania Infantry .... xvii, 95, 110, 114, 116
    Pennsylvania Light, Batteries C and F 131
Personal Recollections of General E. P. Alexander 55
Petersburg, Virginia 13, 180
Philadelphia Brigade 7
Philadelphia, Pennsylvania 2, 13, 15–18, 75, 79, 82, 148, 165, 167, 169, 182, 212, 213
    Broad Street 166

Index

    Chestnut Street... 166
    Fifty-second Street 213
    Sansom Street 166
Philadelphia, Germantown and Norristown Railroad.................................. 167
Philadelphia Mint.. 221
Philadelphia Union League 71
Philippoteaux, Paul... 127, 150
Phillips, Charles A. 131, 135
Philosophy... v
Pickett, George 156
Pickett's Charge 124, 138, 149, 155, 158
Pickett's Mill, Georgia 40
Pipe Creek 21, 25, 45
Pitzer's Woods 86
Pleasonton, Alfred... 14, 27, 84, 115
    attends council of war 150
Plum Run Valley 95
Pope, John viii
Potomac River 7, 146
Princeton, New Jersey 213
Prussian... 41
Pulitzer, Joseph 207

Quaker.. vii, 206

Randall, Francis V. 100, 139, 142
Randolph, Wallace F. 222
Rappahannock River... `3, 123, 124
Read, Lewis Wernwag 168, 176, 179, 180, 197, 213
    biography 169
    removes bullet from Hancock 170
Reading, Pennsylvania 71
Reams's Station 183
    criticism of Hancock 134
Reminiscences of the Civil War 55
Reminiscences of Winfield Scott Hancock 141
Republican Party .... xviii, 3, 204, 210
Reserve Artillery, Union .... xv, 120, 122, 124, 130, 131, 136, 137
    First Volunteer Brigade 121, 131

Index

Third Volunteer Brigade	102
Revolutionary War	21
Reynolds, John F.	22, 25–27, 31, 69, 147, 163
killed at Gettysburg	23, 24, 75

Rhode Island Troops,
    1st Rhode Island Light, Battery A 78, 128
    1st Rhode Island Light, Battery B 78, 128
Richardson, Israel B. xiii
Richmond, Virginia .... xvii, xix
"Richmond Dick,"
    incident with Hancock 90, 91
Ricketts, R. Bruce,
    Batteries F and G 102
Riddle, William 23, 24
Rihl, William H. 5
Rittenhouse, Benjamin E. 120
Riverview Cemetery 209
Roberts, Eliphalet 221
    Hancock's teacher 221
    watches funeral of 221
Robinson, D. 200, 201, 209
Rock Creek 57, 112, 147
Rock of Ages 212
Rodes, Robert E. 41, 42
Roemer, Buddy,
    Governor of Louisiana 231
    declares Hancock Day 231
Roman 44
Roman Catholic 85
Rorty, James McKay 78, 128
Rothermel, Peter F. 149
Round Top, Big 45, 56, 78
Round Top, Little 45, 56, 57, 78, 79, 83–85, 102, 105, 120
Roxborough, Pennsylvania 213
Russell, Oliver [the general's brother-in-law] 200, 201
Rutherford County, Tennessee 95

Saint Cornelius Chapel 199
Saint Louis, Missouri .... viii, xx, 112, 181, 208

Index

Saint Paul 211
Salem, New Jersey 165
Schimmelfennig, Alexander 41
Schofield, John M. 210
Schurz, Carl 41, 42, 48
    challenges General Howard's denial of Chancellorsville 48
    sits with Hancock 57
Schuylkill River 213
Schwartz, Jacob, Farm 163
Scots vii
Scott, Winfield,
    Hancock named for viii
Scully, James B. 142
Sebastopol 169
Sedgwick, John 4, 7, 25, 40, 69
    arrives at Gettysburg on July 2 82
    attends council of war 105, 107
Seminole War vii
Seminary Ridge 42
Seymour, Horatio 71, 208
Shakespearean 119
Shallenberger, George xiii
Shaw, *Mr.* xviii
Shawmont, Pennsylvania 213
Shenandoah Valley 55
Sheridan, Philip H. 184, 197, 208, 210
Sherrill, Eliakim 92, 93, 95
    arrested by Hancock 97
    killed at Gettysburg 179
Sherman, William T. 48, 203, 210, 211, 222
    March to the Sea 40
    reflections of Hancock 203, 204
Sickles, Daniel E. 26, 41, 62, 68, 73, 79, 80, 87, 101, 132, 210
    awarded Medal of Honor 91
    command III Corps 25
    evaluated by General Meade 109
    evaluated by General Warren 88
    kills Barton Key 83
    supports Hancock during Presidential election 211

Index

unauthorized move of July 2	81–85, 88
confuses Hancock	82, 84
wounded	91
Sickles, Teresa [wife of general]	83
Sigel, Franz	40
Signal Corps	46
Sill, *Sergeant*	222
Skelley, Daniel A.	23
Slocum, Henry W.	33, 41, 56, 58, 66–70, 73, 74, 78, 101, 102, 112, 129
accused of inaction	59
attends council of war	105–107
commands XII Corps	56
Hancock turns command to	64
Smith, Kirby	vii
Smith, Orland	44
Smith, William F. [Baldy]	xiii, 207, 210
Smyser, *Dr.*	170
Soldier's Home	124
South Carolina	95
Spangler, George	146
Spotsylvania	183
Stahel, Julius,	
refuses assistance to Hancock	6
Stannard, George J.	100
during Pickett's charge	139–142
Stanton, Edwin M.	71, 167, 168
Stevens, Greenlief T.	28
Stewart, James	133
Stimson, Daniel M.	200
Stock Exchange	211
Stony Hill	87
Stuart, James Ewell Brown [JEB]	15
shadows II Corps on way to Gettysburg	6, 7, 14
Stuckenberg, J. H. W.	xvii
Sudley Springs, Virginia	6
Sugar Loaf Mountain	9
Sumner, Charles	95
Sumner, Edwin V.	40
Surratt, Mary E.	184

Index

Susquehanna River 8
Sutherland, Charles 198, 200, 201
Sword and Olive Branch 59
Sykes, George 85, 101
    attends council of war 105, 107
    needs assistance on July 2 85
    sobriquet, "Tardy George" 85
Syracuse University 65

Tammany Hall 210
Taneytown, Maryland 21, 23, 24, 26, 54, 56, 72, 76, 78, 110
Taneytown Road 43, 147, 163
Taylor, *Dr.* 165
Te Deum 199
Templin Quarry 195
Tennessee 95
Terry, Alfred H. 210
Texas 184
    Hancock as military governor of .... xviii, 184, 205
Thanks of Congress 8, 183
    given to Hancock xix
The Life of Winfield Scott Hancock 192
The Lord's Prayer 212
Thomas, George H. 208
Thompson, James 131
Thomson, J. Edgar 16
Thorn, Peter 72
Thorn, Peter, Mrs. 72, 73
Thoroughfare Gap 5
Tilden, Samuel J. 207
Todd, David 71
Tremain, Henry E. 91
    request the aid of General Zook 87
Trenton, New Jersey 209, 212, 213
Tribune [New York] 3
Trinity Church 208, 210, 211
    Hancock funeral services at 210–212
Trostle Home 91
Trostle Woods 87

Index

Two Taverns, Pennsylvania 41

Uniontown, Maryland 14, 21
United States 16, 17, 71, 203
United States Artillery,
    1st United States, Battery I 128
    4th United States, Battery A 128
    4th United States, Battery B 133
    5th United States, Battery C 100
    5th United States, Battery D 120
United States Constitution vii
United States Congress 92, 95, 183, 207
United States Military Academy .... vii, 1, 2, 7, 13, 40, 41, 58, 85, 181, 199
    Hancock attends vii
    classmates of vii
University of Pennsylvania 169
Upper Saginaw, Michigan 79

Valentine's Day vii
Valley Forge, Pennsylvania 21, 182
Van Dorn, Earl vii
Vanderbilt, Cornelius 207
Vanderbilt, F. W. 207
Vanderbilt, G. W. 207, 208
Vanderbilt, W. K. 208
Veazey, Wheelock G. 116, 121, 139, 142
Veil, Charles H. 23
Vermont 116
Vermont at Gettysburg 141
Vermont Troops 139, 142
    potential source of Hancock's wound 141, 268
    13th Vermont Infantry 100, 139, 141, 142, 144
    14th Vermont Infantry 140
    16th Vermont Infantry 116, 139
Vincent, Strong 85, 102
Virginia .... vii, 1, 2, 78, 204, 207
Virginia Troops,
    3rd Virginia Infantry 132
    28th Virginia Infantry 143

Index

Vodges, Anthony W. 210
Vogel, A. D. 202
von Steinwher, Adolph W. A. F. 73

Wadsworth, James S. 50
Wadsworth. Joseph 17
Wagner, Irving P. 221
Wainwright, Charles S.,
    comments on Hancock 59, 60, 133
Walker, Francis A. 4, 7, 84, 117, 138, 188, 210
    comments of Hancock 139
Walton, J. B. 116
War of 1812 vii
War Office 7
Ward, J. H. Hobart 83
Ward, *Messenger* 200, 201
Warder, B. H. 207
Warren, Gouverneur, K. 61, 62, 68, 73, 208
    attends council of war 105, 106
    views field with Hancock 57
    thoughts on General Sickles 88
Washington Artillery 116
    Battery B 222
Washington, D. C. .. xix, 2–4, 7–9, 15, 25, 40, 68, 124, 183, 197–199, 203, 207
Washington, George .... xix, 21, 182
Waterloo 2, 106, 184
Watrous, Jerome A. 54
Wayne, John xvi
Webb, Alexander S. 9, 129, 153
    seeks assignment from Hancock 7
    assigned the Philadelphia Brigade 7
    at Gettysburg 140, 141, 144
        part of his command fall away from the wall 140, 143
        General Webb repairs the line 140
        heavy casualties to his command 141
        wins Medal of Honor 140, 141
Webster, W. E. 179, 180
Weed, Stephen H. 85
Weekly Times [Philadelphia] 54

Index 339

Weir, Gulian V.	100
commits suicide	100
loses battery	100
Weld, Stephen M.	22, 23
Weldon Railroad, battle of	134
Wells, James	118, 120, 146
Welsh	vii
Welsh, John Lowber	208
West Point [see U. S. Military Academy],	
West Virginia troops,	
7th West Virginia Infantry	102
Westminster, Maryland	14, 163
Hancock arrives there after wounding	163
Wetmore, Prosper M.	17
Wharton, John S.	196
Wheatfield	87, 89, 91, 114
Wheatfield Road	97, 124
Whipple, W. D.	203
White, Luther	166
White Creek	146
White House	xvi
Whittier, Edward N.	57
Whitworth cannon	114
Wiggin, Francis	28
Wilcox, Cadmus M.	81, 92, 97
Wilderness	115, 116, 146, 183
Wilkinson, Morton	98
Hancock praises 1st Minnesota to	98
Willard, George L.	92
Brigade	92, 95
Willcox, Orlando B.	210
Williams, Alpheus S.	107
attends council of war	105
Williams, S.	19
Williamsburg, Virginia	xiii
Williamsport, Maryland	146
Wills, David	163
Wills, Jennie Smyser	163
Wills Home	163

Winchester, Virginia xix
Winkler, F. C. 48
Wisconsin troops,
    2nd Wisconsin Infantry 23
    3rd Wisconsin Infantry 133
Wolson, Wlliam P. 82
Woodlawn Cemetery 195
Woodruff, George A. 128
    Woodruff's Battery I 78, 118
Wormley Hotel,
    Hancock visits before his death 197
Wright, Ambrose R. 98
Wright, Horatio G. 164

York, Pennsylvania 8, 9, 16, 17, 41
Young, David H. .... xvii, xviii

Ziegler's Grove 78, 92, 95, 118
Zook Post, No. 11,
    at Hancock's funeral 221
    named for General Samuel K. Zook 221
Zook, Samuel K. 5, 9, 14, 86, 87, 101
    cursing matches with Hancock 87
    leads Third Brigade, First Division 14
    killed at Gettysburg 87, 221